ORITY.
NCE of the
f GIBRALTAR
C.Spartel
A F R I C A
Almadronis
To Robert, merry Xmas!
Ron
1988
ENEMY'S REAR
Royal Sovereign,100.
V.Adm. Collingwood
Mars, 74.
Belle Isle, 74.
Tonnant, 80.
Bellerophon, 74.
Colossus, 74.
Achille, 74.
Polyphemus, 64.
Revenge, 74.
Swiftsure, 74.
Defence, 74.
Thunderer, 74.
Defiance, 74.
Prince, 98
L'Achille, 74.
blown up during the Action
PE TRAFALGAR: 21 OCTOBER 1805.
D1080282

THE PRICE OF ADMIRALTY

Also by the same author

The Face of Battle
The Nature of War (with Joseph Darracott)
World Armies
Who's Who in Military History (with Andrew Wheatcroft)
Six Armies in Normandy
Soldiers (with Richard Holmes)
The Mask of Command

JOHN KEEGAN

THE PRICE OF ADMIRALTY

War at Sea from Man of War to Submarine

Hutchinson
LONDON SYDNEY AUCKLAND JOHANNESBURG

This edition first published in Great Britain
by Hutchinson, an imprint of
Century Hutchinson Ltd, Brookmount House,
62–65 Chandos Place, London WC2N 4NW

Century Hutchinson Australia (Pty) Ltd
89–91 Albion Street, Surry Hills, NSW 2010

Century Hutchinson, New Zealand Limited
PO Box 40–086, Glenfield, Auckland 10,
New Zealand

Century Hutchinson South Africa (Pty) Ltd
PO Box 337, Bergvlei, 2012 South Africa

Printed and bound in Great Britain by
Butler and Tanner Ltd, Frome and London

ISBN 0 09 173771 0

In memory
of my grandfather
John Bridgman
(1882–1954)
of Toomdeely, County Limerick
and for my son
Thomas John Bridgman Keegan
and my grandson
Benjamin Bridgman Newmark

CONTENTS

Illustrations

Plates

Maps Pages

ACKNOWLEDGEMENTS

My thanks are due first to those who taught me the little I know about ships, seamanship and sailing: John Watson, of Trinity College, Oxford, who taught me to sail in a Fleetwind dinghy at Port Meadow in our freshman term in 1953; the officers of the Royal Military Academy Sandhurst Sailing Club, and particularly Lieutenant-Colonel John Carver, with whom I cruised in the Sandhurst yachts *Wishstream* and *Wishstream II* in the Solent and Channel in 1960–70; the naval historian, the late A. B. Rodger, my Balliol tutor; and my grandfather, John Bridgman, whose lifelong interest in the sea aroused my own. It was he who introduced me to the classics of naval and nautical literature in childhood, made me ship models, told me sea stories and launched me in imagination on the waters. He was the most delightful of grandfathers.

My thanks are also due to the staffs of several specialist libraries: Mr Andrew Orgill and his staff at the Central Library, Royal Military Academy Sandhurst; Mr Michael Sims and his staff at the Staff College Library; Mr John Andrews and Miss Mavis Simpson at the Ministry of Defence Library; and the staffs of the National Maritime Museum Library and the London Library.

I should particularly like to thank friends and colleagues at the Royal Military Academy Sandhurst and the *Daily Telegraph*: Mr James Allan, Mr Conrad Black, Dr Anthony Clayton, Lord Deedes, Mr Jeremy Deedes, Mr Trevor Grove, Mr Nigel Horne, Mr Andrew Hutchinson, Miss Claire Jordan, Mr Andrew Knight, Mr Michael Orr, Mr Nigel Wade and Mr Ned Willmott; Ned Willmott's capacity to answer the most abstruse enquiry about twentieth-century naval history without recourse to printed sources continues to astonish me. I owe warmest thanks of all to Mr Max Hastings, who allowed me the time to write this book.

The manuscript was deciphered and typed by Miss Monica Alexander, whom I once again thank for her skills. It was meticulously edited by Miss Linden Stafford, a copy-editor without peer, and by Mr Dan Frank of the Viking Press and Mr Richard Cohen of Century Hutchinson; Richard Cohen was a source of constant help and encouragement. I should also like to thank Mr Peter Mayer, Miss Christine Pevitt and Miss Gwenda David of the Viking Press and my friend Mr Paul Murphy for their support. As always I owe the warmest thanks to my American Literary agent, Lois Wallace, and to my British Literary agent, Anthony Shell, a schoolfellow at Ampleforth of John Watson, my sailing master, and our Oxford contemporary. Like all his clients I continue as an author only with his constant advice and encouragement. Among friends at Kilmington I should like to thank Mrs Honor Medlam, and Mr Michael Gray and Mr Peter Stancombe, who saved me from being a gardener.

My thanks and love finally to my children, Lucy, and her husband Brooks Newmark (now the parents of Benjamin Bridgman), Thomas, Rose and Matthew, and to my darling wife, Susanne.

John Keegan
Kilmington Manor
3 September, 1988

Illustration Credits

Our thanks are due to the following: The National Maritime Museum, The Robert Hunt Picture Library, E. T. Archives, The Military Archive and Research Service, The Keystone Collection, Ullstein Bilderdienst, The Mansell Collection.

INTRODUCTION

BATTLE AT SEA

How men have fought at sea, in the period from the heyday of the ship of the line to the coming of the submarine, is the subject of this book. It is one I have long wanted to write because, before ever chance turned me into a military historian, it was a naval historian that I wanted to be. Not difficult to explain why: I am English; no Englishman – no Briton – lives more than eighty miles from tidal water, and no Briton of my generation, raised on food fought through the U-boat packs in the battle of the Atlantic, can ever ignore the narrowness of the margin by which seapower separates survival from starvation in the islands he inhabits. The artefacts and memorials of seapower are warp to the woof of British life. HMS *Victory*, cocooned in her dry dock at Portsmouth, is an object as much visited by British schoolchildren as the manuscript of their constitution by American, Napoleon's tomb by French or Lenin's cadaver by Russian. Nelson's Column is the grand centrepoint of the British capital's traffic, and the Admiral Nelson, Hood, Rodney, Albemarle, Jervis, Codrington, Anson, Blake and Collingwood are as familiar city, town or village drinking-places as are the Royal Sovereign – itself a famous ship's name – George or William IV, who was in any case 'the sailor king'.

Most British people possess direct and personal acquaintance with the facts of seapower and the maritime commerce it protects. My family's photograph album is full of images of the trading schooners and ketches in which my grandfather, a small landowner's son from the tidewater of the river Shannon, sailed the west coast of Ireland in his school holidays in the 1890s, on voyages similar to those made by slate-carriers from the North Welsh ports, island traders between the west coast of Scotland and the Hebrides, herring-catchers plying out of Yorkshire and Northumberland ports or spiritsail barges loaded with grain and hay from the East Anglian backwaters for the estuaries of the Medway, Thames and London River itself.

That peaceful commerce, familiar even to the British whose lives connect with it only through the traffic of canal narrowboats and the annual migration to the seaside, intermingles with naval warfare at a multiplicity of points. Sailor sons, husbands, uncles, nephews, clad in the round hat and bell-bottom trousers which are one of Britain's universal legacies to the world, figure in the family tree of the majority of the nation's households. Acquaintance with the ships in which those Jack Tars sailed is part also of the British national experience. Mine embodies two wartime visits: one to a motor torpedo-boat of one of the Channel flotillas, moored in a Dorset port, between sallies against German E-boats, on a naval 'open day' in the weeks before the invasion of Normandy in 1944; another to a fleet minesweeper, of which a family friend was first lieutenant, repairing in the London Docks after damage by a U-boat-laid mine during the last stages of the battle of the Atlantic in 1945. The memory of both crews' sang-froid, light-heartedness and derring-do remains with me to this day.

These impressions are reinforced by others: those transmitted by the extraordinary grace and beauty of the physical means of naval warfare, the hulls, masts, spars, weapons and instruments of the warship. The artistry which went to the making of *Victory*, paradigm of the sailing-warship world, touches anyone who visits her: not only the sublime proportionality of her structure but also the elegance of her joinery and fittings, the delicacy of her classical detail – ogival mouldings to her gun-ports, Doric columns supporting her tween-decks, rococo carving to her bow, Greek-revival colonnades at her stern galleries – and the severe rationality of her standing and running rigging. *Victory* is a cool and deadly instrument of war. But she is also a thing of beauty, as are often her descendants, in wood, iron and steel, in our own day.

The conjunction of the warship's beauty with the deadliness of its purpose raises a second and central question: *why* did men fight at sea at all? For the beauty of such ships, though enhanced by artifice, is fundamentally determined by the nature of the perpetual struggle that the sailor wages with the elements. The run of a ship's lines, the proportionality of breadth to depth and length, the point and counterpoint of its spars and rigging are not a product of the shipwright's whim but the fruit of millennia of experience in pitting wood, metal and fibre against the forces of wind and water. A ship is first of all a vessel for bringing those who sail in her safe from one landfall to another. The perils of making landfall, even across narrow waters, arouse fears which lie very deep in the human psyche. Why, then, add to them those of capture, shipwreck or death at the hands of fellow mariners?

There is, indeed, a profound and powerful set of values that inhibits the waging of maritime war, roughly summarised by the phrase 'fellowship of the sea'. What that implies is a code of mutual self-interest: today's well-found mariner may be tomorrow's derelict, dependent for his life on the help of a passing stranger. All sailors recognise the logic of the code and most abide by it most of the time. But the code of fellowship wars, alas, with an entirely contrary and conflicting interest: that of quick and chance enrichment. Ships, by their nature, are objects of capital intensity. They are valuable in themselves, and what they carry may be more valuable still. The temptation to attack and take a ship, when opportunity offered, could thus all too easily overcome the inhibitions imposed by the sense of risk shared between sailors; when it did so, the practice of war-making at sea was born.

Its institution must have been reinforced by similar motives underlying the institution of organised warfare on land. As Professor William McNeill has pointed out, sophisticated military operations – those entailing mechanisms of command, calculations of strategy and rehearsal of tactics – must have had their origin in campaigns generated by the rewards and opportunities of long-distance trade. Irrigation societies, the first to create the large agricultural surpluses which could support standing armies, were also the first to initiate the practice of sending long-distance expeditions to trade for the commodities – particularly metals and horses – which they did not produce within their own boundaries. Such expeditions were initially mere raids, which seized what they wanted by force; later the irrigation societies found it more profitable to offer manufactured goods for the resources that they sought. But such expeditions always needed protection en route; and the more primitive peoples with which they exchanged trade were tempted by the desirability of the strangers' trade goods to raid in the opposite direction, with the aim of seizing objects of value instead of bartering for them. These raiding expeditions may be seen as a form of piracy on land.

And it is in piracy at sea that we may perceive the origins of naval warfare. Fights between traders and pirates, to whom a trader's ship provided an opportunity for enrichment unattainable by toil, were the small change out of which the larger currency of organised naval warfare grew. Ships were – still are – the most efficient means of transporting bulk cargoes over distance. River voyages may have been the first form that long-distance bulk transportation took; but piracy was a possibility wherever the rivers flowed above or below friendly territory. Once riverine navigators left sheltered waters and took to the open sea, exposure to piracy became an occupational hazard; and all the more so because, for the earliest seaward mariners, navigation was a coastwise affair. Inaccessible offshore and littoral zones, islands, peninsulas and deltas close to trade routes, provided safe refuges for other mariners who chose to practise piracy, though they often combined it with commercial trading, using pirated goods as part of their stock. Hence the 'ambiguous' quality of much piracy, which all students of the practice have identified as one of its salient characteristics.

Pirates, trader-pirates, even pirate rulers were to become a fixed and significant element in the commerce of all inland sea and coastal economies throughout antiquity. They flourished in the Mediterranean, the Baltic, the North Sea, the western Indian Ocean, the Bay of Bengal, the South China Sea and the Sea of Japan from the earliest periods of seaborne trade. And piracy was only suppressed when large polities raised navies to put it down. It was a major achievement of the Ming dynasty in China (1368–1644) that it created a navy which assured safe passage for Chinese traders to ports as distant as those of the Red Sea and East Africa. Maritime peace had come earlier to the Mediterranean. Although not even Athens at the height of its maritime power – founded initially to assure the import of grain from the Black Sea – had been able to extirpate piracy on its trade routes altogether (Greeks had been enthusiastic pirates since the age of Odysseus), the Persian Empire's navy acted as an effective anti-piracy force in the eastern Mediterranean. And the late Roman Republic and early Roman Empire, by the extension of their authority from one end of the Mediterranean to the other, completed the Persians' work. Under the rule of Pompey, in the first century BC, the Roman navy swept much of the inland sea free of pirates. The naval victories of Octavian, later the Emperor Augustus, ushered in a true naval *imperium* which made the seas safe for trade not only within the Mediterranean itself but also along the empire's Atlantic, Channel and North Sea coasts – a peace which was to hold good until the third century AD.

The subsequent resurgence of piracy was a feature of those external barbarian assaults on the empire which culminated in its collapse in the fifth century. And maritime peace was not subsequently to be restored in European waters for over a thousand years – years which comprehended the rise and dominance of the most destructive of all pirate societies, that of the Vikings. The transformation of Viking overseas bases – in England, Normandy and Sicily – into Viking kingdoms imposed an automatic check on their depredations. But it was only with the harnessing of the economies of older-established states – Portugal, Spain, then England and Holland – to the practice of long-distance oceanic trade in the sixteenth century that the principle of freedom of the seas recovered international value. England and Holland in particular hovered uncertainly in their naval policy between the condoning of piracy, for state purposes, and its suppression. But by the seventeenth century a consensus had been reached; the naval ships that state revenues supported, whose efficiency in the defeat of pirates, whether semi-official or the enemy of all, had by then been established beyond question, would in future only fight other naval ships. They would do so to acquire 'command of the sea' – a phrase not yet coined, though its force was implicitly understood by all who sought to exercise it – and command of the sea would in turn determine which states were to be rich and which poor in those parts of the European subcontinent washed by the world ocean.

A similar struggle between navies and pirates – including both semi-official and private operators – had simultaneously been concluded in the Mediterranean, historic home of the maritime predator. Its result was to consign control of the eastern Mediterranean to Islam and of the western Mediterranean to Christendom, represented principally by Spain. But Mediterranean naval warfare of the sixteenth century differed from that waged in North European waters by reason of its distinctively local instrument, the oared galley. The Atlantic warship, by contrast, was a sailing vessel, ill adapted to the ramming and hand-to-hand tactics which characterised galley fighting – as they had done since Greek and Roman times – but a powerful weight-carrier and therefore ready-made to accommodate artillery when artillery achieved a compactly transportable form.

Guns were revolutionised at the end of the fifteenth century. After 200 years of experiment, they suddenly acquired the set of characteristics – solid-cast form with integral 'trunnions' which married into a wheeled carriage – that made them readily adaptable either for easy passage over land or for cross-deck recoil aboard ship. By the third decade of the sixteenth century, wheeled guns had rendered obsolete a thousand years of European castle-building on land, while, arrayed in 'broadside' at sea, they had transformed weight-carrying cargo ships into floating castles of formidable power. 'Broadside' provided states with the potential to wage and win strategic campaigns offshore, and they would shortly begin to do so.

Galleys, too, mounted the new artillery, which also greatly added to their power. A heavy gun trained over the bow of a galley could cause more damage to another than any inflicted by hand-to-hand fighting or even by ramming, in any case the trickiest manoeuvre of sea warfare. But, because galleys were necessarily too narrow to mount guns for cross-deck recoil, they could not deploy them in broadside, nor, in consequence, meet the new sailing warship on equal terms. The galley's narrow configuration made it unsuitable for operations in the heavy weather of great waters; while the sailing-ship powers of northern Europe did not yet seek to penetrate the confines of the Mediterranean. The galley was therefore to survive as a local instrument of naval force for the 200 years in which England and Holland, in competition with the French and Spanish Atlantic fleets, were contesting control of the oceans and the lands that lay beyond.

Contest between these fleets was ultimately resolved by battle, when sea battles could be organised. But encounter between fleets at sea was difficult to arrange in sailing-ship days and, even when a meeting was made, still difficult to contrive in a form which gave victory to one side or the other. Fleets had first to find each other in an environment without landmarks; they then had to choose formations which allowed their firepower to bear; finally they had to hold the enemy in play sufficiently long for firepower to take effect. All three difficulties were to defy easy solution.

Rendezvous proved the least of the problems. For, despite the enormous range of the sixteenth-century sailing ship – the globe was first circumnavigated in 1519–22 by Magellan – and the vast extent of the seas, practical difficulties imposed by intelligence-gathering and position-finding, as well as victualling and the state of the weather, effectively confined a fleet bent on bringing another to battle to short-range sorties from base. Moreover, as long as position-finding and intelligence-gathering were difficult – as both remained until first mechanical and then electronic means appeared to process navigational data or to transmit 'real time' information* – it was only at short range from base that 'command of the sea' could be exercised in any meaningful way. The depths of the oceans meanwhile remained no man's lands, which fleets might beat almost in perpetuity without getting glimpse of each other. Hence the result that no great sailing-ship battle was fought far out of sight of land; Howe's victory of the Glorious First of June in 1794, though the first truly oceanic engagement, took place only 400 miles from the coast of Spain, and was to have no parallel before the coming of the steamship.

Fighting the enemy when found proved difficult at first, and not only at first, because admirals could not readily determine how they should best arrange their ships to attack the enemy. Centuries of engagement in which the issue had been decided by hand-to-hand combat led fleet commanders to believe that tactics suitable for a culmination in boarding were the correct ones. As a result ships whose real power lay in their broadsides were directed head-on at each other, in 'line abreast', when reflection would have revealed that the fleet should have been laid alongside its enemy, in 'line ahead'. The outcome was such messy encounters as Henry VIII's battle with the French off Ryde in 1545 and many episodes of the Armada fight up the Channel in 1588.

By the seventeenth century, however, the North European admirals, particularly the Dutch and English, had grasped that broadside gunnery was the key to victory and were laying their fleets in 'line ahead' – bow to stern with each other, that is, from first ship to last in parallel lines – and fighting the issue out by firepower. The battles that resulted were bloody. Few ships were sunk in these encounters, for the wooden ship was virtually unsinkable by solid shot unless it caught fire. But solid shot caused grievous casualties among crews, as long as ships clung

* 'Real time' is an intelligence term implying that knowledge of one side's intentions or actions is received by the other as, or nearly as, quickly as word of it is passed. Typically it depends on the ability to intercept enemy messages and decipher or decode them at the same speed as the enemy receiving station can do. The triumph of the British crytographic centre at Bletchley Park during the Second World War was to read much German Enigma cipher traffic in 'real time'.

together at man-killing range. Naturally few admirals who sensed casualties mounting chose to sustain punishment, even in the bitter Anglo-Dutch cannonades of the seventeenth century. And the particular circumstances of sailing-ship warfare offered them a ready escape. Because attacking fleets sailed downwind to engage an enemy, and it was attacking fleets which normally inflicted the casualties, the defending fleet automatically retained the option of itself sailing downwind away from battle when battle grew too hot. And so they commonly did.

The consequence was that almost all the great battles of the wooden-wall epoch proved inconclusive, and the pantheon of sailing-ship admirals who fought them – most of them British – are in truth partial rather than decisive victors. Not until the coming of the ironclad steamship would the spectre of annihilation confront an admiral who grievously mismanaged his fleet; and the ironclad era itself would be almost past before – at Midway and the subsequent battles of America's war with Japan in the Pacific – such an outcome transpired. Jutland, the greatest but also one of the earliest clashes of ironclads to occur before the Pacific War, fell short of decision because of uncertainties felt by the opposed British and German commanders as to how a conflict between large fleets of such novel and untested warships should occur. Both were inhibited from pressing the decision by fear of the submarine, a revolutionary instrument of war which was to create its own challenge

Nelson explaining to his officers the plan of attack before the battle of Trafalgar.

to the exercise of 'command of the sea' in the battle of the Atlantic twenty-five years after Jutland was fought. Tactical stalemate may therefore be seen as the determining quality of most action in naval warfare throughout the period from the appearance of the shipborne gun in the sixteenth century until its supersession by the embarked aircraft and the submarine-launched torpedo in the twentieth.

And why, given the forces of nature and impenetrabilities of distance with which sailors have to contend as they make their way across the face of the waters, should things have been expected to fall out differently? The wonder is not that one body of ships should fail to defeat another but that either should have arrived intact and battleworthy at the point of conflict. And yet, at the very end of the sailing-ship era, fleets and admirals had begun to find, fix and defeat the enemy with something akin to regularity. Three admirals, all British – Rodney at the battle of the Saints in 1782, Howe at the Glorious First of June in 1794, Duncan at Camperdown in 1797 – had shown how a decisive battle between sailing ships might be fought. In 1805 a fourth, Horatio Nelson, demonstrated that total victory lay within the grasp of a commander bold enough to seize it.

I

TRAFALGAR

THE WOODEN WORLD

'Like a great wood on our lee bow', Able Seaman Brown of Nelson's *Victory* called his sight of the masts of the French and Spanish fleets, breaking the Atlantic skyline off the coast of Spain at first light on the morning of Trafalgar, 21 October 1805. And 'a wooden world' was what sea officers called navies themselves 200 years ago. The modern visitor who ducks his head to go below one of the ships that survive from that age – *Victory* at Portsmouth, *Constitution* in Boston Navy Yard – will instantly comprehend what they meant. Wood surrounds and encloses him: planed and scrubbed boards of pine or teak 8 inches wide under his feet, sawn baulks of oak a foot and a half square running athwartships overhead, hanging 'knees' cut from whole tree forks at his elbow and pillars of fir, too large for a man's arms to encircle, breaking the deck's run where masts descend to meet the wooden keel and rise to bear the hamper of wooden yards, tops and crosstrees high over poop, waist and forecastle in the open air above.

The smell of wood and its derivatives surrounds him: pine pitch and tar run hot between the cracks of the timbers, filling the vegetable fibres first forced between them; the fibrous odour of hemp from the cables; the sweet tang of vegetable-oil paints and varnishes spread on the wooden fixtures – capstans, cable-bitts, companion ways – that interrupt the deck's floor. And, if the ship could still move, the *sound* of wood would surround him also: timbers – jointed, scarfed, dovetailed, pegged, morticed, fayed and rabbeted – moving with and working against each other in a concerto, sometimes a cacophony, of creaks, groans, shrieks, wails, buzzes and vibrations. Six thousand years of craftsmanship would orchestrate the woodwind of the ship in motion, singing of tolerances between frames and planking, marriages of timbers hard and soft, pliancies and rigidities, give and take, first learned by rule of thumb, then transmitted by word of mouth, finally refined by calculation on a thousand slipways from the Pharaonic Nile to the fiords of Viking Norway.

The great wooden warships that sailed to Trafalgar, and a score of other contemporary oceanic battlefields, were a summary and encapsulation of a culture, almost a civilisation of timber whose roots drive as deep as man's first impulse to leave dry land and venture his life and his future on the bosom of the waters.

Because the great wooden ships, like *Victory* and *Constitution*, that survive to our own age summarise a technology and a society of immense antiquity, and yet catch both, as in a 'freeze frame', at a peak moment of their development, they can convey to the visitor's imagination a picture of the battles they were built to fight far more intense and immediate than any he can conjure up for himself on a battlefield ashore. The battlefields of the sea bear, of course, no physical trace of the events that transpired in those places; wind and water wipe the debris from the surface in a few days, even hours, and the depths engulf the ships and men that fell victim to the action. Land battlefields are marked more lastingly. The soldier's spade leaves scars that may persist for a hundred years, as those of the American Civil War still do. The artillery of more modern wars turns and pockmarks the soil, shreds woodland, sterilises fertile earth, tumbles villages, even whole towns; the landscape of the First World War trench zone will bear the traces of that terrible tragedy long after the great-grandchildren of the actors are in their own graves. And memory relates this or that episode of past battles to landmarks which will stand for all time. Little Round Top at Gettysburg, the ridge at Waterloo, the pass of Thermopylae, the cliffs at Utah Beach will be remembered as places of aggression and suffering as long as collective memory holds.

Yet the exact circumstances, let alone the rhythms and dynamics of land battle, defy easy reconstruction even by the expert visitor to Gettysburg or Waterloo. However precise his understanding of blackpowder tactics, however detailed his knowledge of Lee's or Wellington's regimental dispositions, he will never quite be able to place the people of the past in time and place on the ground that he treads. Was it here, he will ask himself, that Wellington stood when he watched the roofs of Hougoumont take fire – or was it a little further to the right? Did it take five minutes for the head of Pickett's division to breast Cemetery Ridge – or seven – or twelve? Walking the ground oneself will not yield the answer, for, even if one burdens oneself with a soldier's hamper, everything else that worked to deaden or hasten the soldier's step – fear, crowd pressure, the obstacle of fallen bodies – will lack from the simulation. Sight lines, so immediate and easy to establish on a peaceful visit, cannot be those of the day of battle, when smoke clouds, formed bodies of troops, even a neighbour's head and shoulders, intervened to alter a participant's view. However strong the visitor's will to impose the battlefield scene on the landscape before his eyes, it will appear at its sharpest as a fleeting and patchy transparency, monochrome, two-dimensional and ultimately bloodless.

By contrast the gundecks of *Victory* – or any other relic of a sea battlefield – can translate a visitor in imagination directly to the heart of action. Ascending to the open air, he can put his own feet on the spot where Nelson stood at the moment the French sharpshooter's bullet dropped him to the deck; descending below waterline to the cockpit in the lowest level of the ship, he can see the corner, illuminated by a light no stronger than that which helped Surgeon Scott lop limbs and probe wounds for splinters, where Nelson lay to die. On the decks between, along which the sixty guns of *Victory*'s main battery are ranked at 12-foot intervals from stern to stern, he will find himself forced to adopt exactly the same posture, follow the same movements, squint at the same angle of vision as the seamen gunners who laboured there at their cannon 200 years ago. On a crowded day, with visitors jostling for space around him, he will also be able to feel, not merely to visualise, how close was the press of a thousand human beings cramped within 3000 tons of timber shell. The noise will be absent: no rumble of gun-carriage wheels being run up to gun-ports, no babble of orders, no crash of artillery as the guns spoke out. The motion will be absent: no sea sway beneath his feet, no pitch or roll, no heel from the pressure of wind on sails a hundred feet above his head. The fear will be absent, the horror absent, the energy and intensity of action absent; but, more closely than in any other place of past combat that remains on earth, the gundeck will bring to him the reality of human strife. It was actually *here*, he will be able to say to himself, that French shot crashed through the scantlings to decapitate men or cut them in two, here that splinters, as deadly as shrapnel, flew to shred and skewer human flesh, here that those untouched sweated and strained with tackle and handspike to load and lay these 3-ton lumps of iron every minute and a half of action, here that the smoke of discharge hung pea-soup thick between gun-stations to hide one from another, here at last that word came of enemy colours struck and so of respite from carnage, here that the deafened and battle-drugged survivors stopped from the work of killing to reckon their luck and count their friends among the living.

No one then can enter *Victory*'s gundeck without catching some echo of Trafalgar and bearing it away with him; but what took *Victory* and its people to that place, and why they did what was done there, is not so easily grasped. Trafalgar is, after all, just a patch of the Atlantic Ocean, two miles square at most, some forty miles north-west of the Straits of Gibraltar. Only a navigator with chart and compass is equipped to distinguish it from any other patch of the ocean that washes the shores of Spain for fifty miles on either side. Even in Nelson's and Villeneuve's time, it was crisscrossed daily by coasters, fishing smacks and merchantmen whose crews gave not a passing thought to the notion that they were entering or leaving one of the strategic crossroads of history. In our own time, it is entered and left as frequently by ships which often exceed in deadweight tonnage that of Nelson's and Villeneuve's combined. Their crews have their business in waters greater even than Nelson knew, and what brought him and his enemies' 'great woods' of warships to the western approaches of the Mediterranean on Trafalgar Day is a question to which, if they give it any thought at all, they have little answer. Nor do many other mariners – or land-dwellers – of this end of the twentieth century. What *had* drawn the fleets of Britain, France and Spain to battle off Cape Trafalgar on 21 October 1805?

THE STRATEGIC BACKGROUND

To 'defeat the enemy fleet from the land' was what Alexander the Great told his general, Parmenio, should be Macedonia's strategy following the invasion of Persia in the spring of 334 BC. It is a design many warlords have sought to achieve since, rarely with Alexander's success. He had already managed to secure a foothold on the landward side of the continent from which the Persian navy operated and, by moving directly against its bases, struck such anxiety into its captains that they successively abandoned their allegiance to the Persian emperor and made their peace with the intruder. Within a year of setting foot in Asia Minor, Alexander had indeed defeated the Persian fleet 'from the land' and was poised to strike at the heart of the empire.

No warlord more greatly admired Alexander than Napoleon Bonaparte; in exile on St Helena he told Las Cases, his amanuensis, that the study of the life of Alexander was the most perfect education a future soldier could undertake. How keenly must his admiration have been mixed with envy in the aftermath of the collapse (16 May 1803) of the Peace of Amiens, when each of his designs to complete his command of the European continent was checked at some point on its perimeter by Britain's command of the sea. The way to break that command was clear: if he could only land his army on the British coast, as Alexander had landed his in Asia Minor, he could defeat the Royal Navy 'from the land' in trifling time. However, to do so he was faced, not as Alexander had been by the narrow and tideless defile of the Bosporus, but by the nineteen miles of stormy water that separate Calais from Dover. The operation would be similar to 'a large-scale river crossing' (*grosses Flussübergang*), the generals of the German high command would advise Hitler 140 years later in their draft plan for 'Sealion', the plan to invade Britain in the aftermath of Dunkirk. Napoleon – though, like Hitler, he emptied the estuaries of northern Europe to assemble a fleet of flat-bottomed coasters for the attempt – never entertained any such delusion. He had seen as early as 1798, the year of his descent upon Egypt, that a victorious invasion of Britain must turn upon a successful diversion of the British fleet from the seas which they commanded. Then he had written that 'an invasion of Britain' could be made to succeed by mounting expeditions against Egypt or India simultaneously, so forcing the Royal Navy to deploy its fleet far from home in the confined waters of the Mediterranean. In its absence, the French could descend on the British coast and bring the country's minuscule army to battle and defeat on home territory. The trick was to achieve such a diversion in the Mediterranean by preference, if not elsewhere. How was it to be arranged?

At the beginning of the nineteenth century Britain and France constituted a fascinating strategic mismatch. France, with a population of 30 million, was not only the most populous but the most prosperous nation in Europe. It was also, through its victories in the wars of the Revolution and under Napoleon, militarily paramount on land. The sovereign territory of France had been enormously increased by conquest, the Austrian Netherlands (modern Belgium), Nice and Savoy having been annexed and organised as French departments in 1793. The neighbouring territories of Holland, Switzerland and much of northern Italy, established as satellite republics between 1795 and 1798, were fated in the future to undergo similar incorporation, as were the Austrian provinces of the Adriatic coast. Meanwhile the princely states of western Germany, 350 in number, were between 1801 and 1803 summarily reduced to thirty-nine and amalgamated into a Confederation of the Rhine under French tutelage. The terms of the Peace of Amiens in 1801 had obliged France to withdraw from southern Italy and the Greek Ionian islands, but any part of Italy stood subject to reconquest. Finally Spain, intimidated by French power and suspicious of Britain's imperial ambitions, was a potential French ally and would formally become one in 1804, an unhappy prelude to subjection and occupation.

The Atlantic side of the European land mass was, therefore, in the first decade of the nineteenth century almost wholly dominated by France; only remote Portugal, shielded by its mountain chain, lay outside the immediate reach of French armies. The rest of Europe could not count on remaining so. Prussia, still crowned by the military reputation won under Frederick the Great, seemed secure in its Baltic hinterland – but would prove a house of cards in 1806. Austria, traditional enemy of the French kings, had already failed humiliatingly in its efforts to overturn the Revolution. Even Russia, whose troops had intervened far to the west in 1799, had learned to appreciate the ferocity with which French armies moved to the attack.

And those armies were enormous. The Austrian and Russian armies each numbered some 250,000 men; but both were obliged to keep substantial forces on their frontiers with the Ottoman Empire. The Grande Armée, formed after 1802 from the disparate armies of the

Republic and Consulate, reached a strength of 350,000 in 1805, all of which was at Napoleon's free strategic disposal. By 1808 it would number 700,000 soldiers, of whom 520,000 were deployed in the field. Moreover, while the Austrian and Russian armies were heterogeneous in composition, including large numbers of semi-barbaric irregulars as well as drilled infantry and cavalry, the Grande Armée was uniform in composition. It was, indeed, the first modern *operational* army, in which each formation exactly resembled every other and all were equipped and trained for instant and effective co-operation in the field. Its component elements were the *corps d'armée*, virtual armies in miniature, which moved on the line of march ready to manoeuvre in any direction in support of a neighbour. Their artillery was the best in Europe, their logistic arrangements the smoothest, their men the most highly motivated. Motivation, indeed, supplied their battle-winning quality. Europe had in the years since 1789 made the terrifying acquaintance of a new sort of soldier who fought as if he chose rather than was forced to do so. The result was the almost unbroken stream of French victories on land over every adversary from Valmy in 1792 to Marengo in 1800.

Britain had few victories of which to boast from the same period. And that was because its power, though great, could bear against France only in an indirect and erratic way. The British population of only 13 million scarcely sufficed to support a regular army 80,000 strong: but its buoyant industry and commerce yielded cash surpluses which allowed it to subsidise its foreign allies on a generous scale. In 1799, for example, the Cabinet voted to pay £181,000 a month to support 90,000 Russian and 20,000 Swiss troops in central Europe and an additional £44,000 for a Russian army of 17,500 in Holland; as a percentage of national income, almost £200 million in 1800, that annual sum represents about £18 billion at modern rates, or roughly the equivalent of the British defence budget for 1987. But armies that are bought never fight with the will or effect of armies that are under sovereign control. The Russians, good soldiers though they were, proved as bad a bargain as the much less soldierly Austrians and Spanish were to do later.

Bought soldiers – 'the cavalry of St George', from the image on the gold sovereigns in which they were paid – were not the real menace that the offshore British offered to continental France. That menace derived from factors far older and deeper-rooted – factors which had determined the nature of the Anglo-French relationship since the rise of England to maritime power in the sixteenth century and perhaps earlier. Britain, like Japan, is one of the supreme oddities of the international order. Small in population and deficient in traditional natural resources, it emerged as a rival to the far richer and inherently stronger kingdoms of continental Europe because of its dominant geographical position and unique topography. Britain abounds in natural harbours. Its western, southern and eastern coasts offer shelter to shipping in a chain of estuaries, inlets and roadsteads from Milford Haven in Wales, via Bristol, Plymouth, Dartmouth, Portland, Southampton, Portsmouth, the Downs, Medway and Thames, to Harwich in East Anglia. Britain offers safe anchorages to fleets – merchant or military – every sixty miles along its lower coastline. Further, that coastline bestrides every approach route to the far less numerous entrances to the hinterland of continental Europe. France, over twice the size of Britain, offers only five good harbours along its thousand miles of Atlantic and Channel coast – at Rochefort, Nantes, Lorient, Brest and Le Havre. The next 300 miles – Flemish, Dutch and German – provide shelter and egress only at Antwerp, Rotterdam, Amsterdam and Hamburg. The Baltic ports are constricted by the Danish narrows. The Norwegian harbours are imprisoned by their mountain surroundings. And all these outlets to great waters lie within 400 miles of British territory, the most strategic – Brest, Rouen, Antwerp – within 150 miles.

Britain, economically and demographically so unimportant, is thus strategically one of the two or three most significant centres of power in the inhabited world. Had fate robbed it of the chance to unify its social order at an early date, it would have been fought over and exchanged between external sovereigns as frequently as Sicily in the Mediterranean or Ceylon in the Indian Ocean. Because Britain – more particularly England – achieved statehood in the centuries before Europeans learned the technology and technique of oceanic voyaging, it succeeded in defying conquest (except by the Normans, who captured without destroying its unitary government) until such time as it stood ready to venture its own power in the strategic world. Once that moment came, at the very outset of the era of gun-carrying ships, it was to prove not only unconquerable by neighbours but a mighty base in its own right for the carrying of conquest far beyond its own shores.

Much of that conquest was initially peripheral to the affairs of Europe. The establishment of footholds in North America (Newfoundland, 1497) and the Caribbean (Nevis, 1628) was so marginal in extent and location when compared to the empire-building of the Portuguese in Brazil, the Spanish in Mexico and Peru, the Dutch in the East Indies and Asia and even the French in Canada, the West Indies and Africa that, virtually until the end of the seventeenth century, Britain could scarcely be said to count among the oceanic empires. British areas of settlement in North America were extending but the economies of the colonies served the subsistence of the settlers rather than the prosperity of the homeland, while their coastlines dominated none of the great wealth-bearing routes – that of the Spanish treasure convoys from South America or the spice fleets from the East Indies – that fuelled the money markets of continental Europe.

Then, from the beginning of the eighteenth century, Britain suddenly began to acquire overseas possessions that translated the potential of its burgeoning navy into actual power. The capture of the Caribbean islands of the Bahamas and Jamaica in 1670 gave the British a substantial foothold in what was becoming the principal wealth-producing area of the colonial world. The expansion of the Indian enclaves at Bombay, Madras and Calcutta put them into contention for eventual control of the decaying empire of the Moguls. Most important of all, the acquisition of Gibraltar in 1704 and of Minorca in 1708 made Britain a force in the Mediterranean.

The Mediterranean, Europe's 'middle sea', remained the subjective focus of its economic, strategic and cultural life long after the continent's material energies had begun to percolate into the vaster waters of the Atlantic Ocean. It was the sea across which the traditional great powers of the continent – Spain, France, Habsburg Austria, the Italian republics – intercommunicated. It provided the battlefield on which Christendom and Islam, represented by the Ottoman Empire, struggled for dominance on Europe's southern margin. It was a highroad for the transfer of staples and luxuries between Asia, Africa and the West, as well as the outlet through which the tsars of landlocked Russia hoped to break out into the wider world. Above all, it offered to northern Europeans, and particularly to the British, an alternative strategic centre of effort at which they could challenge and perhaps defeat the power of the established continental states.

Gibraltar, Minorca (until 1782, when lost to Britain) and Malta (acquired in 1800) were the levers through which that effort was applied. Fleets, even the highly self-sufficient sailing-ship fleets of the pre-industrial age, need bases at which to resupply, rest and refurbish themselves if they are to keep the seas. France and Spain had such bases in the chain of ports – particularly Cartagena and Toulon – which runs along the northern Mediterranean shore. However, in the absence of significant local adversaries, of whom there was none after the effective defeat of Ottoman seapower at the end of the sixteenth century, neither France nor Spain (strategically France's client from 1700 onwards) had any reason to maintain strong forces in any of them – that is, until the appearance of the Royal Navy, first at Gibraltar, later at Minorca, Sardinia, Elba and Corsica, finally at Malta, during the course of the eighteenth century. If France and Spain had been free to concentrate all their ships in Atlantic ports they would have been positioned not only greatly to reduce British freedom of action in great waters but even to menace the Royal Navy in its home bases and so threaten the security of the British government and people. However, the presence in the Mediterranean of a British fleet demanded that France and Spain divide their navies, keeping a proportion inside the Mediterranean at Cartagena and Toulon.

History demonstrated how wise had been Britain's naval strategy of forcing their enemies to keep their fleets divided. Once and once only had the French and Spanish (assisted by the Dutch) been able to threaten the British effectively. During the course of the American War of Independence, the British found themselves forced to divide their fleet four ways between home, Mediterranean, transatlantic and Asiatic stations – with disastrous effect. At the battle of Chesapeake Bay in 1778 the French succeeded in massing superior numbers against the British in American waters and defeating them. The result was to open the American coast to reinforcements of French troops for the rebellious colonists' army and so decisively alter the balance of advantage on land. It was only through British doggedness in defence of home waters, notably at the battle of the Dogger Bank against the Dutch in 1781, and because of divergent French and Spanish strategic aims, that Britain escaped envelopment. France time and again sought to achieve a superior naval concentration in the Channel, which would have consigned the British to defeat. Spain, obsessed by its desire to repossess Gibraltar and Minorca, as often failed to co-operate, thus sparing the British the consequences of what by every strategic calculation was a military predicament without exit.

One result of the American War of Independence was nevertheless to reinforce the point of a lesson Britain had learned, but temporarily forgotten, long before: not to fight in Europe without allies on land. Very briefly in 1796 a loss of allies reduced it to a state scarcely better than that it had suffered at its strategic nadir in the American War. Following Spain's alliance with France in the Treaty of San Ildefonso (1796), it was forced to withdraw from the Mediterranean and concentrate its overseas fleet at Gibraltar. The French profited from this retreat to mount an invasion of Ireland – frustrated only by ferocious winter weather – and in the spring of 1797 called the Spanish fleet to Brest for a descent on the Channel. It was only the defiant aggressiveness of Admiral Jervis, almost twice outnumbered, at the battle of Cape St Vincent, which prevented the junction and saved the Royal Navy to fight again another day.

That day was to be in the Mediterranean, which the victory of Cape St Vincent once again opened to British naval power. It would never in the future allow the inland sea to be closed to its operations. Early in 1798, on word that the French were preparing a seaborne invasion of Egypt from Toulon, under the young General Bonaparte, the Admiralty organised a squadron for Mediterranean service, entrusted it to Nelson and sailed it south to re-establish the British naval presence on France's alternative maritime frontier.

The consequences of that initiative were to be decisive for British control of the Mediterranean not only during the remaining years of war with Napoleon (effective ruler of France from 1800) but throughout the nineteenth and for half the twentieth century as well. It was not merely that on 1 August 1798, after a sea chase of the highest drama, Nelson found and destroyed Napoleon's battle fleet in Aboukir Bay at the mouth of the Nile. It was not merely that he thereby marooned one of the best of the French Republic's armies on the wrong side of the Mediterranean, consigning it to eventual defeat at the hands of a joint

British–Ottoman army. What shifted the balance of advantage in the inland sea incontestably to the British side was that, as a consequence of Napoleon's expedition to Egypt, Britain acquired the central Mediterranean island of Malta.

Malta, home of the Knights of St John of Jerusalem since 1530, is to the central Mediterranean what Gibraltar is to its western mouth, an almost impregnable fortress from which use of the sea that washes its walls can be permitted or denied at will. However, Malta differs from Gibraltar in a crucial respect: it is the key not to one sea but to a complex of three, all interconnected, each of differing strategic and economic significance, the whole joined at the point where Malta dominates the narrows between Europe and Africa. The three seas are the western Mediterranean, the Adriatic and the eastern Mediterranean with its dependency, the Aegean. Malta, in the hands of a strong naval power, can deny intercommunication between all, thus frustrating the strategic policies of the three great territorial entities which border them. The first is the Latin bloc – Spain, France and Italy. The second is the central European, whose outlet to the sea is via the Adriatic. The third is the Levantine, centred on Egypt and Turkish Anatolia. Political control of these regions shifts and varies, but at the beginning of the nineteenth century, at the moment when Malta fell into British hands, it coincided almost exactly with those broad geographical divisions. France, with Spain its client and most of Italy its possession, formed the Latin bloc. Habsburg Austria, principal power of central Europe, strove through its control of the northern Balkans to dominate the Adriatic. The Ottoman Empire, ruler of Greece and Anatolia and suzerain of Egypt (loosely also of the pirate city-states of Algiers and Tunis), was the paramount power of the eastern Mediterranean.

The strategic freedom of action of all three nevertheless hinged on Malta – more particularly on who owned it and how far the owner's power extended. In 1565, when the tide of Islam was flowing hard to the West, the Ottomans had landed at Malta, besieged the Knights of St John in their Valetta fortress and almost overcame them. They were saved by the intervention of the Habsburgs, who had installed them in the island after the loss of Rhodes and Syrian Tripoli forty years earlier. Thereafter the Knights had been maintained in possession largely by Habsburg protection, and it was only the eclipse of Austrian power in the early campaigns of the French Revolution which had allowed Bonaparte's fleet to occupy the island en route to Egypt in 1798. One of the many French oversights in that spectacular but flawed campaign was to neglect Malta's subsequent defence, allowing a British expeditionary force to land and seize it for George III in September 1800.

The seizure of Malta, in combination with the possession of Gibraltar, determined that thenceforth an 'out-of-area' state, Britain, would be the dominant naval power in the Mediterranean. Possession of the two fortresses actually allowed the British to acquire further footholds on a discontinuous tenancy – Minorca again (1798–1802), Sardinia (while its ruler was at war with France), Sicily (likewise) and Alexandria (after 1801) – which further extended their strategic reach. But none offered the same advantages as did Gibraltar and Malta; not only did those other places, because of their size and relative indefensibility, require occupation by large garrisons which Britain was simply not strong enough to provide. None was as crucially located as either fortress, none as strongly fortified, none as well endowed by nature to receive or shelter a fleet. Sardinia, even Minorca, were splendid ancillaries to British strategic progress in the inland sea, but it was the Rock of Gibraltar and the man-hewn stones of the Malta fortresses that made Britain its overlord.

How did overlordship work for Nelson in the three years of renewed war with France – and Spain – before he brought their combined fleets to battle at Trafalgar? The crux lay in keeping separate the various squadrons into which the French and Spanish fleets divided. Those squadrons were distributed between eight main ports on the French and Spanish Atlantic and Mediterranean coasts. Outside the Mediterranean, they were Brest, Lorient and Rochefort on the French Atlantic coast and Ferrol, Vigo and Cadiz on the Spanish: inside the Mediterranean they were Cartagena in Spain and Toulon in France. The numbers of ships based in each varied with the season and state of campaign. Out of a total of some thirty-five French line-of-battleships and twenty-five Spanish, one third of each navy was commonly in the Mediterranean and the remainder outside.

British dispositions were proportional. The Royal Navy had begun the war against France in 1792 with a superiority of ship numbers which, despite a naval race funded by popular subscription in France, had been maintained. The British had themselves responded with an emergency building programme and had sustained their lead. However, needing as they did to defend their overseas possessions by maritime force rather than local garrisons, they were required to disperse their fleet in several directions simultaneously. Thus, of the 111 ships of the line on the Admiralty's books at the collapse of the Peace of Amiens in May 1803, only some sixty were available for service in home waters and the Mediterranean; the remainder were distributed between the West Indies, North America, India and the East Indies. Even in nearer waters the same pattern of dispersion, imposed by the division of the French and Spanish fleets between their scattered bases, applied: thus in early 1805 the blockading squadron off Brest numbered twelve, that off Ferrol six, that off Toulon eleven and that off the Texel (watching the reduced Dutch fleet) five, leaving a home reserve of only six in the Downs (the Kent roadsteads) and five at Spithead (off Portsmouth). Britain's bare superiority of numbers would not have sufficed to keep an opponent of equal quality confined to port, or even to assure victory had it come out. Worse, both the French and Spanish fleets included ships stronger than any in British service, and the French ships in particular were, unit for unit, faster, more strongly built and more heavily gunned than their British equivalents. Fortunately their crews lacked sea experience, their squadrons were unpractised in manoeuvre and many of the ships themselves were unseaworthy.

Yet Napoleon, in the face of all these inequalities, was determined that his admirals should outwit their adversaries, scatter their ships by stratagem and achieve a concentration sufficient to cover the cross-Channel voyage of his flat-bottomed invasion fleet. The way to achieve that was threefold: to sustain such force *outside* the Mediterranean as to oblige London to match it, thus dividing the Royal Navy's European concentration; *inside* the Mediterranean to diversify the threat to British interests – which included the independence of the Kingdom of Naples and its dependency, Sicily, the security of Malta and, at a secondary level, of Sardinia, as well as the denial of the Ionian islands and Greece to French occupation and the protection of the Ottoman Empire and Egypt – so as to embroil the Royal Navy in strategic dispersal and permit the escape of the Cartagena and Toulon squadrons into great waters. This strategy outside the Mediterranean was to be purely 'maritime'; inside the Mediterranean it was to be by land and sea in combination; thus by sea he would unsettle Nelson, the local commander, with constant sorties from Toulon and Cartagena, while by land his army in the southern Italian province of Apulia, under General Saint-Cyr, would threaten the invasion of Naples, Sicily, Greece, the Ionian islands, Egypt and even the Ottoman capital of Constantinople. Writing to General Brune, his envoy at Constantinople, in early 1804 he said: 'Your mission is of the greatest importance. Whether I [eventually] choose to march on London or to make peace . . . the whole thrust of my strategy is against Britain.'

NELSON VERSUS NAPOLEON

No one was more aware of the complexity of Napoleon's designs than Nelson. A proven master of the tactics of seapower, with the victories of the Nile and Copenhagen to his credit, he was also acutely sensitive to the space and time dimensions of maritime strategy. The course of the Nile campaign remained with him as an awful warning of how a correct spatial perception of enemy intentions may risk being brought to nought by temporal miscalculation. In 1791 he had rightly anticipated that Napoleon's invasion fleet, sailing from Toulon, was bound for Egypt. However, in his haste to overhaul it after bad weather had scattered his blockade, he actually succeeded in arriving at its destination ahead of time. Persuaded that his judgement had been wrong, he quartered the eastern Mediterranean in his efforts to find it elsewhere, going as far as Turkey and Sicily – both possible alternative destinations – before intelligence reassured him that he had been right in the first place and sent him back towards Alexandria. There, at nearby Aboukir, he found and destroyed Napoleon's fleet, but only after it had landed the army and set in train a war which threatened to make France the dominant power in the Levant and give her control of the landward route to India.

These memories dominated his strategic analysis when he arrived once more in the Mediterranean in June 1803. He was determined, he wrote, to safeguard Malta, 'a most important outwork to India, that . . . will ever give us great influence in the Levant, and indeed all the southern parts of Italy. . . . I hope we shall never give it up' (as Britain had originally agreed to do by the Peace of Amiens and Russia had subsequently demanded). Beyond that he wanted troops for the Kingdom of Naples's province of Calabria, to defend it against Saint-Cyr, 'though we must not risk Sicily too far in trying to save Naples'. In any case, there were no troops to be spared from home, with invasion threatening from Boulogne, for such a campaign. As a result his 'first objective' had to be the French fleet at Toulon, 'ever to be kept in check, and if they put to sea to have force enough to *annihilate them*'.

Keeping the French in check imposed special difficulties. The Atlantic blockade (which in 1803 was maintained by Cornwallis with a minimum of twelve ships of the line) was a simpler duty than the Mediterranean. For an Atlantic onshore wind, the 'westerlies' generally prevailing in those waters kept the French squadrons in their anchorages, which were in any case difficult to clear at short sailing notice. An offshore wind, whether easterly or southerly, automatically carried the British covering force to the mouth of the Channel where it could block a French sally towards Boulogne should the wind subsequently shift in the French favour. A French escape in other directions imposed no immediate danger; not only were the distances great enough to permit time for recovery of error, but the destinations the enemy might reach were merely other French or Spanish ports, over which blockade could again be established. Indeed, the only destination at which an escaped French fleet could concentrate in a way to confuse or upset British strategy was on the far side of the Atlantic, in the West Indies – precisely, as we shall see, the shift into which the French were to be driven as the campaign developed.

In the Mediterranean, however, escape was easier and the opportunity for mischief-making by a roving fleet altogether greater. Northerlies – notoriously frequent, unpredictable and violent in the inland sea – drove a blockading fleet off station and allowed one based at Toulon not only to leave harbour unobserved as the weather abated but then to head in any of several menacing directions: south-westward towards Gibraltar and the freedom of the ocean; due south to Sardinia, bearing troops to occupy that almost undefended island; or south-eastwards towards

Naples, Sicily, Malta, the Ionian islands, Turkey and Egypt. The strategic complexities consequent on a French break-out were well known to Nelson, who had experienced the dislocation of an unexpected southerly gale before the Nile in 1798.

He was determined not to be dislocated a second time. In May 1798, when the French were preparing the Egyptian expedition, he had chosen to cover the exits from Toulon at close hand. He was off Cape Sicie, the headland guarding the port's approaches, when bad weather struck and he had been dismasted. Worse, his scouting frigates were scattered in the blow, and without his 'eyes' he had been induced to guesswork in his effort to organise an effective pursuit of Napoleon's fleet. He would not make the mistake of trusting to 'close blockade' again. It was a proper practice in the Atlantic service, where Cornwallis commonly lay almost within sight of land; but there the enormous sea room behind it permitted a fleet to bear out from shore in bad weather without danger to either itself or its mission. In the Mediterranean, where the tolerances were narrower, close blockade was not appropriate. Accordingly, on his return in 1803, Nelson instituted a 'system' of remote blockade, which combined the necessity of narrow surveillance by frigates with the reinsurance of a more distant stationing of his battle fleet.

Because frigates commanded horizons of some twenty miles in all directions, a 'chain' of five sufficed to bring warning of French movement over a distance of 200 miles. The naval signal book had, from small beginnings in the seventeenth century, been brought by different hands, but most recently (1800) and fruitfully by Admiral Sir Home Popham, to a state which allowed a frigate captain to send any message of military significance that he needed to compose. Repeated by the next frigate – always given, of course, sufficient visibility – it would reach the battle fleet they served as fast as hoists could be sent to the yardarm. As the secondary hoists were mechanical, copying a message would take less than five minutes in good weather to carry, through a 'chain' of five frigates, from point of origin to fleet commander over a distance of 200 miles.

The tentacles of the signalling system, therefore, allowed Nelson in 1803 to cast a looser yet more constricting embrace around Toulon than he had been able to devise five years earlier. On arrival, while he was still feeling his way, he kept the battle fleet some forty miles offshore. There it was out of sight of the French lookouts on the high ground above Toulon port, who under the conditions of close blockade could (as Piers Mackesy dissects the situation) 'alert the French fleet the moment Nelson was blown off station by the prevailing northerly gales, and so be halfway to Alexandria before [he] discovered [its] absence. With no dockyard within a fortnight's sail, with provisions inaccessible, with even water unobtainable in the summer nearer than Pula Bay in southern Sardinia', he was absolutely right to shun close blockade under their eyes. During storms he would lie up in the shelter of the Hyères islands, near Marseilles. Later and more daringly, however, as his sureness of touch developed, Nelson withdrew the fleet even further to the south, sometimes to a covering position 150 miles distant off Cape San Sebastian in northern Spain. From that station he detached portions of the fleet to the Maddalena islands, off northern Sardinia, where provisions could be purchased and safe anchorage found in weather too bad for station-keeping nearer the French coast.

Nelson's strategy, in short, foreshadowed that to be applied by the Admiralty in the North Sea a hundred years later when, in order to forestall attempts by the German High Seas Fleet to break out into the Atlantic, the Grand Fleet was kept at anchorages in south-eastern Scotland and the Orkneys, and close surveillance of the German estuaries left to cruisers based on Harwich in East Anglia. However, greater danger attached to Nelson's solution than to his successors', for the North Sea is a long envelope of water with only one exit (discounting the death trap of the Channel Narrows). Its length ensured long warning time, while its conformation restricted enemy activity to a single initiative. In the Mediterranean in 1803–5 such simplicities did not apply. There Nelson had to be on his guard against several potential initiatives at the same time – descents on Egypt, Greece, Sardinia, Sicily, Naples, Malta and a break-out into great waters – with no certainty that, after bad weather, he could overhaul his adversaries once they had escaped.

'I have made up my mind,' he wrote soon after his return to the Mediterranean in July 1803, 'never to go to port till after the battle, if [the French] make me wait a year.' But in the spring of 1804, with his ships worn by sea-keeping, he still had no assurance of where or when he could bring the enemy to fight. 'Bull [the Civil Commissioner in Malta] is sure,' he wrote in the spring of 1804, 'they are going to Egypt; the Turks are sure they are going to [Greece]; Mr Elliot [British Minister at Naples] to Sicily; and the King of Sardinia to his only spot. . . . I trust, and with confidence, they are going to Spithead.' His strategic perceptions were complicated by tactical agitations. Latouche-Tréville, commander at Toulon and best of the French admirals, had an aggressive streak and constantly threatened the battle Nelson sought – but could not be certain of being in the right space–time spot to win. On 5 April 1804, Latouche-Tréville brought his line of battle out of Toulon to sea, in fact on exercise, though Nelson thought it the real thing. On 13 June he emerged again, tantalised Nelson with the prospect of entering a trap the British had baited on the horizon, and then having 'cut a caper . . . went in again'. Nelson was distracted with frustration. It was heightened even further by Latouche-Tréville's unexpected death on 20 August 1804. 'He has given me the slip,' the admiral wrote; 'the French papers say he died of walking so often up to the signal post . . . to watch us.' Tréville was succeeded by Villeneuve, one of the few French ship captains to have made an escape from the Nile and who, fourteen months later, was to be his opponent-in-chief at Trafalgar.

Those fourteen months were to be consumed in a duel of wits between the two admirals, but a duel in which there was to be a third, unseen, player – Napoleon. The emperor – he had assumed that title on 18 May 1804 – not only sustained a larger strategic vision than any of his subordinates could frame; he was also driven by a far more powerful resolution, all the stronger because his ignorance of the sea dissolved the difficulties that they – and Villeneuve in particular – knew to lie between the vision and its realisation. Napoleon truly thought on a global scale, devising plans which comprehended all the war's battlefronts, active and latent, in a single interconnecting scheme. Land, sea, Europe and the Americas, the Mediterranean and the Atlantic, Britain and Austria were each allotted values, each given a place in his timetable of future events, each marked down for an outcome which would drive his strategy to its ordained conclusion. Writing to Decrès, his Minister of Marine, on 29 September 1804, he said:

> We must send off three expeditions: from Rochefort to secure Martinique and Guadeloupe against enemy action and seize Dominica and St Lucia [in the West Indies]; from Toulon to capture Surinam and the other Dutch colonies [in the Americas]; from Brest to capture St Helena. . . . The landing in Ireland [a subsidiary plan] is only the first act. The squadron must then enter the English Channel and sail to Cherbourg to get news of the [Grand Army at] Boulogne. If on arriving off Boulogne it meets several days of contrary winds, it must go on to the Texel, where it will find seven Dutch ships with 25,000 men embarked. It will convoy them to Ireland. One of the two operations must succeed [and] we shall win the war.

In amplification of this large scheme, he issued detailed plans for the movements of the individual squadrons. Villeneuve, from Toulon, was to leave the Mediterranean, detach ships to mop up the British bases in West Africa and proceed to the West Indies. There he was to make a junction with the Rochefort squadron (Admiral Missiessy), which would already be operating against the British islands. When the combined squadrons had recovered the French and Dutch possessions and captured the British islands he wanted, they were to recross the Atlantic and join Ganteaume on the west coast of France. Their forces would then outnumber the British and stand ready to convoy the Grand Army to England.

His naval power was actually about to increase beyond the figure on which his plan turned. Spain, long a co-operative neighbour, would become his ally on 12 December, and the Spanish king would agree to commission '25–29 sail-of-the-line . . . by March 30, 1805'. That date lay beyond those he had set for the sailing of his separated fleets – 21 October for Villeneuve, 1 November for Missiessy, 23 November for Ganteaume. But the Spanish alliance, by extending the range over which the British had to maintain their blockade, strengthened his hand and weakened theirs. By any paper calculation, the cards were falling inexorably his way.

But naval wars, even less than land wars, do not fall out as paper calculations predicate. Villeneuve, Missiessy and Ganteaume all failed to break out of harbour on the dates set, the weather and the strength of Nelson's and Cornwallis's blockades being against them. And the weather – not a hostile factor had the first two actually been able to reach the benign West Indies (hurricane-free each year after October) – was now bound to worsen on the eastern side of the Atlantic. Late autumn did not favour naval operations in Europe in sailing-ship days. Winter threatened a plan of any complexity with miscarriage. The storm-tossed ships of the British blockading squadrons might, at great cost to their gear and sailors' endurance, just succeed in keeping the seas; but the French, with ships not shaken down and crews not trained for cruising, could scarcely hope to fulfil the precise timetable their commander had set for them. Napoleon the general might have found ways of defying winter on land: Hohenlinden had been won in the December of 1800, as Austerlitz would be in that of 1805. Napoleon the admiral could not command the waters. All the probabilities were that foul weather would disrupt his design. So it turned out.

The foul weather that struck did so, however, not in the Atlantic but in the Mediterranean. On 11 January 1805 Missiessy managed to clear Rochefort with five battleships, elude the blockade and sail for the West Indies. However, when Villeneuve got out of Toulon on 17 January, while Nelson was watering at the Maddalena islands, he ran into storms and turned back, attempting to justify himself in a dispatch which read: 'Finding ourselves observed from the first night of our getting out by two English frigates, which would not fail to bring down on us the whole force of the enemy, and it being out of our power to make much sail with ships so much maltreated, we agreed to return.' Napoleon was outraged none the less – 'What is to be done with admirals who hasten home at the first damage they receive?' – though the French sortie had results from which he might have profited. For Villeneuve's escape had provoked one of Nelson's few strategic neuroses: over-anxiety about the security of the eastern Mediterranean. Perhaps because of his intimate association with the court of Naples, where he had conceived his passion for Emma Hamilton, perhaps because of the near-calamity of his chase to the Nile in 1798, he placed the protection of the routes eastward from Toulon higher than those of the routes westward. Though Villeneuve was bound westward, Nelson chose to believe, on hearing news of the escape, that the French were heading for Sardinia or Sicily or Alexandria, and set off, as he thought, in pursuit. As we have seen, all those places lay at more immediate risk in the circumstances of a French break-out than did any other objective. In that sense, Nelson's anxiety and reaction were justified; but his reaction was wrong, and it was only bad weather that saved him from its consequences.

In March he again misread the situation. Sticking to his 'system' of cruising sufficiently far from Toulon to tempt the French out, he was revictualling off Sardina when word reached him that Villeneuve had seized his opportunity and sailed. Nelson at once turned south to block the gap with the North African coast, and stayed in it until 16 April when he got word of Villeneuve's movements. Though he had resolved on this occasion not to go 'to the eastward of Sicily', he was once more in the wrong position, an error he half conceded when, writing on 18 April to Hugh Elliot, British Minister at Naples, that 'I am going out of the Mediterranean', he said: 'It may be thought that I have protected too well Sardinia, Naples, Sicily, [Greece] and Egypt from the French.'

Nelson would enter the Mediterranean for the last time three months later when, landing at Gibraltar on 16 July, he was to set foot on dry land for the first time in two years. By then he would have learned enough of the French admirals' real intentions to resist the temptation of sailing into the eastern Mediterranean. He would turn back into the Atlantic. The facts spoke for themselves. In 1804 before the Spanish had joined the war, the balance of enemy force was one-third Mediterranean, two-thirds Atlantic. By July 1805 only six enemy ships, and those Spanish and based at Cartagena, remained within the Mediterranean. Nearly fifty were distributed between the Spanish and French ports of the Atlantic coast. The preliminaries of Napoleon's plan 'to defeat the British fleet from the land' had been successfully accomplished.

Part of the concentration of force had been achieved entirely by the accession of Spain to Napoleon's cause; that had brought him the twelve ships at Ferrol and the seven at Cadiz. Part represented the continued presence in Brest–Rochefort–Lorient of Ganteaume's ships. What Napoleon hoped was the decisive increment, however, had been added by the arrival of Villeneuve's Toulon fleet in Atlantic waters, after its roundabout voyage which was the dramatic prelude to the Trafalgar battle. That voyage had transformed the struggle between himself and Nelson respectively to exploit and control the Mediterranean 'gaps' into an oceanic game of hide-and-seek. Its chronology, though measured out in day-long voyages of only a hundred miles or less, is as intricate as anything in sea campaigning.

Villeneuve, on eluding Nelson's blockade on 30 March with ten ships of the line, had steered at once for the Straits of Gibraltar. A British frigate got word of the break-out to Nelson only on 31 March. But the French admiral had learnt of the position Nelson was keeping a day earlier, changed course to avoid it, and on 10 April cleared the mouth of the Mediterranean, taking with him five Spanish ships from Cadiz. Nelson was still that day protecting the gap between Sardinia and the North African coast, and it would be another ten days before he too got out of the Mediterranean. Rumour and guesswork were his only guide to Villeneuve's destination. At first he inclined to the view that the enemy was bound for the Channel approaches. Then stronger rumour, gleaned by a call at Lagos Bay in Portugal, persuaded him that the Caribbean was its destination. He set off in chase. 'Although I am late,' he wrote to the Governor of Malta on 10 May, 'yet chance may have given them a bad passage and me a good one. I must hope the best.'

Chance worked as he hoped. Villeneuve was to be thirty-four days on passage, Nelson only twenty-four. Better still, accident delayed Napoleon's order to Missiessy to extend his stay in the West Indies until after he had turned his squadron for home on the prearranged date. Unseen by both fleets, his squadron of five ships passed Villeneuve and Nelson outward bound, thus depriving the former of the chance of concentrating a superior force – it would have numbered twenty-three to eleven – against the British in Caribbean waters and so bringing on a battle of possibly decisive outcome.

Villeneuve, in the event, achieved nothing decisive in the Caribbean. He was expecting to find Missiessy, who had left. He was equally expecting to be joined by Ganteaume, from Brest–Rochefort–Lorient, who – embayed by Cornwallis – did not come. He had orders to wait for forty days until reinforcements did – or did not – arrive, meanwhile doing as much damage to British West Indian interests as he could. He had reached Martinique, the principal French Caribbean possession, on 14 May. Orders subsequently received reduced his waiting period to thirty-five days and on 29 May two ships which had succeeded in slipping unimpeded out of Rochefort did join him. With a force thus numbering eighteen he cruised for a week around Martinique, falling in with a British merchant convoy and capturing fifteen of its ships. Then word that Nelson was present also in the Caribbean – not Egypt where Villeneuve believed he would, as in the past, have headed – prompted him to panic. False reports inflated the number of Nelson's ships, confronting him with the spectre of defeat far from France should they meet, and so turned him homeward. He had, by the spirit if not the letter of Napoleon's instructions, achieved the desired result of drawing the Royal Navy's best admiral and principal striking force to the periphery of the Atlantic operational area.

Nelson meanwhile had been tracking Villeneuve between the Caribbean islands down one false scent after another. On his arrival on 4 June the commander of the St Lucia garrison told him that the French were not at Martinique – though they were – but at Trinidad. On arrival there on 6 June, he learned that he had been misled, headed north and reached Grenada on 9 June. There he discovered that Villeneuve had been at Martinique in the first place but surmised that he must since have moved somewhere else.

Where? To another island? To a Caribbean cruising station? Or back to Europe? 'So far from being infallible, like the Pope,' he wrote in an outburst of self-explanation to the Secretary of the Admiralty on 16 June, 'I believe my opinions to be very fallible, and I therefore may be mistaken that the enemy's fleet is gone to Europe; but I cannot bring myself to think otherwise.' He had in fact turned for home on 13 June, sending the fast-sailing brig *Curieux* ahead of him with news for London. His intentions he summarised in a letter to the British Minister at Lisbon on 15 June: 'I do not yet despair of getting up with them before they arrive at Cadiz or Toulon, to which ports I think they are bound, or at least in time to prevent them having a moment's superiority.'

Once again his obsession with the Mediterranean was to carry him to the wrong place – Gibraltar, on this occasion – but his fleet's superior sailing powers which brought him across the Atlantic ahead of Villeneuve gave him time to retrieve his mistake. On 1 August, having sailed from Gibraltar, he fell in with an American merchant ship which told him it had earlier passed the French steering northwards. He turned in pursuit, to make junction with Admiral Collingwood, who commanded the Brest–Rochefort–Lorient blockade station, there to hear, on 15 August, definite news of Villeneuve's return but also of a miscarried battle. The news was both bitter and sweet for Nelson. It reinforced the fruitlessness of his long chase – 3227 miles out, he understated in his diary, 3459 miles back – but it left open the opportunity for Nelson to be 'living or dead, the greatest man in his profession that England ever saw'.

What had happened turned on his prescient decision to dispatch the speedy *Curieux* from the Caribbean to the Admiralty. Not only did that ship bring word to Lord Barham, the First Lord of the Admiralty, that Nelson was homeward bound. It also brought firm intelligence of Villeneuve's movements. For on 19 June it had sighted the French fleet in mid-Atlantic, also homeward bound. Barham, who woke to this report on 9 July, reacted with instant and courageous decision. The imperative was to catch Villeneuve on the high seas before he could make junction with Ganteaume in Brest–Rochefort–Lorient and achieve Napoleon's long-plotted concentration of superior force. Counting on the unlikelihood of Ganteaume's breaking out, Barham therefore ordered Cornwallis to raise the blockade, send a portion of his fleet under Admiral Calder to patrol off the north-west corner of Spain, Cape Finisterre, and to cruise himself in the Bay of Biscay. These dispositions of battleships, which were supported by the usual screen of frigates, ensured that Villeneuve would unerringly sail into a British net; and that, even if he were joined by ships from the French ports, he would be brought to battle on terms not far from equal.

And so it had turned out, as Nelson learnt when he came aboard Cornwallis's *Ville de Paris* on 15 August. On 22 July Calder, off Cape Finisterre with fifteen ships, had sighted Villeneuve with twenty – six

Spanish, fourteen French – steering to pass to his southward for the port of Ferrol. Calder had cleared for action and formed line of battle. The Franco-Spanish fleet did likewise. But the wind was so light that it was late afternoon before they came within gunshot, and when they did so the tactics Calder chose – to tack up to the French line in succession rather than together – robbed his ships' approach of impact. Individual captains closed boldly with the enemy but none got near alongside, the only measure which assured decision in wooden-wall warfare. British gunnery, as always superior to the enemy's, brought down the masts of two enemy ships which surrendered; it also inflicted far heavier casualties on the enemy than theirs on the British: 641 killed and wounded to 203. Losses of ships and men were not sufficient, however, to justify Calder claiming a victory. Though the action was almost rejoined the next day – impressively at Villeneuve's initiative – fickle winds again frustrated ship-to-ship action and the fleets drew apart. So incomplete was the result that the engagement has no proper name; it is generally known as 'Calder's Action of 22 July'.

In its aftermath, Villeneuve slipped, via Vigo, into the nearby Spanish ports of Corunna and Ferrol, and Calder sailed north to rendezvous with Cornwallis. Nelson, whose mission was to safeguard British interests in the Mediterranean, from which all but a handful of the enemy had departed, was free to take the leave he had not had for two years. As he left the Atlantic, he wrote to a fellow sea-warrior, Captain Thomas Fremantle, in reflection on Calder's miscarried encounter:

> I was in truth bewildered by the account of Sir Robert Calder's victory . . . together with hearing that John Bull was not content which I am sorry for. Who can, my dear Fremantle, command all the success our country may wish? We have fought together [they had been at Tenerife and at Copenhagen] and therefore well know what it is. I have had the best disposed fleet of friends, but who can say what will be the event of a battle? And it most sincerely grieves me that in any of the papers it should be insinuated that Lord Nelson could have done better. I should have fought the enemy; so did my friend Calder; but who can say that he will be more successful than another?

Generously though Nelson's post-mortem on Calder's Action of 22 July reads even today, the truth was that Calder had failed to achieve a victory which Nelson would have died in the attempt to consummate. Calder had not unravelled Barham's strategy of enmeshing the French in a British net, but neither had he drawn together its strings. Napoleon's strategy of concentrating his naval strength in a single theatre of operations for the descent upon England was no further advanced than it had been before Nelson left the Mediterranean. What today is called the 'correlation of forces' revealed in August 1805 the following deployment: the Royal Navy disposed of some fifty-five line-of-battleships, dispersed between the Channel and the north coast of Spain. The French and Spanish disposed of almost the same number, concentrated in two fleets: that of Ganteaume in Brest–Rochefort–Lorient, as always, and that of Villeneuve, temporarily in the north-west Spanish ports. Could the latter but join the former, Napoleon's concentration would be complete and the preliminaries for the descent upon England concluded.

Two eventualities now supervened to frustrate the grand design at its moment of consummation. Napoleon got word of a concentration of land power gathering at his back; and Villeneuve, when freed to sail from the north-western Spanish ports in which he had taken refuge after the 22 July action, chose to go south – away from Ganteaume – rather than northwards towards him.

Napoleon would ever after blame Villeneuve for the collapse of the invasion project – 'Where did my admirals learn that they can make war without taking risks?' – with complete and characteristic unfairness. His decision to strike camp at Boulogne and turn the Grand Army inland, towards the Rhine and ultimately the Danube where the forces of Austria and Russia were mustering for a new (the third) coalition campaign against him, was taken before word of Villeneuve's sailing reached him. He would have had to take the decision he did in any case; a Russo-Austrian coalition threatened his power as the survival of Britain's seaborne empire never could. However, Villeneuve's behaviour was nevertheless perverse to the point of incomprehensibility. What had provoked it?

'In war,' runs one of Napoleon's most famous military maxims, 'the moral is to the material as three to one.' His stratagems had achieved, if not a decisive material superiority over the British in the Atlantic, then at least a material equality. But the moral purpose that might have wrung a victory from that material equality had collapsed. Somewhere and sometime between his leaving Toulon in March and his reaching Spain in July, Villeneuve's nerve had cracked. On 13 August he wrote from Corunna to Decrès, the Minister of Marine:

> I am about to sail but I do not know what I should do. Eight of the [British] line keep in sight of the coast at eight leagues. They will follow us; I shall not be able to get contact with them and they will close on the squadron before Brest [where Ganteaume still was] or Cadiz [effectively empty], according as I make my course to the one port or the other. . . . I do not hesitate to say – to you – that I should be sorry to meet twenty of them. Our naval tactics are antiquated. We know nothing but how to place ourselves in line, and that is just what the enemy wants.

For two days after leaving Corunna he held a course due west into the Atlantic, from which he might have diverged to reach either Brest – where Ganteaume, under exigent orders from Napoleon, would shortly bring his ships out to within gunshot of Cornwallis's blockade – or Cadiz. However, he insisted on interpreting such intelligence as he collected – from his own frigates, from an intercepted neutral – as evidence that the British were in such force to his north that 'they were in a position to meet in superiority the combined forces of Brest and Ferrol'. At nightfall on 15 August, therefore, he altered course to the south and four days later entered Cadiz. Apart from a brief sortie the following day, 20 August, which was checked by the appearance of a small blockading force under Admiral Collingwood, he and the Combined Fleet would remain there until the eve of Trafalgar.

Napoleon's design for the descent upon England had therefore disintegrated; not only had the army, with which the Royal Navy was to be defeated 'from the land', been drawn away into the heartland of the continent; the fleet with which its Channel crossing was to be covered lay scattered almost as far from its necessary point of concentration as it had before he had given the first tug at the ligaments of his strategy. The disintegration had been brought about, however, not by any direct application of British force – Calder's action off Finisterre and Cornwallis's skirmish with Ganteaume scarcely counting – but by the fears and spectres with which five months of oceanic rambling had filled Villeneuve's mind. Napoleon's jibes, threats and draconian orders had fed those fears; worry at the poor state of his ships and members of his crews had sapped his will to resist them; the seeming unwillingness of his fellow admirals, confined to port by British blockade, to share the risks he was running had reinforced them; but in the last resort it was the image of an implacable Nelson – dogging his footsteps, lying in wait for him, anticipating his every move – that had raised them to the level of the unbearable. 'Indeed, Sire,' General Lauriston, commander of the troops embarked on Villeneuve's armada, was to write to Napoleon, 'the fear of Nelson has got the upper hand of him.' What manner of men were they who had fought out this duel for psychological dominance over five months of time and 7000 miles of ocean?

NELSON VERSUS VILLENEUVE

Villeneuve was not born to defeat. A cadet of the old royal navy, which he had joined at fifteen, he had served under the formidable Admiral Suffren in his victorious campaign against the British off Madras and Ceylon in the closing stages of the American war in 1782–3. His lineage was wholly martial. The de Villeneuves of Bargemon in Provence were a military family of great antiquity, intimately connected with the Knights of St John of Malta. A de Villeneuve had served as Grand Master and Pierre Charles Jean Baptiste Silvestre himself was the ninety-first de Villeneuve to belong to the Order.

The coming of the Revolution had thrown his career, as that of all royal officers, into turmoil. The tribunes of the Revolution did not hate the navy as they hated the army; but they needed it less and, as its lower ranks contained as many opportunistic malcontents as any other *ancien régime* institution, they did little to protect its aristocratic professionals from their subordinates' urge to supplant them. The old corps of officers, to which Villeneuve belonged, was dissolved in 1791 and a new establishment created by decree. Some of those appointed to it were – as through the *amalgame* of royal and national guard personnel in the revolutionary army – former commission-holders. Others were merchant officers, warrant officers or men from the lower deck. In October 1793 Jean-Bon Saint-André – the naval member of the Committee of Public Safety – instituted a comprehensive purge, to rationalise the haphazard programme of intimidation, dismissal and occasional guillotining which had racked the officer corps in the preceding two years. Lists of naval officers were posted in their home ports, calling for those suspected of *incivisme* (lack of loyalty to the Republic) to be denounced to the *commune* and the seamen of the *arrondissement*, and their future to be decided by popular vote. This measure not unnaturally accelerated the rate of resignations and emigrations which had so greatly diminished the professional element of the corps of naval officers since 1789. Evidence of its effect is revealed by the composition of the command of the fleet which the revolutionary admiral, Villaret-Joyeuse, took to sea in 1794. Though he himself had belonged to the old royal navy, he had been only a lieutenant three years before. The other two flag officers had been lieutenant and sub-lieutenant respectively, while of his twenty-six captains nine came from the merchant service, one had been a naval rating and one a merchant-service boatswain.

Villeneuve was a survivor of those troubled times. A sometime *rouge* (nobleman) of the *gardes du pavillon*, who with the *bleus* (commoners) provided the old royal navy with its apprentice officers, he had not followed the majority into retirement or exile but in 1793 had sworn an oath of loyalty to the revolutionary Convention and dropped the particule 'de' from his name. As plain Villeneuve he had taken part in the siege of Toulon, then held by royalists with British support, where he had met the young Napoleon. Already a post-captain in command of a ship, he was promoted rear-admiral in 1794 – evidence of how short France was of senior naval officers – and led a squadron in the abortive expedition to Ireland in 1796. In the Nile campaign he commanded the rear of Brueys's fleet. Lying as it did furthest from Nelson's onset, it was not engaged during the crisis of the battle and he was eventually able to extricate some of its line-of-battleships and two of its frigates from the action and sail clear out of Aboukir Bay. For this enterprise – which did not altogether earn the approval of his brother officers – Napoleon christened him 'fortunate', a considerable compliment, since Napoleon thought luck a military talent.

On his escape Villeneuve led the remnant of his division to Malta and played a leading part in the defence of Valetta first against the rebellious Maltese and then against the British when they came to invest the fortress in 1800. With General Vaubois he signed the instrument of surrender which made the island British on 5 September. The quietus in the naval war then kept him out of action until 1804 when, largely through a friendship forged with Decrès, Minister of Marine, in the American war, he was promoted vice-admiral and in August appointed to command at Toulon. The vacancy had been left by the unexpected death of Latouche-Tréville and would have been filled by either Bruix or Ganteaume had they not been commanding respectively the invasion flotilla and the Brest squadron. Villeneuve was certainly no one's first choice for a command of such importance; he succeeded by default.

Napoleon, in the aftermath of Trafalgar, was to launch a famous insult at Villeneuve: that if not a *poltron de coeur* he was a *poltron de tête* – a psychological if not a moral coward. The evidence to support Napoleon's assessment of Villeneuve's progressive collapse of will had come to the emperor in a succession of reports and dispatches, written by his admiral, or his close colleagues, throughout the development of the Trafalgar campaign. Yet it was a low jibe against a man who eventually found the courage first to confront the greatest admiral of the age in open combat and then to choose suicide – or apparent suicide – as a judgement on his own failure. On 21 August, at the end of the cruise to the West Indies, Villeneuve wrote to Decrès from Cadiz in a mood which suggests the onset of nervous breakdown:

> My Lord, whatever be the impression that your Excellency must receive of the circumstances which have not appeared to me to admit of the execution of His Imperial Majesty's vast design, I beg of you to believe that nothing can equal the despair that I am suffering from them and the horror of the situation in which I find myself. But if this great armament which was entrusted to me was inevitably to be the plaything of the winds, in waters absolutely unknown to five-sixths of the seamen who manned these ships; if the state of equipment of these ships, their lack of co-operation and of intelligence did not allow of encountering the slightest obstacles without suffering irreparable injuries, dispersions and the ruin of the project, making us the laughing-stock of Europe; if this armament had ceased to be the enemy . . . so that an engagement . . . could not promise us either success or glory or favourable chances for the fleet at Brest . . . finally if the gallant and estimable Allied Admiral [the Spaniard Gravina] was himself overwhelmed and only followed me with the devotion of despair, it was my duty, after having employed all the perseverance possible in effecting the junctions provided for in His Imperial Majesty's plans, to stop at that point where there could no longer result anything but disasters, confusion and a useless demonstration which would have completed forever the discredit of the Allied Navies.

Fear of 'disasters, confusion and a useless demonstration' were not the emotions which had animated the Villeneuves who had fought at the side of Richard the Lionheart on crusade in the Holy Land or, as legend has it, with Roland in the Pass of Roncesvalles. Such fears had, nevertheless, been present from the start of the campaign, as the letter written by General Lauriston, military commander aboard the fleet, to Napoleon on 22 August makes clear:

I was, from my very first arrival at Toulon, [desirous] of being on good terms with the Admiral. I wrote in this sense to the Minister [Decrès] in order that this would inform him and that this would produce an effect upon him. . . . Your Majesty knows what was my attitude towards him at the time of our first putting to sea; he appeared to be grateful for it until the Minister had replied, perhaps fearing he should be blamed. Since that time he has resumed his proud bearing and sarcastic aloofness towards me, wishing neither to receive advice nor any other counsel. . . . This squadron needs a *man* and above all an admiral who commands confidence and attachment. . . . The captains have no heart left to do well; attention is no longer paid to signals, which remain flying at the masthead for two or three hours. Discipline is utterly relaxed. . . . The greatest resolution is required at this moment. . . . This humiliating cruise has not disgusted me, I am ready to recommence a yet more trying one if only it be with a *man* and that I do not witness the discredit of the navy.

Villeneuve's unsuitability for high command, whether it was intrinsic or the result of the psychological drubbing inflicted by the chase to the West Indies, was borne out by two other documents: the first was the record of a council of war held aboard his flagship, the *Bucentaure*, which his Spanish chief of staff, Escano, made the same day, 8 October. 'A council of war never fights' is a hallowed military maxim; but a council of war need not foment bad blood between comrades-in-arms, and yet that is what Villeneuve allowed his to achieve. 'The French,' Escano reported, 'expressed various opinions with the warmth characteristic of their nation.' Magon (one of Villeneuve's flag-officers) 'refuted [Escano] the chief of staff with scant courtesy; the sensitive and punctilious Galiano [a general commanding embarked Spanish troops] sought to make him retract several expressions, tempers grew warm and Gravina [the senior Spanish admiral present] rising, requested that the vote should be taken without further discussion.' It is difficult to judge whether the recriminations between allies to which Villeneuve had allowed expression and the result of the vote by which he had devolved his authority – it was for staying in harbour – or the devolution of authority itself most clearly demonstrated his failure to show leadership at this critical moment. However, such failure there evidently was, as his half-hearted appeal to action issued to his captains then bore out:

The captains in command will realise from the position and strength of the enemy before this port that an engagement must take place the very same day that the Fleet puts to sea. . . . The Fleet will see with satisfaction the opportunity that is offered it to display that resolution and daring which will ensure its success, revenge the insults offered to its Flag, and lay low the tyrannical domination of the English upon the seas. Our Allies will fight at our side, under the walls of Cadiz and in the sight of their fellow citizens; the Emperor's gaze is fixed upon us. The motives of emulation are also the guarantees of a day honourable alike to the forces of our respective Sovereigns and to the glory of all the valiant men who will bear their part therein.

Pessimism and defeatism ooze from every sentence of this circular letter. The hopes it expresses are half-hearted; the emotions it seeks to arouse are lukewarm; the appeal to action it evokes – in particular the veiled allusion to Napoleon's withheld displeasure – is minatory rather than inspiring. No wonder Lauriston yearned for 'a *man*' to head the fleet; no wonder, either, that he identified the brooding presence of Nelson as the factor which had unmanned Villeneuve. For, where Villeneuve saw difficulty, Nelson glimpsed opportunity; where Villeneuve found in bad weather and damage to his ships the pretext for inaction, Nelson saw nothing but everyday challenge to be overcome; where Villeneuve shrank from action, Nelson sought by every means to bring it on; where Villeneuve anticipated defeat, Nelson believed in victory. Every difference between them was trumpeted by the tone of his famous memorandum to his captains, the counterpart of Villeneuve's circular of 28 September, written on 8 October and known ever after as 'the Nelson touch'.

It is a brilliantly straightforward statement of intention. 'I have made up my mind,' its substantive passages begin, 'that the order of sailing is to be the order of battle', and goes on to analyse in the closest particulars how the battle must then develop, culminating in a totally confident prediction of the outcome: 'If the van [leading division] of the enemy tacks [turns into the wind] the captured ships must run to leeward of the British fleet, if the enemy wears [turns away from the wind] the British must place themselves between the enemy and the captured and disabled British ships, and should the enemy close I have no fears as to the result.' This memorandum superseded one written earlier during the cruise to the West Indies, the preamble to which applied to both and left his captains in no doubt as to what he intended: 'The business of an English Commander-in-Chief being first to bring an enemy's fleet to battle and on the most advantageous terms to himself (I mean that of laying his ships close on board the enemy as expeditiously as possible) and secondly, to continue them there, without separating, until the business is decided.' When his captains came aboard *Victory* off Cadiz on 29 September, the day of its rejoining the fleet, and the day after Villeneuve had written his limp circular, he outlined to them over dinner both the spirit and letter of his intentions. 'When I came to explain to them the "Nelson touch",' he wrote immediately afterwards to Emma Hamilton, 'it was like an electric shock. Some shed tears, all approved – "It was new – it was singular – it was simple", and, from admirals downwards, it was repeated – "It must succeed, if ever they will allow us to get at them! You are, my Lord, surrounded by friends whom you inspire with confidence." '

Nelson's capacity to inspire derived most strongly from his dramatic personality and extraordinary character; but it was reinforced by his appearance, and his record of service, the first physical evidence of the second, which in turn set him – but also the majority of his fellow sea-officers – altogether apart from the French and Spanish contemporaries. Villeneuve's pathetic allusions to his sailors' – he could also have included his officers' – lack of sea time and fighting experience simply did not apply to the Royal Navy, as Nelson's own account of his life story perfectly testified. Written in 1799, after the Nile, it is both a masterly abstract of autobiography and a shorthand record of the Royal Navy's operations in his lifetime – as well as being a striking refutation of those charges of egotism and self-dramatisation which are usually laid against his character. It states simply that, soon after being sent to sea with his uncle, Captain Suckling, at the age of twelve, he had served on an Arctic expedition and a voyage to India, taken part as a lieutenant in the American war, fought ashore (and been blinded in one eye) in Corsica in 1794, served in three Mediterranean naval actions in 1795, the blockade of North Italy in 1796 and of Cadiz in 1797, fought in the battle of Cape St Vincent and lost his right arm in landing operations at Tenerife in the same year. In 1798 he had conducted and won the campaign of the Nile and commanded the squadron sent to protect Naples from French invasion (where he had met Emma Hamilton). 'Thus may be exemplified my life,' he concluded, 'that perseverance in any profession will probably meet its reward.' Of his most celebrated – and remarkable – exploit, the victory of the Nile, he made no more reference than to direct the reader 'to the printed narrative', while as a general comment on his career he went no further than to suggest that 'difficulties and dangers do but increase my desire of attempting them', a neat Anglo-Saxon expression of Alexander the Great's *pothos*.

Nelson's modesty in this document – he could, of course, as Wellington recalled from their only meeting, be embarrassingly immodest at times – concealed a great deal: that he had acquired a ferocious reputation as a ship-taker, in particular through his leadership of the boarding parties that had stormed the *San José* and the *San Nicolas* at Cape St Vincent; that he was a master of ship and fleet management, as his refitting of his own flagship and its companions after the great storm in the Gulf of the Lion during the Nile campaign testified; that he had the actor's gift of attracting the attention but also the devotion of subordinate officers and – a more difficult task – men; and that he was a revolutionary tactician. His decision to risk the shallows of Aboukir Bay at the Nile, a decision to be repeated three years later at Copenhagen, marked him out as an innovator and anticipated his solution of the problem of bringing decision to battle on the high seas so triumphantly achieved at Trafalgar.

Extraordinary though Nelson's life had been, however, it was not qualitatively different from those of many of the officers who were to serve under him in the approaching battle. Among those equal to him in length of service, for example, Collingwood had fought ashore at Bunker's Hill, commanded ships at the battles of the Glorious First of June and Cape St Vincent and been continuously on blockade in the Atlantic in 1800–2 and 1803–5. Hardy had served in the Mediterranean in 1793–6, fought at Cape St Vincent, the Nile and Copenhagen and was famous in the navy for his capture of the French frigate *Mutine*, of which he had subsequently been given command. And Fremantle, a ship captain since 1793, had been with Nelson in both Corsica and Tenerife, had captured enemy gunboats in 1795 and a frigate in 1796 and commanded a man-of-war at Copenhagen.

These, of course, were the great men of the Nelsonian navy, Hardy and Fremantle almost the closest members of Nelson's 'band of brothers'. But humbler men in the Trafalgar fleet had comparable records of service. Andrew Green, for example, a lieutenant of HMS *Neptune*, had been at the siege of Toulon in 1793, with Nelson in Corsica in 1794, and in Admiral Hotham's action with the French in 1795. He had been wrecked and taken prisoner in the same year, then gone to the West Indies, where he had fought in a siege and a ship action. He had been at Copenhagen and earlier in 1805 was mentioned in dispatches for commanding boats in an attack on a Spanish convoy. Samuel Burgess, a lieutenant in HMS *Prince*, had been a midshipman at the Glorious First of June and in the capture of privateers in 1794 and 1795, had taken part in the Dutch expedition of 1799 and had fought in a night action against a French ship in 1801. Thomas Colby, lieutenant in HMS *Thunderer*, had fought at the battle of Camperdown against the Dutch in 1797, against the French off Ireland in 1796 and again against the French in Indian waters in 1804. John Hindmarsh, a lieutenant in the frigate *Phoebe*, had been at the Glorious First of June, at the Nile, where he lost an eye, in the capture of forts at Naples and Gaeta in 1799, at the Algeciras and Gibraltar actions in 1801, wounded again the same year in the capture of a privateer and wounded in the battle of Alexandria in 1801.

These men were somewhat more experienced than the majority of officers in the Trafalgar fleet, but not exceptionally so. Their records of service are replicated, in part if not in full, across the whole roll of Nelson's officers. Of the seventeen lieutenants and officers of equivalent rank abord HMS *Victory*, for example, ten had been in action at least once before, including one who had been at both the Nile and Copenhagen. Aboard the *Spartiate*, a 74-gun ship, four out of the six lieutenants had been in action; aboard the *Mars*, also a 74, three out of six; aboard the *Swiftsure*, 74, five out of five; aboard the *Thunderer*, 74, four out of four.

Neither the French nor the Spanish complements of the Combined Fleet could match this record of action and sea service. The senior officers, who had held rank before the Revolution and the era of blockade, which for so long confined their ships to harbour, knew the ways of the sea and of battle. Dumanoir, second-in-command to Villeneuve, had been a frigate captain in the expedition to Egypt and second-in-command at the Algeciras action of 1801. Magon, third-in-command, had fought in European and West Indian waters in the American war. Cosmao-Kerjulien, captain of the *Pluton*, had served in the West Indies and fought in Calder's action. And Infernet of the *Intrépide* had been in the battle of the Saints in the West Indies in 1782. Of the Spanish commanders, Gravina's combat experience went back to the great siege of Gibraltar in 1782, when he had commanded a gunboat; so too did that of Alava, second-in-command; while Cisneros, third-in-command, had been a ship captain at Cape St Vincent.

But the more junior Spanish and French officers – many of the latter, as we have seen, inducted from the merchant service or promoted from the lower deck – were simply not the equivalents of their British opposite numbers, lacking both battle experience and naval sea time – many of them any sea time whatsoever. And between the common seamen of the British and combined fleets there was scarcely a comparison to be made. Saint-André's abolition of the corps of seamen gunners (5400 strong) in 1793 on the grounds that they constituted 'an aristocracy of the sea' had had a disastrous effect on the republican navy's fighting ability, which had not been corrected by the Directory's efforts to found the corps anew. The navy's establishment of able seamen was not the equivalent of its British counterpart; it contained far too high a proportion of men whom the Royal Navy would have rated no better than 'waisters' and 'landsmen'. To compensate for that weakness the French component of the Combined Fleet had a large number of uniformed soldiers aboard. They were the men under General Lauriston's command and comprised 1800 men of the 2nd Infantry Regiment; another 1800 men of the 16th Infantry Regiment, 1150 of the 67th and 120 artillerymen were embarked as a landing force. They would do duty in battle, but they were not seamen, nor even marines, those disciplined sea-soldiers who were to fight so effectively aboard Nelson's ships. The Spanish seamen were of even lower quality. 'Herdsmen and beggars' was how Villeneuve wrote of them to Decrès on 24 September; these were the products of the Spanish conscription service and by his reckoning they formed five-sixths of the Spanish crews. The gunners, best of the men aboard, were inexperienced and under the command of army artillerymen.

The British seamen, by contrast, were masters of their trades. Some had learned those trades willy-nilly, for the Royal Navy had from the middle of the eighteenth century consistently manned its ships in war by impressment; by 1805 pressed men made up at least half of each ship's crew. However, there is a widespread misconception about the press, supplied by the gruesome imagery of the 'press gang' and its supposed practice of kidnapping and shanghai-ing townsmen and villagers from their homes and workplaces. That was not how the press worked. The powers of the impressment service were, and always had been, strictly limited to conscripting within the seafaring population. Its size by 1805 was about 300,000, if fishermen and longshoremen were counted in with merchant seamen; and from that total some 120,000 were serving in the navy. About half were volunteers, the majority British nationals but a significant minority – 8 per cent in HMS *Victory*, more in other ships – foreigners. The rest were pressed and – a new element – 'quota' men, supplied by the inland counties, usually by offering minor criminals the choice of sea service as an alternative to gaol. Quota men were unfamiliar with the sea but probably willing to learn its ways. Pressed men were usually skilled seafarers who accepted conscription as an occupational hazard. N. A. M. Rodger, a scholar of the eighteenth-century navy, has recently shown that press gangs collected volunteers in significant numbers, while unwilling victims frequently submitted to impressment without resistance. The rise in pressing imposed by the necessities of the Napoleonic wars aroused resentments which broke out in the Spithead and Nore mutinies of April and May 1797; but the former was a strike (for better pay and conditions) rather than a rebellion, the men making it clear that they would sail if the French put out, while the latter, though more seditious, collapsed because the grievances expressed by the Spithead mutineers had been remedied.

Nelson's crews were thus a homogeneous body of high seafaring quality. Their number, compared to those in merchant ships of similar size, was high (one man to two tons displacement as opposed to one to ten, on average), for two reasons: the first was the need to work the guns, the second that to handle sails with a dispatch unknown in merchantmen. These duties were not mutually exclusive. Men whose duties were aloft when the captain was making and shortening sail would go below when action stations were beaten, because then ship-handling was reduced to bare simplicities. Naval battles could not be fought in heavy weather. The guns could not be brought to bear nor ships laid alongside each other. Contrarily, the weather that permitted cannonade and boarding did not require crews to man the yards or running rigging.

It was therefore true, as Samuel Leech, a Napoleonic veteran of the lower deck, tells us, that 'each task has its man and each man his place. A ship contains a set of *human* machinery in which every man is a wheel, a band or a crank, all moving with wonderful regularity and precision to the will of its machinist – the all-powerful Captain.' But, while some men had only one task, others had at least two: the service of the guns and that of the motive power of the ship – sails and rigging. Fore, main and mizen-top men doubled at both. 'Waisters', who worked at the least-skilled tasks of pulling and hauling in the waist of the ship, also doubled as gun crew in action, since each team of twelve included a number needed only for muscle power. The remainder of the ship's company were all specialists of high and low calling. They included the commissioned officers, the warrant officers, the marines, the gun captains, the craftsmen and the 'idlers', so called because they did not turn out for watch.

In a first-rate ship of the period 'idlers' included the master-at-arms and the ship's corporal (responsible for discipline), the armourer and his three mates, the sailmaker and his four mates, four 'holders' (who stowed the stores), two coopers, the yeomen of the boatswain, gunner and carpenter, a midshipman's steward, a captain's sweeper, three surgeon's attendants, five admiral's servants, two captain's servants, two officers' servants, two butchers, three hairdressers, a painter, a poulterer, two tailors, three purser's assistants, two sanitary men ('captain of the head and mate'), three crew cooks, a fifer, a caulker and a clerk.

The officers of a first-rate ship, besides the captain, numbered, in the commissioned ranks, eight lieutenants, three marine officers and (as embryo officers) eighteen midshipmen; warrant officers included the (sailing) master and his half-dozen mates (who might become officers), the surgeon, chaplain and purser; and, in a class not admitted to the officers' wardroom, the gunner, carpenter and boatswain – the latter responsible for the ship's sails and rigging.

Gunner, boatswain and carpenter were the ancient mariners of a ship's crew; as 'standing' officers, they remained in it whatever its circumstances – at sea, in harbour or 'paid off'. Its fabric and essential equipment – guns, spars, rigging and sails – were in their charge and they were jealous of their rights, which many of them reckoned to include surreptitious misappropriation of government property. Admiral Duncan, victor of Camperdown over the Dutch, is alleged to have told his boatswain in HMS *Edgar*, John Bone, 'Whatever you do, Mr Bone, I hope and trust you will not take the anchors from the bow', a delightful revelation of the status a 'standing' officer could acquire in a ship and the lengths to which he might be tempted to go, since it took most of the ship's company to shift the weight of an anchor by main force.

'Standing' officers were drawn from the cream of the lower deck and, for all the allegations of peculation to which they were subject, devoted seamen; a disproportionate number of boatswains, as we shall see, were killed at Trafalgar. The commissioned ranks, lieutenants, midshipmen and, increasingly, master's mates came from families of gentle birth, often with established traditions of naval service. Nelson was the nephew of a naval captain; Andrew King and Bligh, lieutenants in *Victory*, were respectively brother and son of admirals; Captain George Duff, killed commanding the *Mars*, had his son aboard as a midshipman, while two other Duff brothers were also in *Mars* as master's mate and volunteer first-class, the latter to be a fatal casualty; in *Belleisle* four officers were the sons of naval officers while another had three brothers in the service; in *Revenge* two officers also had three officer brothers; *Spartiate* and *Achilles* were both commanded by the sons of admirals, *Africa* by the son of a captain RN, the cutter *Entreprenante* by the son of a lieutenant.

The French and Spanish navies of 1805, for all the ancient military lineage of some of the officers serving aboard their ships, simply could not match their British adversaries in dedication to service or in the habit of 'following the sea'. Many British officers might, by family background, seem to have had only the most distant connection with seafaring; a high proportion were the sons of doctors, clergymen and lawyers, a smaller proportion the sons of landed gentlemen and a very few the sons of noblemen; but, however tenuous the individual association, the body of British naval officers were steeped in their nation's maritime tradition. In that sense it is irrelevant that a quarter of the officer entrants to the Royal Navy between 1793 and 1815 were in fact the sons of naval officers and another eighth the sons of officers of the army, itself essentially an amphibious force; the remaining five-eighths, however unmaritime by background, were members of a society which felt the rhythm of the sea in the pulse of its daily life, knew that their country lived by its commerce and believed that their freedoms would die unless the command they exercised over it was defended in its deeps. How was that command defended?

NAVAL WARFARE IN THE AGE OF SAIL

By the autumn of 1805 the Royal Navy had already fought nine naval battles in its effort to contain the hegemonistic urge released by the French Revolution. They were the Glorious First of June, fought in the Bay of Biscay in 1794; the Ile de Groix, again fought in the Bay of Biscay, and the Mediterranean battle of Hyères, both in 1795; Cape St Vincent, fought in the Atlantic off Spain, and Camperdown against the Dutch off Holland in 1797; the Nile in 1798; Copenhagen and Algeciras, fought near Gibraltar in 1801; and Calder's action, in the Bay of Biscay on 22 July 1805. It had also conducted and supported a score of amphibious operations designed to assault the French continental empire at its periphery and capture its possessions and those of its satellites beyond the seas. The list included the siege of Toulon in 1793; and the operations against Pondicherry and Chandernagore in India in the same year, against the Seychelles in 1794, against the Dutch possessions of Cape Town, Trincomalee in Ceylon and Malacca and Chinsura in the East Indies in 1795, against Colombo in Ceylon and Amboyna in the East Indies in 1796, at Acre in the Levant in 1799, against Malta in 1800 and in Egypt in 1801. It also included several expeditions to the West Indies, where British possessions stood cheek by jowl with French, Spanish and Dutch, the landings in Flanders in 1793, on Corsica in 1794, at Quiberon (an early Bay of Pigs-style fiasco) in 1795 and in Holland in 1799.

This chronicle testifies both to the extraordinary strategic outreach achieved by navies in the days of sail and to the degree to which such outreach had been incorporated into the Nelsonian navy's routine. Not yet constrained, as later fossil-fuel fleets would be, by the endurances imposed by the capacity of their coal bunkers or oil tankers, Britain's wooden walls, creaking south, west or eastward at fifty or sixty miles a day, could keep the seas and cover distances without the need to touch land for periods never achieved before or since. Liberated from the danger of bad landfalls by the great eighteenth-century advances in hydrography and navigational technique, advances to which the British government and the Royal Navy had made decisive contributions, manned by crews conditioned by childhood frugality to find preserved shipboard fare comparatively bounteous – Dr Rodger has demolished the belief that Jack Tar lived on rotten beef and verminous hardtack – the Royal Navy during the Revolution and the Napoleonic years almost effortlessly sustained a network of maritime control and intervention over more than half the globe's surface. Despite voyage times of as much as 200 days, that imposed by the 12,000 sea miles from Plymouth to the East Indies, British admiralty could make its force felt as distantly as the western approaches to the Pacific, its furthest regular outreach, as well as in the comparatively nearby theatres of the Caribbean, the coast of South America and the Mediterranean coastline of the Ottoman Empire. That was the measure of the power exercised by the men who met to sit beneath the windvane crowning the Board of Admiralty building at the northern end of Whitehall, any shift of which might send a squadron of two-deckers lumbering seaward from the Downs or Spithead to block a Dutch sortie to interrupt the Baltic timber trade, a Spanish effort to run a Peruvian bullion cargo into Cadiz or a French tentative to land an invading army in the Kent levels.

Yet, for all the fine texture of the strategic mesh woven by the Admiralty across the French fleet's outlets to great waters, it was by battle at sea that the enemy's freedom of action was ultimately restricted. However, the nine full-blown engagements fought by the Royal Navy during the Revolution and the Napoleonic wars had succeeded in limiting that freedom only temporarily. True, the Royal Navy had not suffered a defeat; indeed, it had not been beaten in a clear-cut action since the Third Dutch War of the previous century. However, of the nine battles fought, four had been indecisive engagements with the French – Groix, Hyères, Algeciras and Calder's action – while three of the five victories had been won against allies of France rather than France itself. Only the Glorious First of June and the Nile counted as unequivocal defeats of French power. The other victories – Cape St Vincent, Camperdown and Copenhagen – had been won respectively against the Spanish, the Dutch and the Danes. They had had the effect of severely diminishing Spanish naval capability in the first case and of effectively eliminating that of the Dutch and the Danish in the second and third cases. The Royal Navy had greatly profited by the results. Camperdown and Copenhagen had granted it the release of discounting thereafter the North European naval presence – a relaxation of strategic tension it had not known since before the rise of the Dutch navy in the seventeenth century. The hammering given the Spanish at Cape St Vincent had greatly weakened, though not wholly demolished, the southernmost pillar of the anti-British naval coalition. But, even despite the outright decisions of the Glorious First of June and the Nile, twelve years of successful naval campaigning still left the Royal Navy, at the end of 1805, a dominating rather than predominant force. Why was it that mastery of the seas still eluded its crews and captains?

The orthodox, but still probably the conclusive, answer is that the Royal Navy kept striving to win its battles in a fashion that negated the effort made. Naval warfare remained the prisoner of tactics – linear tactics – which reduced even the most elaborate strategy, at its culminating point, to a simple struggle of unit of force against unit of force, single broadside against single broadside, ship against ship. Armies imprisoned by the same linear tactics since the beginning of warfare had just begun to escape their limitations. Thitherto the danger of being 'outflanked' – having the end of a formation overlapped by the enemy force marching across it – had obliged commanders to arrange all their force in a continuous line which, given success in massing equal numbers, geometrically matched the extent of the opponent's. The development of long-range weapons, in the shape of mobile field cannons and the refinement of drills, was now allowing generals with an inventive and forceful turn of mind to bring portions of an opposing army under attack at a distance to weaken their formation by fire to which musketry offered no riposte, and then to launch superior force against the weakened portion. Frederick the Great in the mid-eighteenth century had been an initiator of the technique, which Napoleon had more recently brought to a high degree of perfection.

But land warfare differs from warfare at sea in the crucial respect of the surface on which it is fought: the land offers a variety of declivities, elevations, screens and obstacles which are not present on the open sea. Intelligent use of such topographical features had always been a weapon of the successful land commander; its integration with the new tactics of long-range fire and the massing of reserves had enormously enhanced his power to achieve victory; consequently its systematic application to the tactics of the defensive could, as Wellington would show in the Peninsula, nullify the new tactics of the offensive and transfer the advantage to the army which stood its – carefully chosen – ground.

Yet, if the sea does not offer the option of topographical advantage to the warrior, it does offer another: that of the elements. Wind, tide and current, but particularly wind, are of cardinal significance to the sailing-ship sailor. On land in the days of black-powder warfare there was a marginal advantage to be gained by an army which could station itself upwind of the envelope of blinding white gunpowder smoke that enfolded a battlefield as soon as action was joined. The same marginal advantage accrued at sea. However, the additional advantages of taking station upwind – 'to windward' – were not marginal at all. Because sailing ships make ground against the wind only with difficulty, a fleet 'on the leeward station' – downwind, that is, of its opponent – had effectively surrendered to the enemy the option of choosing the moment of action. It had lost the initiative, had to await attack rather than deliver it and, to that extent, was at its opponent's mercy. True, occupation of the leeward station allowed a fleet to slip away if action grew too hot; but that, by definition, was not a battle-winning tactic. The leeward station suited the navy of a power whose eggs were not all in the basket of maritime victory. It therefore suited the navies of France and Spain which, in the wars with Britain, had traditionally been content to forgo the windward station. It did not suit the Royal Navy, whose *raison d'être* was victory. It had consistently sought the windward, and its admirals has usually pressed their attacks home. Yet they had not always, not indeed very often, decisively beaten the enemy. Why was that?

The answer is that a perfectly proper concern to impose order upon the potentially chaotic nature of sea warfare had resulted in over-organisation, order becoming an end in itself. The phenomenon has been called 'formalism' and has been meticulously analysed by Professor Michael Lewis, a pioneer of tactical analysis in British naval history. His starting-point is the observation that, in the absence of a flexible, comprehensive and easily communicable system of signals, the natural tendency of individual ship captains in a battle fleet was to seek out the nearest enemy ship and concentrate fire upon it. However, unless arrayed at regular intervals in a 'line of battle', several attacking ship captains might choose the same target, with disastrous consequences for the victim but no concertedly destructive effect upon the enemy fleet as a whole. During the seventeenth century and particularly in the wars against the Dutch the Royal Navy experimented with a variety of means to avert that tendency and to multiply the force of the single ship. One was known as 'doubling', by which a group of ships overlapped the front (van) or rear of the enemy's line, seeking to surround and so overwhelm an inferior group; another was known as 'massing', in which the same effect was sought by a simple concentration against a portion of the windward side of the enemy's line; and the third was known as 'breaking', in which a group of ships would pass through a gap in the enemy's line from the windward and attack it from the leeward side. 'Breaking' would, in the very long run, prove to be the correct solution of tactical difficulty in sailing-ship warfare; but it would have to await a revolution in signalling and, consequent on that, the dissolution of a naval way of thinking against anything but the most formal linear organisation.

Linear organisation recommended itself because it could be prearranged and then enforced by the code of naval discipline. As early as 1691 a set of fighting instructions had been issued which established 'line to line' as the preferred method of combat at sea. In 1703, at the outbreak of the War of the Spanish Succession, the instructions were reissued in a form which was not to alter for eighty years. By 1744, during the War of the Austrian Succession, they became the permanent fighting instructions, from which officers diverged literally at pain of death. Byng, shot '*pour encourager les autres*', was executed not because he had lost the battle of Minorca (1756) but because he had done so in breach of the permanent fighting instructions and so confronted his court-martial with no choice but to condemn him to the firing-squad.

Yet, as experience had already amply demonstrated, the 'line to line' formation imposed by the permanent fighting instructions not only did not but physically *could* not achieve the effect intended by those who had framed them. The ideal was straightforward. An attacking fleet arrayed itself upwind of the enemy in three divisions, van, centre and rear, so as to coincide with the enemy line downwind of it. At a signal from the commanding admiral, the leading ship turned to run down on the enemy and those behind it conformed. However, because of difficulties in intervisibility – captains of ships distributed along a line could not easily see a flag hoisted in the centre – conformation with the executive order was sequential instead of immediate. Thus the ship second in the line began to turn only when it saw the leader do so, and so on along the line's length. As a result, the first ship arrived within gunshot of its enemy counterpart well before the last ship did so, and the simultaneous assault which it was the purpose of the instructions to ensure did not occur. The heads of the two columns were engaged before the centres, and the centres before the rearward divisions. The battle therefore developed piecemeal, allowing the enemy commander, should he find his van or centre overpressed, to break off action and depart downwind.

This was not merely a theoretical outcome. It was exactly what had happened in numbers of naval battles between the British on the one hand and the French, Spanish and Dutch on the other, fought in obedience to the Admiralty's fighting instructions from the end of the seventeenth until almost the end of the eighteenth century. The battles of Barfleur (1692), Malaga (1704), Cape Henry (1781) and Chesapeake Bay (1781), all conducted in strictly linear fashion, left the British the nominal masters of the local waters but returned results which in no sense could be counted as victories. Chesapeake Bay, in particular, was a strategic disaster. Its outcome was to leave Cornwallis's army marooned without naval support on the Yorktown peninsula, to condemn it to surrender and thus ensure the defeat of Britain in its war with the American colonists.

Hindsight supplies the charity to understand how the British admiralty and its sailors had so hamstrung themselves in their efforts to achieve the successes which their pre-eminence as seamen and warriors ought to have delivered into their grasp. Hindsight enables us to see that navies had arrived in the eighteenth century at a state of development that armies would not until some 200 years later and were subject, in consequence, to difficulties in the tactical management of battles for which no precedents or parallels from other forms of warfare offered a solution; 210 years after the battle of Malaga, the European armies on the Western Front would find that the firepower they generated nullified their capacity to manoeuvre on the battlefield. The British, perhaps precisely because of their essentially maritime approach to war-making, rapidly perceived that the means of breaking the stalemate lay in the construction of a machine which would combine the qualities of manoeuvre and firepower within itself. They characterised this conception as a 'landship' and only later, when a prototype had actually been built, christened it a tank.

Landships did indeed revolutionise the nature of land fighting; but they were not to become decisive weapons until the first stages of the Second World War when their intrinsic capabilities for manoeuvre and firepower were supplemented by the exterior capabilities of massive and rapid resupply of the tank's necessities – fuel and ammunition – and centralised comprehensive and 'real time' command. The first was supplied by mechanical transport, the second by radio. In concert, these capabilities transformed individual landships into genuine land fleets, fit to strike and manoeuvre, on favourable terrain, with almost the same power and freedom that navies had enjoyed since the seventeenth century.

Hindsight also enables us to see that the wooden man-of-war, for all its outwardly antiquarian appearance, was in fact an astonishingly efficient, highly developed, even 'modern' instrument of war. Its designers had endowed it with capabilities, particularly those of 'endurance' in the widest sense, which the naval architects of later generations would seek in vain to supply to their creations. The sailing man-of-war, for example, took its means of motion from the winds, which are constant, or nearly so, costless and immune to interruption. It could carry within its hull almost all that its crew and fabric required by way of supply – preserved victuals, water, timber and cordage – for voyages of many months. HMS *Victory*, for example, was designed to store enough biscuit, beef and beer, the sailor's staples, for 850 men for four months and enough powder and shot for estimated expenditure in a three-year commission. A great deal of necessary maintenance – repairs to sails and 'setting up' the rigging – was carried out daily at sea as a matter of course. Position-finding was, since the invention of a reliable chronometer in the 1760s, as accurate as it would remain until the development of radio. Damage control in the event of action was usually well within the capacity of the crew unless fire, a rare eventuality, took hold. Above all, the offensive potentiality of the ship was ferocious: the first broadside from a first-, second- or third-rate, if well aimed and well timed, could disable an opponent completely, leaving it defenceless against boarding or further salvoes.

The artillery power of the sailing man-of-war is best conveyed by comparison with that exerted by contemporary armies. Napoleon's Army of the North of 1815, that destined to give battle at Waterloo, took 366 guns of 6-pounder to 12-pounder calibre into the field. The force of artillerymen needed to work this 'cannon park' numbered 9000, and the train of horses to draw it, its ammunition limbers and its supply wagons at six horses to a train some 5000. Horse fodder, at 20 lb per horse per day, amounted to 50 short tons, a supply which also had to be collected and transported at heavy additional cost in human and animal labour. By contrast, Nelson's Trafalgar fleet of twenty-seven ships mounted 2232 guns, of which the lightest was 12 lb in calibre and the heaviest 68 lb. The force of men needed to work this cannon park, at twelve to two guns (since only one broadside was manned at a time) was some 14,000, their daily supplies some 3 lb per man (liquids, which had to be transported at sea as they did not on land, added another 8 lb), while the motive power to manoeuvre the whole artillery force and its crews (though not the attendant capital costs) came free. In short, the gun power of Nelson's Trafalgar fleet exceeded that of Napoleon's Waterloo army six times; and if it had had to be transported by land – at a speed five times less – it would have required over 50,000 gunners and 30,000 horses, as well as a daily supply of some 300 short tons of fodder and 75 tons of food; the comparable daily intake of solids and liquids aboard Nelson's fleet was 70 tons. In brief, six times as many guns, of much heavier calibre, could be transported daily by Nelson's fleet as by Napoleon's army, at one-fifth of the logistic cost and at five times the speed.

The potency of this highly advanced weapon of war was, however, circumscribed by two extrinsic though interconnected factors: rigidity of the naval signalling system that had prevailed throughout the eighteenth century and the consequent rigidity imposed on the contemporary admiral's mind. In his ships he had military instruments whose equivalents the land commanders would not possess until the middle of the twentieth century; strategic in their capacity to detach themselves from fixed points of supply, tactical in their power to deliver overwhelming force at the critical offensive point. As we have seen, however, his inability to articulate them *en masse* at the moment of contact with the enemy had driven him to adopt exactly the same expedient as generals would find themselves forced to accept at the outset of the twentieth century: that of exerting equal pressure along the whole length of a line of engagement for want of means to identify and concentrate against the critical point. Eighteenth-century battles at sea, it is not going too far to say, resembled First World War battles on land. They were characterised by the same concern for prearrangement, the same 'flank to flank' rules of engagement, the same lack of 'hands on' control as soon as action was joined and the same failure to return a decisive result – though fortunately not by the same catastrophic cost in human life. N. A. M. Rodger has shown, for example, that in ten selected single-ship actions of the eighteenth century British casualties totalled only 64, or 6.4 per action, which may be taken as a representative toll. To advance into the nineteenth century: the six great engagements of the Glorious First of June, Cape St Vincent, Camperdown, the Nile, Copenhagen and Trafalgar cost only 1403 British lives, a remarkably small percentage of the total of crews present, reckoned as some 50,000.

Sparing life, however, if the accompanying outcome was indecisive, little consoled a sea service whose purpose was victory. Several British admirals of the eighteenth century, of whom Byng was one, experimented at the risk of professional – even personal – extinction with tactics more likely to yield a decisive outcome. The crucial trick was not discovered almost until the end of the eighteenth century and then by accident. Rodney, manoeuvring his fleet against the French, under de Grasse, near Martinique in the West Indies on 12 April 1782, encountered the enemy on an opposite bearing; that is, they were sailing to pass, not intercept, each other. A shift in the wind suddenly allowed the British to make ground towards the French and, instead of laying alongside, Rodney sailed groups of his ships through the French line, encircled groups of theirs and hammered several into defeat. The result of this Battle of the Saints was the first clear-cut success the Royal Navy had achieved since the seventeenth century.

However, the example of the Saints could not of itself transform overnight the battle procedures of the Royal Navy. They were too deeply ingrained in the navy's mentality and the battle itself too much of an oddity; the British for once had approached from downwind of the French, neither fleet was in an orthodox formation to engage, and it was a trick of the weather, rather than a command decision, that had brought about the encounter. The Saints was celebrated at the time and remembered later. It was even to be repeated, in closely similar form, sixteen years after, when Admiral Adam Duncan defeated the Dutch fleet at Camperdown off Holland on 11 October 1797. There too it was circumstances rather than deliberate choice that caused Duncan to abandon orthodoxy. Alarmed that the shallow-draught Dutch fleet was about to escape his pursuit into coastal waters where his deep-keeled ocean-goers could not follow, he signalled his captains to attack in the chase formation the fleet had already adopted. This extempore order achieved its object. The British did succeed in cutting the Dutch off from safety by penetrating their line in double-column formation. However, the resulting battle cost the victors as heavily as the vanquished and certainly taught no lesson that an admiral anxious to preserve his professional reputation would risk repeating on a subsequent occasion.

Yet the Saints and Camperdown clearly indicated the *only* means by which one sailing fleet could defeat another in a mobile engagement on the open sea. It was a means fraught with danger: the long approach in line abreast, when the attacking fleet, its broadsides masked, exposed the fragile bows of its ships to the enemy's guns, entailed the risk of crippling damage before ever any could be done in return. The passage through the enemy's line required the most skilful ship-handling. And the 'gathering' of the fleet once it had passed through and assumed the leeward station demanded more of a commanding admiral's executive powers and the signalling system at his disposal than either had yet been known to deliver.

Some inspirational appreciation of the revolutionary nature of the Saints must nevertheless have lodged in Nelson's mind; and when to it was added his grasp of the potentialities offered by the most recent advances in British naval signalling, the resulting intellectual brew yielded the truly original tactical plan for Trafalgar. Of the two ingredients, the signalling contribution was the decisive one. Signalling, like the tactical formations so dependent on it, had scarcely altered in the Royal Navy from the end of the seventeenth until the end of the eighteenth century. Admirals communicated their intentions by hoisting flags in series at appointed positions on fore-, main- and mizen-masts; but the hoists, like the Chinese 'alphabet', were ideograms. Unless the signals officers aboard accompanying ships had the hoists by heart, they could not decipher. To get a small number of flag ideograms by heart was simple; but the difficulty of adding to an individual's mental stock directly limited the number of hoists that could be made with any certainty of rapid comprehension. Admirals thus had to keep their orders simple, even though the changes of course and activity they wished, and ought to have been able, to order were complex and manifold.

Efforts were made to move from a system of ideograms to an alphabetic signalling method, notably by Admiral Kemenfelt in the 1780s; but the effort was not rationalised until 1800, when Home Popham, who deserves to be commemorated among the greatest of British admirals, devised a truly alphabetic signal book which, first published in 1803, at last put a flexible, comprehensive and instantly communicable range of signals at a sea commander's disposal. The vocabulary signal book, of which fifty new copies were distributed to the British Cadiz fleet in early September 1805, designated ten coloured flags to give the numerals 1–0 or the letters A–K in single hoists (I and J – which was also no. 9 – counted as one letter). Two-flag hoists from 10 to 25 gave all the other letters of the alphabet, and by their use individual words could be spelt out separately. By reference to an index, 3000 numbered sentences – 0 to 999, 1000 to 1999 and 2000 to 2999, the three series differentiated by a separate indicator – could also be sent and received. As a result, any order, or even thought, that recommended itself to an admiral could be transmitted and received as quickly as flags could be sent to the yardarm, telescopes trained and appropriate pages in a signal book turned up. To give an example, the famous Trafalgar signal, 'England expects that every man will do his duty', required eight hoists of three flags each for the first eight words and four of seven for 'duty', which was not a separate entry in the Popham book. Often-used executive orders, 'Make all sail possible with safety to the masts', for example, sent by *Victory* four times during the battle (signal book no. 307), could be made in a single three-flag hoist.

Telescopes, invented in 1608 and in common use by the mid-eighteenth century, extended accurate recognition of flags to at least a mile in clear weather. Their use could not overcome one of the principal difficulties of intercommunication, which is that the leading and rearward ships of a fleet in line ahead (one following the other) have difficulty in observing hoists made at the yardarm of one in the centre, where custom dictated the admiral's flagship should be. However, this difficulty was ameliorated by (1) the practice provided for in the signal book of hoists being repeated, with appropriate differentiation of their origin, by intermediate ships; (2) the repetition of hoists by accompanying frigates standing out of the line and so visible to many neighbours in it, as was done notably by *Euryalus* at Trafalgar; and (3) the adoption of parallel columns, as at Trafalgar, which allowed ships in the second-in-command's column a clear view of the admiral's hoists and so the opportunity to repeat them for the benefit of rearward ships in his column.

'Psychological change', as Professor Sir Michael Howard observed in his notable 1986 Roskill Memorial Lecture, 'always lags behind technological change.' As he also observes, the psychological acceptance of significant technological change usually depends upon the making of a mental leap by a single individual, or by several individuals struck simultaneously by the same thought. In the early 1900s it was Admiral Sir John Fisher who, with the Italian naval architect Cuniberti, grasped that improvements in optics, the chemistry of propellants and the metallurgy of artillery – which, combined, promised enormously to increase the range at which accurate armour-piercing shells could be delivered – predicated the creation of the 'all-big-gun ship'. Equally, at the beginning of the nineteenth century, it was Nelson who grasped that the signalling evolution predicated, through the proper retraining of his subordinate captains, the realisation of the intrinsic power of sailing-ship fleets to deliver decisive victory at sea. Trafalgar was to be the result.

Ten of Nelson's Trafalgar captains had served under or with him before, notably Fremantle of the *Neptune* and Tyler of the *Tonnant*, who had been at Copenhagen, but also Berry of the *Agamemnon*, who had been his flag-lieutenant at the Nile, and Bladen of the frigate *Phoebe*, who had been his signal officer in the same battle. These were men who had felt the electricity of Nelson's personality both on campaign and in action. If the others in the fleet had not personally been touched by it, they had lived for a decade in its field of force and were tense with expectation to serve it in person. 'The officers who came on board,' Nelson wrote to the Secretary of the Admiralty of his return on 28 September in *Victory* to the fleet waiting off Cadiz, 'forgot my rank as commander-in-chief in the enthusiasm with which they welcomed me. As soon as these emotions were past, I laid before them the plan I had previously arranged for attacking the enemy; and it was not only my pleasure to find it generally approved, but clearly perceived and understood.' To Lady Hamilton, with an uncharacteristic touch of reserve in judging his fellows, he wrote, 'Some may be Judases, but the majority are certainly much pleased with my commanding them.'

Events were to prove that the fleet harboured no Judases, not even a doubting Thomas. The captains, even the crusty fellow admiral, Collingwood, were keen to be disciples. On 29 September Nelson dined half of them aboard *Victory* and the other half the following night, so as to expose his plan to them. He had already outlined it to an old comrade-in-arms, Captain Keats, at Merton, his English home, before leaving for the Mediterranean. There, walking in the garden, he had explained that 'No day can be long enough to arrange a couple of fleets and fight a battle according to the old system.' The 'old system' meant, of course, that of laying a fleet in line ahead to the windward of the enemy, flank to flank, and fighting for a victory by simple weight of cannon power. He intended, instead, to divide his fleet into columns and attack with them abreast. 'I would go at them at once, if I can, about one-third of their line from the leading ship. What do you think of it? I'll tell you what I think of it. I think it will surprise and confound the enemy. They won't know what I am about. It will bring forward a pell-mell battle and that is what I want.'

The enthusiasm with which the captains greeted his presentation of these intentions to them direct was spontaneous and unanimous. There was no dissent, no request for clarification or amplification when he circulated it as a formal order to them on 9 October:

> The whole impression of the British fleet must be to overpower from two or three ships ahead of their commander-in-chief, supposed to be in the centre, to the rear of their fleet. I will suppose twenty of the enemy's line to be untouched; it must be some time before they could perform a manoeuvre to bring their force compact to attack any part of the British force engaged, or to succour their own ships, without mixing with the force engaged. . . . Something must be left to chance; nothing is sure in a sea fight beyond all others. Shot will carry away the masts and yards of friends as well as foes, but I look

with confidence to a victory before the van of the enemy could succour their rear, and then that the British fleet would most of them be ready to receive their twenty sail of the line or to pursue them should they endeavour to make off.

Here was a recipe for a sort of fight not deliberately attempted by the Royal Navy since its epic tussles with the Dutch in the seventeenth century. It was also, faint hearts would have warned, a recipe for defeat should the plan miscarry. The fighting instructions might constrain the chances of success; but they also enshrined a great deal of hard-won experience about the course of fighting at sea and were not lightly to be disregarded. Nelson, moreover, could offer his captains no guarantee that his plan would work. He had never before commanded a fleet action in the open sea. The Nile and Copenhagen, great victories though they had been, had been fought in protected waters against ships lying at anchor. He was therefore gambling with an idea and plotting a course into the dark. Only his own self-confidence could sustain him in the days of waiting before action was joined, only his reputation as a fighter carry his captains with him into the uncertainty that lay ahead.

BATTLE OFF CAPE TRAFALGAR

There was, indeed, no certainty that the French would oblige with a battle. On 24 August Napoleon, who had joined the invasion army waiting at Boulogne three weeks earlier, ordered it to break camp and march into the heart of Europe. Pitt, the British Prime Minister, had achieved a diplomatic coup, persuading Russia and Austria to make common cause once again with his own country in a third coalition against France. The new alliance imposed a reversal of strategic priorities on Napoleon. If the defeat of Britain had been at the head of his list in early August, the avoidance of defeat by Britain's allies had taken its place three weeks later. He would now have to seek battle near the Danube as soon as the Grand Army could be got there. In the meantime, the navy must pursue a subordinate object. Instead of covering the passage of his principal striking force to the coast of Kent, it must re-enter the Mediterranean again to 'succour' (one of Nelson's favourite words) his detached expeditionary forces in Italy and above all to prevent a junction of the British and Russian armies in the Mediterranean against their rear. Villeneuve, he ordered on 14 September, was to pass the Straits of Gibraltar, pick up the Spanish squadron remaining in Cartagena and make for Naples, where he would stand across the junction point of the British troops based in Malta and the Russians coming from the Black Sea. At long range, this move was designed to protect the flank of the Grand Army in its long trans-

European traverse from the Channel shores to the approaches of Vienna.

Across the distance which separated Villeneuve from imperial headquarters, however, even the force of the Napoleonic will attenuated. Villeneuve prevaricated. His Spanish confederates, at the council of war of 8 October, argued the dangers of proceeding to sea, and the French could not overcome. By then they knew that Nelson, whom the Admiralty, alerted to Villeneuve's pressure in Cadiz on 2 September, had recalled from leave on 13 September, was with the British fleet offshore. Their sense of inferiority, with worn ships and uncertain crews, unmanned them. For all the strong language and allegations of cowardice exchanged, no consensus for battle could be agreed. 'The commanding officers of all the vessels reported that they were ready to set sail,' the Spanish admiral Escano wrote to Madrid, 'lacking nothing but good crews, which we could never remedy . . . [but] the result of the voting was that they should remain at anchor.'

Ultimately it was personal, not collective, pique that was to drive the Combined Franco-Spanish Fleet to sea. Napoleon, anticipating Villeneuve's faintheartedness, had dispatched his rival, Vice-Admiral François Rosily, to supersede him on 9 October. Learning shortly after Rosily's arrival in Madrid on 12 October that he was on his way, Villeneuve was stung to action. One resolution of the council of war had been that the Combined Fleet should proceed to sea in the event of the enemy's 'dividing the force of his squadron in order to protect his trade in the Mediterranean'. On 18 October he got word that four of Nelson's battleships – a force under Admiral Louis detached to escort a Malta convoy through the Straits – had left the main fleet. This could be judged the 'favourable opportunity' on which the council of war had agreed to act. Accordingly he hoisted the signal to weigh anchor and at six in the morning of 19 October the frigate *Sirius*, waiting outside Cadiz, signalled to the fleet below the horizon, 'Enemy have topsails hoisted.' An hour later it hoisted signal no. 370, 'Enemy ships are coming out of port.' The hoists were made to the next frigate in the signalling chain, *Euryalus*, which in turn signalled no. 370 to *Phoebe* with the accompanying admonition – superfluous in a service schooled to such discipline – 'Repeat signals to lookout ships west'. And so no. 370 travelled down the chain, from *Phoebe* to *Naiad*, *Naiad* to *Defence* (a line-of-battleship), *Defence* to *Colossus* and *Colossus* to *Mars*, standing in Nelson's line of battle itself, forty-eight miles from the mouth of Cadiz harbour. The news reached Nelson at 9.30. He immediately ordered 'General Chase south-east' and steered to place the fleet between Cadiz and the Straits of Gibraltar. The opening move of the battle of Trafalgar had begun.

Nelson knew exactly what he was about; by contrast, for Villeneuve the decision to sail was a venture into the unknown. *Sirius*, like a bird of ill omen, hovered on the outer arc of the Combined Fleet's radius

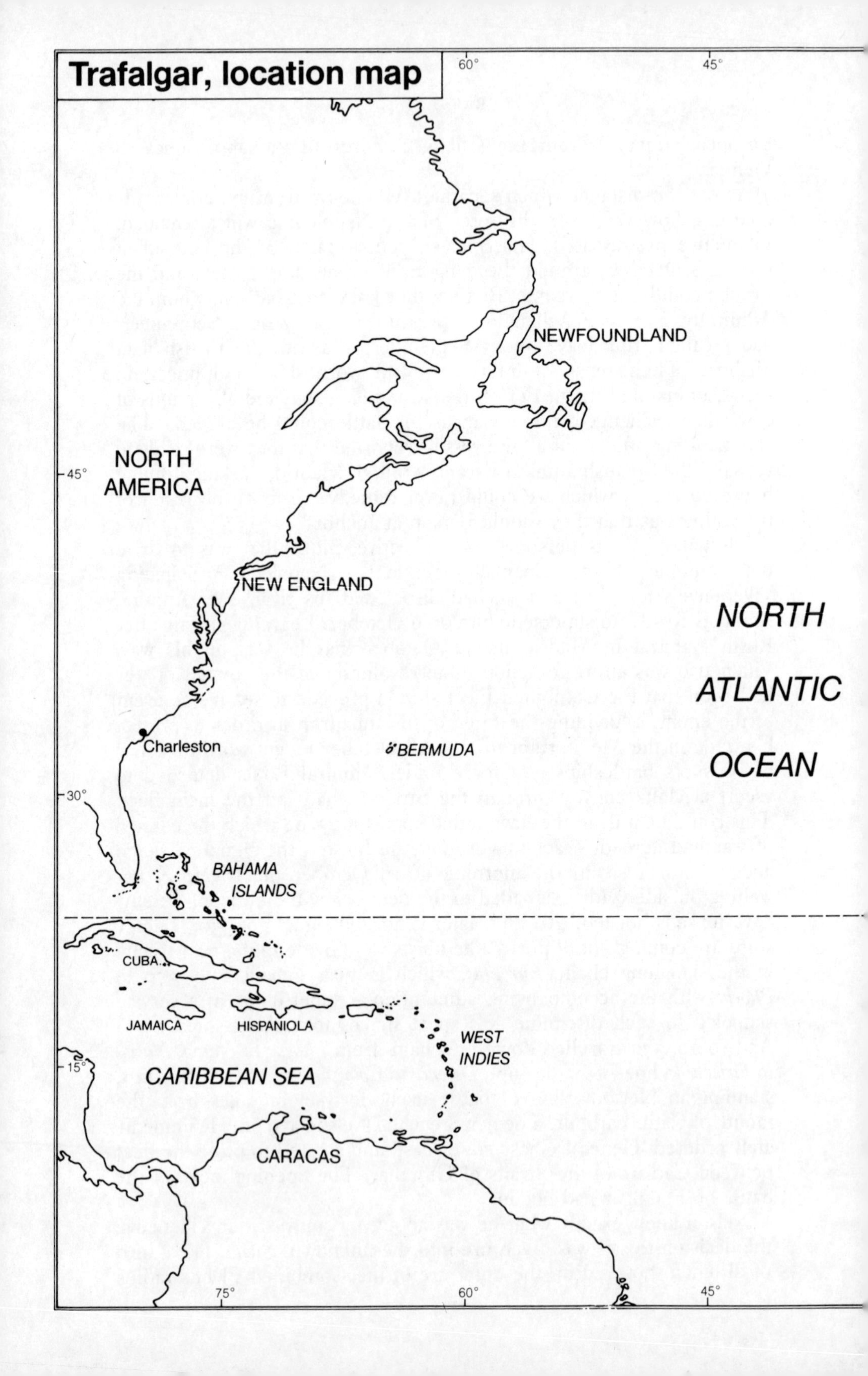
Trafalgar, location map
60°
45°
NEWFOUNDLAND
NORTH
AMERICA
45°
NEW ENGLAND
NORTH
ATLANTIC
OCEAN
Charleston
BERMUDA
30°
BAHAMA
ISLANDS
CUBA
JAMAICA
HISPANIOLA
WEST
INDIES
15°
CARIBBEAN SEA
CARACAS
75°
60°
45°

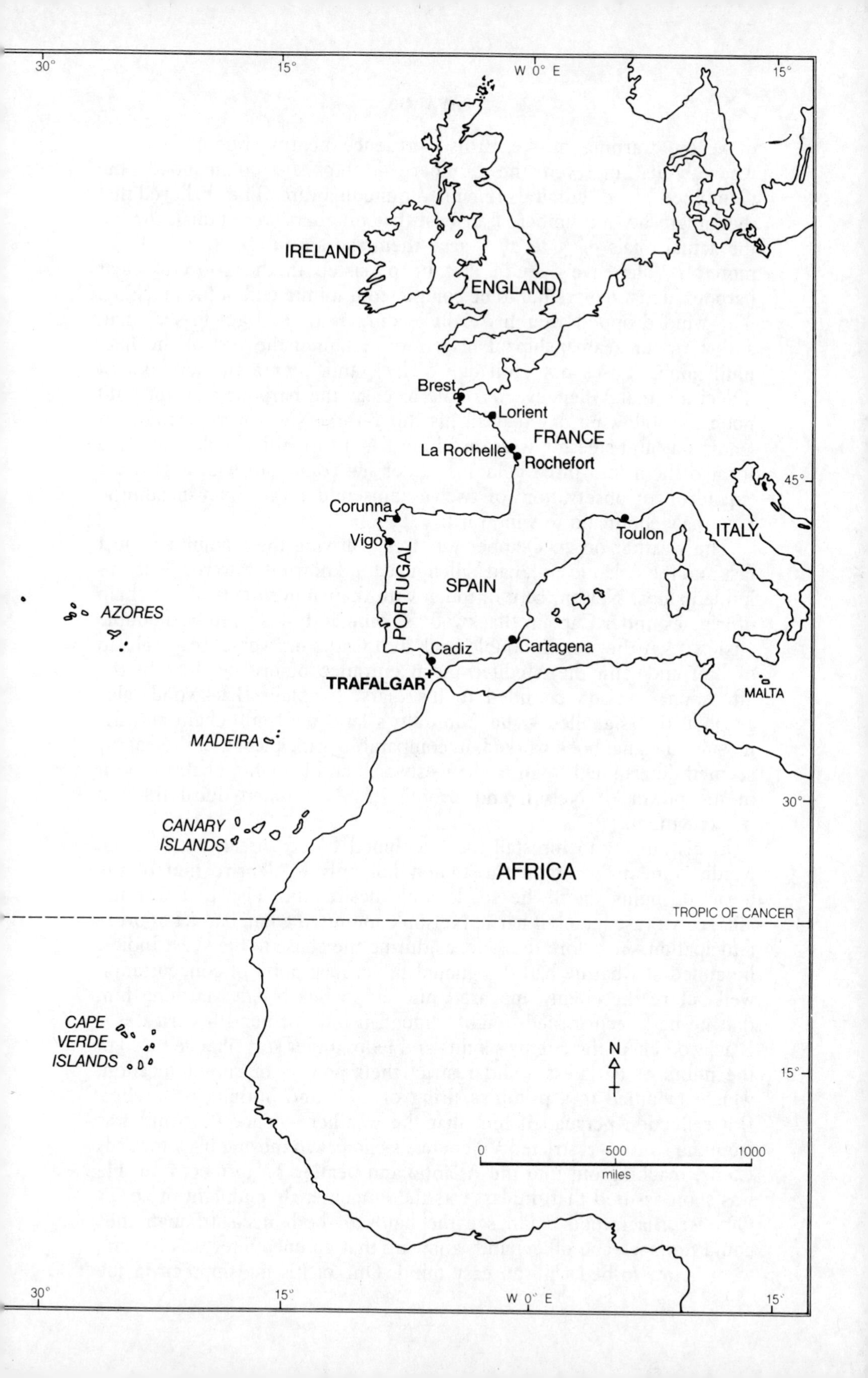
30°
15°
W 0° E
15°
IRELAND
ENGLAND
Brest
Lorient
FRANCE
La Rochelle
Rochefort
45°
Corunna
Vigo
Toulon
ITALY
PORTUGAL
SPAIN
AZORES
Cadiz
Cartagena
TRAFALGAR
MALTA
MADEIRA
30°
CANARY
ISLANDS
AFRICA
TROPIC OF CANCER
CAPE
VERDE
ISLANDS
N
15°
0
500
1000
miles
30°
15°
W 0° E
15°

of vision, warning of the British presence nearby; but of Nelson's whereabouts, or even the number of ships he commanded, the Combined Fleet's admirals remained quite unaware. They believed that they might be outnumbered, at best that numbers were equal, though the actual totals – 33 to 27 – gave them the advantage. It was all the more to Villeneuve's credit that he persisted in the effort to clear harbour, a manoeuvre not to be completed until the end of the morning. The wind dropped after his eight leading ships had got to sea; that, and the poor seamanship of his crews, detained the rest of the fleet until noon. It was not until one o'clock and after a further bout of indecision that Villeneuve was able to clear the harbour and not until noon the following day that all his thirty-three ships were seaward of Cadiz Bay and steering westward in cruising formation. Villeneuve had formed them into three columns under his command with a separate 'squadron of observation' of twelve ships under the Spanish admiral Gravina's command to windward.

The weather on 20 October was fresh, driving the Combined Fleet fast into the Atlantic and, had Villeneuve but known it, towards Nelson's hidden ships. Nelson, kept in touch with their movements by his chain of frigates under Captain Blackwood's command, was riven by a double anxiety: that they might double back into Cadiz or, worse, reach ahead of him and gain the Mediterranean entrance before he did. 'In the afternoon,' Nelson confided to his diary, 'Captain Blackwood telegraphed [i.e. signalled – the Admiralty's land telegraph chain and the new naval signal book worked on comparable principles] that the enemy seemed determined to go to the westward; and that they shall *not* do if in the power of Nelson and Brontë [his Neapolitan ducal title] to prevent them.'

In his anxiety to forestall the Combined Fleet's break-out into the Mediterranean, where it threatened not only to deprive him of the 'peace-bringing' battle he so devoutly desired but also of doing the alliance's cause material harm, Nelson committed a familiar act of over-anticipation. As before the Nile, as during the chase to the West Indies, he aimed at what he had designated the crucial point of concentration well before the enemy appeared, the empty sea briefly alarming him that he had been misled. Night, though it did not blind his frigates – Blackwood kept the enemy's lights and loom under surveillance through the hours of darkness – did restrict their powers of communication, which dwindled to a primitive firing of guns and burning of torches. But reflection persuaded him that the weather – since the wind was from the south – restricted Villeneuve's choices to moving back towards Cadiz, reaching out into the Atlantic and beating on to meet him. He was soon assured that the last was the outcome. By midnight of 20/21 October Blackwood could see the lights of both fleets (though they could not see each other) and, knowing that an encounter was certain, went below to bed with an easy mind. One of his midshipmen in the

Euryalus, Hercules Robinson, wrote later to his father that the ship took its 'place between the two lines of lights, as a cab might in Regent Street'. Nelson recorded what he himself saw shortly afterwards in his diary: 'Monday October 21. At daylight saw enemy's Combined Fleets from east to E.S.E. Bore away. Made the signal for the order of sailing, and to prepare for battle. The enemy with their heads to the southward.' It would now only be hours before the cannon of the battleships spoke.

Cannonade was the instrument of decision in sailing-ship warfare, but seamanship was the craft which determined whether or not cannonade should take effect. Twentieth-century seamen, attuned to consider the weather only as a cause of greater or lesser difficulty in their peregrinations, can scarcely begin to reckon the impediments which had hampered Nelson in his efforts to bring the Combined Fleet to battle or the Combined Fleet to give it on terms favourable to itself.

Speed of movement, for one thing, was laboriously slow by the standards of mechanical propulsion. In the great chase to the West Indies during the previous summer, a passage facilitated by the benign and constant pressure of the trade winds blowing from the equator, the hourly advance over the ground had been no more than five miles for each fleet. In Nelson's and Villeneuve's transatlantic passages it had been even lower. The British frigates, built and rigged for fast passage, had sometimes made ten knots as they swooped about between the fleets. The fleets themselves had made nothing like that speed. Nor had they been able to keep the same steady course as when on traverse between Europe and the Americas four months before. Shifts and surges of the inconstant coastal wind had sent topmen aloft and hands to braces and sheets in every watch, to shorten and make sail and trim the yards to a backing and filling wind. Nelson's fleet, trained by years of sea-keeping, had better succeeded in holding formation during its manoeuvres to stand between Villeneuve and his objective. Villeneuve had seen his heterogeneous squadrons fall higgledy-piggledy about the sea in their efforts to make ground first westward and then to the south. Squadrons and individual ships had overrun or fallen away from each other in response to his orders to keep station. The exigencies of the approaching battle would demand even more of both fleets' ship-handling capacities, capacities scarcely present at all in many of the Spanish crews.

On the morning of 21 October the winds fell light. Battle at sea in the sailing-ship age was impossible in fresh weather, and fresh weather would have spared the French and Spanish fleets the agony they were about to undergo. The rain squalls which had disturbed the night receded and at ten to six the *Achilles*, one of Nelson's 74-gun battleships, hoisted the signal, 'Have discovered a strange fleet.' It was nearest to the Combined Fleet which, illuminated by the sun rising on the eastern horizon, stood between the British and land. The enemy ships were nine miles distant and soon the cliffs of Cape Trafalgar, showing white in the morning light twenty miles away, would be visible also. Lieutenant Barclay of the *Britannia* recorded that 'the eastern horizon was beautifully adorned with French and Spanish ensigns'.

Nelson, as he had planned, had the weather gage – that is, the Combined Fleet was downwind of his, the correct circumstances for an orthodox approach to a flank-to-flank engagement. Of course, Nelson had no such outcome in mind. He intended the 'order of sailing' to be the 'order of battle', and the order of sailing was not to be a mere parallel formation but a pair of spearheads aimed at the gaps in the Combined Fleet. Such gaps were naturally present: ships normally sailed at a cable's (200 yards) distance and it was into that interval that he intended to plunge. He also counted, with realism, on the enemy's poor seamanship opening larger gaps.

With never yet explained prescience, Villeneuve had anticipated Nelson's intention. Some memory of what had transpired at the Saints and Camperdown, combined with his appreciation of the Nelsonic urge to victory, may have persuaded him that, in his adversary's first command venture on the open sea, he would eschew the formalities and drive in for an all-or-nothing result. At any rate, as early as the previous December, he had foretold how Nelson would choose to attack, and he repeated his forecast in a final instruction to his captains dated the morning of the battle: 'The enemy will not confine himself to forming in a line of battle parallel with our own and in engaging us in an artillery duel . . . he will endeavour to envelop our rear, to break through our line and to direct his ships in groups upon such of ours as he shall have cut off, so as to surround and defeat them.'

Additionally, Villeneuve warned that captains must not rely upon signals to direct the action of their individual ships. With almost Nelsonic bravura ('No captain can do very wrong if he places his ship alongside that of an enemy'), Villeneuve enjoined that 'a captain who is not under fire is not at his post'. And, in anticipation of the 'pell-mell' battle that Nelson wanted, he had instructed that 'the formation being broken, every effort must be exerted to go to the assistance of the ships assailed and to close on the flagship, which will set the example.'

However, the 'pell-mell' battle was still some six hours distant from the fleets' first sighting of each other at daybreak. Much remained to be done before they could fight. The ships must clear for action. The admirals must dispose the final battle formations. And the British had to make their long approach across the water separating them from the French and Spanish.

A sudden change of heart and plan by Villeneuve was the most dramatic preliminary. At 7.30 am, perceiving that he could no longer expect to break into the Mediterranean and hoping that, if action went against him, he might reach the safety of port with at least part of the fleet intact, he hoisted the order to wear on to a northerly course and

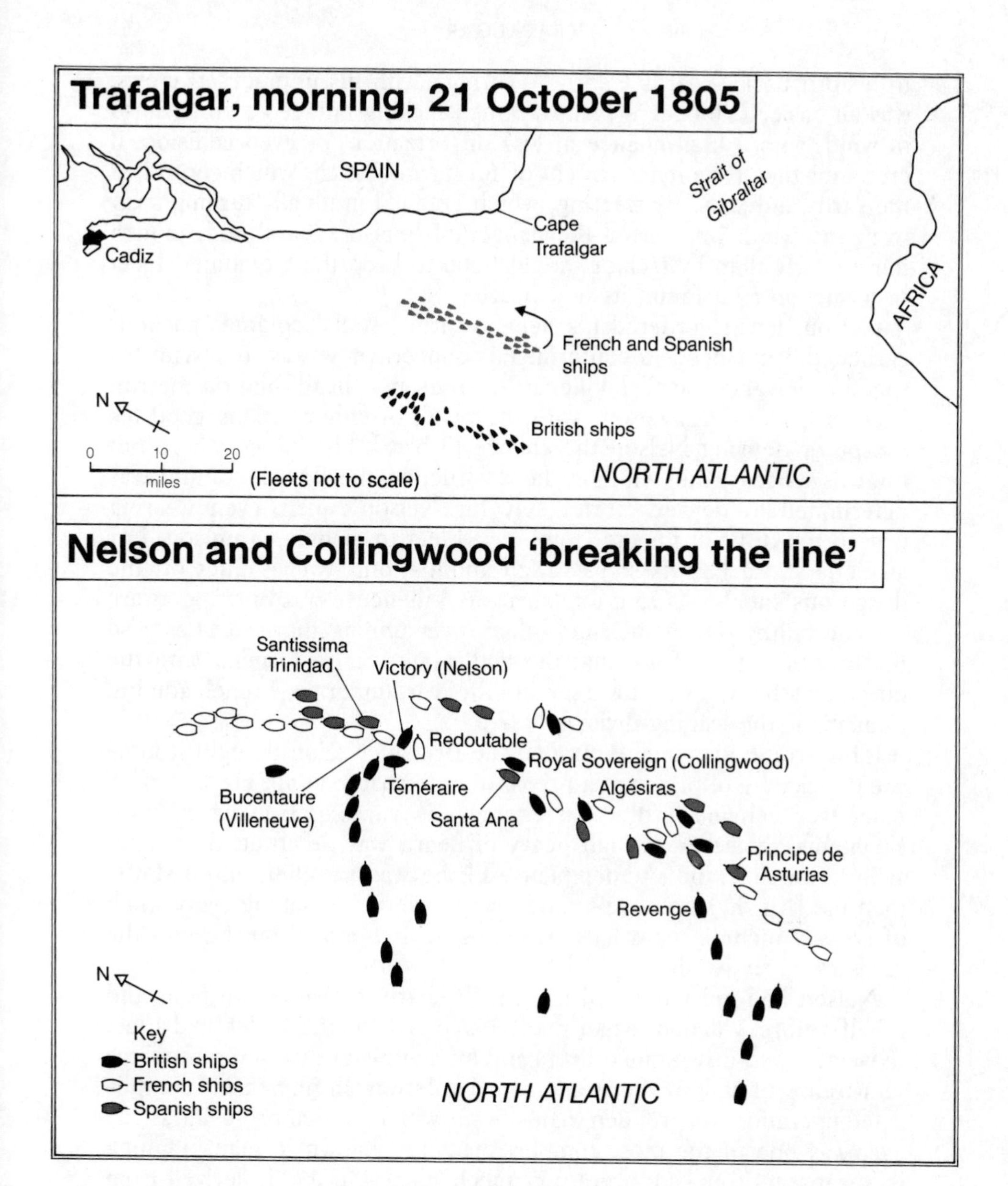

Trafalgar, morning, 21 October 1805
SPAIN
Strait of Gibraltar
Cadiz
Cape Trafalgar
AFRICA
French and Spanish ships
British ships
N
0
10
20
miles
(Fleets not to scale)
NORTH ATLANTIC
Nelson and Collingwood 'breaking the line'
Santissima Trinidad
Victory (Nelson)
Redoutable
Royal Sovereign (Collingwood)
Téméraire
Bucentaure (Villeneuve)
Algésiras
Santa Ana
Principe de Asturias
Revenge
N
Key
British ships
French ships
Spanish ships
NORTH ATLANTIC

to head it back towards Cadiz. 'Wearing', with his unpractised crews, was an easier manoeuvre than 'tacking'; tacking entailed turning head to wind, with a high chance of loss of formation, or even collision, if crews mistimed the management of sheets and braces which controlled the yards and sails. By wearing, which entailed gradually turning away from the wind, he averted the danger of 'missing stays' and, though more slowly than by tacking, could hope to keep the Combined Fleet in formation as it found its new bearing.

Nelson, having ordered his fleet to form parallel columns an hour earlier, did not need to conform. His concern now was to sustain his speed of advance, so that Villeneuve would not 'head' him on the run back to Cadiz – draw away, with the result of either making good his escape or denying Nelson the chance to break his line anywhere but towards its rear, thus eluding the destruction the British admiral was determined to deliver. Fortunately for Nelson's plan, even wearing proved too difficult for the Combined Fleet to manage in unison. For an hour and a half its ships yawed about – only twelve miles off the dangerous shoals of Cape Trafalgar, as Villeneuve was only too aware – some falling out of the line, others overrunning the next ahead; so that it was not until ten that the battle line was re-formed, with the difference that van was now rear and the rear, under the French admiral Dumanoir, the leading division.

This erratic manoeuvre puzzled the British; Nelson thought it indicated a change of plan, not a preparation for battle at all. He was more than ever convinced that the enemy was running backing to port. Villeneuve, however, though heavy of heart, was determined to fight; sailing 'on the wind', under plain sail, he was travelling more slowly than the British, who were sailing 'by the wind' and setting every stitch of canvas, including auxiliary 'studding sails' boomed out beyond the yards to maximise their speed.

Nelson had hoisted signal no. 13, 'Prepare for battle', an hour and a half before Villeneuve had made his signal for the Combined Fleet to wear. It had driven the officers and men of his twenty-seven warships to a frenzy of action. Preparation for battle was an immensely complicated operation in a wooden man-of-war which, in that proto-industrial age, was one of the most complex machines known to man. Though its means of propulsion were non-mechanical – in that it derived from a natural rather than a stored source of energy – almost anything else aboard was very mechanical indeed. The 'standing' rigging of shrouds and stays, which supported the masts and distributed the strains exerted by the wind on the yards and sails in a variety of redundant ways, had to be duplicated where possible. The bosun of each ship, one of the key 'standing' officers, instantly led his crew of mates to reeve extra sheets to the sails, braces to the yards and stays and shrouds to the masts. These were the ropes by which sails were loosed or tightened, yards trimmed amidships, forward or abaft, and the lower, top and topgallant masts stiffened against the pressure of the wind. If sheets or braces were shot away, the ship's handling would be impeded; loss of stays or shrouds might bring the masts – huge compound baulks of Norwegian or Newfoundland fir – crashing down. Yards – the *Victory*'s mainyard was a hundred feet long – threatened even more damage; a shot through the braces that held them against the mast would drop them straight on to the deck, so braces were duplicated with chains. The bosun and his mates also rigged nets to check the flight of splinters (after cannonballs the deadliest of projectiles in a sea fight) and launched the smaller boats to ride astern.

The carpenter and his crew meanwhile were assembling what a later age would call 'damage control' equipment – wooden plugs to stop shot holes, particularly those made below the waterline (as would happen when a ship presented its lower sides on a roll), sheets of lead, hides of leather, 'shot boards' and buckets of nails to hammer the makeshifts home. The carpenter's crew also put out the spare tiller and 'relieving tackle' against the danger of the main tiller or wheel being smashed – both frequent occurrences; the smashing of the rudder head, which could also occur, was an almost irretrievable catastrophe.

The gunner, the 'standing officer' who came into his own before battle, had a dozen tasks to supervise. The magazines, where the powder charges were stored, had to be opened, the spark-proof lanterns in sealed enclosures lit, water-soaked felt curtains at the doors rigged, other fire curtains hung about the decks. Water-filled buckets of slow matches – lengths of smouldering fuse – also had to be distributed to each gun, against the danger of the flintlock firing mechanism failing (this was a British precaution; the French and Spanish guns, like field artillery pieces, were fired by slow match in normal practice). Ready-use charges – flannel-covered tubes of gunpowder, 'distant' holding 11 lb for the opening shots, 'full' holding 8 lb and, issued latest of all, 'reduced' holding 6 lb, respectively painted in black, blue and red – had to be broken out and prepared for issue. Some of the 'distant' charges were sent to the guns at once, the rest kept for safety in the magazine. Extra cannon-balls, in addition to those regularly stored in the shot garlands near the guns, had to be sent up from the hold. They were carried by marines and seamen – 'idlers' – not needed at the guns or to work the ship. The gunner also saw to the mobile fire-engine, which could be run on wheels to wherever fire had taken hold, dropping its intake hose through a port into the sea; fire was by far the most dangerous occurrence aboard a wooden man-of-war in peace or war.

The gunner, though master of the arsenal, was not directly responsible for the ship's armament in action. That collectively was the concern of the lieutenants of the gundecks and individually of the gun captains. Each deck had two lieutenants appointed to it in a man-of-war, one forward, one aft; in a three-decker, mounting 104, 100 or 98 guns (the Spanish contingent also included the gigantic four-decker

Santissima Trinidad with 140 guns and the *Principe de Asturias* and *Santa Ana* with 112), two lieutenants were assigned to the 32-pounder battery on the lower deck, the 24-pounders on the middle deck and the 12-pounders on the upper deck. The gundeck lieutenants' duty was to keep the batteries in action, seeing to the supply of ammunition and shifting crews as men were killed, guns bore successively on the enemy or were disabled. The duty of keeping individual guns in action fell to the gun captains, senior seamen who practised each gun's crew and fired the piece when it had been loaded (or reloaded) and trained on the enemy. A 32-pounder, weighing three tons with its carriage, needed a crew of twelve men, excluding powder monkeys, to serve and lay it. A thick breeching rope secured it to strong points on the ship's side, to check its recoil. Gun tackles, on which the 'gun numbers' heaved after each firing, ran it up to the port. Hand spikes, levered under the carriage, trained it to left or right. Elevating wedges under the breech raised or depressed the muzzle as the range altered. The gun captain gave the appropriate orders, supervised the loading – swabbing out if a round had been fired, to remove scraps of burning cartridge, then the insertion of fresh one, then the ball, finally a wad to hold it in place – then cleared the vent (touch hole), tore the cartridge by sliding a sharp rod down the vent, inserted a quill containing fine powder to mingle with that from the torn cartridge and finally stood back with the firing lanyard in hand while the number two cocked the flintlock firing mechanism.

Fifteen such 32-pounder gun crews stood under their captains at ten-foot intervals along the lower deck on a first-rate like the *Victory*: 225 men in all. Only one broadside of guns, those facing the enemy, was manned; though if the ship 'went aboard' two of the enemy simultaneously in close combat – and that was to happen at Trafalgar – the crews would double up as best they could. Nowhere else in the military world of the gunpowder age was such power concentrated, not even in the strongest and most powerful of land fortresses. It was an extraordinary testimony to the skill of contemporary shipwrights that the shock of discharge and recoil of so dense a mass of artillery could be borne and distributed by the ship's timber structure.

It was additional testimony to the shipwright's skill that the impact of full broadsides could be absorbed by the same structure, sometimes again and again, without causing such ships to disintegrate. But disintegrate they did not. Shot would bring masts and spars crashing down; shot, striking lucky, might let the sea in below the waterline; shot would kill crew members, sometimes by the score; but, unless the flash of close discharge started a fire (more likely the result of accident or carelessness), cannon could not destroy a wooden man-of-war. They could rob it of its means to move, by devastating spars and rigging; they could overcome its power to fight, by dismounting guns from their carriages; they could occasionally leave it waterlogged and unmanageable by puncturing its hull and breaking its rudder; but they could scarcely ever sink it. The most deadly damage they could do to it as a fighting machine was by secondary effect from the timber structure itself: shot – solid, it must be remembered, not explosive – in striking ribs, scantlings, decks, indeed anything wooden, split off razor-sharp splinters a few inches, sometimes several feet, long, which – travelling at speeds close to that of the primary projectile – became terrible man-killing instruments. Captain Hardy, as we shall see, was hit in the shoe by such a splinter and lucky enough only to be bruised. Others were transfixed or disembowelled.

It was for that reason that one of the most important routines of clearing for action was to send as much loose timber below or over the side as possible: mess tables and benches, the officers' furniture, sea chests, cabin partitions, companion ways (replaced by scrambling nets) were struck into the hold; more easily replaceable items went into the sea. The carpenter of the *Defiance* noted a sheep pen, eight wardroom berths, four hen coops and an arms chest heaved overboard.

Finally arms – muskets, pistols, cutlasses, pikes – were issued by the gunner and stacked handy about the decks, the decks sluiced with water against fire, and sand sprinkled on top, partly to give a better grip to the bare feet of the gun crews, partly 'for the blood', as a Spaniard new to sea-fighting was told on the *Santissima Trinidad*.

Some British ships, like the *Neptune*, had cleared for action as soon as the French fleet was sighted; others had waited for Nelson's signal no. 13. By 11 am, two were ready and most piped hands to dinner: cold meat on the tiller head for the officers of the *Bellerophon* (putting out the galley fire was a priority in clearing for action), cheese and a half-issue of grog on the *Tonnant*, salt pork and half a pint of wine on the *Victory*. Aboard the *San Juan Nepomuceno*, Commodore Churruca called the chaplains to give general absolution to the crew. There were no chaplains aboard Napoleon's ships; on King George's (it was a Monday) men made such private prayers as they chose. Nelson, alone in the privacy left to him before his cabin partitions were struck below, penned his famous address to the Deity: 'May the Great God, whom I worship, grant to my country and for the benefit of Europe in general a great and glorious victory . . . and may humanity after victory be the predominant feature in the British fleet'; Lieutenant Cumby, aboard the *Bellerophon*, had already made his own prayer on rising – 'to the Great God of Battles for a glorious victory to the arms of my country, committing myself individually to His all wise disposal and begging His gracious protection for my dear wife and children'; later, when the words of Nelson's prayer had become famous, Cumby often 'reflected with a feeling of pride how nearly similar [his own] were [to those] of our immortal leader'.

Private prayer struggled against the clamour of bands and boasts helping men to nerve themselves for battle. Fifes, drums and trumpets on the upper decks of the British and Combined Fleets alike beat out the rhythms of 'Britons Strike Home' and 'Ça ira'. Second-Lieutenant Samuel Ellis, Royal Marines, of the *Ajax*, 'was much struck by the preparations of the bluejackets' when sent below with orders as the fleets drew together. 'The majority . . . were stripped to the waist. A handkerchief was bound tightly round their heads and over their ears to deaden the noise of the cannon, many men being deaf for days after the action. The men were variously occupied; some were sharpening their cutlasses, others polishing the guns' (some also chalking slogans on the barrels – '*Bellerophon*, Death or Glory' on that ship) 'as though an inspection was about to take place instead of a mortal combat, whilst three or four, as if in mere bravado, were dancing a hornpipe. Occasionally they would look out of the ports and speculate as to the various ships of the enemy, many of which had been on former occasions engaged by our vessels.'

Aboard *Victory*, Nelson with his instinct for inspiration had toured the gundecks once the crew had closed for action. 'This will be a glorious day for England,' he predicted, 'whoever lives to see it.' A premonition of death, which afflicted him before all his battles, was strong upon him. 'I shan't be satisfied with twelve ships this day, as I took at the Nile.' He wanted twenty, as he told many that morning, a larger number than that taken in all the battles of any of his predecessors put together. Aboard *Minotaur* Captain Charles Mansfield addressed all hands in a speech of a force and brevity a Greek captain might have found before Salamis: 'I shall say nothing to you of courage; our country never produced a coward. For my own part I pledge myself to the officers and ship's company not to quit the ship I may get alongside of till either he strikes or sinks – or I sink. I have only to recommend silence and strict attention to the orders of your officers. Be careful to take good aim, for it is no purpose to throw shot away . . . God save the King!' Churruca, aboard the *San Juan*, though already seized by despair – Villeneuve's order to wear, with its consequent disarrayal of the Combined Fleet, had driven him to say that it was 'lost' – struck a defiantly aggressive note. 'My sons,' he cried from the quarterdeck rail, 'in the name of the God of Battles I promise eternal happiness to all those who today fall doing their duty. On the other hand, if I see any man shirking I will have him shot on the spot.' He then called for three cheers for His Most Catholic Majesty; theologically, there was nothing unsound in Churruca's mixture of ritual, exhortation and threat. The *ancien régime*, to which his Spain still belonged, recognised the legal right, indeed duty, of officers to kill shirkers or fugitives on the battlefield; and the internal division of armed forces – between cavalry and infantry, sailors and mariners – was in part designed to ensure that one force would coerce another if necessary, a public secret which explained the strong antipathy traditionally prevailing between these different branches.

The time taken up by these speeches and ceremonies – Villeneuve had his ship's eagle standard paraded about the decks of the *Bucentaure* to shouts of 'Vive l'Empereur' and 'Vive l'amiral' – was granted by the wind, which remained light and fitful all morning; so light that the Combined Fleet, with the wind on the beam, made no more than a mile an hour northward while the British ships, even with the wind behind, the best point of sailing for square-riggers, advanced at less than walking pace. For nearly three hours, from eight to eleven, the fleets stood in full view of each other but at barely shortening range, presenting a spectacle of the greatest beauty as well as deadliest menace. 'I suppose no man ever before saw a sight of such beauty,' reflected Captain Edward Codrington of the *Orion*, 'or rather as we did, for I called all my lieutenants up to see it.' Perhaps no man had: the Armada had brought more ships together, but not in the ordered lines of formal naval warfare. Trafalgar was to be not only the last but the largest battle of the sailing-ships age organised, at least in its preliminaries, by the rules worked out over two centuries of gun-to-gun engagement at sea. Both fleets were under full sail, the British with studding sails also set, and many of the ships were fresh with paint. Although the Spanish favoured a red, white and black colour scheme, and the French black with white, Nelson had insisted that all ships in his fleet be repainted in buff and black, so that uniformity would avert mistakes of identity amid the smoke of close action. The white sails, varnished spars and bright sides of sixty men-of-war, slipping slowly towards each other over a square mile of Atlantic water, made indeed a sight such as no man ever before saw or would see again.

Both fleets were also bright with ensigns – gold and red, tricolour, union flag – and with signals, on the British side that for 'close action' which Nelson had ordered should be kept flying throughout the battle. At 11.15 he had caused another to be hoisted aboard *Victory*, the famous 'England expects'. Originally the words proposed were 'Nelson confides that every man will do his duty'. One of his officers proposed 'England' instead of 'Nelson'; then John Pasco, whom he had appointed signal lieutenant, pointed out that 'expects' was a numbered hoist, 'in the book', while 'confides' was not. And so the final form was chosen. Collingwood, leading the second column in *Royal Sovereign*, complained before it was read to him that he wished 'Nelson would stop signalling. We know well enough what to do', but approved when it was read to him. It was generally communicated throughout the fleet, to a mixed reception: 'I have always done my duty,' an officer sent to read it below decks heard a gunner mutter. On *Defiance* Captain Philip Durham turned up all hands to hear it. They greeted it with cheers and then 'Everything being ready – matches lit – guns double-shotted with grape and rounds and decks cleared – we piped to dinner and had a good glass of grog.'

Drink, hard to come by in a land battle unless the men had been able to fill their canteens with spirit beforehand (veterans commonly did so; the commissary of the British Third Division had a whole barrel of rum rolled into a square at Waterloo), was a useful, almost a vital palliative of nervous tension in the last interval of waiting for action. It was alcohol – half a pint of rum daily was, until 1824, Jack Tar's ration – that made the cold, wet and relentless physical labour of everyday shipboard life physically tolerable. In the approach to battle it was a psychological necessity. Sailors drank and were merry, in the clinical sense almost literally so.

The battle that, at a few minutes to noon, approached second by second would divide into five separate actions. Nelson had anticipated three, by his plan for a tripartite division of the Combined Fleet's line. The other two would fall out by happenstance, contingencies he had also anticipated without being able to provide in detail for their conduct ('The remainder of the enemy's fleet . . . are to be left to the management of the Commander-in-Chief,' as the memorandum ran).

Actions one and two would be brought about by the penetration of the Combined Fleet's lines of battle by Nelson's and Collingwood's columns respectively; though that there would be a penetration Nelson could of course not guarantee at all. The danger of his plan lay in the advantage it gave to the enemy in the last few hundred yards of the approach, when their broadsides could play unanswered against the fragile bows of his lead ships and, if aimed straight and timed correctly on the roll, drive salvoes of shot the length of his decks, dismounting the guns and decapitating or dismembering the crews; alternatively, and given the continental navies' preference for firing high, the same salvoes might dismast the leaders, stopping them dead in the water and dislocating the advance of those ships next in line astern.

However, if the enemy salvoes did not strike sure then Nelson's plan would bring on two separate but closely proximate actions in the Combined Fleet's centre, as the British passed through and then bore up to leeward, trapping their chosen targets between the wind and their broadsides.

The other two actions, which might or might not coalesce with the first, would occur as the rear ships of the two columns made their way into the fight: as the columns were over 2000 yards long and the speed of approach less than 4000 yards an hour, there would be an appreciable delay before they did so.

The fifth action would involve the van of the Combined Fleet which Nelson intended to separate from the centre and rear. He expected it to double back ('to bring their force compact to attack') and join in the support of the ships already embattled, though with even more delay than the rear of his own columns would get into action. The elapsed time of the engagement he could not predict, though, as we have seen, he was determined to keep it short, so 'as to make the business decisive'. He had hoped to attack early in the day for that reason, and the lightness of the wind had fed his frustration. As things were to fall out, the action of the battle was to be compressed into a little more than four hours, from just before midday until late afternoon.

The first shots were fired, by the general agreement of logs which differ widely in timing, at two minutes before noon by the French ship *Fougueux** at Collingwood's *Royal Sovereign*. It was a full broadside and it fell short, scuffing the surface of the sea with plummets or the ducks-and-drakes puddles of ricocheting shot. Collingwood ordered the crew to lie down, certainly not out of soft-heartedness; though not a flogger – he preferred to shame his sailors into subordination – he was hard of spirit and gave that order for entirely practical life-sparing reasons. It could not have been given on land, where erectness under fire was a means of intimidating the enemy. At sea, where the wooden walls hid the crew from sight, it was wholly sensible – and would be given again at battles as distant in the future as Jutland and the Falklands. It was all the more necessary that it should be given on *Royal Sovereign*, which, fresh out of dockyard with a clean copper bottom, had drawn so far ahead of the rest of Collingwood's column that it was nearly fifteen minutes before the next in line was heavily engaged; hence the gruff old admiral's rueful reflection that 'I thought it a long time after I got through their line before I found my friends about me.'

Collingwood's was just the first of the British ships to break the enemy line, prompting Nelson to exclaim, 'See how that noble fellow Collingwood carries his ship into action.' But he indeed went into battle as if in a single-ship fight. Nelson, though lagging a little behind, carried his neighbours with him and thus inaugurated the first of the collective engagements it had been his intention to bring on. 'My

* *A note on ship names*

Fougueux means *Fiery* and was a traditional ship's name in the French navy; so too were *Redoutable*, *Intrépide*, *Formidable*, *Héros* and *Neptune*; the name *Intrépide* dated to the War of the Spanish Succession. Most French ship names, however, were new and some ships had borne second names with the change of the political tide since 1789. *Redoutable* had previously been *Suffren*, after a royal admiral.

It is a considerable confusion that navies tended not to change the names of ships captured from the enemy, and then sometimes passed on a foreign name to a new construction. This explains why there was both a French and a British *Swiftsure* at Trafalgar, as well as the British *Belleisle*, *Téméraire*, *Spartiate* and *Tonnant*. The French *Swiftsure*, which had fought under Nelson at the Nile, was captured off the Barbary Coast in 1801. *Tonnant* and *Spartiate*, by contrast, were Nile prizes of Nelson's and *Belleisle*, formerly the *Formidable*, a prize from the battle of the Ile de Groix. *Téméraire* was a British-built ship named after a prize taken at the battle of Lagos, off Portugal, in 1759. It is coincidence that there were *Neptunes* in both the British and French fleets; the names were traditional. It is a common misbelief that there was a British as well as a French *Achille*; the British ship, as previously given in the text, was *Achilles*.

British ship names were largely traditional; Nelson's Trafalgar *Swiftsure* was the fifth of that name. However, the appearance of some names, like *Victory*, *Defence* and *Britannia*, in wars as far apart as the Seven Years and the Napoleonic is explained not by rebuilding but by longevity. Those three were the same ships, laid down respectively in 1765, 1763 and 1762. When constructed of seasoned oak frames and properly maintained, men-of-war could serve successfully for decades. *Orion*, built in 1787, had fought at the Glorious First of June, the Ile de Groix and the Nile. Spanish ship names, usually religious, were almost entirely traditional; there had been a *Santa Ana* in the Armada (as on the other side there had been a *Victory*).

line,' he had written in the 'Nelson Touch' memorandum, 'would lead through about their centre . . . so as to ensure getting at their Commander-in-Chief on whom every effort must be made to capture.' The concentrated mass of *Victory*, *Téméraire*, *Neptune* and *Leviathan*, bearing down on the point where Nelson guessed Villeneuve to be, was aimed almost at the right point. As Collingwood's *Royal Sovereign* led in, the ships of the three enemy admirals – Dumanoir, Gravina, Villeneuve – broke out their flags, previously concealed. *Victory* was steering to pass between *Bucentaure*, on which Villeneuve's flag had sprung out, and *Santissima Trinidad*, next ahead. But *Bucentaure*, drawing ahead at the last moment, closed the gap, forcing Hardy, *Victory's* captain, to choose the space astern. That too narrowed as the *Redoutable* closed up. 'I cannot help it,' Nelson was heard to say. 'Go on board where you please. Take your choice.' At 12.45 *Victory*'s bowsprit crossed *Bucentaure*'s stern and, Hardy having the helm put down to 'double' the enemy line, found the ship's starboard side grazing *Redoutable*'s port. The British *Neptune* crossed between *Victory* and *Bucentaure*, heading for the *Santissima Trinidad*. *Leviathan* and *Téméraire* followed through, the former to engage the French *Neptune* which had fallen a little out of the line, the latter to join *Victory* in its struggle with *Redoutable* on the French ship's unengaged side.

There had been gunfire before physical contact. In strictly formal terms, those known to Nelson's predecessors, there should have been a great deal of gunfire before any ship had 'gone aboard'. In fact the French and Spanish *Héros*, *Santissima Trinidad*, *Bucentaure* and *Redoutable* had fired at least four broadsides before the British had answered. The first ranging shots had fallen short or skipped over, puncturing sails. Then a broadside had hit home, killing and wounding men on *Victory*'s upper deck. A shot from another had killed John Scott, Nelson's secretary, from a third a file of eight marines and from a fourth bruised Captain Hardy's foot with a splinter, drawing from Nelson, at his side, the famous remark (did it prompt Wellington's 'Hard pounding gentlemen. We will see who can pound the longest'?): 'This is too warm work, Hardy, to last long.' Shortly afterwards a shot smashed four spokes of *Victory*'s wheel (without touching the helmsmen but forcing the ship to tiller-steering below) and two others brought down the mizen-topmast and the foresail. By the time *Victory* herself was ready to fire, thirty of her crew had been wounded and twenty killed, a full third of the casualties she was to suffer throughout the battle.

The French and Spanish had as yet not lost a man; but as *Victory* passed slowly through the enemy line her gunners fired first the port 68-pounder cannonade on the poop (heaviest of the calibres mounted by either fleet) and then, gun by gun as they came to bear, the whole of her port broadside. The effect of several thousand balls of grapeshot and fifty-two solid shot on the timbers and personnel of *Bucentaure* was

Santissima Trinidad, 136 guns, flagship of the Spanish Admiral Cisneros at Trafalgar; in 1805 she was the largest and was also thought the most beautiful ship-of-the-line afloat. She was dismasted and captured in the battle and sank in the great gale afterwards.

HMS *Victory*, as painted by Constable. The subject was suggested to him after hearing an account of the battle from a Suffolk man who had been in Nelson's ship.

RIGHT Nelson shot down in the Quarterdeck of *Victory*; a contemporary impression by Denis Dighton, who also produced authentic reconstructions of Waterloo.

Swiftsure (French), *Bahama* (Spanish), *Colossus* (British) and *Argonaute* (French), closely engaged, Trafalgar, early afternoon.

'Scene from the Mizzen starboard shrouds of HMS *Victory* at Trafalgar' by William Turner; the battle had a powerful effect on the imagination of contemporary British painters.

'HMS *Victory* entering Gibraltar harbour', after the battle and great gale, by Clarkson Stanfield; Stanfield's reputation as the leading marine artist of his day guarantees the picture's accuracy.

TOP Vice-Admiral Sir Cuthbert (later 1st Baron) Collingwood (1794–1810), who commanded the lee column of the British fleet in *Royal Sovereign*.
ABOVE Captain (later Rear-Admiral Sir) Thomas Masterman Hardy, Bt. (1796–1839), captain of *Victory*; he was at Nelson's side when the admiral was mortally wounded.
ABOVE RIGHT Vice-Admiral Horatio, 1st Viscount Nelson (1758–1805), at prayer.
RIGHT Vice Admiral Pierre Charles Jean Baptiste Sylvestre (Comte de) Villeneuve (1763–1806), commander of the Combined Franco-Spanish fleet.

catastrophic. Sweeping the open decks above and, through the flimsy stern galleries, the gundecks below, the torrent of metal shattered wood, dismounted guns and killed or disabled men in dozens.

'We fired five broadsides into her,' wrote Able Seaman John Brown, which may have been an exaggeration, 'knocked all her Counter [stern] in', which was not. As *Victory*'s followers passed astern of *Bucentaure* they repeated the effect. Captain Jean-Jacques Magendie, compressing the agony of the *Bucentaure* into two paragraphs of his after-action report, wrote:

All the rigging was cut to pieces, the masts damaged by a number of shot, the guns in the upper decks dismounted. I was wounded by a splinter ... the Admiral [Villeneuve] ordered the few men remaining on the upper decks – they were now useless, having no guns left and no rigging to work, all being cut to pieces – to go below to the 24-pounder gundeck. The enemy ships appeared to leeward of us; they were followed by the rest of the line ... two 74s were on our beam, very close to windward, into whom we fired as vigorously as possible; the main and mizen masts fell, shot through and masked the starboard side, the colours were secured to the stump of the mainmast; the 24-pounder battery was totally dismounted and the 36-pounder battery had lost very many men, all the hands still able to serve were sent there; worked to clear away the masts from the ship so as to be able to make use of the 36-pounder battery.... The ship, having only the foremast standing, fell away and broke her jib-boom against the *Santissima Trinidad*, they being very close together ... an instant later our foremast fell.... Our rigging completely dismantled, totally dismasted, having lost all our men in the upper works, the 24-pounder battery entirely dismounted and abandoned ... the starboard side masked by the masts; unable to defend ourselves, having nearly 450 men killed and wounded; not being supported by any ship ... not even having a boat in which [the admiral] might put off [to shift his flag], all of them having been riddled with shot as well as the one which we had kept, cowered before the battle, we were cut off in the midst of 5 enemy ships which were pouring a very hot fire into us. I went on deck again at the moment when Admiral Villeneuve was constrained to strike [surrender], to prevent the further slaughter of brave men without the power of retaliating, which was done after three and a quarter hours of the most furious action, nearly always at pistol range. The relics of the Eagle were thrown into the sea, as were also all the signals.

Magendie's account telescopes time and events and was written in part to justify a surrender; it nevertheless starkly conveys the experience of a single ship overwhelmed by the gunfire of a superior concentration, an experience which was to be that of several French and Spanish men-of-war throughout the afternoon of Trafalgar. Nelson had wrought better than he had hoped, thanks to Dumanoir's aimless dissociation of his ten ships from the general action, which gave the outnumbered British a superiority overall of 27:23 and, at the critical points, of considerably more than that. But *Bucentaure* had been notably unlucky: making allowance for the ordeal of its neighbours *Redoutable* and *Santis-*

sima Trinidad and for that undergone by the British *Royal Sovereign*, *Bellerophon*, *Colossus* and *Téméraire*, it probably exchanged fire with more enemy ships than any other at Trafalgar. It had certainly been fired into by *Victory*, *Neptune*, *Leviathan*, *Conqueror*, *Britannia* and *Agamemnon*. *Conqueror*'s broadside seems to have been the decisive stroke, the one that caused Villeneuve to have the imperial eagle cast overboard.

Bucentaure's horrible suffering resulted principally from Nelson's choosing it as his target ship, thus condemning it to the fire of those which followed *Victory* through the gap. It was also partially the result of Villeneuve, Magendie and their brave crew trying to give what they got. An artillery duel on land inflicted the cruellest punishment known in contemporary warfare; but not even that of a great fortress ever achieved the concentration and weight of fire of a first-rate's broadside; if a ship's crew is reckoned the equivalent of a battalion of infantry ranked in close order, it underwent, at the moment of a 'raking' broadside such as *Bucentaure* received five times, a killing effect no group of soldiers ever experienced. It was because *Bucentaure*'s crew stuck literally to their guns, instead of fleeing into the bowels below waterline (as others elsewhere in the Combined Fleet did) that the list of dead eventually reached its appalling total.

Redoutable, on which *Victory* had 'gone aboard' following the French ship's brave but unavailing efforts to block the gap through which Nelson sailed, was bent on different tactics. Jean Lucas, her fiery little captain, did not fully subscribe to the artillery doctrine of contemporary sea warfare. He recognised the superiority of both British ship-handling and gunnery and had therefore determined to oppose it by musketry and boarding. His reasoning was not without logic. As he doubted the capacity of his gundecks to overcome the power of his opponents', he would seek instead to 'decapitate' the enemy with which he locked yardarms; kill the British ship's officers and sail-handlers, overwhelm the defenders of its upper deck and then capture the ship by physical assault. Accordingly he had trained his crew in marksmanship and grenade throwing. He wrote in his report:

> My ideas were always directed to fighting by boarding. . . . I had had canvas pouches to hold two grenades made for all captains of guns. . . . I had 100 carbines fitted with long bayonets on board; the men to whom they were issued were so well accustomed to their use that they climbed halfway up the shrouds to open musketry fire. All the men armed with swords were instructed in broadsword practice every day and pistols had become familiar arms to them. The grapnels were thrown about so skilfully that they succeeded in hooking a ship even though she was not exactly touching us. When the drums beat to quarters, each went to his station ready armed and with his weapons loaded; he placed them near his gun in nettings nailed between each beam.

A particular concern of Lucas was to crowd marksmen into the tops – Nelson forbade the practice because he believed that sending powder into the tophamper was a cause of fires in battle – from which they could sweep the decks of the grappled enemy ship.

Victory, cannoning off *Bucentaure*, locked yardarms with *Redoutable* five minutes later, and Lucas at once put his 'musket and board' tactics into practice. While the *Victory*'s gunners loaded and fired down below, Lucas had the lids of his ports shut, to prevent boarding, and ordered his musketeers to open fire above. *Redoutable*'s ceasefire confused *Victory*'s crew. For a while they continued to fire, some of the crew throwing buckets of water across the gap to douse outbreaks of flame which threatened both ships. Then, believing *Redoutable* had struck her colours – indicating surrender – they arrested the loading sequence. Meanwhile Lucas's sharpshooters had done their worst work. At about 1.35 Nelson, who was walking the quarterdeck with Captain Hardy at his side, was hit in the chest by a musket-ball from *Redoutable*'s mizzen-top. Hardy turned to see him on his knees, supporting himself with the fingertips of his one hand. 'My backbone is shot through,' the admiral said, an extraordinarily accurate self-diagnosis, and was then swept up by a marine sergeant and two others to be carried below.

A very great confusion now reigned on both ships. Hardy, appalled by the casualties the *Redoutable*'s musketeers and grenadiers were inflicting among the quarterdeck 12-pounder crews, sent them below to join those at the 24- and 32-pounders. At the same time he called for marines to come up, fearing that the French might try to board. Second-Lieutenant Lewis Rotely, Royal Marines, who took the order, found it almost impossible to execute:

> I need not inform a seaman of the difficulty of separating a man from his gun! In the excitement of action the marines had thrown off their red jackets and appeared in their check shirts . . . there was no distinguishing marines from seamen – all were working like horses. . . . A man should witness a battle in a three-decker from the middle deck, for . . . it bewilders the senses of sight and hearing. There was the fire from above, the fire from below . . . the guns recoiling with violence, reports louder than thunder, the decks heaving and the sides straining. I fancied myself in the infernal regions, where every man appeared a devil. Lips might move but orders and hearing were out of the question; everything was done by signs.

Rotely managed to collect about twenty-five men and led them up 'to a purer air'. As he did so, *Victory*'s gunners, who had already once ceased firing in the belief that *Redoutable* had struck, did so again, giving the French a breathing space. Lucas, meanwhile, seeing British crewmen emerging on to *Victory*'s quarterdeck, believed that the moment of boarding for which he had prepared his crew so energetically was at hand. 'I ordered the trumpet to sound (it was the recognised signal to seamen boarding parties in our exercises). They came up in such perfect order with the officers and midshipmen at the head of their divisions that one would have said it was only a sham fight. . . . I gave orders to cut away the slings of the main yard and to lower it to serve as a bridge. Midshipmen Yon and four seamen succeeded in getting on board the *Victory* by means of the anchor.' In the fight that followed, a total of nineteen were killed and twenty-two wounded; Captain Charles Adair, commanding the *Victory*'s Royal Marine detachment, died from a musket-ball in the neck, 'while encouraging his men in the poop of the gangway'.

Lucas's boarding tactics would probably not have succeeded; his two-decker crew was outnumbered by that of the three-deck *Victory* and had already suffered disproportionate casualties. But at that moment, in any case, *Redoutable* was run aboard by *Téméraire* which, after exchanging fire with the *Santissima Trinidad* and losing its main-topmast and foreyard to a broadside from the French *Neptune*, was almost out of control. Seeing *Redoutable* looming up out of the smoke, it fired its port guns into her and then locked alongside. Lucas at first refused a demand to strike, ordering 'several soldiers who were near me to answer this summons with musket shots'. Shortly afterwards, however, recognising that 'the stern was absolutely stove in, the rudder struck, the tiller, the stern post . . . shot to pieces . . . an 18-pounder gun on the main deck and 36-pounder cannonade on the forecastle having burst . . . [and] all other decks covered with dead buried beneath the debris and the splinters [so that] out of the ship's company of 643 men we had 522 . . . killed and wounded', he accepted that he could not maintain resistance. One of *Victory*'s midshipman, John Pollard, had already avenged Nelson by shooting one marksman after another out of *Redoutable*'s mizen-top. Shortly afterwards the mast, which bore Lucas's ensign, collapsed across the *Téméraire*'s poop. The fight in the centre of the Combined Fleet's line had gone definitively the British way.

Collingwood's fight, initiated six ships further to the rear, had begun earlier than Nelson's and was to prove larger in scale, more confused and ultimately more destructive. Because the van of the Combined Fleet, under Dumanoir, held its course for another hour after Nelson's breaking of the line, turning back only after the worst had been done to Villeneuve and the ships of his centre, and because the rear of Nelson's column had trailed far behind the leaders, the struggle between the commanders had been fought on almost equal terms, with some half-dozen ships on either side. Collingwood's fourteen ships, coming successively into action against the fifteen ships of the Franco-Spanish rear, had to fight them all, as the wind and line of bearing brought them abreast of each other.

Royal Sovereign, fresh out of dockyard with a clean copper bottom, had drawn ahead of her followers – *Mars* and *Tonnant* – and was the first of the British fleet to exchange fire with the French. Nelson had proposed in the memorandum that Collingwood should choose a break-in point at the twelfth ship from the rear. So he may have intended;

but at the moment of encounter he found himself heading for a gap between the eighteenth, *Santa Ana*, and nineteenth, *Fougueux*, and it was with it that he made his entry. His officers had been reading off with their sextants the angle of declination from the truck of the *Santa Ana*'s mainmast, which gave the range. At 11.58 this declination was four degrees ten minutes, which indicated a range of a thousand yards, and at that moment *Fougueux* opened fire. *Santa Ana* shortly followed suit, and then the *Monarca* and *Pluton*, together with *Indomptable*, which was steering to leeward out of the line. Some shots struck home in the hull, rigging and sails but the range was still too long for serious damage to be inflicted. *Royal Sovereign*, drawing closer where artillery would tell, held her fire.

In the last moments before impact, *Fougueux* tried, like *Redoutable* in Nelson's chosen gap, to forge ahead, making more sail even at this instant of crisis. *Santa Ana* did the contrary, backing one of her topsails to check her advance ('backing' filled the front of a sail with wind). However, these complementary manoeuvres were timed slightly too late. 'Steer for the Frenchman and carry away her bowsprit,' ordered Collingwood. The evident intention intimidated *Fougueux*'s captain, and he backed a topsail also, leaving just sufficient gap for *Royal Sovereign* to pass through. As she did so, her port gunners fired their broadside into *Santa Ana*'s stern and then, though *Fougueux* and the more distant *Indomptable* fired also, bore up to windward, came alongside *Santa Ana* and went aboard.

'I told brother Tom,' one of *Royal Sovereign*'s gunners wrote home later to his father, 'I would like to see a greadly battle. . . . But to tell you the truth of it, when the game began, I wished myself at Warnborough [Hampshire] with my plough again; but when they had given us one duster, and I found myself snug and tight, I . . . set to in good earnest and thought no more about being killed than if I were at Murrell Green Fair, and I was presently as black as a Collier.' Collingwood, admiral though he was, moved among his gunners to encourage and to direct their fire. It seemed that the enemy's was slacking. Then he was hit. 'Did I but tell you,' he wrote later to his wife, 'how my leg was hurt. It was by a splinter – a pretty severe blow. I had a good many other thumps, one way or the other; one in the back, which I think was the wind of a great shot, for I never saw anything that did it.' Shortly afterwards the ship's sailing master was mortally wounded. 'A great shot almost divided his body; he laid his hand upon my shoulder and told me he was slain. I supported him until two men carried him off.' *Santa Ana*, her fire made clear, was still in the fight.

Her fire continued heavy enough to mangle *Royal Sovereign*'s next astern, *Belleisle*, as she came into action. Hargood, her captain, had announced to his officers, 'Gentlemen, I have only this to say: that I shall pass under the stern of that ship.' In the event he did pass under the stern, and *Belleisle* received so heavy a fire from *Fougueux* that he was knocked flat by a splinter, while the rest of its broadside dismembered and decapitated crewmen about him. Second-Lieutenant Paul Nicolas, Royal Marines, wrote that 'those only who have been in a similar situation to the one I am attempting to describe can have a correct idea of such a scene. My eyes were horror-struck at the bloody corpses around me, and my ears rang with the shrieks of the wounded and the moans of the dying. At this moment, seeing that almost everyone was lying down, I was half disposed to follow the example and several times stooped for the purpose, but – and I remember the impression well – a certain monitor seemed to whisper "stand up and do not shrink from your duty".'

Hargood had been steering to come alongside the *Indomptable*, but the vagaries of *Fougueux*'s movement carried the two ships together in the smoke and they went aboard. A gunner below decks of *Belleisle* recalled:

At any moment the smoke accumulated more and more thickly, stagnating on board between decks at times so densely as to blur out the nearest objects and often blot out the men at the guns from those close at hand on each side. The guns had to be trained, as it were, mechanically by means of orders passed down from above, and on objects that the men fighting the guns hardly ever got a glimpse of . . . the men were as much in the dark as if they had been blindfolded . . . every man was so isolated from his neighbour that he was not put in mind of his danger by seeing his messmates go down all round. All that he knew was that he heard the crash of the shot smashing through the rending timbers, and then followed at once the hoarse bellowings of the captains of the guns calling out to the survivors 'Close up there! Close up!'

Belleisle and *Fougueux*, both disabled by the weight of fire they had thrown into each other, fell off to leeward in a private battle, widening the gap *Royal Sovereign* had opened in the line. Next into it sailed *Mars*, which chose *Pluton* as its target ship. Both were 74s, so that the first exchange of broadsides should have been on equal terms. *Pluton*, however, manoeuvring more skilfully, managed to rake *Mars* – that is, engage her from an angle at which the guns of *Mars* did not bear – and so get the advantage. 'In a few minutes,' wrote Midshipman James Robinson, 'our poop was totally cleared, the quarterdeck and fo'c'sle nearly the same, and only the Boatswain and myself and three men left alive.' George Duff, commanding, consulted his captain of marines, Thomas Norman, about making reply, but the light wind had temporarily fallen and Norman said he could not judge the firing angle because of the smoke. Duff went off to lean over the quarter-rail and was just telling Midshipman Dundas Arbuthnot (aged sixteen) to go below and have the guns trained further astern when *Fougueux* fired again; Duff's head was struck off by a shot which then killed two seamen. The maintopmast fell and the foremast began to totter. Two midshipmen, a master's mate, seventeen seamen and eight marines were now dead, forty-four seamen and sixteen marines were wounded, and Captain

Norman was mortally struck. *Mars* fell away out of control, presenting her stern to the French ship *Pluton*, which fired in another destructive broadside.

Collingwood's original gap had now become a focus of confusion as British ships further down his column pushed in and the French and Spanish of the original ordered line bore up to engage and fell away, their behaviour being determined by causes as various as bravado, battle damage and loss of heart. *Tonnant* had followed *Mars* into action and found herself between the Spanish *Monarca* and the French *Algésiras* – 'so close,' Lieutenant Hoffman recalled, 'that a biscuit might have been thrown on either of them'. *Tonnant*'s gunners fired into both. 'Our guns were all double-shotted,' wrote Hoffman, and 'being so close, every shot was poured into their hulls and down came the Frenchman's mizen-mast, and after our second broadside the Spaniard's fore and crossjack [mizen] yards.' (*Monarca* rehoisted her colours when danger passed.)

Admiral Charles Magon, flying his flag aboard *Algésiras*, was a fire-eater of the brand of *Redoutable*'s Lucas. He was for boarding, and by quick sail management got his ship's bowsprit lodged in *Tonnant*'s rigging; while sharpshooters in his own poured fire down on to *Tonnant*'s deck, he ordered a boarding party to assemble and escalade the British ship by the bowsprit. As it gathered on the forecastle, however, *Tonnant*'s carronade gunners fired grape into it and almost all were killed or wounded. Only one French seaman survived to scramble across the gap and then, wounded in the leg by a pike thrust, to have his life spared by Lieutenant Hoffman as a cutlass was poised over his head.

Tonnant's battle with *Algésiras* was to last another hour, conducted with cannon at such close range that both ships caught ablaze and were saved only by the British ship's fire-engine playing its jet on both hulls. Magon, reported his captain, Laurent Le Tourneur, meanwhile 'went about everywhere encouraging us by his presence and displaying the most heroic coolness and courage'. He paid the price for his self-exposure at such short range. After he had been wounded in the arm by a musket-ball and in the thigh by a splinter, his officers begged him to go below. He refused and shortly afterwards was shot in the chest and killed.

Algésiras had by then lost her foremast and soon afterwards her remaining mast toppled, pitching the sharpshooters in the top into the sea. Her 18-pounder battery had already fallen silent and now the British gunners 'so crippled [our 36-pounder battery] that they forced us to cease fire,' reported Commander Le Tourneur. A British boarding party jumped across to take possession, found Magon's body at the foot of the poop ladder and 77 dead and 142 wounded Frenchmen below decks.

Algésiras, out of control, drifted away from *Tonnant*, with the boarding party left aboard as a 'prize crew' (to bring it into a British port). The focus of action at the rear of the Combined Fleet now shifted to the Spanish ships *Bahama* and *Montanes*, which *Bellerophon*, *Tonnant*'s follower, had steered to pass between. *Bellerophon* – 'Billy Ruffian' – was a famous ship in the Royal Navy, a veteran of the Glorious First of June and of the Nile, and was to become more famous after Trafalgar. John Cooke, her captain, was a daredevil officer who, as a frigate captain, had already taken six French ships in single-ship actions. Like Nelson he had disdained disguising himself for the coming action. Urged by one of his officers to remove his captain's epaulettes, he had answered, 'It is too late to take them off. I see my situation but I will die like a man.'

Cooke was to be dead within the first half-hour of action, killed as he was reloading his pistols on his quarterdeck. *Bellerophon* was by then in the gravest situation any ship was to undergo in the battle, worse even than that of the French *Redoutable* or the British *Téméraire*. Passing through the Combined Fleet's line she had exchanged fire with *Bahama* and *Montanes*; emerging on the other side she was confronted by the French *Swiftsure* and *Aigle* which had fallen out of formation. Both poured into her 'raking' fire as she was borne on to their broadsides. Turning head to wind and 'luffing' (shaking the wind from her sails) to slow her motion, *Bellerophon* went aboard *Aigle*, locking fore to main yardarms, and at once found herself in a brisk small-arms fight. Of *Aigle*'s 750 crew 150 were soldiers, who packed the tops and rigging as marksmen and grenadiers.

A French grenadier, with a lucky throw, was to threaten *Bellerophon* with the deadliest danger to which any of the Trafalgar ships was to be exposed throughout the battle. Later in the action *Aigle*'s gunroom (fortunately not a powder store) was to be set on fire by burning shot-wads from British guns; but now the grenade thrown from the *Aigle* popped in through a lower-deck port and exploded, so 'forcing open the door into the magazine passage', reported Lieutenant Price Cumby, who had taken command on Cooke's death. The grenade also started a fire. This was a potential catastrophe, for a fire in the magazine was the only means by which a wooden man-of-war could be destroyed outright. Extraordinary precautions – involving a system of double doors and water-soaked felt curtains – were taken to see that fire did not break out by mishandling of powder, while the common projectiles of sailing-ship warfare, being solid shot, could not of themselves generate an outbreak. The incursion of a grenade was an unanticipated eventuality, threatening disaster; from it *Bellerophon* was spared only by eccentric accident. 'The same blast which blew open the store-room door,' reported Cumby, 'shut the door of the magazine, otherwise we must all in both ships inevitably have been blown up together.' The immediate crisis was finally overcome when the *Bellerophon*'s gunner gathered hands to throw water into and over the magazine – 'hung' through the orlop deck (the lowest deck) into the hold so that all its external surfaces could be doused in exactly such a crisis – and to 'put the fire out without its having been known to any persons on board except those employed in its extinction'.

Grenades elsewhere were inflicting heavy casualties on the crew: one wounded twenty-five of *Bellerophon*'s men. Their success in the fire-fight encouraged *Aigle*'s crew in an attempt to board and some crawled out from the forecastle along *Bellerophon*'s spritsail yard; the sortie was checked by the quick thinking of a seaman named Macfarlane who loosed the spritsail yard brace, dropping the interlopers into the sea. That was the last French attempt at boarding; but *Aigle*'s gunners still manned their pieces and *Bellerophon* also suffered from the fire of *Bahama*, which lay only a little further distant. Two other ships also lay close enough to direct fire at her, and shortly afterwards a fifth came up and also engaged.

Cumby (who was to be promoted substantive captain after the battle for the way in which he fought his ship) described the scene as he reached the quarterdeck: 'This would be about a quarter-past one o'clock, when I found we were still entangled with the *Aigle*, on whom we kept up a brisk fire, and also our old opponent on the larboard [port] bow, the *Monarca*, who by this time was nearly silenced, though her colours were still flying. At the same time we were receiving the fire of two other of the enemy's shipssss, one nearly astern of each other on the larboard quarter' (these were the *Bahama* and the French *Swiftsure*). 'I must say,' wrote another officer, 'I was astonished at the coolness and undaunted bravery displayed by our gallant and veteran crew, when surrounded by five enemy's ships [the fifth was the *San Juan Nepomuceno*, which came up from astern] and for a length of time unassisted by any of ours.'

San Juan was not long in the battle. Soon after engaging the *Bellerophon* she was taken under attack by the 98-gun *Dreadnought*, one of the furthest astern of Collingwood's column, driven off and forced into a single-ship fight. Commodore Churruca, *San Juan*'s commander, was a notably brave officer, but mistrust of Villeneuve's leadership had sapped his fighting spirit. His ship had already had a damaging brush with *Tonnant*. Now, outgunned by *Dreadnought*, it fought bravely for a few minutes until he was mortally wounded by a cannon-ball which almost severed his right leg. 'It is nothing – go on firing,' he is reported as saying, and ordered the colours to be nailed to the mast. However, news of his mortal wound spread to the gundecks – in which *Dreadnought*'s fire had killed a hundred men – and, since no surviving subordinate took decisive command, the crew quickly struck.

San Juan, originally the last ship in the Combined Fleet's line, had clashed with *Tonnant* and *Dreadnought* by overreaching those ahead of her. The main engagement in the rear was to be between those which had kept station – *Argonaute*, *Argonauta*, *Achille*, *Principe de Asturias* –

and the remainder of Collingwood's column which was now coming into action, *Colossus*, *Achilles*, *Revenge*, *Defiance* and their followers. *Argonaute* was overcome in minutes by the fire of *Colossus*, which next turned its broadsides on to *Bahama*, stricken in the fight with *Bellerophon*. Soon after *Bahama*'s mainmast was brought down and her captain, Galiano, killed by a shot in the head, his subordinate officers held a summary council of war and decided to strike. *Colossus* then found herself near the French *Swiftsure*, a survivor of the fight with *Bellerophon*, and swiftly beat her into surrender also. *Achilles*, next astern of *Colossus*, devastated the Spanish *Montanes* (also a survivor of the fight with *Bellerophon*) and then engaged *Argonauta* in a fight that was to last an hour. As *Argonauta* drifted out of action, *Achilles* engaged first her namesake *Achille* and then the Spanish *Berwick* (named for the son of James II who had fought against Britain in the War of the Spanish Succession). Half an hour's firing forced the Spaniard to strike also; the British officer who went aboard found 51 dead, 200 wounded and a dearth of officers, 'the quarter-deck [their battle station] having thrice been cleared' by shot.

Revenge, one of the most famous names in the Royal Navy, was next astern of *Achilles*, and commanded by one of Nelson's leading gunnery experts, Robert Morrison. 'We shall want all our shot when we get close in,' he had told his crew. 'Never mind their firing.' His well-trained gunners first brought down the mizen-mast of *Achille*, then engaged the Spanish *San Ildefonso* and *Principe de Asturias* simultaneously, a fight which lasted for twenty minutes until the last four of Collingwood's division – *Defiance*, *Polyphemus*, *Thunderer* and *Defence* – drew into action. Relieved by their arrival, *Revenge* brought down two of *Achille*'s masts, forcing her out of action, and then found herself within gunshot of *Aigle*, which had fallen back from her fight with *Bellerophon* but was still operational. *Revenge* was now too badly damaged to finish off *Aigle* – she had had the unusually high number of nine shots below the waterline and suffered heavily in lost masts and rigging – but *Defiance* was close at hand. Her captain, Philip Durham, formed the impression that *Aigle* had struck and sent away a boarding party which, all the ship's boats having been riddled, swam the intervening distance. It was led by a master's mate, Jack Spratt, who clambered aboard by the rudder chains and then fought hand to hand on deck while *Defiance*'s guns continued to play on *Aigle* below. The cannonading shortly started a fire which the French captain decided he could not hope to extinguish while sustaining resistance and he accordingly hauled down *Aigle*'s colours. Her decks by then, Colin Campbell, one of *Defiance*'s master's mate, recalled, 'were covered by dead and wounded [since] they never heave their dead overboard in time of action as we do'; the explanation, had he but known it, was that a Catholic widow needed the evidence of burial of her husband's body if she was to remarry.

The fight at the rear of the line of battle was now lost to the Combined Fleet. Fourteen British ships – thanks particularly to the ferocious aggressiveness of the *Belleisle*, *Mars*, *Colossus* and *Achilles* which had respectively engaged six, five, three and four of the Combined Fleet – had overcome sixteen of the enemy. The last encounters of this phase of the battle were between Gravina's flagship the *Principe de Asturias* and HMS *Prince*, whose broadsides wounded the admiral but could not bring her to strike before fugitives from further up the line, *San Justo* and the French *Neptune*, came to Gravina's assistance and caused *Prince* to draw away.

Principle de Asturias was by then the only ship in the rear division which had not struck her colours or fallen out of contention, but the van division, under Dumanoir, had so far not been engaged at all. For two hours Dumanoir had led his ten ships away from action, despite Villeneuve's frantic signals to bring him back, and it was only at two in the afternoon, when the signs of heavy engagement in his rear left him no excuse for holding on, that he ordered his division to retrace its steps. Some tacked, some wore; it made little difference in the light airs; *Scipion* had to launch boats to drag its prow round.

The return of the van, whose presence would have made a telling difference if they had participated from the start, was to achieve little. *Héros*, *Rayo*, *San Augustin* and *San Francisco de Asis* made no attempt to intervene but steered directly for Cadiz across the head of the mass of men-of-war. *Formidable*, *Duguay-Trouin*, *Scipion* and *Mont Blanc* steered for the rear, but held off half a mile to windward of the action, Dumanoir himself in the lead. Only two ships, the Spanish *San Augustin* and the French *Intrépide*, commanded by the appropriately named Infernet, steered for battle.

Dumanoir's group ran into the rear of Nelson's column, exchanged fire with two of its last ships, *Spartiate* and *Minotaur*, and despite its superiority of numbers managed to lose *Neptune* to *Minotaur* after a very short exchange of fire; the British ship lost only three men killed and suffered minor damage to its masts. The Spaniards' heart was not in the fight.

San Augustin's crew and captain were a bolder bunch. Captain Felipe Cajigal had apparently determined to come to the rescue of the *Santissima Trinidad*, lying dismasted in the centre of the line of battle, and passed through the leading ships, probably between the fifth and sixth, to steer for his admiral. The odds were against him, however. As he cleared the stern of the British *Neptune*, *Leviathan* took him under attack, fired several broadsides, wore ship and came alongside to board. 'Having been boarded twice,' reported Captain Cajigal (this was an exaggeration), 'I had not sufficient men to repel a third boarding, the few who remained being on the gundecks, continuing to fire into the other ships which were closing round at pistol range.' He was obliged to strike.

Infernet, aiming for his admiral in the *Bucentaure*, was engaged six ships up the line by the *Africa*, a 64 whose bad sailing had made her late for the battle. Outgunned, *Africa* kept up the exchange for forty minutes until *Orion*, also a late arrival, came up to sustain the attack. Infernet, despite being engaged with two of the enemy and having been fired into by four others which had departed in pursuit of Dumanoir's fugitives, defied all thought of surrender, brandishing a sword he threatened to use against anyone who even spoke the word. He and one of his lieutenants, Gicquel des Touches, found time to be amused by the antics of a French colonel, a veteran of Napoleon's victory at Marengo, who was trying to shelter behind the captain's body ('Colonel,' Infernet enquired, 'do you think I am sheathed in metal?'). However, as the minutes wore on, *Intrépide*'s predicament became more and more extreme. 'At five o'clock,' reported Infernet, 'the wheel, the tiller-sweep, the tiller-ropes and the tiller were shattered. . . . At 5.15 the mizenmast fell; four or five minutes later the mainmast did the same. . . . At 5.35 pm the foremast fell; I was then left without masts or sails; seeing myself surrounded by enemies and not being able to escape, having, moreover, no French ships in sight to come to my assistance, the enemy keeping up a terrible fire into me, having about half my crew killed . . . I was obliged to yield to the seven enemy ships that were engaging me.'

Infernet's reluctant surrender was the last substantive event of the general action. By that time all the British ships engaged had either ceased firing or were about to do so; *Revenge* logged her last shots, fired presumably against *Principe de Asturias*, at 6.15; but that may have been a mistake of time-keeping. Half an hour before, the most spectacular event of the battle had occurred when the French *Achille* blew up; in one of the last encounters, bloodless on the British side, *Prince* had somehow set fire to her fore-top, from which flames had spread rapidly to the decks and then below; the floors had begun to burn, dropping guns down through the ship and sending flaming debris with them. As the fire took hold in the orlop (the lowest deck), the crew began to abandon ship – *Prince* had lowered boats – but flames touched one of the magazines before all got off. 'In a moment,' a British observer recorded, 'the hull burst into a cloud of smoke and fire. A column of vivid flame shot up to an enormous height in the atmosphere and terminated by expanding into an immense globe, representing, for a few seconds, a prodigious tree in flames, speckled with many dark spots, which the pieces of timber and bodies of men occasioned while they were suspended in the clouds.'

WHAT HAD HAPPENED?

The long swells of an approaching gale had now begun to disturb the square mile of sea on which the survivors of the battle rode, portent of an ordeal worse for many than the battle itself. The Trafalgar gale, one of the late equinoctial storms which regularly send Atlantic shipping running to port at the onset of autumn, raged from the evening of Monday, 21 October, to Sunday, 27 October. It was at its height on the night of Wednesday, 23 October, but many survivors thought it the worst experience at sea they had ever known. Ships' logs recorded 'strong gale' and 'hard gale', technical language which would later translate into force 9 or 10 on Admiral Beaufort's scale of wind intensities. Yet for a moment there was time to take stock, or at least to pause. 'About five o'clock,' wrote Paul Nicolas, the marine lieutenant of HMS *Belleisle*, 'the officers assembled in the Captain's cabin to take some refreshment. The parching effects of the smoke made this a welcome summons . . . still, four hours' exertion of body with the energies incessantly employed, occasioned a lassitude, both corporeally and mentally, from which the victorious terminations so near at hand could not arouse us.'

Shortly afterwards they learned that Nelson was dead, news which sent a pang of genuine mourning through the fleet. It was clear nevertheless that the British had won a great victory. But quite how great the confused evidence of their eyes could not yet disclose. Hardy had told Nelson in his last minutes that he was certain fourteen or fifteen of the enemy had been taken. 'I had bargained for twenty,' Nelson answered. Broken and dismasted ships lay all about, those of the enemy with British prize crews, often very small, aboard. Even so, the exact reckoning was hard to make.

Some of the Combined Fleet, it was clear, had got away. Dumanoir had led four out of action – *Formidable*, *Scipion*, *Suguay-Trouin* and *Mont Blanc* – hoping to rejoin the remnants of the French fleet elsewhere. Storm-driven, he was eventually to be brought to battle on 22 November by Admiral Strachan's squadron off the north coast of Spain and forced to surrender. Ten under Gravina had got away in various states of disorder and were heading for Cadiz: *Neptune*, *Indomptable*, *Pluton*, *Argonaute*, *Héros*, *Principe de Asturias*, *Montanes*, *San Francisco de Asis*, *San Justo* and *San Leandro*. That left nineteen either destroyed, like *Achille*, or surrendered to the British: *Bucentaure*, *Intrépide*, *Aigle*, *Berwick*, *Argonauta*, *Algésiras*, *Fougueux*, *Redoutable*, *Neptune*, *Monarca*, *San Augustin*, *Santissima Trinidad*, *Santa Ana*, *Rayo*, *Bahama*, *Swiftsure*, *San Juan Nepomuceno* and *San Ildefonso*.

Dumanoir's fugitives had suffered hardly at all in the battle. In their running exchange with the rear of the British line the heaviest total of casualties suffered was 22 dead in *Formidable*. Neither she nor the others had been severely engaged. Some of those which had got away with Gravina, however, suffered severely. *Argonaute* had 55 dead and *Pluton* 60, the results of their close-range encounters with *Colossus* and *Mars*. *Principe de Asturias* had suffered 54 fatal casualties in her exchanges with the rear of Collingwood's column; *Prince*, *Defiance*,

Revenge, *Dreadnought* and *Thunderer* all logged that they had fired into or at her. On the other hand, many of Gravina's covey of refugees from the battle had escaped lightly. *San Francisco* had 5 fatal casualties, *San Leandro* 8 and *San Justo* none at all.

The terrible mortality had fallen on those ships which had been chosen as targets by the leaders of the British columns, had been encircled in the course of the action or had fought with unusual zeal, categories which in some cases overlapped.

Santissima Trinidad belonged to the first. She had been fired into by *Victory* as that ship broke the line to engage *Bucentaure* and was next taken under attack by the third and fifth ships of Nelson's column, *Neptune* and *Conqueror*. *Africa*, a latecomer into action because of her poor sailing qualities, then joined in. The four-decker *Santissima Trinidad*, the largest ship in the world, with 140 guns, was a match for any of her opponents, perhaps for two put together, but their combined broadsides nullified her advantage in weight of metal and her very bulk may have offered the British solid targets that smaller ships did not. Several British shot hit her masts below deck, others ravaged her standing rigging, and first the mizen, then the main fell into the sea. 'Her immense topsails had every reef out,' wrote one of *Conqueror*'s officers. 'Her royals were sheeted home, but lowered; and the falling of this majestic mass of spars, sails and rigging plunging into the water at the muzzles of our guns, was one of the most magnificent sights I ever beheld.' Cisneros, *Santissima*'s admiral, still refused to strike, though he had 200 dead below decks and was himself wounded; an emissary from *Africa* was politely sent back to his ship with the assurance that *Santissima* was still in action, though she lacked any spar from which to display her colours; but the truth was that she had been beaten into inactivity and was taken without resistance by *Prince* at the end of the battle. *Santissima*'s hull had been penetrated so frequently by shot that her pumps could not keep pace and, exceptionally for a wooden man-of-war, she foundered at sea in the night of 24/25 October.

Santa Ana, chosen by Collingwood of *Royal Sovereign* as a target ship in his run-in, furnishes an example of the effects of exposure to an enemy's first broadside. Alava, the Spanish admiral aboard, five years later told Hercules Robinson, one of *Royal Sovereign*'s officers, that his ship's fire had killed 350 men (a threefold exaggeration, but an index of the horror) and though he fought on afterwards for a couple of hours, like an old hidalgo, like 'a man of honour and a cavalier, the first broadside did his business, and there was an end of him'. There seems no doubt that a first broadside, like a first salvo in a land battle, was exceptionally effective. It was fired with guns loaded at leisure, and so shot, powder and wads were packed as carefully together as they were ever likely to be; it was delivered from guns aligned with a care impossible to achieve in the heat of action; and it was timed to match the ship's roll with a closeness that the noise and confusion of battle ruled out of practice. A well-aimed and well-timed first broadside, like an equivalent first salvo of musketry by well-drilled infantry, was probably worth the half-dozen following. *Royal Sovereign* had given *Santa Ana* such a discharge and had reaped the benefit.

Bucentaure, also a target ship, had paid the price of suffering a first broadside, as had *Redoutable*. Both had subsequently been surrounded and suffered outnumbering attacks, *Bucentaure* from *Victory*, *Neptune*, *Leviathan* and *Conqueror*, to whom she had eventually struck. The worst experience of encirclement may, however, have been suffered by *Fougueux*, which reported having been fired into by seven ships as they passed or came alongside. Her casualty list, 546, was almost the highest in the fleet and, though inflated by losses suffered in her subsequent wreck, is nevertheless an index of the devastation she had suffered from British gunnery in the course of the battle.

Intrépide and *San Augustin*, with 242 and 184 fatal casualties respectively, were exemplary in conduct and paid the price. Like *San Juan Nepomuceno*, which drew up from the last place in the Combined Fleet's line to take an unequal share of action, both might have avoided heavy engagement had they chosen to follow the example not only of most of Dumanoir's disengaged division but of ships initially close to the focus of fighting, like *San Justo*, *San Leandro* and *Neptune*, which frankly took little part in the fight, falling out of line at the British approach and making no effort to get back into it once action was joined.

San Augustin, in its effort to lend assistance to the *Santissima Trinidad*, was quickly intercepted and severely handled by *Leviathan*, though it might have been by any other British ship of the centre, most of which by that time – 4.30 pm – had won their individual battles and were still ready to engage. *Intrépide*'s intervention was even bolder, an essay in pure heroism of which neither Trafalgar nor any other battle of the long Anglo-French rivalry at sea yields the equivalent. Infernet, a son of the Revolution if there was one, ex-cabin boy and rough-spoken Provençal, had determined to rescue Villeneuve and the *Bucentaure* if wit and flesh could stand. His lieutenant, the Marquis Gicquel des Touches, an officer from the world Infernet could never have hoped to enter, let alone inspire to hopeless venture before 1789, remarked that Infernet 'wanted to rescue Admiral Villeneuve and take him on board, and then to rally round ourselves the ships that were still in a fit state to fight. He would not have it said that the *Intrépide* had quitted the battle while she still could fight a gun or hoist a sail. It was a noble madness, but though we knew it we all supported him.'

Infernet's noble madness took, by his estimation, the action of seven British ships to contain. That, as the testimony of British officers already cited suggests, may have been an exaggeration; but Infernet's bravery cannot be exaggerated. Of all the ship captains opposed to Nelson's at Trafalgar, not excluding the ferocious homuncule Lucas of *Redoutable* – four feet four inches tall – Infernet, in the words of Lieutenant

Humphrey Senhouse of HMS *Conqueror*, 'deserves to be recorded in the memory of those who admire true courage'.

Had there been more commanders of the stamp of Infernet, Lucas or Cajigal, of the *San Augustin*, in the Combined Fleet, Nelson's Trafalgar enterprise might have perished through its very recklessness. He had counted, as we have seen, on compensating for inferior numbers by the unorthodoxy of his approaching manoeuvre. Its unexpectedness he had to some degree over-estimated: Villeneuve had warned his captains to anticipate a breaking of the line from the windward and the British approach had certainly not surprised them. At a secondary level Nelson had counted on the inaccuracy of the enemy's gunnery to spare him the consequences of exposing the unarmed and unprotected bows of his leading ships to broadside fire until his own superior gunnery could take effect. There he had calculated better. Neither *Royal Sovereign* nor *Victory* (though there are ninety shot holes in the Trafalgar foresail preserved aboard) was disabled on the approach, nor any of their immediate followers.

In the close action both flagships lost many spars and much rigging; *Royal Sovereign* her main- and mizen-masts, *Victory* her mizen. Five other British ships lost masts: *Tonnant* her three topmasts, *Bellerophon* her main- and mizen-topmast, *Téméraire* her main-topmast, *Mars* her main-topmast, while *Belleisle* was dismasted. Many other suffered shots in major spars which left them tottering and caused their loss later; *Colossus* lost her mainmast the following night. The complete list of damage suffered by *Prince*, not one of the most heavily engaged, is an index of the effect even passing broadsides could have on a wooden man-of-war. Her bowsprit, three lower masts, main-topmast and gaff were badly damaged. She had several chain plates (to which the shrouds were secured) shot away and nine shots below the waterline, causing heavy damage to her timbers. Several gun-ports were destroyed, her stern and transoms badly damaged and three guns dismounted. After the battle she had to refit at Gibraltar.

Remarkably, few of the British ships were badly damaged in their hulls. *Revenge* and *Neptune* both logged nine shots below the waterline, *Leviathan* eight. *Téméraire* was, of course, much knocked about all over and *Colossus* had four ports stove in by collision with *Argonaute*. However, a meticulous catalogue of damage aboard *Victory*, drawn up by Midshipman Richard Roberts, confirms that the essential structure of the ship was intact. He mentions much damage to the 'wales, strings and spirketting', but these were lateral timbers above the waterline. The head and stern had been cut by shot; they had been the most exposed on the run-in. Of damage to the ship's great internal timber skeleton he noted only 'several beams, knees and riders shot through and broke'. In bad weather the ship was making twelve inches of water an hour, with which the pumps could easily cope.

Indeed, only two men had been wounded on *Victory*'s lower gundeck, in which the 32-pounders were mounted. The bulk of the casualties had been suffered on the exposed quarterdeck and main deck, where the officers, marines, sail-handlers and some of the 12-pounder crews stood unprotected by great timbers. There it was musketry and grape from the upper-deck guns of *Victory*'s opponents which had inflicted the heavy losses. *Victory* had suffered altogether 57 killed and 102 wounded, the majority struck by solid shot, musket-balls or splinters. Nelson had been hit by a musket-ball, Scott, his secretary, by a round-shot, Lieutenant William Ram by a shot which came out of the deck at his feet, throwing up splinters that wounded five seamen.

The relatively small loss of the British fleet – 449 killed and 1214 wounded out of a total strength of some 18,000, or about 2.5 per cent mortality (compare some 19,000 killed and wounded out of 67,000 in Wellington's army at Waterloo) – confirms the correctness of Nelson's pre-battle appreciations and battle tactics. He had taken one tremendous risk: that, in the approach, the Combined Fleet's gunnery would cripple his leading ships and throw his columns into disorder. That risk survived, the second factor on which he had counted to win predominance for the British had come into play. They had indeed succeeded in devastating their opponents with their first broadsides as they passed through the enemy line; and, when they had 'gone aboard' their target ships, their gun-handling – coolness of aim, rapidity in reloading – had achieved fire superiority.

The enemy's own reports, and those of British officers who went aboard the prizes, testify unequivocally to the results. Lucas of the *Redoutable* said he knew 'of nothing on board that had not been hit by shot and that the decks were everywhere strewn with dead, lying under the debris'. *Redoutable* had lain between *Victory* and *Téméraire* for at least two hours, in which time she might theoretically have suffered eighty broadsides into each beam. That total is intrinsically improbable; 7000 solid shot fired at ranges of a few yards would have pulverised any wooden hull, however strong. Yet terribly punished she undoubtedly was; Lucas's observation that 'a great number of the wounded were killed on the orlop deck' (that below waterline) suggests that *Victory* and *Téméraire* did indeed depress their guns to fire down through the ship, with catastrophic effect not only on the human occupants but also on the structure itself. *Redoutable* had to be abandoned on the evening of the following day after water in the hold had overcome the pumps.

Midshipman William Badcock of *Neptune*, who went aboard *Santissima Trinidad* after she had surrendered, found 'her beams . . . covered with blood, brains and pieces of flesh, and the after parts of her decks with wounded; some without legs and some without an arm'. *Santissima Trinidad* had at one time been simultaneously under fire from *Neptune*, *Africa* and *Conqueror*, the latter raking her from astern, which may explain why Badcock noticed so many of the wounded aft.

Captain James Atcherley, Royal Marines, going aboard *Bucentaure* to secure her magazine, found 'the dead, thrown back as they fell, among the middle of the deck in heaps . . . shot passing through these had fearfully mangled the bodies. More than four hundred had been killed and wounded, of whom an extraordinary proportion had lost their heads. A raking shot, which entered on the lower deck, had glanced along the beams and through the thickest of the people; and a French officer declared that this shot alone had killed and disabled nearly forty men.' An officer of *Achilles* on going aboard *Berwick* – a ship comparatively late into action which had fought only *Achilles* and *Defence* – 'counted upon her decks and in her cockpits and [cable] tiers, fifty-one dead bodies including that of her captain'. She also contained 200 wounded. *Defence*, by contrast, had only 7 dead and 29 wounded, though she had exchanged fire also with (and taken) the *San Ildefonso*.

The estimation of firm casualty figures among the French and Spanish crews defies exact reckoning, for so many men, fit and wounded alike – confined below while tiny British prize crews tried to work their ships – were to be drowned during the great gale that followed Trafalgar. The reported total of 4408 fatalities in the Combined Fleet must allow for many drownings; but the figure for wounded, 2545, calculated among the survivors of the gale – eighteen out of thirty-three ships – suggests, when contrasted with the British total of 1214 wounded in twenty-seven ships, that Franco-Spanish casualties were three times those of the British overall. The worst British casualties absolutely were in *Victory* herself (57 dead), the heaviest relatively in *Téméraire* (47); *Prince*, as we have seen, had not a man touched. These compare, among those for enemy ships that survived the battle and gale, with figures of 103 killed in *San Juan Nepomuceno* and 104 in *Santa Ana*.

In whichever fleet, however, a disproportionate share of casualties had been suffered by officers. The Combined Fleet had six ship captains killed, together with a commodore and three admirals (the Royal Navy, by contrast, lost Nelson and two captains – Cooke of *Bellerophon* and Duff of *Mars*). The toll among officers of the hardest-pressed French and Spanish ships is awesome. Le Tourneur (who was eventually to succumb from the effect of his own wounds) reported the deaths aboard *Algésiras* of Admiral Magon, two lieutenants and a midshipman and wounds to eleven officers. *Redoutable*, Lucas reported, had lost almost its entire 'executive': what that meant in practice was that two of six lieutenants had been killed and three wounded, five of the eleven sub-lieutenants and midshipmen killed and four wounded, and four of the eight marine officers killed and three wounded. Only seven out of twenty-nine officers went untouched, and they included the surgeon and purser, whose stations were below. Among officers in the Combined Fleet whose station was expressly above deck, that is to say the captains, twelve out of the thirty-three, or over a third, were either killed or wounded.

In the British fleet, deaths and woundings among the fighting and sailing officers varied between one-sixth and one-third, according to duties. Captains suffered 22 per cent casualties, lieutenants 19 per cent and marine officers 18 per cent. All or many of these officers would have had their stations on the quarterdeck, unprotected by anything but the bulwarks and hammock nettings, where they would have been exceptionally exposed to sharpshooting from the tops and rigging of enemy ships alongside. Sailing officers, in particular the masters, whose duty was to supervise sail-handling and steering, which could only be done above decks, suffered 30 per cent casualties. Boatswains, whose responsibility was for the spars and rigging, suffered 33 per cent; it may be guessed that some went aloft in the course of the action and were killed or wounded by fire into the tophamper, by falling spars or by themselves falling.

By contrast, only one carpenter in a British ship became a casualty: carpenters' responsibilities lay with the hull and kept them below decks, often below the waterline. There were no casualties among surgeons, whose action station was below waterline, and only four among administrative officers – secretaries and clerks. Midshipmen, the most junior and youngest officers, suffered 12 per cent casualties; among volunteers first-class, embryo midshipmen of tender years, only 8 out of 118 in the fleet became casualties. The supposition must be that the captains sent them out of harm's way at the start of action.

The total casualties among British officers was 37 killed and 102 wounded, out of some 800 captains, lieutenants, masters and masters' mates, midshipmen, volunteers and marines, or over 17 per cent. Casualties among the sailors, on the other hand, amounted to 1524 out of some 17,000, or nearly 9 per cent. As the action station of the majority of sailors was below decks, where they were protected by stout timbers on four sides, the discrepancy further bears out the supposition that it was exposure above decks – to musketry as well as roundshot – rather than mere presence in battle that constituted the greater danger in sailing-ship warfare, even at the very last stage of its refinement at the beginning of the nineteenth century.

If that is the case, then the conventional representation of the dominant trend in sailing-ship warfare – as a struggle between ships and their great guns, rather than between their crews – is necessarily called into doubt. The leading historians of sailing-ship warfare – with exceptions, that of Professor John Guilmartin being the most notable – have consistently argued that as seapower became oceanic, its instrument, the line-of-battleship, increasingly adapted to sea-keeping, and its armament, the heavy artillery cannon, ever more destructive of hulls and spars, but particularly hulls, fighting at sea progressively ceased to be 'man killing' and became instead 'ship killing'. Taking the conflict between the Spanish Armada and Queen Elizabeth I's fleet in the Channel as their starting-point, they have demonstrated that admirals consistently sought to turn their collections of ships into cohesive fleets, articulated by a single will from the centre – a development parallel to that which generals were working with their armies on land – and to defeat the opponent by collective action rather than through the sum of individual successes.

The evidence, as we have seen, however, is that collective fleet action did not work. The long record of Anglo-French engagements at sea from the end of the seventeenth until the end of the eighteenth century yields no example of a decisive victory, nor even of much 'ship killing'. Fleets clashed, flank to flank. Broadsides were exchanged. Masts toppled, hulls were punctured, men killed. But, when darkness or the elements or some other extraneous factor intervened, the fleets drew away with little substantial damage suffered by either.

The conventional resolution of the conventional representation of trends in sailing-ship warfare is that indecision stemmed from a fault of control; had admirals enjoyed the power to concentrate the gunnery of their fleets against the whole length of an enemy's battle line simultaneously, then a 'shock' would have been delivered against which no line could stand. However, because, in the absence of a comprehensive system of signals, such power was lacking, battle lines escaped the effect of shock and engagements at sea petered out in stalemate. Trafalgar, a 'revolutionary' battle in its effects, owed its nature to revolutionary tactics; but those tactics, so the argument runs, were chiefly the product of a revolution in control, brought about by the innovation of Home Popham's telegraphic signalling system. It was because Nelson had at his disposal the means to direct his ships wherever he wanted them to go at whichever moment he chose that he could risk the experiment of 'breaking the line from to windward', and so encompass the destruction of the Combined Fleet.

Such a resolution requires for validity, however, a demonstration not merely that the signalling revolution permitted the controlled breaking of the enemy's line but that 'ship killing from the windward' was also a form of tactics intrinsically superior to 'ship killing from the leeward'. It requires, in short, evidence that Nelson defeated the Combined Fleet not simply by preventing it from taking the wind and running away at a moment of its choice – the option conventionally held to have invalidated traditional tactics – but by sinking, burning or ungunning its ships.

No such evidence presents itself. *Achille*, it is true, took fire and eventually exploded, but that was the result of a conflagration in the fore-top, spread to the hull when the foremast fell. The fire was most probably started by the presence in the fore-top of musketeers festooned with powder cartridges, a source of danger Nelson himself had always recognised, and averted in British ships by forbidding marines or sailors to fight as musketeers in the tophamper. *Santissima Trinidad*, *Redoutable* and *Argonauta* admittedly sank after the battle; but they did so at the height of a great gale, when their depleted crews' efforts to work the pumps and repair damage below waterline was overcome by the extreme motion of the hulls. None of the British ships, badly shot about as some were aloft and alow, foundered. The relatively intact crews of even the worst damaged succeeded not only in mastering the inflows but in rigging jury spars and sails adequate to get steerage-way and ride out the ferocious weather. The least-damaged ships took prizes under tow and got four into Gibraltar. The eleven casualties among the seventeen surrendered Franco-Spanish ships (two were recaptured) were burnt or abandoned to the elements because of the severity of wind and sea.

The incontestable conclusion, therefore, is that it was 'man killing', not 'ship killing', that won the battle of Trafalgar. The evidence of the captains of the Combined Fleet itself supports this judgement. It may be argued as follows: deduct from the total of thirty-three ships present those in the centre and rear that did not fight – *Montanes*, *San Justo*, *San Leandro* – or fought barely at all, the Spanish *Neptune*. Further deduct eight of the ten ships of Dumanoir's division which took only a running part in the action – *Héros*, *San Francisco*, *Rayo*, *Duguay-Trouin*, *Mont Blanc*, *Formidable*, *Scipion* and the French *Neptune*. That reduces the real total of combatants the British twenty-seven faced to twenty-one. Of these several, notably the *Principe de Asturias*, *Argonaute*, *San Ildefonso* and *Pluton*, were engaged comparatively late, because they lay in the line at points the British did not choose for a break-in. *San Ildefonso*, for example, was attacked only by *Defence*, last in Collingwood's column, and *Pluton* only by *Mars*, the rear ship of the group Collingwood led against the central mass.

This means that the decisive fighting of the battle centred on four ship 'clusters': *Santissima Trinidad*, *Redoubtable* and *Bucentaure*, which were the targets of Nelson's break-in; *Indomptable*, *Santa Ana* and *Fougueux*, the targets of Collingwood's; and, further down the line, *Aigle*, *Achille* and their neighbours, which sailed at points where the leaders of the rest of Collingwood's division broke in. Six of those eight ships struck their colours (*Achille* blew up, *Indomptable* got away but in a devastated condition). All struck because of appalling loss of life. None – *Achille* apart – was 'killed' in any material sense.

What happened, on the contrary, was that British gunnery slaughtered their occupants, above and below decks, though probably above rather than below, in droves. *Santa Ana* had 104 killed and 137 wounded. *Fougueux*'s captain reported three-quarters of the crew killed or wounded, *Aigle*'s two-thirds, *Redoutable*'s five-sixths, while *Bucentaure* had 450 casualties and *Santissima Trinidad* 400 killed and 200 wounded. These must be compared with the worst losses in the British fleet of 57 dead aboard *Victory* and 47 dead aboard *Téméraire*.

THE AFTERMATH

Trafalgar was, in short, a massacre. As massacres go, it compared not at all with the worst of what Napoleon – or Wellington – was wreaking or would shortly wreak on land. The total of 8500 killed and wounded out of some 50,000 present (17 per cent) must be set against 13,500 casualties among 59,000 at Marengo (23 per cent), 78,000 among 226,000 at Borodino (35 per cent) and 55,000 among 192,000 at Waterloo (29 per cent). However, it was a figure unprecedented in sea fighting and, even though inflated by the drownings of crews wrecked in the gale that followed the action, one which set the battle altogether apart from any fought in the 250 preceding years of wooden-wall warfare. In its human horror, it both emphasised how half-hearted had been the urge to victory of all European admirals before Nelson and anticipated how very much more brutal naval warfare would become once truly ship-killing – and therefore mass man-killing – weapons appeared to lend Nelsonian naval tactics of do-or-die attack their essential point.

It was an ironical but also a logical outcome of Trafalgar that Nelson should have been its principal victim. The greatness of Nelson as a commander, like the greatness of Wellington, whom he resembles not at all in personality but closely in intellect, was to have comprehended the essence of the form of warfare he practised and reduced it to an operational procedure. What Wellington comprehended was that the firepower of infantry, when infantry was disposed in careful conformity to the topography of a defensive position, would, under scrupulous, direct and personal management, defeat any attack thrown against it; and by defeating it create the circumstances in which counter-attack would deliver victory. He had grasped, in short, that the *defensive* was the stronger form of war between gunpowder armies and devised a 'system' – his word – to capitalise on that perception. Nelson had perceived an opposite truth: that the *offensive* was the stronger form of warfare between gunpowder navies, given an equally scrupulous, direct and personal management of ship firepower, and to his chosen form of management he also gave the term 'system'. Both indeed had 'systems', but with this difference: Wellington's system, depending though it did on his immediate personal presence, did not expose him continuously to the fire of the enemy at close range; Nelson's, by contrast, did exactly that. As a result, while Wellington survived sixteen battles as a commander at the cost of some near misses, Nelson succumbed in his first command of a general engagement at sea to a point-blank shot.

It was also in the logic of the Nelsonian system that casualties should have been heavy among the crews, very heavy among the officers, of the leading British and their opposed 'target' ships, and that those ships themselves should have suffered major, in some cases disabling, damage. The 'old system' which Nelson had rejected had been an effort to defeat a whole fleet by the action of another whole fleet; his new system was an attempt to defeat a whole fleet by the devastation of a few of its parts. Hence the wide discrepancy between damage done to and lives lost in *Bucentaure* on the one hand, for example, and in *Rayo* on the other. *Bucentaure* had been caught, while *Rayo* had run away; but it was the point of catching *Bucentaure* to make *Rayo* run away. Its fate could be settled at leisure when the integrity of the Combined Fleet had been sundered.

The human consequences of the Nelsonian 'system' were barbaric. His own last two and a half hours of life, probably more exactly reported than those of any other human being, thanks to the meticulous memoir written later by Dr William Beatty, *Victory*'s surgeon, convey all too realistically the agony undergone by a badly wounded man carried down to the orlop deck of a man-of-war in the course of action. 'Drink, drink', 'fan, fan', were the words Nelson most frequently uttered, in between describing to Beatty with remarkable precision the sensations of a man who had suffered two broken ribs, a punctured lung, two broken vertebrae and a damaged artery. Besides thirst and heat, he also complained of the noise of the discharge of *Victory*'s 32-pounder battery on the deck over his head, repented his sins, grieved for his family and called for his friends. Apart from a preliminary and quickly abandoned probing for the lodged ball, Beatty could do nothing for his patient. He continued, therefore, with amputations, splinter extractions, wound debridage and limb-splinting among his other patients. Fortunately only 25 of *Victory*'s 102 wounded were categorised 'dangerously' and only four subsequently died. Dr Beatty was clearly an efficient surgeon, but it was a factor in the effectiveness of his ministrations that he had two assistants and that the number of their patients did not overwhelm them.

The worst hit of the French and Spanish ships were charnel houses, their orlops overflowing with wounded, many others lying unattended among the guns. And the agonies of the wounded were soon compounded by the vicious hull motion imparted by the gale and then by the terror, frequently realised, of drowning below decks.

Three of the British prizes, *Argonauta*, *Redoutable*, *Santissima Trinidad*, proved unmanageable under tow and had to be abandoned. *Redoutable*, under tow by *Swiftsure*, lost her remaining mast on 22 October and parted her cable next day. *Swiftsure* had sent boats, despite the ferocious weather, and managed to take off some of the prize crew and 'a great number' of the crew, but many, including most of the wounded, went down with the ship in the darkness. 'We could distinctly hear,' wrote Midshipman George Barker, 'the cries of the unhappy people we could no longer assist.' *Santissima Trinidad* lasted until 24 October. She was attended by *Neptune*, *Ajax* and *Prince*, the latter trying to maintain a tow, but failing; 400 bodies had been thrown overboard, 300–400 wounded were in the orlop and survivors took turns continuously at the pumps, which were struggling against fifteen feet of water in the hold. Eventually the signal was received from Collingwood to abandon the prizes and *Prince*'s boats got under the stern to take off the people. 'What a sight when we came to remove the wounded,' wrote Lieutenant John Edwards; 'we had to tie the poor mangled wretches round their waists, or where we could, and lower them down into a tumbling boat, some without arms, others no legs, and lacerated all over in the most dreadful manner. About ten o'clock we had got all out, to about thirty-three or four, which I believe it was impossible to remove without instant death.'

Intrépide and *San Augustin* were abandoned by the British, the prize crews setting them on fire as they left. *Aigle*, *Berwick*, *Fougueux* and *Monarca* went ashore in British hands. *Monarca*, with a British prize crew on board (most of whom got drunk as soon as they took possession), stranded with the loss of 150 Spaniards. Aboard *Berwick* 200 drowned. She had anchored, but some of the prisoners, who were not under control and feared the storm worse than the shore, cut the cables and let her run on to rocks. *Fougueux*, the first of the prizes to be lost, suffered the worst of fates. Full of wounded, she broke the tow passed her by the frigate *Phoebe* and began to founder during the night of 21 October. Pierre Servaux, her master-at-arms, reported that the water had risen almost to the orlop deck. 'Everywhere one heard the cries of the wounded and the dying, as well as the noise and shouts of insubordinate men who refused to man the pumps and only thought of themselves.' Next morning, as *Fougueux* neared shore, Servaux managed to swim off; 'only about 30 men got to land,' her commander reported, 'who in addition to those whom the English had on board, might amount to 110 or 120 men remaining out of a ship's company of 682 souls who were on board the day that we put the sea.' *Bucentaure*, whose crew managed to retake her from her British prizemasters at the height of the gale (as did that of *Algésiras*), went ashore at the entrance of Cadiz harbour; most of those aboard were saved, but the majority of her company had transferred to *Indomptable* and were lost in that ship's wreck. *Algésiras* struggled into port intact. The Combined Fleet suffered two other casualties. *Santa Ana*, recovered adrift in a sortie led from Cadiz by some of the fugitives of the battle, went ashore together with *Rayo*, which belonged to the reserve party.

The wrath of the elements, therefore, ultimately wrought far greater damage to the Combined Fleet than the firepower of the Royal Navy. Sixteen ships escaped the encounter to sail again under French or Spanish colours. Four survived as British prizes. One, *Achille*, had been destroyed by explosion in action. Twelve had foundered or run ashore in the great gale. It was that outcome which allowed Napoleon, in his only public reference to Trafalgar, to remark that 'storms caused us the loss of several ships after an imprudently undertaken engagement'.

The strategic results of Trafalgar far overreached this contemptuous dismissal. Napoleon might have abandoned his grand design for a descent upon Britain before the battle had been fought. In two battles of his own – Ulm in October and Austerlitz in December 1805 – he might devastate the armies of the Third Coalition and destroy it as a diplomatic instrument opposed to his power. But his long-term object of defeating his maritime enemy 'from the land' was in no wise advanced by that result. Britain continued to retain its Mediterranean possessions of Gibraltar and Malta. It continued to sustain garrisons and allies in Sicily and Sardinia. It was shortly to add to its chain of oceanic calling-places on the route to India the island of Madeira and the port of Capetown, the one conceded by the Portuguese, the other captured from the Dutch. Further, in a succession of strokes at the periphery of Napoleon's European empire, it was to diminish the stock of naval units available for inclusion in his central striking force while greatly enlarging the area in which the Grand Army had to deploy its occupying force. In September 1807 a British amphibious expedition took possession of the Danish fleet, the first move in a major extension of British power into the Baltic. In November the British shanghai-ed the Portuguese fleet, thereby negating the point of a French invasion of Portugal. And in June 1809 they opened the first round of the war in the Iberian Peninsula which was to embroil a quarter of Napoleon's disposable military force in a strategically irrelevant diversion of effort from his main purpose of making the continent a French hegemony.

Overseas, meanwhile, the Royal Navy steadily recaptured the French and Allied possessions returned to Napoleon by the Peace of Amiens and took those which had previously escaped its strategic grasp – Guyane, Martinique, Guadeloupe in and near the Caribbean, Senegal in West Africa, Mauritius and Reunion in the Indian Ocean and the Dutch island of Java, jewel of its colonial crown, in the East Indies. For a brief period, between his defeat of Russia at Friedland in 1807 and the tsar's return to the Allied cause in March 1812, Napoleon might theoretically count on the availability of some 160 line-of-battle-ships, French and satellite, to oppose some 110 British. However, scattered as Napoleon's naval resources were between a dozen ports, many landlocked behind choke points, like the Baltic Narrows which the Royal Navy controlled, the ships which composed his theoretical *masse de manoeuvre* availed him not at all. The French navy's efforts to invade Sicily, recover lost islands in the West Indies, incorporate Turkey into his closure of Europe to British trade (the 'Continental System'), disrupt Britain's Indian convoys, interdict the maritime supply of Wellington's army in Spain, all failed; and failed at the cost of losing squadrons and small fleets to the British whenever the efforts were made. The extension of British naval power was as inexorable as the steady diminution of the French navy which, except in a few hurried and humiliatingly frustrated dashes from one port to another, was never again after Trafalgar to take to the high seas. Trafalgar had made the high seas British Sovereign territory, so that it was indeed 'those storm-beaten ships upon which the Grand Army never gazed that stood between it and the dominion of the world'.

Indeed, the real heroes of Trafalgar were as much the ships as the men who manned them. 'Ships,' Admiral Mahan also wrote, 'have a personality only less vivid than that of the men who fought in them.' Nelson's wooden walls – Villeneuve's, too, one might say, had he not led them to defeat – exemplify a triumph of human ingenuity for which one would seek far to find a parallel. Some 300 years before Trafalgar was fought, iron and bronze founders had perfected instruments of destruction before which the castles that had dominated Europe's strategic landscape for 500 years were to topple in a few decades, and before which armies were to wilt and disintegrate on every battlefield where powder and ball opposed their ranks. It would require a revolution in the techniques of fortification and military drill and discipline to offset the power that cast cannon brought to land warfare before equilibrium was restored and generals could campaign again by the rules evolved over 3000 years of combat. The art of the shipwright, by contrast, was to undergo no such upheaval. Altogether without prescience, European shipbuilders had already, at the moment of the appearance of the 'great gun', arrived at a form of wooden ship design which assured its capacity to breast great waters and the elements which disturbed them, to sustain the shock of artillery discharge in broadside and to absorb the impact of solid shot that broadside battery threw.

Victory was, of course, a much larger ship than any of its European predecessors of the immediately pre-gunpowder age – the merchant 'cogs' and 'round ships' of the fifteenth-century Channel and Baltic. Yet in fundamental construction it differed from them not at all. They were immensely strong and stiff load-bearers, designed to carry a large press of sail on several masts, ride out Atlantic storms and store bulky and heavy cargoes – barrels, baulks of timber – on their lower decks. Because of the high intrinsic weight of such cargoes the danger attendant on their shifting in a seaway, and the need to 'take ground' at calling places where deep water did not provide anchorages or moorings, the skeletons of the North European load-carrier benefited from progressive over-compensation by the men who built them. Keelsons were added to keels, ribs doubled and trebled, stringers and wales thickened, crossbeams cut ever more massively. When, at the beginning of the sixteenth century, it was decided that such ships should become gun-carriers, no fundamental adaptation of their hulls proved necessary at all. Ports, with closing lids, to keep the sea out, were cut between the ribs, gun-carriages devised, restraining tackle designed to anchor carriages to timbers, and, almost overnight, stout merchant ships were transformed into powerful men-of-war. Their complements of cannon weighed no more than the cargoes they had previously carried; nor did the shock of discharge strain them more than tempests or groundings had done before.

Even more strikingly, these great wooden skeletons – *Victory*'s hull contained 300,000 cubic feet of timber, that yielded by a hundred acres of woodland – proved extraordinarily resistant to gunshot. The spans of a man-of-war were easily toppled, its upper works – bulwarks, stern galleries, beaks, figurehead and plank sheer – quickly pulverised. But its fundamental structure was stouter stuff. On *Victory*'s return to Dover in December 1805, eighty shot-holes 'between wind and water' were counted (at places which let in the sea), all of which had been plugged by her own carpenter's crew during and immediately after the battle. Damage to her spars had reduced her sailing qualities, but her sea-keeping and status as a gun platform were still intact.

'Wooden wall', in short, was an exact as well as metaphorical characteristic of the sailing man-of-war. Unlike the masonry fronts of the 'artillery trace' fortresses on which the European dynastic states had poured out their millions in the seventeenth and eighteenth centuries, man-of-war hulls did not fracture or collapse when struck by solid shot. They admitted the projectile and then elastically regained their shape. They splintered, but with nothing like the lethal effect on their occupants that stone and brick fortresses inflicted on their defenders. They rarely exploded, burnt or sank. Even after the heaviest of poundings, they usually brought the survivors among their crews, given good weather, home to harbour. Little wonder that their sailors – for all the labour at capstans, sheets and braces their means of motion imposed, for all the repetitiveness of sluicing and swabbing the discipline of shipboard life required, for all the immutability of watch and watch about, for all the danger of work aloft, for all the harshness of naval punishment – came to feel an almost mystic affection for them. Little wonder, either, that the few survivors of the wooden world – *Vasa*, *Victory*, *Constitution* – command the awed veneration of a later generation. Any great wooden ship, but particularly the wooden man-of-war, is a monument to human ingenuity of a unique sort. Nothing else made by man to coax power from the elements while defying their force has ever so perfectly embodied his intentions. The successors of the wooden man-of-war would go further, shoot further and hit harder than anything wrought from oak, fastened by copper and rigged with flax and hemp; but no product of the shipwright's art – perhaps not even the nuclear submarine – would ever serve the purposes of those who pay and those who command so narrowly. The passing of the age of wooden ships, which had made their last great encounter at Trafalgar, marked a moment of fundamental change, by no means for the better, in human history.

2

JUTLAND

THE FALL OF THE WOODEN WALLS

Victory was to be damaged in war once again after *Trafalgar*. On the night of 10/11 March 1941, a German 500 lb bomb, dropped during a raid on Portsmouth naval dockyard, fell into the dry dock which had been the ship's home since 1922. It exploded between the dock walls and the ship's hull, blowing a 20-foot gap in the masonry and a hole 8 feet by 15 in *Victory*'s side. The elasticity of her timbers once again worked to save her from destruction.

Had the bomb fallen into water, however – and *Victory* remained afloat in Portsmouth harbour until 1922 – the explosion must have sunk her, for water conducts shock far more efficiently than air. Had the bomb actually struck her, the probability must also have been that *Victory* would have been destroyed by fire. Explosive projectiles spelt death to wooden ships. The detonation of the filling was a primary source of fire, the scatter of red-hot metal splinters into their timbers a multiple source of secondary outbreaks. It was chiefly for that reason that wooden ship fleets had, by unspoken mutual agreement, eschewed the use of explosive projectiles long after they had become a common medium of firepower in warfare on land (the dangers of handling and fusing such shells aboard ship was a significant but secondary deterrent).

Until thirty years after Trafalgar the main armament of all line-of-battleships continued to be smooth-bore cannon firing solid shot. The ships themselves, thanks to the introduction of iron bracing into their timber construction, had grown considerably since 1805. Tonnages of nearly 4000 tons – *Victory*'s was 2600 – had been achieved (though it was recognised that the dimensions of natural timbers precluded further enlargement) and auxiliary steam-engines, working retractable screws, assisted the propulsion of such hulls in calms and light airs. The appearance of the gundecks, however, seemed immutable; they remained unobstructed open spaces running the whole length of the ship, with gun-carriages ranged behind ports at ten-foot intervals from bow to stern.

Admirals, however, could not forever deny the trend of technology. Indeed, in the acquisition of auxiliary vessels admirals, both in the Royal and French navies, proved remarkably adaptive to contemporary ship-building developments. Steam, iron, the paddle and the screw were readily adopted as means of construction and propulsion for tugs, tenders and gunboats. It could only be a matter of time before such machinery and materials were introduced into capital ship construction. When the moment of change occurred its ramifications were wide and rapid. As early as 1822 the French general Henri Paixhans, an artillery expert, had advocated the construction of a fleet of steam gunboats firing explosive shells which, he claimed, would make France paramount at sea and lay the grounds for avenging Trafalgar. By 1837 the French navy adopted shell-firers and two years later the Royal Navy followed suit. The persistence of peace fortunately precluded the two trying their new guns against each other's wooden walls. However, when Russia's Black Sea fleet surprised Turkey's at Sinope in 1853, the former firing shells, the latter traditional solid shot, the result was devastation. It was already too late for the British and French navies to add any anti-shell protection to the wooden walls sent against Russia in the Crimean War that began the following year; but fortunately the Russian wooden walls did not challenge them to battle. However, the warning was too strong to be ignored; and it was reinforced by the success in action against Russian fortresses in the Baltic of three small purpose-built French gunboats, *Tonnante, Lave* and *Dévastation*, whose ironclad hulls proved equally impervious to solid shot and explosive shell.

In a rash of activity after the Crimean War, the French and British admiralties reacted accordingly. France, in 1859, put to sea a shell-firing ship, *Gloire*, whose wooden hull had been sheathed in iron armour. The following year Britain launched an equivalent ship, *Warrior* (now preserved near *Victory* in Portsmouth dockyard), which is rightly regarded as the first battleship of the modern age. *Warrior* was steam-propelled, shell-firing, iron in construction from keel to bulwarks and heavily armoured as well. Seeing her lying at anchor beside the surviving wooden walls of the Channel Fleet, Palmerston said she looked 'like a black snake among the rabbits'.

The naval rabbits disappeared in the following decade as if by a plague of myxomatosis. The first iron gunboat constructed by the South in the American Civil War drove the North's fleet of traditional wooden ships ignominiously into harbour. Coastal and river operations between the two navies were thereafter exclusively conducted with steam warships, purpose-built and hastily improvised, and iron in construction whenever possible. Meanwhile the navies of the traditional great powers were transforming themselves year by year into fleets of black snakes. After 1865 all the Royal Navy's new ships were built of iron; the most modern of the old were cut down and ironclad. By the next decade all navies with a claim to be regarded as modern had battle fleets exclusively composed of iron ships driven by steam, mounting shell-firing guns and protected over their engine-rooms, magazines and gun batteries by plates of metal armour.

Yet most battle fleets remained small until the end of the century. Britain's radical and adventurous dismantling of her wooden walls in the 1860s confronted her naval rivals – France and Russia – with costs they did not choose to meet; from their starting position of relative inferiority, both countries felt the obstacles to equalling or exceeding the size of the Royal Navy to be insuperable. As late as 1883 Britain's battleship total was larger than that of the next three European navies – those of France, Russia and the new German empire – put together at 41 to 33. The newly unified Kingdom of Italy had only three major warships, and those future naval titans, the United States and Japan, had none at all.

By 1897, only fifteen years later, the balance had radically altered. Britain's relative economic decline and her competitors' absolute increase in wealth and productiveness had made the Royal Navy, though still the largest fleet in the world, inferior to France, Russia and Germany, with 62 as against 66 battleships; calculated against all other naval powers, including Italy, the United States and Japan, the ratio was 62 to 96. This reordering of the balance of naval power was explained in part by unit-cost factors; the shift from wood to iron, sail to steam and smooth-bore to rifled artillery had entailed huge increases in the construction costs of individual ships. Even for a state as wholly dependent for its world position on a great navy as was Victorian Britain, these costs were too large to be met by conventional budgetary outlay. However, it was also explained by deliberate decisions taken among its fellows. France, an expansionary imperial power with colonial interests in places as far apart as West Africa and Indo-China, had decided it needed a large navy. The United States, its frontiers established on the Pacific as well as the Atlantic coasts of the North American continent and with a growingly hegemonic stake in the politics of the whole hemisphere, decided likewise. Italy had conceived naval and imperial ambitions in the eastern Mediterranean and its dependent seas, Japan in the northern Pacific. Above all, the new German empire chose to consider that a place among the foremost states of the world consistent with its economic and military power could be achieved only by the building of a large High Seas Fleet.

The German navy counted initially for so little beside the consistently triumphant German army – victor in the brilliantly abrupt campaigns of 1866 and 1870 against Austria and France which made Prussia the leading state in central and western Europe – that it was originally commanded by generals. General Stosch, the first imperial admiral, regarded the navy as a 'living coastal defence' and left it equipped with seven armoured frigates he hoped would help to spare German port cities from French and Russian naval attack in the event of war. General (later Admiral) Caprivi, who succeeded him, enlarged the fleet to eighteen major warships, also adding numbers of torpedo-boats in the belief, first given currency by the French admiral Théophile Aube, that the torpedo promised a cheap means of reversing the positions of weak navies *vis-à-vis* the battleship powers – particularly Britain.

However, when Caprivi left office in 1888 Germany was still no more than 'a sea power of the second rank', Bismarck's characterisation, which he and the bulk of the German high command thought it proper it should remain. It was the accession of a new Kaiser in the same year, Wilhelm II, that transformed the German navy's future. Kaiser Wilhelm, a grandson of Queen Victoria, had been brought up in the shadow of the Royal Navy. He admired its traditions, he was jealous of its reputation and he envied the power its still predominant strength conferred on his grandmother's kingdom. 'Wilhelm's one idea,' his mother, Victoria's daughter the Empress Frederick wrote, 'is to have a Navy which shall be larger and stronger than the Royal Navy.' In 1891 the first steps were taken with the launching of a true battleship, *Brandenburg*, and by 1897 Germany had eight such ships afloat. However, that counted scarcely at all beside the Royal Navy's sixty-two. What Wilhelm needed for the translation of his daydreams into reality was an ordered programme of naval construction and a coherent plan for the employment of the resulting fleet. In June 1897, with the appointment of Rear-Admiral Alfred Tirpitz to the office of State Secretary for the Navy, he acquired the services of a man who could design both.

Tirpitz has been described by Professor Holger Herwig, the leading historian of the Imperial German Navy, as 'ruthless, clever, domineering, patriotic, indefatigable, aggressive yet conciliatory, pressing yet patient, and stronger in character and drive than the three Chancellors and seven heads of the Foreign Office who were destined to be his co-actors on the political stage.' In office Tirpitz was to display two priceless abilities. The first was to coax from the German parliament funds sufficient to build a large fleet in ways that did not conspicuously add to the citizen's tax burden, thereby averting the fiscal resistance which might have killed the High Seas Fleet in embryo; the second was to argue a strategy which offered a realistic chance of nullifying British naval power from a basis of German inferiority – marginal inferiority, it is true, but inferiority nevertheless. Tirpitz called his strategy *Risikogedanke* – 'risk theory'. The Royal Navy, by his analysis, had been accustomed since Trafalgar to go where it chose and do what it would across the watery globe. If a German navy could threaten, even at heavy cost to itself, such losses to the Royal Navy that its ability to confront one of its other naval rivals – France, Russia, the United States – was thereby compromised, it would shrink from the challenge. In doing so it would concede to Germany a freedom of action of its own in international politics and thereby open the way for Berlin to move from great power (*Grossmacht*) to world power (*Weltmacht*) status.

Tirpitz's analysis was persuasive. Moreover, it had been influenced by the larger analysis of the foremost naval thinker of the age, the American Alfred Thayer Mahan. Mahan, whose *Influence of Sea Power upon History* had appeared in 1890 – and by which the Kaiser, who read it in 1894, had been instantly converted to 'navalism' – believed in the intrinsic superiority of ocean-going ('blue water') fleets over coast-defence forces as a means of extending state power. He propagated faith in the decisive battle (*Entscheidungsschlacht*, the Germans termed it), or its threat as the crux on which 'blue water' strategy must turn. Trafalgar, his 'favourite battle', perfectly exemplified the way in which he held fleets should be used. Because it showed how a numerically inferior fleet might nevertheless overcome a stronger, even in the stronger's home waters, its example was an encouragement to both Tirpitz and the Kaiser, who drew from it the conviction that a High Seas Fleet of carefully calculated size might win for Germany the long-term advantage that Nelson had given Britain.

Mahan's thinking worked on the Kaiser chiefly as means to enrich his naval fantasies, which were many and varied. Between 1893 and 1914 he spent no less than 1600 days – four and a half years – at sea in his luxurious steam yacht *Hohenzollern*, cruising in her between the Baltic and the Mediterranean, often wearing the uniform of an imperial *Grossadmiral* (great admiral), a rank he created for himself. When appropriate he also appeared as an admiral of the fleet of the Royal Navy and occasionally in the admiral's uniform of the Russian, Swedish, Danish, Norwegian or Greek navies. He reserved alone to himself among German ruling princes the right to wear the uniform of a naval executive officer, in which he once attended a performance of Wagner's *Flying Dutchman*, and, of course, he outfitted his sons in sailor suits.

He was also given to designing battleships on the backs of envelopes, in the belief, to which Hitler was also to show himself prone, that an ideal design which had eluded the professional naval architect might somehow fall from the pen of an enthusiastic amateur; his particular obsession was with the 'fast capital ship', a vessel combining the strength and firepower of a battleship with the speed of a cruiser (this contradiction in terms, to be fair, was an obsession of Tirpitz's opposite number, Admiral Sir John Fisher).

Tirpitz, though genuinely grateful for the Kaiser's wholehearted commitment to German naval expansion, was a realist, not a fantasist. Had he never read the works of Mahan (which in fact he caused to be translated into German), he would neverless have arrived at Mahan's point – which was that the single-minded use of a navy in the service of rational state policy would overcome structural deficiencies in a nation's relative status among others. Thus Britain, though small in population, deficient in high-value resources and originally backward industrially, had succeeded, by exploiting its highly advantageous location athwart the trade routes of northern Europe and by the acquisition of bases controlling trade routes further afield, in acquiring world power wholly disproportionate to its objective military strength. Between the fourth quarter of the eighteenth and the third quarter of the nineteenth century it had made itself – despite the loss of much of North America – the largest empire the world had ever known, successor to the Mogul emperors of India, master of the continent of Australasia, dominant power in the West Indies, controller of the South African Cape and its hinterland, commercial overlord of China and parts of Latin America, ruler of Egypt and wide areas of East and West Africa, and a significant power in Arabia, the East Indies and the South Pacific. It had also retained its traditional footholds in the Mediterranean, to which it had actually added since the creation of the unified German state. Germany, by contrast, had awesome military strength; but, because of its late rise to great-power status and inherent disadvantages of access to the high seas, it had missed its chance to translate military strength into colonial grandeur. 'Risk theory' offered the opportunity of reversing that situation.

'Risk theory', moreover, was not just the stuff of ink and paper. Tirpitz, almost from the outset of his strategy-making, put a figure to it: sixty capital ships (the dominant ship-types in the fleet). This figure was to include forty battleships and twenty large cruisers, the latter designed to scout ahead of the fleet and engage the enemy as a preliminary to general action. Such a figure still conceded superiority to the Royal Navy, which persisted at a strength of some sixty battleships and looked to do so in virtual perpetuity. However, by sophisticated (today it would appear specious) argument, Tirpitz justified settling for a balance that gave the British a 50 per cent numerical preponderence by invoking a supposed German qualitative advantage. The argument turned on the superiority of German crews, ships, equipment and tactics, and the capacity of Germany to maintain its fleet in North Sea harbours at a permanent state of readiness for war, while the Royal Navy, distracted by the need to man stations as far distant as Hong Kong, Trincomalee, Bermuda, Vancouver and Perth, enjoyed no such strategic stability.

Tirpitz did not, however, expect the British to acquiesce in a direct German challenge to the Royal Navy's power. Contrary to popular conceptions, he did not plan to conduct an open naval race. His design was to make ground on his rival by stealth, increasing the size of the German battle fleet and of its component ships by barely perceptible stages. 'The patient laying of brick upon brick', he called it, entailing the addition of about 2000 tons' displacement to each successive class of battleship, and an increase of capital ships at the rate of about one a year. The programmed finances of his first Navy Bill of 1898 fell well within these limits. But its popularity and its results diminished his caution. To the alarm of the British the Second Navy Bill of 1900 elicited funds for the doubling of the fleet, and the Supplementary Bill of 1906 (others were to follow in 1908 and 1912) heightened it further. For all Germany's resolve 'to operate carefully like the caterpillar before it has grown into a moth', British hypersensitivity to a naval challenge from any direction, but particularly from a point as close to home as the North Sea, ensured that caterpillar and moth came under immediate parliamentary, press and public scrutiny. In November 1904 the traditional 'two-power standard', which laid down that Britain must maintain a fleet equal in size to that of the next two combined, was revised to include a 10 per cent margin. Further, with the promotion the previous month of Admiral Sir John Fisher to the post of First Sea Lord, the Royal Navy was plunged into the most radical reorganisation it had ever undergone, designed to transform it from a sprawl of far-flung squadrons at the margins of empire to a rationalised instrument of world power with, at its centre, a great striking force based on Britain.

Much of the reserve fleet of old and antiquated ships held in dockyards against the contingency of war – 'a miser's hoard of useless junk', in Fisher's characteristically vigorous dismissal – were struck off the strength. Three historic overseas stations – Australia, China and East Indies – were amalgamated into an Eastern Fleet based in Singapore; the South Atlantic, North America and West Africa stations were subsumed within an expanded Cape Station; the Pacific Station was abolished altogether. Much of the abolished stations' complements of sloops and gunboats went with them; 'an enemy cruiser', Fisher forecast, 'would lap them up like an armadillo let loose on an ant-hill.' The net result of Fisher's programme of scrappings was to reduce the Royal Navy by 154 units. With the crews and money saved he achieved a doubling of the size of the home fleet to seventeen battleships; the Mediterranean Fleet was reduced from twelve to eight; only the Atlantic Fleet, with eight battleships, was left at its former strength. Overall the result was to create by 1905 a battle fleet in home waters twenty-five strong, when Germany still had only fifteen, of which five were old.

In 1905, moreover, Fisher inaugurated a new round of battleship construction which consigned all existing types to obsolescence. Since the beginning of the century an idea had been germinating among the naval architects of the advanced countries that current battleship design did not unify in a single hull the many advances that the different technologies of propulsion, protection and armament now made available. Battleships were still driven by reciprocating engines, intrinsically inferior to the new turbine as a source of power, and, because of the long stroke of their upright pistons, requiring a wasteful diffusion of armour about the engine spaces for their protection against shellfire;

the rotary turbine, by contrast, lay low in the ship's hull. Improvements in gun design, giving greater range, now exposed ships to the danger of plunging fire, requiring, because of armour's very great weight – a quarter-ton per square foot of 12-inch plate – that the decks as well as sides be protected. However, this in turn imposed a height restriction on the sides of the armoured box which formed the 'central citadel' of a battleship to win weight-carrying capacity for the lid. Certainly, the development of such armoured citadels demanded the largest possible delivery of shell-weight to crack them open. The former philosophy of deluging an enemy ship with a 'hail of fire' from many guns, large and small, to cause damage indiscriminately ought rationally to yield to a practice of attacking it with one calibre, and that the largest possible, of armour-piercing shot only. The development in the 1890s of fuses which would retard detonation of a shell's filling until the shell had pierced through a ship's armour brought that practice within the realm of the possible. And improvements in range-finding optics, range-estimating machinery (the 'gunnery clock', a proto-computer) and gunnery practice realised gunnery enthusiasts' ambition of hitting targets at greatly increased ranges. Admiral Percy Scott, the Royal Navy's foremost gunnery enthusiast and a dynamic innovator who brooked no opposition from traditionalists, quickly succeeded after 1903 in increasing the percentage of hits achieved from 30 to 80 per cent and in lengthening the range at which accurate fire was delivered from 2000 to 7000 yards. Scott's revolution entailed little more than centralising fire control in a ship (instead of allowing turrets to fire independently) and training fire-control officers accurately to observe and correct the fall of shot. The abrasive manner in which he brought about his 'revolution' won him enemies throughout the fleet; but Fisher, his principal supporter, met complaints with a dismissive 'I don't care if he drinks, gambles and womanises; he hits the target.'

The outcome of Fisher's technological star-gazing and Scott's down-to-earth gunnery drills was to be a battleship, *Dreadnought*, of truly revolutionary design. Constructed and launched in record-breaking time between October 1905 and February 1906, *Dreadnought* embodied all those disparate features of which Fisher had noted the significance. She was turbine-driven, giving her a contemporary cruiser's rather than a battleship's speed, more robustly and rationally armoured than any ship afloat, and armed exclusively with armour-cracking guns, ten 12-inch mounted in five turrets. She was, moreover, intended as only the first of a series, among which were to be included a class of 'all-big-guns' ships, sacrificing protection to speed, which would come to be called 'battlecruisers'. Their role would be to sweep away the protective screen of an enemy battle fleet, bringing on a Trafalgar-style encounter of capital units with a minimum of preliminaries.

Dreadnought was not designed with the intention either of nullifying the Tirpitz programme or of fighting a future German battle fleet in the North Sea. She represented a technological leap into the future, undertaken to forestall pre-emption by the naval architects of whatever competitor, France, Russia, Germany, Japan, the United States or Italy; both the last two had recently authorised or adumbrated the building of battleships too close to *Dreadnought*'s design for safety. However, the effect of *Dreadnought*'s appearance was indeed to nullify the Tirpitz programme and to threaten a German North Sea fleet with defeat. Tirpitz grasped the implication as soon as he heard of *Dreadnought*'s launch. It confronted him, moreover, with a triple difficulty. The first was to accept that his fifteen existing battleships had been outdated overnight; the second was to win from the German parliament the funds to build modern replacements; the third was to preserve the camouflage of his 'brick by brick' competition with the Royal Navy. He bit the bullet of supersession with courage; bearding parliament he undertook with characteristic high-handedness – and success; a Supplementary Naval Bill for the construction of three dreadnought-type battleships and a battlecruiser was passed, at the threat of his resignation, in May 1906; and open confrontation with the Royal Navy he decided would henceforth have to be accepted as a component of his 'risk theory'. It would be seen whether Britain's determination to remain the world's leading sea power would be made good in hard cash, spent on replacing its own battleships that *Dreadnought* had outdated.

The Anglo-German naval race was on; but because of Tirpitz's success in concealing first the keel-laying of Germany's first dreadnoughts and then the funding for the construction of their successors its start was slow. Then in 1909 Britain, committed to a programme of constructing only ten new capital ships by that year and five each in 1910 and 1911, confronted the discovery that Germany planned to build sixteen between 1908 and 1911, giving Britain an advantage of only four. Germany, moreover, could apparently build faster than Britain, by finding funds to stockpile material ahead of time and by adopting techniques of prefabrication that British shipyards had not learned. At the best estimate Germany would have seventeen new capital ships to Britain's twenty in 1912; some estimates put the ratio at 21:20 in Germany's favour. Germany, moreover, had now adopted the turbine as a means of propulsion and, though favouring guns of slightly smaller calibre than the Royal Navy's, was building ships clearly superior in armoured protection and internal subdivision. No British alarmist was yet claiming that the ships of the High Seas Fleet were unsinkable; but it was in that direction that the trend of their design was incontestably moving.

This 'naval scare' of 1909 drove the British Admiralty, parliament and ultimately the people into a frenzy of competition. The 'navalist' party was strong in Britain; so too were its opponents, who deprecated the diversion into warship-building of funds which might have been spent on social measures or not spent at all. However, in the words of the German naval attaché in London, Captain Widermann, 'the nervous tension, not to say fear of the German fleet, increased so much in England that in the spring of 1909 it presented a spectacle which was unworthy of the tradition of the first sea power.' The Liberal government's programme was for four new dreadnought constructions that year; the Admiralty and Conservative Opposition's demand was for six; eventually an arrangement was agreed by which four would be laid down in 1909 and another four in 1910, if the necessity was demonstrated. In the event – which required much putting of Germany's rate of dreadnought construction in the worst light – the demonstration was made, providing Winston Churchill, then Home Secretary, with the pretext for one of his most memorable aphorisms: 'The Admiralty had demanded six ships; the economists offered four; and we finally compromised on eight.'

Writing after the First World War, however, Churchill conceded that he and Lloyd George, principal opponents of the 'eight' and 'six' programmes, though 'right in the narrow sense . . . were absolutely wrong in relation to the deep tides of destiny. The greatest credit is due to the First Lord of the Admiralty, Mr [Reginald] McKenna, for the resolute and courageous manner in which he fought his case and withstood his [Liberal] Party on this occasion.' What Churchill with hindsight saw was that, without the four 'contingent' dreadnoughts of 1909, the High Seas Fleet might well have had as many or even more dreadnoughts afloat in 1914 than the Royal Navy. This was all the more likely given Krupp's ability to fabricate guns and turrets at a faster rate than its British competitors. 'In a word', by the judgement of Arthur Marder, Olympian adjudicator of the Anglo-German naval race, 'it was the contingent four capital ships of 1909 that gave the [Royal] Navy its rather bare margin of security in the critical early months of the [First World] War.'

HIGH SEAS FLEET VERSUS ROYAL NAVY

War – large-scale war – when it came in August 1914 was an eventuality for which the Royal Navy's bare margin of material security would not compensate for its marked lack of attention to strategic or even tactical thought. Professionally the Royal Navy had grown complacent. For all its dedication to the Trafalgar ideal and the Nelsonian memory it had no clear-cut vision of how Trafalgar might be refought in modern conditions and no proven battle leaders. Not only was there no Nelson among its higher ranks, an admiral with two or three solid victories at sea to his credit; at the next level down there was not even an equivalent of the 'band of brothers', captains experienced in blockade, squadron or single-ship actions. Anti-slaving, gunboat diplomacy and the coastal operations of the Crimean War had provided the fathers and grandfathers of Britain's sea-officers of 1914 with a taste of action (not always palatable; Admiral David Jones, sent to lead a fleet against Russia's Pacific port of Petropavlovsk during the Crimean War, had chosen to blow his brains out on his own quarterdeck rather than face the responsibility of command under enemy fire). Late Victorian and Edwardian empire had offered not even those opportunities. Such British naval officers of August 1914 as had fought at all had, paradoxically, most often done so on land, leading 'naval brigades' of sailors acting as gunners or infantry in the Boer War, the Boxer Rising in China in 1900 and against the Sudanese in 1896–8. David Beatty and Roger Keyes, to become respectively the outstanding capital-ship and cruiser leaders of the war, had both made their names originally in land operations, Beatty running boats up the Nile to fight the Mahdi, Keyes storming Chinese forts during the Boxer Rising.

Not only was experience lacking; so, too, was talent. 'There is,' remarked Winston Churchill as First Lord of the Admiralty just before the outbreak of war, 'a frightful dearth of first class men in the [admirals] lists.' After 1918 he amplified his judgement thus: 'We had competent administrators, brilliant experts of every description, unequalled navigators, good disciplinarians, fine sea officers, brave and devoted hearts; but at the outset of the conflict we had more captains of ships than captains of war.' An exemplar of the deficiencies that troubled him was Vice-Admiral Sir Douglas Gamble, commanding the 4th Battle Squadron, who, in the words of a brilliant junior, 'won't admit that a knowledge of war is the least necessary for any officers until they come to [admiral's] rank, but how they are to learn it then I don't know . . . the old school will not admit that anyone junior to them can have any ideas at all.' The 'old school' were at only three generations from Nelson himself, who had opened his mind at its fullest to his juniors and delighted in enlarging their ideas. Not only was it deplorable that its members should have extirpated the Nelsonian spirit in personal relations; it was worse that they pooh-poohed the value of formal education in command. The Naval War College, founded in 1909, offered a course of instruction in naval tactics to commanders and captains; but their practice in fleet movements was highly mechanical, while the value placed on the course by admirals was low. What they – and therefore almost every other officer in the navy – esteemed was command of a ship at sea with its responsibilities of seamanship, navigation and leadership of the crew. That was entirely understandable in Nelsonian terms; in Nelson's day, service with the fleet was the exception and detached duty, which taught habits of self-reliance, was the norm. However, an undesired effect of Fisher's reforms was to diminish self-reliance by the drawing of the ships of the navy, small as well as great, into ever larger fleets. The trend was unavoidable; the appearance of the torpedo required that high-value battleships should be protected by ever deeper screens of lighter ships, cruisers and -

originally specifically anti-torpedo vessels – destroyers. It might have been resisted, nevertheless, had admirals recognised that screening was best performed by quick-thinking and independent-minded juniors. Nothing of the sort occurred. 'Follow senior officer's motions' had become a fetish instruction, which juniors violated at the peril of ruining their careers.

The instruction applied most strictly of all to the captains of capital ships and commanders of capital-ship squadrons. Nelson, we know, confidently divided his fleet at Trafalgar into two columns, but initially thought of dividing it into three. What would become the Grand Fleet of 1914 was supposed to fight as one division – 'following senior officers' motions'. The old fighting instructions, consigned to abeyance in the wooden navy by the 1780s and disregarded altogether by Nelson, achieved a renaissance as soon as the Napoleonic wars were over. Orders for engagement in a single line were reissued in 1816 – pedantry commonly springs from the jaws of victory – and those orders were still in force at the outbreak of the First World War. Their longevity is made to seem all the more extraordinary by the improvements in signalling available to Nelson's naval great-grandchildren. Not only had the Morse code, efficiently transmitted by powerful signalling lamp, come to supplement the easily obscured telegraphic flag hoist; so too had wireless. This latter innovation, because of difficulties in supplying adequate electric power, was still an erratic means of communication in land warfare. Afloat, where engine-rooms generating thousands of horsepower supplied current in superfluity, wireless already worked excellently by 1914. Admirals nevertheless clung to the flag hoist as their favoured means of intercommunication, despite the greatly extended distances over which fleets operated, at speeds up to ten times higher than those prevailing at Trafalgar, and in conditions where smoke was a permanent, not intermittent, factor affecting visibility.

British admirals chose to plan for war as if still commanding wooden walls by the 'flank to flank' principle because they believed even more fervently than wooden-wall admirals had done that victory lay with the fleet that most quickly, accurately and densely laid down firepower on the enemy. For of all the technical revolutions which had overtaken navies since the supersession of the wooden wall in the preceding half-century – steam propulsion, iron construction, armour protection, steel artillery – it was the improvement in naval armament that most dramatically impressed. Iron construction had improved the seaworthiness of ships and greatly extended their lives. Steam propulsion had trebled the best speed of battleships, multiplied that of the frigate and sloop equivalents four or five times and liberated all types from reliance on the elements. But guns had increased their range tenfold and threw shells which would have pulverised any present-day battleship with a single shot; they could indeed, if striking into a magazine – the protection of which was the principal purpose of armour-cladding – disintegrate the most modern battleship also.

Such examples of naval warfare as recent history offered – the Spanish-American battles of Santiago and Manila Bay, the Russo-Japanese battle of Tsushima – all testified to the power of the large gun. The Spaniards had lost all their ships to American gunnery in the battles of 1898; the Russians, after circumnavigating the globe to reach Tsushima in 1904–5, lost all but a handful of fast cruisers to Japanese gunnery, and those escaped only by running away. British admirals had what seemed incontestable fact on their side, therefore, when they insisted that it was the role of individual ship captains to crowd into formations almost as dense as those of Trafalgar (2½ cables, or 500 yards, was the standard interval between the Royal Navy's ships in battle formation in 1914; at Trafalgar it had been one cable), 'follow senior officers' motions' and fire as fast as ammunition could be sent from the magazines.

Such tactics, if effectively employed, would be as successful as those of the Japanese at Tsushima; but, if unsuccessful, fatal – for the time factor is pitiless in war at sea. A fleet heavily damaged by an opponent cannot count on topography to shield its retreat; unnavigable areas are few and, even if enlarged by minefields or the threat of submarine attack, offer nothing like the opportunity for effective rearguard action that rivers, marshes, forests and mountains do to a stricken military force on land. A strategy based on the premise of tactical success alone – victory in a duel of great guns – risks going wrong both quickly and irreversibly. That was the worm in the apple of British naval doctrine before 1914. It harked back to the triumph of Trafalgar; but it was fated to work through a technology which threatened disaster to the miscalculating side.

It was precisely on this possible outcome that Tirpitz's 'risk theory' was based; his challenge to the Royal Navy was that of a confrontation in the North Sea close to Germany's home ports which might well end in material catastrophe for the High Seas Fleet; but, if it did not – and he believed that the superior construction of German ships made that unlikely – then it would end in strategic disaster for the British. Robbed by mischance in battle of its numerical preponderance, the Royal Navy must concede absolute control of home waters to its enemy and thereafter either acquiesce in Germany having access to the high seas and in a combination of other powers acceding to its first place in the maritime world – or both.

Fortunately for Britain's strategic future, there were men at the head of the Royal Navy in the years before 1914 who grasped the flaw in Tirpitz's analysis. As Mahan, the most incisive observer of British naval affairs, had perceived, 'Great Britain . . . cannot help commanding the approaches to Germany' (he might have written 'northern Europe') 'by the mere possession of the very means essential to her own existence as a state of the first order.' What Mahan meant was that Britain had risen to world power because she had exploited her location across the sea routes which led from great waters to the ports of northern France, the Low Countries, Scandinavia and European Russia. Confronted by Tirpitz's challenge, the Admiralty, then Fisher and Churchill in particular, reassessed current plans to exploit Britain's intrinsic ability to dominate Germany's exits into great waters. They decided to do so by holding the fleet at a much greater distance from German ports than was traditional. Their calculation was that exit between Britain and France through the nineteen miles of the Channel Narrows could be discounted; the Germans would not risk it. That focused the danger on their attempting to exit through the top of the North Sea between southern Norway and the Orkneys and Shetlands, some 600 miles, or thirty hours' steaming distance, from Germany's naval bases on the Ems, Jade, Weser and Elbe estuaries. Common sense thus argued that the Royal Navy's main bases should be relocated from the Channel and east coast to Scotland, where, as it happens, several of Britain's plethora of magnificent natural harbours are found – at Rosyth, near Edinburgh, in the Cromarty Firth and in Scapa Flow among the Orkney Islands. Thus, at a stroke, Tirpitz's strategy of risking all on an engagement at Germany's very doorstep was exploded. In future, Germany's High Seas Fleet – though presented with the opportunity (which it would take) of bringing Britain's east coast towns under attack – might have to voyage a whole day's steaming from its safe havens, under threat of submarine and surface torpedo attack throughout, before bringing the Grand Fleet to 'decisive battle'. If such a battle supervened, the High Seas Fleet could not determine beforehand whence the Royal Navy might appear, as it could have done when Harwich, the Thames and the Channel Narrows were its enemy's only sally ports. Further, if action went awry, it faced the ordeal of a retreat in disarray, certainly of many hours, perhaps at night and in bad weather, to its firm base.

In the last years of peace, therefore, Tirpitz found himself thrown back in his calculations of relative advantage over disadvantage on to qualitative arguments: in particular, those turning on the superiority of German ships as gun platforms. For, despite all the money raised by taxation and imperial loans, he had not been able to equal, let alone exceed, the size of fleet the British people were prepared to support. In July 1914 the last month of the great European peace which had endured since the downfall of Napoleon in 1815, the Royal Navy counted twenty dreadnought battleships on its strength, nine 'dreadnought-type' battlecruisers and forty-one pre-dreadnoughts; twelve dreadnoughts and one battlecruiser were building. The High Seas Fleet, by comparison, had only thirteen dreadnoughts, five battlecruisers and twenty-two pre-dreadnoughts; seven dreadnoughts and three battlecruisers were building. The modern capital-ship ratio was therefore 29:18 and potentially 42:28; moreover, by the requisitioning of three dreadnoughts nearly completed for the Turkish and Chilean navies, Britain was shortly to raise the initial ratio to 32:18.

A numerical inferiority of little better than one to two held out little hope for Germany of worsting the Royal Navy in a Mahanian *Entscheidungsschlacht* (decisive battle). Tirpitz could nevertheless realistically calculate on the High Seas Fleet's ships performing better in action than the British. *Dreadnought*, true, had been a phenomenon; and German dreadnoughts were not to be propelled by turbines until the third-generation 'Kaiser'-class ships were laid down in 1909. It was also true that German dreadnoughts, until as late as 1914, were smaller than their British equivalents and more lightly armed. *Dreadnought* had 12-inch guns; its successors had 13.5-inch and those which came into service in 1914, the ships of the 'Queen Elizabeth' class had 15-inch (*Erin, Agincourt* and *Canada*, the dreadnoughts being built for the Turkish and Chilean navies in 1914, had 14-inch guns). The German ships, by comparison, had 11-inch guns at first, then 12-inch and 15-inch only in the two ships of the 'Baden' class, which did not fight in the First World War. However, all German dreadnoughts had qualities their British equivalents lacked. They were, for one thing, very strongly armoured; their 'belts', running along the waterline across their vitals, were consistently made one or two inches thicker than those of British ships of the same date of building. The German ships were also broader in the beam than their British equivalents, and this made them more stable gun platforms; they were also internally subdivided by watertight compartments with an elaboration no British dreadnought matched. Internal watertightness was the key to survival in action. Short of a shot into the magazines – and battle experience was to enable the Germans to identify crucial magazine weaknesses earlier than the British – only internal flooding could sink a dreadnought. The liner *Titanic*, sunk by collison with an iceberg in 1912, was a notionally watertight ship; but its internal bulkheads did not connect with the main deck overhead, with the result that, as each partition was overtopped by the inflow, the next segment of the ship was flooded and it eventually sank. German dreadnoughts were constructed on the honeycomb principle, which required that a majority of cells be punctured before residual buoyuncy was lost. British ships, though also built as honeycombs, had fewer cells. Buoyancy was therefore threatened sooner and the damaged ship risked foundering unless it slackened speed and pulled out of action to repair damage.

Tirpitz was thus right to regard his dreadnoughts as battleworthier than the British; his two most modern battlecruisers, *Derfflinger* and *Lützow*, were certainly the best of their type afloat, a match for the 'Queen Elizabeth' class of battleships in speed and protection and not far behind them in hitting power. British battlecruisers, by comparison, were dangerously under-armoured; and the older British battleships were both under-armoured and insufficiently subdivided for safety.

Dreadful experience would also demonstrate that British magazine protection was fatally inferior to German, a defect which in itself would cause the largest loss of life and material at Jutland. However, Tirpitz was deluding himself to regard British officers and crews as inferior to his own. German sailors were picked men, and well trained during their compulsory service; but service was short and the trainees often landlubbers. The Royal Navy's sailors were long-service men and drawn in the majority from exactly the same centres of seagoing life as had supplied Nelson – the West Country ports, the Thames and Medway towns, the Scottish firths and estuaries, the Welsh havens and the Irish sea loughs. Many had family traditions of naval service, and this was particularly the case with the British officers. By direct descent, five of Nelson's 'band of brothers' – Blackwood, Thompson, Cottesloe, Fremantle and Troubridge, as well as Hood, from an earlier tradition – were represented in the Royal Navy of 1914; by indirect descent, scores more. The German army, through its long tradition of recruitment from the East Elbian squirearchy, could show an equivalent roll of von Arnims, Schwerins and Kleists. The German navy could not follow suit. Its officer corps had modelled itself socially on the Kaiser's elite of guards and cavalry officers. Its professional and academic credentials were impeccable. Its readiness to go down with its ships was unquestioned. But its innate seamanship and understanding of the sea – which not even the severest critics of Britain's seadogs would have thought of doubting – remained unproven. German naval officers, particularly when closeted with the Kaiser, drank toasts to 'the day', the occasion when they would put the Royal Navy to the test. No one doubted that in a day of battle they would display supreme heroism. What had not yet been tested was their capacity for the long haul, the seasoned sailor's uncomplaining edurance of sea-keeping, year in, year out, including the sequence of small, unresolved actions, missed chances, accidental ship losses and occasional setbacks which were a historic navy's routine fare. For 'heroic sacrifice' (*Sichopfern*) they were certainly ready; the long watches were another matter. Not even they themselves, when war with the Royal Navy confronted them on 4 August 1914, knew how well they would keep them. 'The English fleet,' Admiral Reinhard Scheer, the High Seas Fleet commander at Jutland, was to say, 'had the advantage of looking back on a hundred years of proud tradition which must have given every man a sense of superiority based on the great deeds of the past.' The German novelist Theodor Fontane expressed the same idea more dramatically: 'We do not have a trace of this confidence . . . we are not mentioned in the Old Testament. The British act as though they *had* the promise.'

THE WAR AT SEA BEFORE JUTLAND

The German navy's belief that the British were held fast by a 'promise' led it to expect that the Grand Fleet – as the squadrons in home water were constituted in August 1914 – would sail forth on the outbreak of war to seek decisive fleet action. For such an action the Grand Fleet was certainly materially prepared. The Sarajevo crisis found it practising mobilisation and preparing for a royal review at Spithead. As the crisis deepened, demobilisation was cancelled and the review – involving 24 dreadnoughts, 35 pre-dreadnoughts and 123 smaller vessels – culminated in the dispatch of the most modern battleships and battlecruisers to their war stations in Scotland. By 4 August, when Britain's ultimatum to Germany expired, the Grand Fleet could have made the descent upon the German naval bases in the Heligoland Bight that the High Seas Fleet expected; but it did not.

The reason was twofold: first, the British had decided against 'close blockade' in favour of 'distant blockade', a perfectly sensible policy in view of their domination of the High Seas Fleet's access, via the Scotland–Norway gap, to great waters; second, equally sensibly, Jellicoe, the Grand Fleet's commander, feared the damage German submarines and minefields could inflict on his ships in German home waters. The German, like the British, navy had by 1914 learned enough from its experiments with submarines, and had sufficiently developed their seagoing qualities, to form submarine squadrons for offensive purposes. 'Contact' mines, detonated when struck by a ship, and moored to the sea-bed by a cable which held them just below the surface, had been developed during the Crimean War and by 1914 were in use by all advanced navies. Despite these menaces the Royal Navy was to succeed in convoying the British Expeditionary Force to France unscathed; but on 6 August it lost a destroyer, *Amphion*, to German mines, besides suffering a succession of false alarms of submarine attack against its anchorages.

It was not until 28 August that anything resembling 'the day' materialised. Then Commodore Roger Keyes, the commander of the Harwich cruiser force on the east coast, persuaded the Admiralty to let him risk a sortie into the Heligoland Bight in the hope of intercepting one of the destroyer patrols that were regularly sent there by the German High Seas Fleet commander, von Ingenohl. Keyes achieved his intended surprise and, when some German light cruisers steamed out of the estuaries to the destroyers' rescue, called up Beatty's three battlecruisers, which were covering his movements, and, with the help of their shattering long-range broadsides, smashed three German ships in short order. There was time for Keyes to come alongside one of the foundering victims, *Mainz*, and for an echo of Trafalgar to sound across the water separating them.

A young [German] officer who had been zealously superintending the removal of the wounded ... was now standing motionless on the poop. Keyes, anxious to push off before [*Mainz*] capsized and guessing what was perhaps in the young man's mind, shouted to him that he had done splendidly, that there was nothing more he could do, and that he had better jump on board quick; and he held out his hands to help him. But the boy scorned to leave his ship as long as she remained afloat, or to accept the slightest favour from his adversary. Drawing himself up stiffly, he slipped back, saluted, and answered 'Thank you, no'.

This German Casabianca and a shipmate who was a son of Admiral von Tirpitz were subsequently plucked from the sea; but his behaviour warned that the High Seas Fleet's urge to 'heroic sacrifice' was no theatrical attitude. The warning was reinforced four months later when British battlecruisers once again caught an inferior German force at a disadvantage. In November, at the battle of Coronel, Germany's detached southern squadron of commerce raiders had surprised some antiquated British cruisers in the Pacific and destroyed them. Churchill and Fisher (returned to the Admiralty as First Sea Lord on 29 October), in a boil of anger, had taken the risk of depriving the Grand Fleet of two of its battlecruisers, *Invincible* and *Inflexible*, to send them into southern waters in pursuit. On 8 December, 1914, Spee, the German squadron commander, called imprudently at the British Falkland Islands, where the battlecruisers had paused to take on coal in their search for him, detected his mistake as the first salvo of heavy shells straddled his ships, and ran for it. The salvoes remorselessly tracked him down, broke his light-armoured decks open and sent him and the crews of four of his five ships to the bottom. At no stage, however, did any German officer ask for quarter or even look like striking. Watched by a godson of Wagner, who happened to be a spotting officer in one of the British battlecruisers' tops, they sank into the South Atlantic with colours flying in a spectacular ironclad *Götterdämmerung*.

German willingness to risk superior odds was demonstrated closer to home in the winter of 1914 when the High Seas Fleet twice mounted raids against English east coast towns. It had been recognised by the Admiralty that the withdrawal of the battle fleet to distant blockade stations in Scotland and the Orkneys exposed ports further south to the danger of hit-and-run attack. However, it was surprised in every sense by the daring of the German descents on Yarmouth on 3 November and Scarborough, Hartlepool and Whitby on 16 December. The battlecruisers raced south on both occasions, some of the battleships on the second, but the High Seas Fleet nevertheless got clean away. It was a particularly worrying endorsement of anxieties about subordinate British officers' independence of mind that one of the battleship divisional commanders, Arbuthnot, had refused to open fire on the German raiders when he had them in clear view because he had not received an order from his superior to do so.

The first winter of the naval war therefore closed on an uncertain note. The British had won a single clear-cut victory at the Falklands – in Beatty's words, 'the most decisive battle of the war'. They had also shown themselves superior in a cruiser action in home waters. But they had twice failed to nail the High Seas Fleet when it had 'come out' in strength; and they had also suffered some humilating and avoidably costly ship losses – that of the brand-new dreadnought *Audacious* to a random mine in October, of the old cruisers *Aboukir, Cressy* and *Hogue* to the torpedoes of a single U-boat, U-9, in September, and of the pre-dreadnought *Formidable* to U-24 in the Channel in December. The German navy, on balance, persuaded itself that, as the weaker party, it had acquitted itself creditably. So in material terms it had; but unknown to itself it had also suffered a disabling immaterial blow. Through the capture and recovery of three cipher books – one for merchant, small ship, zeppelin and U-boat use taken by the Royal Australian Navy from a German freighter in the Pacific, one for diplomatic use hauled up from a wreck on the bed of the North Sea, one for the High Seas Fleet itself found on a cruiser wrecked in the Baltic and sent on by the Russian navy – the Admiralty had acquired the key to the whole German maritime and overseas cipher system. The use it was to make of its ability to read German secret traffic was to be flawed; even so, from October 1914 it was to enjoy an advantage over the High Seas Fleet without price or parallel.

Suspicion of this advantage was to prompt the weightiest German sortie against the Royal Navy in the opening stages of the war. The German high command could not blind itself to the evidence of apparent British foreknowledge of its plans, which had, for example, underlain the Grand Fleet's reaction to the Scarborough raid. However, as in the next war, when the *Abwehr* grasped at any straw of explanation for British foreknowledge of *Wehrmacht* operations, short of confronting the unthinkable conclusion that its Enigma cipher system had been broken, the German admirals determinedly discounted the thought that its ciphers were compromised, preferring to believe that dockyard spies were betraying fleet movements – or the more popular conception that 'neutral fishing vessels' on their routes of egress from the Ems, Jade and Weser, particularly where they crossed the Dogger Bank, were in fact clandestine British spy ships.

Rear-Admiral Franz Hipper, commanding the German battlecruiser force (1ST Scouting Group) therefore proposed in January 1915 that the High Seas Fleet undertake a dual mission to sweep the Dogger Bank clean of spy ships and, profiting by the deprivation of intelligence that would inflict on the British, go on to lay an offensive minefield in the Firth of Forth, the approach waters to the British battlecruisers' base at Rosyth.

The resulting battle of the Dogger Bank, 24 January 1915, was unsatisfactory to both sides. German perversity in discounting the possibility that its ciphers were being read gave the British clear advance warning of the sortie, which was mounted with three battlecruisers, *Seydlitz, Moltke* and *Derfflinger*, plus the heavy cruiser *Blücher*, supported by four light cruisers and eighteen 'torpedo-boats'. 'Torpedo-boats' were the German equivalents of the British destroyers, but smaller, weaker and slower ships; their design was a misconception which would dog the High Seas Fleet's chances of fighting on equal terms throughout the war. *Blücher* was also a misconceived design; she had been laid down at a time (1907) when Fisher's battlecruiser idea was not properly understood by the navy across the water and thus, though fast and well armoured, was undergunned. Hipper was obliged to include her in his First Scouting Group, since she fitted nowhere else, but she did not really belong there.

Beatty's Battlecruiser Fleet, by contrast, was homogeneous. It consisted of *Lion, Tiger, Princess Royal, New Zealand* and *Indomitable*, supported by three light cruisers and thirty-five destroyers from Harwich and covered at a greater distance by a force of pre-dreadnoughts and cruisers from Scotland, with the Grand Fleet itself sailing as a long-stop. Beatty's battlecruisers were more than a match in themselves for Hipper's. *Indomitable* and *New Zealand* were 25-knot ships armed with 12-inch guns; *Princess Royal, Lion* and *Tiger* (certainly the most beautiful warship in the world then, and perhaps ever) were 28-knotters armed with 13.5-inch guns. Beatty, moreover, had the advantage of foreknowledge of Hipper's movements and could spring a trap, which he successfully did. His cruisers found and fixed Hipper early in the morning of 24 January, and, though Hipper turned at once for home, the British battlecruisers' superior speed allowed them to overhaul him until, at the unprecedented range of 20,000 yards, they opened fire and began to score hits.

Fighting instructions then let the Germans out of the trap. The captain of *Tiger*, misapplying a Grand Fleet battle order, joined *Lion* in concentrating its fire on the leading German ship, *Seydlitz*, leaving the second, *Moltke*, to engage *Lion* unopposed. *Lion*, in consequence, was so badly hit that she had to fall out of line, thereby equalising the odds to four-to-four; Beatty's signal to sustain the attack against the whole enemy line was simultaneously misread by his subordinates. The result was that all their fire was concentrated on the rearmost of the German ships, *Blücher*, while the others proceeded to pull steadily away for the safety of home.

They did not escape unscathed. *Seydlitz*, in retreat, was hit by a 13.5-inch shell which penetrated an after turret roof and started a catastrophic fire. Admiral Reinhard Scheer described the consequences:

In the reloading chamber, where the shell penetrated, part of the charge in readiness for loading was set on fire. The flames went high up into the turret and down into the munition chamber, and thence through a connecting door, usually kept shut, by which the man from the munition chamber tried to escape into the fore turret. The flames thus made their way through to the other munition chamber, and thence again up to the second turret, and from this cause the entire gun crews of both turrets perished almost instantly. The flames rose as high as a house above the turrets.

The death toll was 165 and the detonation of 14,000 lb of propellent threatened the magazines, which would have disintegrated the ship. An officer and two ratings, with extraordinary bravery, nevertheless found their way into the magazine arms, succeeded in working the flooding valves to admit 600 tons of water and thus saved the ship. *Seydlitz*, though down by the stern, retained propulsion and sustained her escape.

Blücher, the slowest ship of the fleet, did not escape. Since she was now the target of four British battlecruisers, she was progressively devastated. A German zeppelin, L-5, was overhead and observed her agony, reported by an officer aboard: '*Blücher* was left behind as our forces steamed off and she was unable to follow. The four English battlecruisers fired at her together. She replied for as long as she could, until she was completely shrouded in smoke and apparently on fire. At 1207 she heeled over and capsized.' A survivor – out of 1200 embarked 234 were saved from the water – describes her last moments.

The shells . . . bore their way even to the stoke-hold. The coal in the bunkers was set on fire. Since the bunkers were half empty the fire burned merrily. In the engine room a shell licked up the oil and sprayed it around in flames of blue and green. . . . The terrific air pressure resulting from explosion in a confined space . . . roars through every opening and tears its way through every weak spot. . . . As one poor wretch was passing through a trap-door a shell burst near him. He was exactly half-way through. The trap-door closed with a terrific snap. . . . Men were picked up by that terrific air pressure and tossed to a horrible death among the machinery.

Moore, Beatty's subordinate, who had taken over command of the Battlecruiser Fleet when *Lion* was crippled, did not resume the pursuit of Hipper after *Blücher*'s sinking. In Fisher's characteristically trenchant verdict he 'ought to have gone on, had he the slightest Nelsonic temperament in him, regardless of signals. In war the first principle is to disobey orders. Any fool can obey orders.' However, the prevailing spirit of the Royal Navy was of course against that; much of the misunderstanding over Beatty's signals resulted from the fact that Nelson's most often used Trafalgar hoist, 'Engage the enemy more closely', had been deleted from the book and nothing substituted to replace it. Beatty himself, who had transferred from *Lion* first to a light cruiser and then to *Princess Royal*, tried to make up the distance lost but without success. His Battlecruiser Fleet had fallen too far behind the fugitives, and the Grand Fleet, which the Admiralty with its foreknowledge of Hipper's intentions might have positioned to intercept, was still further away. Dogger Bank was incontestably a British victory; but it was an incomplete one, which damaged and alarmed the High Seas Fleet but did not defeat it.

Moreover, the Germans had learned an important lesson from the battle which eluded the British. Damage to *Lion* had been severe – hits allowed 300 tons of water to enter the ship, greatly diminish her speed, rob her of all electrical power and threaten fire in her magazines – but it did not disable her. Despite her light armouring, *Lion* appeared to have survived her rough treatment at the hands of the German battle-cruisers well; she had had only twenty wounded and one man killed. In truth her escape had been narrower than anyone aboard, or later in the Admiralty, appreciated. The fire started in her 'A' (forward) turret lobby might easily have spread downwards into her ammunition-handling rooms, thence into her magazines and destroyed her. By good luck, the quantity of ammunition present in her turret lobby was small, the resulting fire small also and consequently rapidly extinguished. In consequence, the intrinsic danger of fire transmission was not recognised and no measures undertaken to limit the amount of ammunition – particularly propellant – held in the lobby or to elaborate 'anti-flash' devices in the turret trunk which led into the vitals of the ship. The Germans, by contrast, were alerted to such dangers by the turret fire in *Seydlitz* and modified both structures and practices in their ships accordingly; anti-flash shutters were multiplied and the amount of combustible material held in or near the turrets greatly reduced. These modifications were to prove of the greatest life- and ship-saving importance in the next engagement between the two fleets.

Any immediate repetition of the Dogger Bank battle was, however, now forbidden by the Kaiser, who chose to preserve the High Seas Fleet for a decisive action timed to coincide with a dramatic improvement of German fortunes on land; meanwhile he preferred to concentrate on submarine warfare, for a brief period inaugurating something like an unrestricted sinking campaign against merchant shipping sailing to allied ports. For over a year – during which Ingenohl was replaced in command by Pohl and then Pohl by Scheer – the High Seas Fleet kept to its North German ports, occasionally venturing into the Baltic against the Russians but not risking a confrontation with the Royal Navy. Not until 5 March 1916 did it appear in strength in the North Sea again, and then very briefly; while its only major action against Britain, the Lowestoft raid of 24/25 April, proved a repetition of those of 1914 – as soon as the High Seas Fleet was opposed, in this case by the lightest of forces, it broke off action and headed for home. Tirpitz's pre-war 'risk theory' had now apparently been stood on its head; any risk threatening the High Seas Fleet was deemed too heavy to bear, forcing it back into port and leaving the freedom of the same, as for a hundred years, to the Royal Navy.

'Risk theory' might have petered out as mere bravado had not Pohl's successor proved a sailor of Nelsonian stamp. Reserved in expression and unassuming in manner, Scheer achieved high command only because fatal illness removed Pohl from it. Once established in office, however, he showed a capacity for dismissing difficulty as marked as Pohl's had been for exaggerating it. It was on the strengths rather than the weaknesses of the High Seas Fleet that he concentrated. A torpedo specialist, he believed that his surface and submarine forces had the capacity to inflict unacceptable damage on the Grand Fleet if it were manoeuvred into unfavourable circumstances – 'risk theory' in its purest conception – and throughout the spring of 1916 he struggled with plans designed to bring about that outcome. The Lowestoft raid was an attempt at that result but one, he judged in retrospect, directed too far southward to entrap the Grand Fleet in his toils. Throughout May 1916 he refined plans for a more extended operation, which would run his opponents' battleships and battlecruisers on to a series of submarine-laid minefields, and allow his capital ships to pick off casualties and detached units at small cost to himself. The High Seas Fleet now counted sixteen dreadnoughts and five battlecruisers to the Grand Fleet's twenty-eight and nine; it also had six pre-dreadnoughts fit to stand in the line of battle. The balance of force, given numbers building, could not improve in his favour. He concluded that it was now or never for a decisive fleet action and in the early morning of 31 May 1916 ordered his squadrons to sea in the hope of returning to port with losses fewer than those he believed he could inflict.

THE IRONCLAD WORLD

The ironclads – the term armourclads, Professor Bernard Brodie has percipiently suggested, better characterises their nature – in which Sheer and Jellicoe steamed to their rendezvous were ships unlike any on which navies before or since had counted for victory. *Victory* and all the men-of-war of the wooden world had been, it is true, specialised in function; none the less, they did not differ in construction, means of propulsion or essential configuration from their merchant sisters which, in the last resort, it was their function to protect. Indeed, some contemporaries of *Victory* maintained by the East India Company doubled as cargo and gun-carriers, not without success; while *Victory*, with its 21-foot depth of hold containing stores for four months' cruising, was a considerable bulk-carrier in her own right.

Dreadnought, by contrast, had no space to carry anything but fuel for her own propulsion, munitions for her armament and supplies for her crew. Of the three commodities, fuel was by far the bulkiest; the amount carried determined the 'endurance' of the ship – the distance she could steam, at varying speed, before needing to refuel. *Dreadnought*, carrying some 2000 tons of coal, would burn that amount in five days' steaming at 20 knots; *Victory*'s endurance was, of course, limited only by her capacity to load food and drink. Oil, to which Britain turned in the design of her latest pre-war dreadnoughts, extended endurance (by some 40 per cent) because of its greater efficiency as an energy source. However, its loading, as a proportion of the ship's displacement and capacity, was constrained by the same competing demands as coal had been. Those were the weight and space necessarily devoted to machinery, armour and armament. In *Dreadnought*, displacing 18,000 tons, armour amounted to 5000 tons, machinery to 2000 and weapons to 3000. Armour was not bulky; machinery and weapon spaces were. Roughly a third of the ship's length was occupied by the engine and boiler rooms and nearly another third by the turrets, their trunks and the magazine complexes at their base.

The crew, in consequence, were almost as cramped for living space as Nelson's sailors had been in *Victory*. His 800 men were crowded into the 150 feet of the lower deck, taking watch and watch about to sling their hammocks. The thousand men of *Dreadnought*, three times *Victory*'s length though she was, therefore had to sling hammocks where they could too; by an odd reversal of traditional design, they slept aft, the officers forward. The standard arrangement confined 'the lower deck' to the hundred forward of the bridge and the officers to a complex of small cabins over the screws.

Both areas lay outside the 'armoured belt' which protected machinery and magazines against shells. In action, however, the living spaces would be empty, for every man in the crew had duty which took him into the ship's central fighting zone. Here lay a crucial difference between the functions of the crew in wooden-wall warfare and those of the armourclads. At Trafalgar those functions had been few: a minority of the crew continued to act as sailors, handling sails above deck; another small minority – officers and marines – also remained in the open, to command or to act as small-arms men. A tiny minority of specialists working in the powder rooms, the sick bay or at damage control kept to the bowels of the ship; but the vast majority worked as members of gun teams.

On a dreadnought, the division of fighting labour was immensely complex. There was, to begin with, the division between the propulsion team and the rest of the ship's company. Engineer officers and stokers formed a third of a coal-burning ship's crew, in which the stokers were beasts of burden, carting up to 20 tons of coal each hour from the bunkers to the stokehold and throwing it into the furnaces. Theirs was the hardest but also the lowliest work in the ship. Almost as hard, though intermittent, was the work of the ammunition crews. They handled the machinery that transferred projectiles and charges from the shell and powder rooms at the bottom of the turret trunks and sent them up the hoists into the gun chambers. Then the turret crews handled the ammunition and fed it into the guns.

The laying and training of the guns were the responsibility of the gunnery officer, who, in British ships by 1914, controlled fire centrally through a 'director'. The crew of this range-finding device, located high on the ship's superstructure, estimated the initial range of engagement, observed the fall of shot and signalled corrections to the individual turrets through a transmitting room inside the armoured belt. The gun crews of the secondary armament (suppressed in *Dreadnought* but reincorporated in her successors) manned individual gun positions, against destroyer and cruiser attack, but fired independently. They had their own ammunition-handling arrangements and teams. In the Royal Navy a battleship's marines traditionally worked one of the main turrets and several of the secondary armament mountings.

Finally the crew comprised a group of command and battle specialists. On the bridge were the captain, navigators and signallers, almost as exposed as Nelson and his entourage had been at Trafalgar (though a little-used armoured 'conning-tower' offered ultimate protection). Below decks were the damage-control teams, trained to work fire-hoses and plug shell holes in emergency, and the surgeon and his medical party. The torpedo gunners (torpedoes would be rarely fired by battleships in action, since the ranges at which they engaged were too great) were a free-ranging team who supervised the ship's electrical system. Scattered about action stations were telephonists and clerks, transmitting and recording messages within the ship. Finally, there were the engineer parties, detached from the main engine-rooms, who kept the auxiliary machinery – steering, hoisting and turret-training gear, largely hydraulic – in operation.

The navy's complement of seamen and fighters had thus become enormously complex in a hundred years of technical revolution. The wooden navy had 'rated' men in only four ways: as able seamen, fit to go aloft or serve guns; as less than able seamen, consigned to labouring or servile work; as craftsmen in timber or sailmaking; and as marines. The dreadnought navy had a dozen rates. Marines had lost their distinctive function and became gunners. However, among seamen there were shell and charge handlers, turret crews, gun-layers, range-takers, rate-takers, telephonists, signallers; in the propulsion crew, an entirely new category, mechanics, artificers and electricians as well as stokers; while among officers there were five separate hierarchies – the gunnery officer's, the navigator's, the signal officer's, the engineer commander's and the (paymaster) supply officer's, as well as the captain's own command.

Dreadnought still lived by many of the wooden walls' routines; messmates ate in groups of eight or ten, drawing a common meal from the galley and slinging their hammocks in the space left when the table was cleared away. The lash had been abolished, but discipline was exigent and rum still a cherished mitigation of the hardship and boredom of shipboard life. Officers were a caste apart, perhaps even more so than they had been in the cheek-by-jowl intimacy of wooden-wall life. Leave was short and infrequent. The 'exigencies of the service' and the safety of the ship stood above all other values in the sailor's life.

Further, there was one overriding difference between the function of the Grand Fleet's ships and that of their modern predecessors. They, though ships of war, were evidently branches of the same tree from which all coevals had been hewn; just as their crews, in the overwhelming majority, served the sea rather than the navy. *Dreadnought* and its descendants were fighting machines alone, while their crews – regulars in the Royal Navy, conscripts in the German – knew no sea life outside the fleet. *Dreadnought* would have been quite useless for any purpose other than that which dictated its design; and its purpose dominated the life and outlook of those who served in her. The achievement of the highest possible speed, most rapid and accurate gunnery and highest exactitude in manoeuvre were her company's overriding aims. Each man aboard had, in his individual task, a part to play in their realisation. Battle alone would prove how well the tasks had been learned.

THE BATTLE OF JUTLAND

Hipper's battlecruisers of the High Seas Fleet began to leave their North Sea ports on 31 May at one in the morning; Scheer with the battleships followed him at 2.30. Altogether twenty-two battleships, five battlecruisers, eleven cruisers and sixty-one torpedo-boats put to sea. The modern capital ships were organised into two battleship squadrons of eight dreadnoughts each and the 1st Scouting Group of five battlecruisers. The best speed of the dreadnought squadrons, determined by their slowest ships, *Posen*, *Rheinland*, *Nassau* and *Westfalen*, was 20 knots; but it was further reduced to 18 knots by the presence of six predreadnoughts in the 2nd Squadron, which Scheer had included in his sortie to bulk out numbers. The 1st Scouting Group, by contrast, had a best speed of 26 knots, and was committed to the role of finding and 'fixing' the enemy's fleet until the heavier ships came up.

Scheer's plan did not envisage a decisive action. Realistically he recognised that his inferiority in numbers of ships and in weight of broadside (400,000 – 200,000 lb, reflecting the lighter calibres of his ships' main armament) ruled out a German Trafalgar. He hoped, nevertheless, to come off the better by entangling the Grand Fleet with a U-boat line he had deployed off the British bases and by inflicting losses on ships and squadrons temporarily separated from the main body. The High Seas Fleet was to steer due north, towards the outer mouth of the Baltic, the Skagerrak, by which the Germans were to name the ensuing battle. News of its sortie was trusted to draw the Grand Fleet southward to a rendezvous.

News of the sortie came to the Grand Fleet, however, far quicker than Scheer had reckoned. Thanks to the insecurity of his ciphers, the Admiralty had detected his intention to 'come out' as early as 16 May, when his U-boats had departed for their patrol lines, and it was

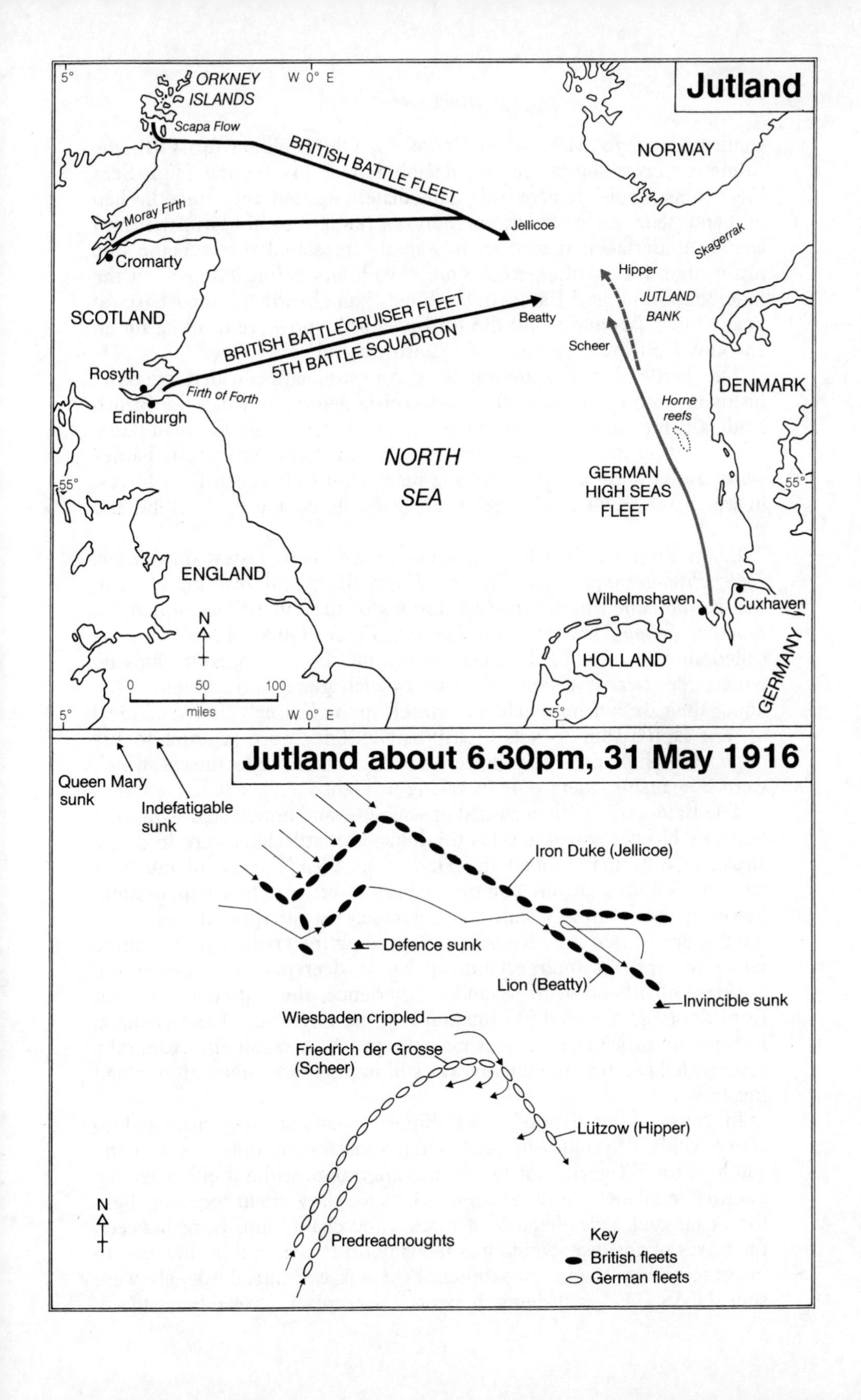
Jutland
5°
ORKNEY ISLANDS
W 0° E
Scapa Flow
BRITISH BATTLE FLEET
NORWAY
Moray Firth
Jellicoe
Cromarty
Skagerrak
Hipper
JUTLAND BANK
SCOTLAND
BRITISH BATTLECRUISER FLEET
5TH BATTLE SQUADRON
Beatty
Scheer
Rosyth
Firth of Forth
Edinburgh
DENMARK
Horne reefs
NORTH SEA
GERMAN HIGH SEAS FLEET
55°
55°
ENGLAND
Wilhelmshaven
Cuxhaven
N
HOLLAND
GERMANY
0 50 100
miles
5°
W 0° E
5°
Jutland about 6.30pm, 31 May 1916
Queen Mary sunk
Indefatigable sunk
Iron Duke (Jellicoe)
Defence sunk
Lion (Beatty)
Invincible sunk
Wiesbaden crippled
Friedrich der Grosse (Scheer)
Lützow (Hipper)
N
Predreadnoughts
Key
British fleets
German fleets

confirmed on 30 May, when Room 40, Old Building (40 OB), the Admiralty cryptological centre, deciphered orders for the High Seas Fleet to assemble. Jellicoe was immediately warned and, since he had on hand plans for a search operation or 'sweep' of his own, the third already undertaken that year, he rapidly translated that scheme into firm orders for an offensive action. Two hours before Hipper left the Jade, the Grand and Battlecruiser Fleets had already left their bases at Scapa Flow, Cromarty and the Firth of Forth and were heading for an encounter off the west coast of Danish Jutland.

The battle that was to follow is conventionally divided by naval historians into five phases: the battlecruiser action, in which the British made a run to the south and then, on encountering the German battle fleet, a run to the north; the first and second encounters of the battleships; and a night action, involving many clashes between light forces, in which the High Seas Fleet made good its escape to the Elbe and the Jade.

Beatty's Battlecruiser Fleet now comprised his six fastest ships, *Lion, Tiger, Princess Royal, New Zealand, Queen Mary* and *Indefatigable*, and was accompanied by the fast battleships of the 5th British Squadron, *Barham, Valiant, Warspite* and *Malaya*. These 'Queen Elizabeths' (so called after the first of their class) were the most formidable ships on either side, heavily armoured, with 15-inch guns, and capable of 25 knots; their design approached as closely to the Kaiser's cherished ideal of 'fast capital ship' as was then possible. They were superior to any other battleship and barely slower than the fastest battlecruisers, which were safe against them only by taking to flight.

The Battlecruiser Fleet passed unscathed – and undetected – through Scheer's U-boat patrol line (as the Jellicoe's battleships were to do), a stroke of luck that robbed the High Seas Fleet's sortie of much of its point, besides gravely compromising its security. In compensation, however, the Admiralty staff had perversely misinterpreted the cipher intelligence passed it by Room 40. Regarding the cryptologists as mere fact-gatherers, the interpretation of whose decrypts was properly the business of officers with seagoing experience, the staff did not elicit from Room 40 the vital information that the High Seas Fleet changed its wireless procedure on leaving harbour. As a result the Admiralty assured Jellicoe that the enemy was still in port nine hours after it had put to sea.

In consequence Beatty's and Hipper's battlecruisers managed to arrive within fifty miles of each other, some ninety miles west of the south of the Skagerrak, at two in the afternoon, without either having knowledge of the other's proximity. Chance drew them together; light forces on each side detected a neutral merchant ship, lying between their axes of advance, which was blowing off steam, and in diverting to investigate they found each other. Fire was exchanged, signals were sent (HMS *Galatea*: 'Enemy in sight. Two cruisers probably hostile in sight bearing ESE course unknown'), and the battlecruiser forces were ordered by their commanders to change course and steer for each other.

By the sort of mischance that would have been excusable at Trafalgar, when flags were the only medium of intercommunication, but not at Jutland, where radio provided a means of duplication, Beatty's fast battleships missed his hoist directing them towards the Germans and persisted in a prearranged turn northward to rendezvous with Jellicoe. The result was that Beatty led his lightly armoured battlecruisers to challenge Hipper's ships unsupported. Thus when, at 3.45 pm, action was joined it did not go in the British fleet's favour.

On sighting Beatty's ships, Hipper ordered a turn to draw them down on to Scheer's battleships following forty miles in his rear. The British were silhouetted by the sun in the western sky and showed up crisply in the German range-finders. 'Suddenly my periscope revealed some big ships,' recorded Georg von Hase, gunnery officer of *Derfflinger*. 'Black monsters; six tall, broad-beamed giants steaming in two columns.' The British range-takers had also acquired targets, but as Beatty ordered a change to a parallel course von Hase passed instructions to the turrets: 'Direction on second battlecruiser from Left [*Princess Royal*] 102 degrees. Ship making 26 knots, course ESE, 17,000 [metres range]. Our target has two masts and two funnels, as well as narrow funnel close to the foremast. Deflection 19 left, Rate 100 minus. 16,400 [metres range]. Still no permission to open fire from the flagship.'

A few minutes later, however, Hipper signalled 'open fire' and the German battlecruisers began observing and correcting their fall of shot. Beatty, whose range-takers had overestimated the distance separating the two lines and who was occupied in getting a radio message off to Jellicoe, did not yet respond. Eventually, some five minutes after the Germans had begun to engage, Beatty's flag-captain ordered the 'open fire' on his own responsibility.

Because British range-finding was inferior to German (a function of the better quality of German optics), the Battlecruiser Fleet, which outranged the 1st Scouting Group, had allowed itself to run within the fire-zone of the enemy's guns. Hipper's 11- and 12-inch armaments were therefore straddling and scoring hits on Beatty's 12- and 13.5-inch gun ships when more prudent ship-handling would have denied them the opportunity. Bad signalling also misdirected British gunnery, so that one of the five ships in Hipper's line (*Derfflinger*) was spared altogether from attack by Beatty's six for nearly ten minutes. The consequences were not long delayed. At 4 pm *Lion* was hit on Q (the Royal Marine) turret and damaged so gravely that a magazine explosion was barely averted. A huge fire was started and Beatty's flag-captain pulled her out of the line to take her from the danger zone. The Germans believed her finished. Shortly afterwards *Indefatigable*, which had been exchanging salvoes with *Von der Tann*, also suffered hits.

Lion's were to prove survivable; *Indefatigable*'s were not. One salvo penetrated her thinly armoured deck. Another, hitting near her fore turret, set off a fatal internal explosion: she turned over almost instantly and sank.

Numbers were now equal. 'I gazed at this in amazement,' recalled Beatty's flag-captain. 'There were only five battlecruisers in our line. . . . I glanced quickly towards the enemy. How many of them were afloat? Still five.' Beatty now ordered his light forces into action in the space, 15,000 yards wide, separating the two battle lines. Light cruisers and destroyers, engaged by the German battlecruisers' secondary armament, tried to launch torpedo attacks against the enemy heavy units; Hipper's light forces swung into action against them. Then, while light cruisers and detroyers fired their 6- and 4-inch guns against each other, the 'Queen Elizabeths' of the 5th Battle Squadron, redirected at last on to their proper targets, opened concentrated fire which tossed columns of water larger than any yet seen around the German battle line. Suddenly the odds were again in Beatty's favour – nine against five, and greater range and weight of shell on his side. German gunnery did achieve one more success: *Queen Mary*, hit by a full 12-inch salvo, erupted in two great internal explosions, turned over and sank. However, under the cumulative effect of Beatty's much heavier gunnery, Hipper's line was running ever deeper into danger. Well-aimed salvoes were falling about his ships every twenty seconds, some were scoring hits, and the British officers on the battlecruiser and battleship bridges who could see enough to judge the course of the action were certain that the destruction of the 1st Scouting Group was at hand.

At 4.30 pm Beatty received a signal from one of his advanced light cruisers that she had 'sighted enemy battle fleet, bearing approximately SE, course of enemy N'. The implication was incontestable. If Beatty held on with his run to the south, he would arrive under the guns of Scheer's battleships against which his Battlecruiser Fleet could not hope to stand, even with the support of the 5th Battle Squadron. At 4.40 therefore he signalled orders for a turn-away, towards Jellicoe's approaching squadrons, and the run to the north began.

Goodenough, commanding the British light cruisers which had made the sighting of Scheer's ships – it was the dense clouds of black smoke emitted by their coal-burning engines, working at full revolutions, which had drawn him towards the eastern horizon – held on far into the danger zone while he established their number and bearing. When he at last turned away he was followed by torrents of shells, any one of which would have obliterated him or a consort. Forty large shells fell within 75 yards of *Southampton* as she made her escape at 25 knots towards Jellicoe, zigzagging between the shell fountains to confuse the German range-takers. Beatty's battlecruisers had meanwhile put enough sea room behind them to be out of danger. However, the fast battleships of 5th Battle Squadron, misled by an ambiguous flag signal, had not. They were a full five minutes late in turning away, during which interval *Barham* and *Malaya* were hit, *Malaya* heavily. One of her secondary batteries was knocked out and she was holed beneath the waterline. Then the fast battleships' advantage in gunpower told in reply. Several German battleships and battlecruisers were struck by salvoes from the retreating British ships, *Seydlitz* so hard that she risked sinking.

The run to the north, though a withdrawal, was therefore as much a British success as the run to the south had been a British setback. Both had been preliminary engagements. Shortly after 6 pm the battle fleets themselves at last drew within range of each other. Their covering screens of cruisers and light cruisers had already been in action and the Germans had fallen under the guns of Beatty's battlecruisers, with disastrous result; three cruisers – *Wiesbaden, Pillau* and *Frankfurt* – suffered crippling damage. Yet so too had a British destroyer, *Shark*, overwhelmed by heavier fire, and a cruiser, *Chester*, in which the boy hero of Jutland, Jack Cornwell, VC (who stayed by his gun when mortally wounded) was killed. There were to be still more losses before the dreadnoughts began their artillery duel. Two British armoured cruisers, supporting Jellicoe's battleships, came under fire from Scheer as they steamed ahead of the Grand Fleet; *Warrior* was rapidly wrecked and *Defence* blown up, both hit by shells against which their thin sides offered no protection and at ranges over which their 8-inch guns could not reply.

There was to be yet another British catastrophe before Jellicoe's and Scheer's battleships saw each other. Three battlecruisers, *Indomitable, Inflexible* and *Invincible*, oldest and weakest of their type, were accompanying the Grand Fleet. At one minute after 6 pm *Lion* had come within sight of Jellicoe, who signalled to Beatty, 'Where is the enemy's battle fleet?' The answer was ambiguous but it persuaded the commander that he must anticipate imminent action and deploy from column into line – that is, from an approach at right angles to a course parallel to the German fleet's. That was the formation best suited for the concentration of maximum gunpower on the enemy, since it allowed all turrets a clear field of fire. As his six columns began their fifteen-minute deployment into line, the *Invincible*, steaming ahead of the main formation, out of sight of Jellicoe but in sight of Beatty, also came within view of the Germans. It was an unlucky rendezvous. Cloud and mist, which had so far concealed their presence, suddenly parted to reveal the isolated squadron of three battlecruisers to the leading German battleship, which at once opened fire. *Invincible*, the leading ship, was the focus and she was hit repeatedly. At 6.33 pm a shell penetrated the roof of Q turret amidship, the flash travelled down the turret trunk, and in an instant her magazine exploded and blew her into halves. Among the six survivors of her thousand men was Wagner's godson, who had been observing the fall of shot from the highest point in the ship.

It was not *Invincible*'s loss which prompted Beatty's notorious remark, 'There seems to be something wrong with our bloody ships today.' That had been drawn from him by the destruction of *Queen Mary*. However, all the British battlecruisers, indeed all the British capital ships, were flawed by a fundamental design defect: that insufficiency of 'anti-flash' devices between the turrets and the magazines noted earlier. Because of *Seydlitz*'s near-fatal internal fire at the Dogger Bank, the High Seas Fleet's ships had been modified to avert the passage of flank down their turret trunks. The British fleet's had not, a third of its battlecruisers having been destroyed in consequence. Fortunately the surviving battlecruisers were not to bear the brunt of the ensuing action, while the battleships, which were, had external armour sufficiently thick to keep out the projectiles which had damaged the *Invincible* and Beatty's ships so fatally.

Moreover, Jellicoe's battleships were to join action with Scheer's on highly advantageous terms. Ambiguous and intermittent though the signalling of his advanced forces had been, he was the more fully alerted of the two commanders of the approach of his opponent. Hipper had been able to warn Scheer of the imminence of fleet action with no clearer signal than 'Something lurks in that soup. We would do well not to thrust into it too deeply.' Scheer, who had so far believed that he had the British battlecruiser fleet in a trap, now had to grapple with the anxiety that it might be supported by the rest of the Grand Fleet, yet he had no clear indication of its location. Jellicoe not only knew Scheer's positions and heading; he could also calculate that his own heading put him between Scheer and his line of retreat to the North German ports and, therefore, so long as daylight and the accuracy of his gunnery availed he could 'Trafalgar' the enemy by cutting them off and annihilating them.

The Grand Fleet's twenty-eight battleships, deploying from columns to line as they passed the wreck of *Invincible* – many British sailors, so sure were they of victory, thought her German and cheered – now enjoyed the advantage of the light that earlier in the day had been the enemy's and could pick out their targets clearly on the western skyline. 'To Scheer's range-takers, Jellicoe's ships were indicated on the horizon ahead of us [only] by the firing of heavy-calibre guns. The entire arc stretching from north to east was a sea of fire. The muzzle flashes were clearly seen through the mist and smoke on the horizon, though there was still no sign of the ships themselves.'

The opening range was about 12,000 yards, well within the reach of the guns on the leading British ships which, by classic tactics, had 'crossed the T' of the German line and were pouring fire at its head. British observers were convinced they were scoring a succession of hits and sinking ships. Several German battleships – and battlecruisers, leading the fleet – were indeed hit in this exchange; twenty-two shells struck altogether, but none sank a ship. The German line inflicted thirty-three hits in return, all on British battlecruisers, cruisers and the fast battleships of the 5th Battle Squadron. Jellicoe's battle line was not touched: as it steamed imperturbably onward, steadily closing the range and interposing itself more deeply between the High Seas Fleet and home, Scheer's nerve cracked. After only ten minutes' engagement, he ordered a 'simultaneous turn-away' to take his fleet out of danger.

The German ships disappeared instantly and mysteriously from the British range-takers' field of vision as the smoke and gathering dusk of a misty evening enclosed them. Although they might have turned south, Jellicoe correctly guessed that Scheer had chosen the quickest way out of danger and turned due west, towards the British coast. He ordered an alteration of course southward, to better his chances of cutting off the Germans' retreat, and held onward. So too, for some ten minutes [from 6.45 to 6.55 pm), did Scheer, until, gambling that he might thus escape across the rear of the Grand Fleet, he signalled a reversal of course and began to steer due east. His intention was to reach the coast of Jutland and then work his way home behind the minefields fringing it in German territorial waters.

His order, however, was timed too early. Overestimating the speed of Jellicoe's advance, he failed to cross behind the Grand Fleet's rear but ran straight into it. At about 7.10 he suddenly found himself under fire once more from the British battleships, his T crossed, his weakest ships, the battlecruisers, in the van, and last light silhouetting his line while it hid the British. This 'second encounter' of the battlefleets went far worse than the first for the Germans. They scored only two hits on Jellicoe's line (both on *Colossus*), while the British scored twenty-seven in return, all on the already heavily stricken battlecruisers.

Less than ten minutes of this treatment persuaded Scheer to break off action. The first shots had registered at 7.10 pm. At 7.18 he signalled a second 'simultaneous turn-away' to his battle line, having meanwhile ordered the battlecruisers to 'charge' the enemy and his light cruisers and torpedo-boats to lay smoke and mount a torpedo attack. Hipper's 'death ride' – the allusion was to the last charge of Prussia's armoured horsemen in 1870 – put all but one of his ships out of action. The torpedo attack was more profitable. Jellicoe deployed his own light cruisers and destroyers against it as the Germans approached and caused most to launch at extreme range, or not to launch at all. Nevertheless twenty-one torpedoes travelled the distance, forcing Jellicoe to order a general 'turn-away' and individual ship captains to manoeuvre sharply. No hits were scored, but by the time Jellicoe resumed his pursuit Scheer had put himself some ten to eleven miles from the Grand Fleet, comfortably out of range, and was heading south for home with the British abreast of him to the east and slightly to his rear.

Light was failing fast as the last phase of the battle – to become known as 'the night action' – opened. The sun set at 8.24 pm. At 8.30 Scheer ordered his squadron of six pre-dreadnoughts to go to the help of his battlecruisers which, lying to his east, were still under fire from Beatty's; his, in turn, were running ahead of Jellicoe's line of advance. While the pre-dreadnoughts exchanged fire with Beatty's fleet, Hipper's battlecruisers made good their escape; eventually, as Beatty's range-takers lost definition on the darkening horizon, so did the pre-dreadnoughts. Theirs had been a hopelessly brave intervention and it was fitting that they were able to disengage unscathed.

While the darkness thickened, the battle fleets converged on southerly courses in complete ignorance of each other's whereabouts. In the six miles of sea that separated them there were to ensue nine encounters between German and British light forces and British light forces and the German battle fleet. In the third the British cruiser *Southampton* sank the German cruiser *Frauenlob* by torpedo. In the fifth British destroyers attacked the German dreadnoughts at ranges which closed to a thousand yards and damaged one by ramming. In the sixth a British destroyer put a torpedo into a German pre-dreadnought, *Pommern*, found its magazine and blew it up. In the seventh a British armoured cruiser, *Black Prince*, was set on fire by salvoes from a German dreadnought and also blew up. The eighth and ninth were destroyer actions, in which one German torpedo-boat was lost.

While these brief and chaotic encounters, the last timed at 3.30 am on 1 June, were taking place, the High Seas Fleet, holding to its southerly course and making several knots less than the Grand Fleet, had passed behind the British and got safely to the coast of Jutland and its minefields. It was in sore straits. One of its battlecruisers, *Lützow*, had sunk, and of the four remaining only *Moltke* was still fit to fight. A pre-dreadnought had blown up and four light cruisers and five torpedo-boats been lost. Altogether ten of its capital ships were damaged, *Seydlitz* and *Derfflinger* so badly that they were not to leave dockyard until September and December respectively. A total of 2551 sailors had been killed and some 500 wounded.

Nevertheless the fleet was home – even if *Seydlitz*, twice grounded on the approaches to the Jade, had to be hauled ignominiously into harbour stern first. Moreover, the fleet had inflicted far greater damage than it had suffered. Three British battlecruisers, *Indefatigable, Invincible* and *Queen Mary*, three armoured cruisers, *Black Prince, Defence* and *Warrior*, and eight destroyers were sunk. A total of 6097 British sailors had been killed and some 500 wounded, while five British capital ships had suffered hits by 11-inch shells or heavier, notably *Lion, Tiger* and *Warspite*. Despite the British losses, however, the balance of forces had not been significantly altered. The Grand Fleet still outnumbered Scheer's by twenty-eight dreadnoughts to sixteen, and it had left the scene of action only after seeing Scheer into waters where it could not follow. Yet it had not 'Trafalgared' the Germans, nor had it deterred them from contemplating another North Sea sortie. As Scheer reported to the Kaiser on 4 July, 'The High Seas Fleet will be ready the middle of August for further strikes against the enemy.'

True to Scheer's word, the High Seas Fleet did put to sea, on 19 August, and steamed north to bring the English east coast town of Sunderland under bombardment. His approach was covered, however, by ten of the zeppelins he had not been able to take to Jutland, and when one reported that the Grand Fleet was bearing down on him from the Scottish anchorages he reversed course and raced for home. The Admiralty cryptographers had detected his sortie, and were to do so again when he next put to sea in October, with the same humiliating outcome. That was to be the High Seas Fleet's last open challenge to the Royal Navy. In April 1918, when it slipped out of port once more, its mission was mere commerce raiding against the Scandinavian convoys. An engine-room accident in one of the battlecruisers, causing the battleships to reduce speed also, then obliged Scheer to call off the operation and return to port. That marked the end of 'risk theory' and anticipated surrender and the journey to Scapa Flow by only seven months.

For more than half the war, therefore – from 1 June 1916 until 11 November 1918, twenty-nine months in all – the High Seas Fleet was at best 'a fleet in being', and for its last year scarcely even that. Much explains its inactivity: the growth of the Grand Fleet's strength relative to its own (Britain launched nine capital ships between 1916 and 1918, Germany only three), the addition of the American to the British dreadnought fleet after April 1917 and the Kaiser's increasingly neurotic opposition to the running of any naval risk whatsoever. However, the central factor in the reduction of the High Seas Fleet to an inoperative force was the action of Jutland itself. Germany had built a navy for battle. In the only engagement fought by its united strength it had undergone an experience its leaders did not choose – any more than the leaders of the Combined Fleet after Trafalgar chose – to repeat. What had happened to deter it from fighting again?

THE EXPERIENCE OF ACTION

Of major importance to the understanding of Jutland is a recognition that equals did not fight equals. Trafalgar had been a contest between ships of the line and, though some were stronger than others, notably the hundred and hundred-plus-gun ships, the majority had been roughly equal in their ability both to give and receive punishment. Such was not the case at Jutland. The late nineteenth-century diversification of ship-types, prompted by the development of the torpedo and the turbine, whose principal products were the battlecruiser, the destroyer and the submarine (though the last played no part in the events of 31

May 1916), pitched 'weak' ships against 'strong' in permutations sailors had never known hitherto. In the central phase of the battle, when Jellicoe's battleships had fought Scheer's, the fight had been between equals. So, too, had it been while Hipper's and Beatty's battlecruisers had struggled for advantage in the opening encounter. But battlecruisers had also fought battleships, at great disadvantage to themselves, and cruisers and destroyers capital ships – as well as each other – at suicidal risk. In all ships, moreover, the efforts of 'fighting men', traditionally defined – those who manned the bridge or the guns – had been supported by those of others in the bowels of the ship, stokers, engineers, ammunition handlers, who had no sight of the enemy at all but were none the less quite as much combatants, by reason of shared risk-taking, as the seamen most directly exposed to enemy fire. What experience had these warriors undergone off Jutland on 31 May 1916?

Battlecruisers versus battlecruisers

First sightings between the ships on which the outcome of the battle was to turn were glimpsed and distant. Hipper's line of battlecruisers, with the advantage of light, saw Beatty's at 3.20; Beatty's did not make out Hipper's until a few minutes later. 'At 3.22,' reported an officer in *Princess Royal*, 'we first sighted the enemy. 5 battle cruisers faintly distinguishable a very long distance away, accompanied by some torpedo craft. First of all their smoke, and later the outline of their masts, funnels and the upper part of their hulls became visible from the control positions aloft, but from the turrets' (which had periscopes for 'local control' of fire if the director broke down) 'only smoke could be observed until some time later.'

The gun control positions, located over the bridge on the foremast, were sixty feet above the turrets, an advantage of height which added some 2000 yards to effective range of vision. The position was unprotected, and those in it were cut off from the rest of the crew while action lasted. A midshipman of HMS *Neptune*, one of Jellicoe's battleships, describes the preparations he made for running his action station.

> Access could be gained either by ascending an interminably long iron ladder running up the interior of the mast, or by climbing up outside the tripod by means of iron rungs rivetted on the struts. Experience of the difficulties of ascent had induced me some time ago to have made a blue jean bag, in [which] I always kept [essential] gadgets – ear protectors, binoculars, a stop watch, a pistol, a camera, a respirator, scarves, woollen helmet and so forth. It was armed with this weighty 'battle bag' that I clambered up the starboard strut of the foremast, past the steam siren (which sizzled ominously as I approached it . . .), through a belt of hot acrid funnel smoke, and finally into the top through the lubber's hole.

Masts were not, however, as they had been at Trafalgar, a deliberate target of dreadnought gunnery; and, because gun-laying was so much

TOP HMS *Iron Duke*, Jellicoe's flagship at Jutland; launched in 1912 and mounting ten 13.5 inch guns, *Iron Duke* was representative of the most powerful pre-war Dreadnoughts. BELOW HMS *Warspite*, of the 5th Battle Squadron which fought with Beatty's Battlecruiser Fleet at Jutland; those 'super Dreadnoughts' had the speed of battle cruisers and the armament (15-inch guns) of the most modern battleships.

The battle line of the Grand Fleet steaming in line ahead to its encounter with the German High Seas Fleet at Jutland.

The battlecruisers *Indomitable* and *Inflexible* steaming to engage the German battle line, May 31 1916; both these 'I' class battlecruisers survived Jutland.

BELOW The battlecruiser *Seydlitz* in Wilhelmshaven after Jutland.

CENTRE HMS *Lion* (left) suffering a hit on Q turret by *Lützow* at 4pm from a range of 16,500 yards; emergency flooding of the magazine saved the ship.

BOTTOM The bow and stem of HMS *Invincible*, about 7p.m. 31 May 1916, resting on the shallow bed of the North Sea; HM Destroyer *Badger* is approaching to search for survivors.

Admiral Sir John (later 1st Earl) Jellico (1859–1935) Commander of the Grand Fleet at Jutland, aboard HMS *Iron Duke*. TOP RIGHT Vice-Admiral Sir David (later 1st Earl) Beatty (1871–1936), commander of the Battlecruiser Fleet at Jutland: his flamboyance and impetuosity exceeded his abilities. CENTRE Admiral Franz (later Ritter von) Hipper (1963–1932), Commander of the First Scouting Group of German battlecruisers. RIGHT Admiral Reinhard Scheer (1863–1928), commander of the German High Seas Fleet at Jutland; Admiral Prince Heinrich and the German Crown Prince to his left and right.

more accurate in 1916 than in 1805, and fore-tops made a small target, none suffered a direct hit in the course of the action. Gunnery control officers were trying to hit hulls and particularly turrets which, even if heavily armoured, were the access points to magazines.

A director officer in HMS *New Zealand*, fourth ship in Beatty's line, described his sensations at the moment fire was opened:

I had great difficulty in convincing myself that the Huns were in sight at last, it was so like Battle Exercise the way in which we and the Germans turned up on to more or less parallel courses and waited for the range to close sufficiently before letting fly at each other. It all seemed very cold-blooded and mechanical, no chance here of seeing red, merely a case of cool scientific calculation and deliberate gunfire. Everyone seemed cool enough, too, in the control position, all sitting quietly at their instruments waiting for the fight to commence.

Cool the beginning of action may have been; once the shells started to fly even the steadiest crews in the control top were infected by the drama of action. They, comprising the spotters, who observed the fall of shot – 'over', 'short' or 'straddle' (when shells were observed to fall on both sides of an enemy ship), the latter usually meaning a hit – and the rate-takers, who measured the convergence or divergence of the opposing battle line, had the best view in the ship of events, better even than that of the captain and the bridge party, who lacked their high-powered optics. The range-takers in the range-finding tower below the control top had a larger view of individual ships, because of the high magnification of their instruments, but also, because of their instruments' narrow field, an incomplete one. The crew of the transmitting station, to which range, rate and fall of shot were transmitted and where computation of the correct bearing and elevation of the guns was worked out by 'gunnery clock' and sent to the turrets, saw nothing. The crew of the director tower, from which the guns were fired centrally at the moment when an instrument indicated the ship was steady between its rolls to port and starboard, saw something. Although they were masters of the main armament, however, their view was much more constricted than that of the men in the control top. Hence the intensity of communication between spotters and rate-takers in this most exposed of positions – as the director officer in *New Zealand* explained:

The control officer is making allowance for own ship altering course, judging as to enemy's course both as observed and deduced from the plotting in the transmitting station, receiving short reports for the T.S. and giving monosyllabic replies, overhearing quick questions and answers between the spotter and the rate-keeper, as well as general gunnery reports given and received, which are noted and acted upon or, if not of immediate interest or not requiring reply, ignored. The conversation in the gun control top runs something like this:

'Did you see that?'

'No.'

'Down 400 [reduction of range]; close the rate 200 [reduce estimation of battle lines' convergence].'

'Can't'.

'Make it one.'

'Down 400 on the plot.'

'Put it on and close 100.'

'Rate 250 closing.'

'Shoot.'

'Ship altering course to starboard, rate 200 closing.'

'Stand-by, splash [enemy shell falls close by].'

'Up 200.'

Occasionally there is a check in this endless babble, but almost immediately it is fired with renewed activity by a sharp challenge up the voice-pipe, 'T.S. – Foretop', to ascertain if the control position is still in action. . . . Occasionally there comes the variation of 'Hail falls' or 'the-ship-is-picked-up-and-thrown-down-again-angrily'. Hail falling is the result of an enemy shell falling short and bursting on impact with the water throwing a large number of small fragments of shell high into the air which fall on the thin sheet-iron roof of the control top, making a noise like a heavy fall of hail. . . . The-ship-is-picked-up-angrily . . . is due to an enemy shell hitting the ship's armour and being unable to penetrate, when the whole of the force of the detonation is imparted in the hull of the ship . . . once the side of the control top was struck and detonated, but only by quite a small fragment of shell, which did no harm . . . those shells which burst or detonate inside the ship did not seem to have the same effect of shaking the ship as those which burst in the armour.

This phenomenon is probably explained by the exterior 'work energy' of a hit on the armour transmitting itself to the whole structure of the ship. The work energy of a penetrating shell, by contrast, was dissipated inside the spaces surrounding the point of impact and absorbed by the layers of compartmentation. Hence the result, noted by numbers of survivors, that the crew in unaffected parts of a damaged ship could remain quite unaware of disaster in another; thus a midshipman in HMS *Malaya*, serving in the torpedo control tower, who went forward at the end of the action, 'was surprised to see a large shell hole in the upper deck near No. 3 6-inch gun starboard . . . when the battery was finally lighted by an emergency circuit, it was a scene which cannot easily be forgotten – everything burnt black and bare from the fire; the galley, canteen and drying-room blown and twisted into the most grotesque shapes and the whole deck covered by about 6 inches of water and dreadful debris. . . . The men below decks and in other stations away from the actual damage had never dreamed that we had suffered such damage or casualties.'

Such a direct hit on a lightly armoured and unprotected sector of the ship killed or wounded everyone in the vicinity. On armour, however, shells exerted erratic effects. In Q turret of HMS *Tiger*, hit on its armoured roof at 3.55 pm by an 11-inch shell from *Moltke*, two men were killed outright and a midshipman mortally wounded. Four other members of the crew were wounded, but another three were able to remain at duty and help the survivors bring the turret back into action. A turret officer recorded: 'The dead were placed to one side, the wounded given first aid and necessary substitutes were brought up from below to replace casualties.' A quick survey of the damage revealed that the more fragile machinery and instruments had been disabled but that the guns and loading gear could still be worked; as the directors of strategic bombing were to discover in the Second World War, it is almost impossible to destroy high-grade steel machinery with explosive, however accurately delivered. 'The left gun cage was soon put right by removing a fragment of armour,' the turret officer continued; 'but the wire of the right gun-loading cage was seriously jammed . . . so the left gun continued loading normally, and the right gun used the secondary loading method . . . the turret was fired by percussion firing when the other guns were heard to fire, the correct elevation and bearing being maintained from the director receivers, which were fortunately undamaged.'

Tiger had, nevertheless, been lucky to escape. Had flash from the penetrating German shell entered the ammunition hoist, the magazine would have detonated and destroyed the ship. This, subsequent investigation revealed, was because the British crews, in their determination to achieve the highest possible rates of fire in gunnery competitions, had removed anti-flash devices from the magazine trunks without realising that cordite flash in the turret labyrinth was the gravest danger to which battle exposed dreadnoughts.

What might have happened in *Tiger* came even nearer to happening in *Lion*. Her Q turret was hit by a 12-inch shell from *Lützow* at 4 o'clock, which killed everyone in the gun-house. One of the gun-numbers, as he died, involuntarily sent the loading cage of the right gun down into the working-chamber with cordite in it. A fire, spreading apparently down the turret's electrical cables, ignited the cordite in both the cage and the working-chamber; and fire then passed down the turret trunk towards the magazines. The turret officer, Major F. J. W. Harvey, managed with his dying breath (he had lost both his legs) to order that the magazine doors be closed and the magazine flooded. The giving of this order, for which he was posthumously awarded the Victoria Cross, saved the ship.

The fire which the shell started below the turret was fatal to all the crew in the working spaces above the magazine. As the ship's chief gunner reported:

> [It] passed down the main trunk into the shell-room and handling-room and up the escape trunk into the switchboard compartment. In this latter compartment were stationed, beside the switchboard men and certain of the electrical repair party, the after medical party under the charge of a surgeon. All these men, together with the magazine and shell-room crews, were killed by the cordite fire . . . [their] bodies and clothes were not burnt and, in cases where

the hands had been raised involuntarily, palms forward, to protect the eyes, the backs of the hands and that part of the face screened by the hands were not even discoloured. Death to these men must have been instantaneous.

Queen Mary, *Tiger*'s and *Lion*'s consort, suffered similar – though worse – damage and did not survive. About 4.26 pm, after several earlier hits, she was struck on one of her forward turrets. A cordite fire entered the forward magazine and the resulting explosion blew off the forepart of the ship. Shortly afterwards a hit on X turret blew up the after magazine and the remains of the ship capsized. Gunner's Mate E. Francis, a survivor of X turret crew, describes the sequence:

Then came the big explosion [the detonation of the forward magazine] which shook us a bit, and on looking at the pressure gauge I saw the [hydraulic] pressure had failed [hydraulic power trained the turret, elevated the guns and worked the ammunition lifts and loading rammers]. Immediately after that came . . . the big smash and I was dangling in the air on a bowline, which saved me from being thrown on to the floor of the turret. . . . Nos 2 and 3 of the left gun slipped down under the gun, and the gun appeared to me to have fallen through its trunnions and smashed up these two numbers. Everything in the ship went as quiet as a church, the floor of the turret was bulged up and the guns were absolutely useless. . . . I put my head up through the hole in the roof of the turret and I nearly fell back through again. The after 4-inch battery was smashed right out of all recognition and then I noticed the ship had an awful list to port [X turret, behind the bridge, gave no view of the missing foreparts of the ship]. I dropped back inside the turret and told Lieut Ewart [the turret officer] the state of affairs. He said, 'Francis, we can do no more than give them a chance; clear the turret.' 'Clear the turret,' I called out, and out they all went.

Francis and Midshipman Lloyd-Owen of X turret were to be among *Queen Mary*'s twenty survivors, of a crew of 58 officers and 1228 men. *Indefatigable*, also blown up by a magazine explosion, sank at two minutes past four with the loss of all but two of her crew of a thousand. These holocausts, with the later loss of *Invincible*, a sister battlecruiser, were to be the great tragedies of Jutland, because of their unexpectedness; the old armoured cruisers, *Black Prince* and *Defence*, were sunk later in the action with comparable loss of life, but these were casualties which, while they shocked, surprised no one, since neither should have been allowed within range of dreadnoughts. The battlecruisers, though 'risk' ships, were expected to have been proof against running salvoes in the preliminary to the main action, even if unsuitable to stand in the line of battle; *Seydlitz* and her sister ships indeed passed that test. For the British, the vulnerability of the *Invincible*, *Indefatigable* and *Queen Mary* to German long-range armour-piercing fire was to be the most unsettling outcome of all the events of the Jutland encounter.

Battleships versus battleships

Yet, at the time, so sublime was British confidence in the superiority of their own material and battlecraft that the loss of *Indefatigable* and *Queen Mary* was denied by many who witnessed it. A midshipman in HMS *Malaya*, one of the fast 'Queen Elizabeth' battleships accompanying the Battlecruiser Fleet, remembered that 'our enthusiasm knew no bounds when we passed a sunken ship with survivors swimming round her. We never dreamt that it was one of our own battlecruisers, but it was the *Indefatigable* . . . the same thing occurred when we passed the wreckage and survivors of the *Queen Mary*. Even when a man on some wreckage waved to us, we thought it must be a German wanting to be picked up.' *Malaya*'s crew, 'bored stiff at the prospect of another uneventful sweep', were 'jubilant' when they realized that they 'were at last in for a proper action . . . so much so, that when a German shell landed abreast us on the port side about 500 yards short there was a positive cheer.'

Observers in *Tiger* and *New Zealand*, which had been close to *Queen Mary* when she blew up, preserved no such sense of immunity. A spotting officer in *New Zealand* saw 'a small cloud of what looked like coal dust come out from where she was hit' and then the ship disappear in 'a terrible yellow flame' and 'a heavy and very dense mass of black smoke'. When *Tiger* was abreast of the wreck, its propellers still revolving, and 'men crawling out of the top of the after turret', there was another large explosion. 'The most noticeable thing was the masses and masses of paper which were blown into the air as the after portion exploded. Great masses of iron were thrown into the air and things were falling into the sea around us.' To an observer in the conning tower of *Tiger*, 'the whole ship seemed to collapse inwards. The funnels and mast fell into the middle and the hull was blown outwards. The roofs of the turrets' (solid sheets of armour weighing some 70 tons) 'were blown 100 feet high, then everything was smoke.'

This was an awful warning of the true impact of German shellfire if it found a vulnerable point. Clearly visible in spotting glasses, and sometimes to the naked eye, shells were at first watched dispassionately. 'They always seemed to be coming straight for one's eye . . . [they] appeared as dots getting larger and larger, till they burst short or droned past and fell beyond us. . . . Ricochets were also clearly visible, turning end over end, and making a noise like the rumbling of a distant train.' In *Colossus*, later in the action, an officer recalled 'the extraordinary clearness with which we were able to see a large shell which ricocheted over and which was painted yellow with a black band'.

As battle intensified, and the effect of shellfire striking armour could no longer be ignored, anxieties were heightened. 'It is a curious sensation,' remarked a Midshipman in HMS *Neptune*, 'being under heavy fire at long range. The time of [shell] flight seems more like 30 minutes than the 30 or so seconds that it actually is. A great ripping gush of flame breaks out from the enemy's guns some [ten] miles away, and then follows a pause during which one can reflect that somewhere in that great "no-man's-land" 2 or 3 tons of metal and explosive are hurtling towards one. The mountainous splashes which announce the arrival of each successive salvo rise simultaneously in bunches of four or five to an immense height.'

'The warm red glow of a "hit",' the observer went on, 'is easily distinguishable' on enemy ships 'from the flash of a salvo and is extremely pleasant to look upon.' At the receiving end, such 'warm red glows' – which, if successive salvoes were accurate, might occur at 20-second intervals – were terrible in their effect. Within the first hour of action, warm red glows had obliterated two of the British battlecruisers. The British battleships – and all the German capital ships – made stouter targets. But the physical damage caused by the shell from a dreadnought's main armament striking inboard even on a heavily armoured battleship were extremely destructive.

Commander Walwyn, the executive officer of HMS *Warspite*, one of the four battleships attached to Beatty's Battlecruiser Fleet, described what he found when sent by the captain to investigate damage, later established to have been caused by *Seydlitz*, about 5.30 pm. He decided, for speed's sake, to go above rather than below decks, 'put up my coat collar and run like a stag, feeling in a deuce of a funk' (a major difference between wooden-wall and ironclad battles was that, in the latter, the decks were deserted; only the captain and his command party on the bridge were in the open air). The executive officer was nearing the point of reported damage when '12-inch shell came through side armour on boys' mess deck. Terrific sheet of golden flame, stink, impenetrable dust and everything seemed to fall everywhere with an appalling noise. Called for No. 2 fire brigade, and they ran up from the flat below, and we got hose on, and put out a lot of burning refuse . . . several of the fire brigade were ill due to the sweet, sickly stench but there was no sign of poison gas.' (Shell fumes lingering in confined spaces were a major medical hazard.) 'The shell hole was clean, about a foot in diameter; big flakes of armour had been flung right across the mess deck, wrecking everything. Many armour bolts came away. Magazine flooding cabinet was completely wrecked, and all voice pipes and electric leads overhead were cut to pieces, smoke was pouring up through holes in the deck.' Hits on the *Warspite* continued. Shortly afterwards Commander Walwyn was 'told a shell had just burst in the Captain's lobby'.

Went aft again and found my cabin had been completely removed overboard . . . hole about 12 feet square in the centre of the deck. Lots of burning debris in my cabin, which we put out; in the middle of the heap was my wife's miniature, without its case but otherwise perfect. . . . There were about four bursts in the lobby . . . went along by No. 5 fire brigade and saw we had been heavily hit portside. Helped with fire brigade ... plugging out fire mains and trying to stop water getting down ventilating trunks. Columns of water pouring through hole in deck overhead, must have been from enemy shoots [shells falling alongside]. ... A shell had come in further forward and hit X turret barbette armour, killing several of No. 5 fire brigade and wounding a lot more. ... I realised we could not effectively stop hole in side, and decided we must at all costs stop water getting to the engine room. We plugged [ventilation] by big sheets of rubber shoved down with deal flats. ... Blast of shell momentarily put out lights, but candles were instantly re-lit. ... Electric light bulbs broke in vicinity of shell bursts.

The damage here had been caused by an unexploded shell, from which two stokers were found trying to chip the fuse; 'I luckily stopped the little effort.' Meanwhile another 12-inch shell came into the galley ('there goes my dinner,' said a stoker), and then the executive officer was told *Warspite* had been hit under the engineers' office. 'It looked very bad, as a large triangular piece [of armour] had been blown out of the main belt about a foot above the water. The fresh water and oil fuel tanks' (*Warspite* was one of the Royal Navy's first oil-fuelled ships) 'had been blown to pieces. ... Men trying to plug the hole, but tons of water were coming in and washing them back all the time.' Seeing that plugging was impossible, he eventually ordered them to fill the whole affected compartment with hammocks: 'It took 600 hammocks to fill up ... which effectually stopped the trouble but not till late that night. Body of the [unexploded] shell was afterwards found in the bathroom.'

Damage was now being suffered and reported at close intervals. In the next few minutes a shell burst in the starboard secondary battery and 'a sheet of flame came down through slits of sliding shutters ... heard a lot of groaning'. When he went forward, he found the burst had started a fire in the ready-use cordite among the guns of the starboard secondary battery, which had 'frightfully burnt' two gun crews. It was also blazing around the conning-tower, through the slot of which 'signalmen and messengers peering out ... looked like thrushes in a nest, gaping and shouting "Put the fire out". We eventually got a steam main connected and got water.' The fire had also taken hold below, in the navigating officer's cabin, and was burning a store of 400 life-jackets nearby, 'the stench of burning rubber being perfectly awful ... smouldering wooden uprights of doors kept on breaking out again ... decks were all warped and resin under corticone [deck covering] crackling like burning holly ... everything in the fore superstructure was wrecked and it looked like a burnt-out factory all blackened and beams twisted everywhere ... a 12-inch had come through the after funnel, through beef-screen [meat storage area] and smashed the second cutter [ship's wooden boat] to matchwood. On its way through the beef-screen it had carried a whole sheep with it, which was wedged into the gratings. At first I thought it was a casualty.'

That the carcass of a sheep could be mistaken for a human casualty testifies to the appalling nature of wounds that high-explosive projectiles inflicted in the confined spaces of armoured ships. Astonishingly, despite all the damage, *Warspite* was to suffer only four fatal and twenty-six non-fatal casualties in the whole course of the action, the majority being burn cases. Throughout, its crew were to display an amazing insouciance. After an early shell-burst, one damage-control party was found 'busy souvenir hunting'; the marines of 'port 6-inch ammunition supply were playing cards on the deck quite happily' while fire was raging on the starboard side; and, while the executive officer was busy with damage control in the mess decks, 'two stokers came to me . . . and begged me to take watches, letters, etc., found on men who had been knocked out. It struck me as so incongruous, as if it mattered a bit when we might all of us go at any minute!'

In fact, despite a great deal of superficial damage and flame and a constant barrage of noise – 'deafening and rather nerve-shattering. You could not hear youself speak and had to shout in anybody's ear' – *Warspite* was not dangerously injured by any of the fifteen 11- and 12-inch shells that struck her. One of her guns was put out of action, but her turrets, magazines and engine-room remained intact, even though for a brief period (from 6.19 to 6.45 pm) she was the principal target of the German battle line. Her steering engines had jammed, because of overheating by severe use, and she circled helplessly between the fleets until the fault could be corrected. In that period she was struck eleven times, but only five shells caused damage that interfered with the normal working of the ship and in all cases essential functions were quickly restored. *Warspite*'s escape was due to the duplication of systems – hydraulics, steam lines, electrical cables – common to all dread-noughts, and to the great strength of the 'Queen Elizabeths' as a class. They were the best as well as the newest ships at Jutland and their performance vindicated their design.

Warspite was the hardest hit of British battleships at Jutland; *Malaya* and *Barham* next hardest with seven and six hits respectively. All, however, belonged to the fast 5th Battle Squadron supporting the battlecruisers. Indeed, the only battleship of the line of battle proper to suffer heavy shell hits was *Colossus*, built in 1909 and so a comparatively old dreadnought. At about 7.15 pm two 11-inch shells from *Seydlitz* struck her superstructure. One deflected harmlessly; the other caused splinter damage, and started a fire, but it was quickly put out. *Colossus* suffered most not from a direct hit but from 'a short', the effects of which are described by a midshipman stationed on the conning tower: 'All the officers and men on the forebridge had very narrow escapes, but only Leading-seaman Beddow, the range-taker at the forebridge range-finder, was hit, his right arm being practically severed just below the shoulder. He later had to have his arm amputated . . . but had it not been for the Captain of Marines who improvised a tourniquet out of a handkerchief and a bit of stick... he would certainly have bled to death.'

The immunity of the bridge parties at Jutland was perhaps the most striking feature among human experiences of the battle. W. S. Chalmers, who stood beside Beatty on the bridge of *Lion*, describes the exposure of the bridge party and their sensations:

On the bridge we were blissfully ignorant of the fact that two large shells had exploded in the ship: the rush of wind and other noises caused by the high speed at which we were travelling, together with the roar of our own guns as they fired, four at a time, completely drowned the noise of bursting shell. There was no doubt, however, that we were under heavy fire, because all round us huge columns of water, higher than the funnel, were being thrown up as the enemy shells fell into the sea. Some of these gigantic splashes curled over and deluged us with water. Occasionally above the noise of battle, we heard the ominous hum of a shell fragment and caught a glimpse of polished steel as it flashed past the bridge.

The bridge party remained unaware of the shell strike on Q turret which almost destroyed the ship until 'a bloodstained sergeant of Marines, hatless, his clothes... burnt' arrived to report. Chalmers 'looked over the bridge. No further confirmation was necessary; the armoured roof of Q turret had been folded back like an opened sardine can, thick yellow smoke was rolling up in clouds from the gaping hole, and the guns were cocked up in the air awkwardly... strange that all this should have happened within a few yards of where Beatty was standing, and that none of us on the bridge should have heard the detonation.'

The bridge parties of the German ships enjoyed a similar immunity during the battleship-to-battleship phase of Jutland, though they were to be struck more often than Jellicoe's. *Colossus*, as we have seen, was the only British ship of the battle line to suffer direct hits. *König*, *Grosser Kurfürst*, *Markgraf* and *Kaiser*, by contrast, were hit by nine, three, two and two shells from Jellicoe's battle line, while *Markgraf*, *Kaiser* and *Helgoland* were also hit by the Battlecruiser Fleet. *König* and *Grosser Kurfürst* were hit hard; but neither suffered the punishment undergone by *Lützow*, *Derfflinger* and *Seydlitz*, struck by twenty-four, twenty-one and twenty-two heavy shells respectively. Their survival in action was indeed testimony to the high standards of German warship construction, even though *Lützow* had eventually to be abandoned on the passage home.

Her captain described her end, early on the morning of 1 June: 'After it became clear that it was not possible to save the ship, because she had 8300 tons of water in her and was on the point of heeling over, I decided to send off the crew.... She was so down by the bows that the water came up to the control tower and the stern was right out. On my orders the ship was sunk by a torpedo fired by G-38 [a German torpedo-boat]. She heeled over and after two minutes swiftly sank with her flag flying.'

The only other German capital ship not to return from Jutland was the heroic pre-dreadnought *Pommern*, destroyed during the night action by a torpedo fired from the destroyer *Onslaught*. The German pre-dreadnoughts were not elaborately subdivided and had no underwater protection. The explosion broke *Pommern* in half. There were no survivors from her crew of 844.

That terrible toll is largely explained by the near-impossibility of finding survivors on the surface of the sea during the hours of darkness. That some did survive her wreck is suggested by the aftermath of the *Queen Mary* and *Indefatigable* disasters in which eleven were picked up; only *Invincible*, devastated by the worst of the Jutland explosions, went down with all hands. *Pommern*'s broken hull remained afloat for at least twenty minutes after the torpedo strike. The surmise is that the ship was destroyed by a succession of explosions, beginning in the magazine of the secondary armament and spreading to where the 11-inch charges and shells were stored. Men in the tops and on the bridge must have been thrown into the sea, and others in the upper decks would probably have been able to make an escape. All were subsequently lost to the darkness and the cold.

Those most at risk to internal explosion – indeed, without hope of escape at all – were the ammunition and engine-room crews. Ammunition handlers, if at the flashpoint, suffered instantaneous extinction. Stokers and mechanics might undergo a protracted and awful agony. That must certainly have been the fate of the engine-room crews in *Pommern*, as well as in *Indefatigable* and *Queen Mary*, trapped in air pockets below decks, plunged in darkness, engulfed by rising water, perhaps also menaced by escaping superheated steam and machinery running out of control.

The details of the last minutes in those engine-room spaces are mercifully hidden from us. Some impression of what the victims underwent is conveyed by the experience of the engine-room crew of *Warrior* the British armoured cruiser attacked by *Derfflinger* and other German battlecruisers at about 6.20 pm. *Warrior*, which was, inappropriately, attempting to support the British battlecruiser line, suffered hits by fifteen heavy shells, one of which struck at the waterline, causing flooding in the whole engine-room space.

Warrior escaped further punishment because German fire then shifted to *Warspite*, circling out of control nearby; but the damage caused had trapped the survivors of the engine-room crew in the working spaces. There were initially eight of them. The officer in charge tried to lead them out of the engine-room but was defeated. He 'found by the glimmer of the sole remaining oil lamp, that the water was coming over the floor plates, and the crank pits were full up and the cranks were swishing round in the middle of it.' *Warrior* was not a turbine but a reciprocating-engine ship, in which massive pistons worked in cylinders up to the height of the engine-room space, perfectly safely while the ship was proceeding normally, but at great risk to the engine-room crew as soon as anything went awry. The engineer officer first

tried to ease the engines and shut off steam, fearing further accidents, but by this time the water was breast high over the floor plates, and he decided the only thing to do was to clear out. But by this time the ladders were inaccessible as the floor plates were dislodged, and there was every chance of being drawn into the racing cranks. They climbed up over pipes and condensers, holding hands to prevent the swirling water carrying them away. Unfortunately their chain was twice broken, with the result that several men were jammed somehow and drowned. The remainder climbed from one vantage point to another as the water rose until they reached the upper gratings, but by this time it was quite dark, and having no purchase anywhere they could not dislodge the gratings overhead, and apparently found themselves doomed to certain death. Not only were they expecting to be drowned, but escaping steam almost suffocated them, and they kept splashing the oily water over their faces to keep themselves from being peeled. Some men had wrapped scarves round their heads to protect themselves, and all kept as much of their heads as they could in the water. The surprising thing was that the engines went on working till the water was half-way up the cylinders and only stopped then because the boilers were shut off. And this agony of terror went on for nearly two and a half hours in pitch darkness and apparent hopelessness. . . . A stoker petty officer . . . absolutely refused to recognise the horror of the situation and kept talking and cheering them all up . . . they kept hold of each other to save their lives as long as possible, but one by one they kept dropping off and getting lost and drowned in the water, till at last there were only three of them left. [The engineer officer] himself would have been lost, having slipped from his hold and finding himself being drawn into the machinery, but the petty officer held on to him and kept him up until he recovered somewhat. They thought at one time that the ship had been abandoned . . . then they felt a noticeably cold stream of water coming in . . . and from this they apparently had the idea that the ship must be under way, and therefore in tow of someone, which encouraged them. At last they heard some order being 'piped' round the ship and they all shouted together and this led to their rescue.

There was to be no rescue for the engine-room crew of the battleship *Pommern* any more than there had been for those of the battlecruisers *Queen Mary* and *Indefatigable*. The crews of the turbine-engined battle-cruisers were spared the horror of crushing and dismemberment by cranks and pistons as the shattered hulls of their ships carried them down into the deeps. The older *Pommern*, a juggernaut of the sea, must have mangled many of her stokers and mechanicians as she made her last plunge. In all three ships the escape of propulsive steam would have flayed men alive before they finally drowned.

The modern battleships had nevertheless proved their worth. Action had demonstrated that the British and even the German battlecruisers were too lightly armoured and too scantily subdivided to stand up to salvoes of heavy shells – as were also the German pre-dreadnoughts, among which the *Pommern* had been an unlucky victim. The five dreadnoughts, by contrast, had survived each others' exchange of fire without injury to their vitals. Even *Warspite*, the worst damaged, though it had been hit by fifteen heavy shells – thirteen fired by the German battleships – had suffered a surprisingly small toll of casualties: 14 killed and 32 wounded. Many of the casualties were caused by the seventh hit, which struck in the starboard secondary battery, ignited cordite and burnt many of the gun crews.

British – and German – battleship casualties were overall remarkably light. The 5th Battle Squadron of fast battleships, operating with the battlecruisers, lost 103 killed altogether – 26 in *Barham*, 14 in *Warspite* and 63 in *Malaya*, in which a cordite fire caused 102 casualties in the starboard secondary armament battery. Only one ship of the battle fleet proper suffered any fatal casualties at all – *Marlborough*, which lost two killed. The German battleships were harder hit, particularly *König*, in which 45 sailors were killed, mainly gun crew in the port secondary armament batteries. The total of German battleship casualties was 107 killed and 139 wounded (compared to 283 killed and 139 wounded in the battlecruisers), the effect of twenty-six hits by British shells of 12-inch and larger calibre. All these hit and casualty figures must be set against the totals of battleship heavy shells fired – 1904 by the Germans, 1539 by the British – most of which were directed at each other. The percentage of hits achieved among shells fired did not exceed 5 per cent by the British or 3 per cent by the German battleships. Individual ships made better practice: the champion was *Iron Duke*, Jellicoe's flagship, with seven hits on *König* out of forty-three 13.5-inch shells fired at a range of 12,600 yards – the score that killed so many of *König*'s crew.

Little is known about casualty-evasion technique at Jutland. Several British captains at Trafalgar had made their crews lie down on the decks during the approach to action, while numbers of the enemy deserted their posts during battle for the safety of the orlop or the hold, both below waterline, when action grew hot. Circumstantial evidence suggests that few British or German sailors lay down at Jutland. It appears to have been thought a dereliction to do so; moreover, battle tasks generally required that officers and men remain upright. All crew members stationed in turrets, magazines or ammunition-handling spaces, however, were issued with 'anti-flash' gear, which covered their hands and heads. This proved an effective protection as long as cordite fires did not flash over into magazine conflagrations.

Even so there were terrible incinerations of human beings in several ships which escaped explosion. In *Malaya*, where a serious fire was started in the cordite supply of the starboard 6-inch-gun battery, 'the most ghastly part,' a midshipman remembered, 'was the smell of burnt human flesh, which remained in the ship for weeks, making everybody have a sickly nauseous feeling the whole time'. A similar pollution must have affected *König*, as well as the battlecruisers *Seydlitz* and *Lion*; in the latter a cordite fire erupted after the turret had been unroofed, but not before a sick-berth attendant had gallantly made his way inside to render first aid to the wounded. After the flash, he was removed – badly burnt and unconscious – from beneath the bodies of two of the turret party. They and everyone else 'in the "silent" cabinet, gun-house working-chamber handling room and shell room' had been burnt to death.

The smaller ships

At Trafalgar ships too small to 'stand in the line of battle' – frigates, brigs and cutters – had taken no part, except as repeating signal stations or emergency command vessels. At Jutland ships smaller than dreadnoughts had been in the thick of action, as was intended and expected. Torpedo-boats, destroyers and cruisers, light and heavy, had fought each other but had also fought battleships and battlecruisers – the cruisers inappropriately, for they were merely inferior versions of the capital ships, but destroyers and torpedo-boats as a function of their design. Torpedo-boats had been conceived, immediately after Whitehead's invention of the first efficient self-propelling torpedo in the 1870s, as a cheap though perhaps expendable means of bringing large and costly ironclads under attack. Their development had inspired an alternative theory of naval strategy, which argued that torpedo-boat fleets put weak naval powers potentially on an equal footing with strong (its supporters formed the so-called *Jeune École*). That theory was mistaken; its realisation would depend on the perfection of the submarine, a development not to be completed until the appearance of the nuclear-propelled submarine in our own time. However, the torpedo, the torpedo-boat and even the early and primitive submersible imposed important restrictions on ironclads' freedom of action and required significant alterations to their design and tactical employment. One was the incorporation of underwater barriers in the ship's hull, culminating in the torpedo 'bulge', a feature long since abandoned by naval architects but subsequently adopted and refined, in the form of 'spaced armour', by tank designers. A second was the multiplication of secondary armaments. HMS *Dreadnought* had had almost none. Fisher revelled in its 'all-big-gun' design and its speed was considered to give it sufficient protection against torpedo attack.

A doubling of the range and tripling of the speed of torpedoes between 1906 and 1914 called the 'all-big-gun' philosophy into doubt. Doubt was enhanced by consonant improvements in the speed, endurance and sea-keeping qualities of torpedo-boats, which by 1914 were capable of keeping company with capital ships in fleet operations in all but the worst weather. As a result, room had had to be found in battleships and battlecruisers for large numbers of anti-torpedo-boat guns, of up to 5-inch calibre, with consequent complications to the layout of their armoured belts and magazine protection. As we have seen, many of the casualties suffered in capital ships at Jutland were caused by fire in the secondary armament, where arrangements for the safe handling of cordite propellant were necessarily less elaborate than in the supply systems of the big-gun turrets.

Torpedo-boats and destroyers – the latter originally the enemies of the former, but by 1916 simply their equivalent in a larger version – remained potent threats to capital ships, despite the multiplication of secondary armaments designed to destroy them. However, for all their speed – British destroyers easily exceeded 30 knots in the sort of easy sea conditions prevailing at Jutland – torpedo-craft were acutely vulnerable to shellfire, even to the shells fired by each other's 4-inch guns. In exchange for speed they sacrificed every vestige of protection, so that a hit by any calibre of shell penetrated the hull and might strike into the vitals of the engine-rooms or magazines. Even a hit below water could cause damage sufficient to overwhelm the pumps and take the ship to the bottom.

Light cruisers, though larger, were scarcely more robust. Their function was to scout for the battlecruisers and hold torpedo-boat and destroyer flotillas at bay, for which their heavier armament, guns of 6-inch calibre or so, well fitted them. However, should they encounter capital ships, they were wholly at their mercy and could only hope to escape destruction by using their high speed to put sea room between themselves and danger. The so-called armoured cruisers, forerunners of the battlecruisers by which they had been wholly eclipsed, had no place at all in a major fleet action between dreadnoughts. Slow, weak and undergunned, they were little menace to light cruisers or torpedo-craft and were victims to anything larger. The British lost three at Jutland – *Black Prince*, *Defence* and *Warrior*. The last foundered as a result of battle damage; the other two blew up with the loss of all on board.

Defence and *Warrior* suffered their fatal damage on the same mission. Subordinate ships of the Battlecruiser Fleet, they mounted a 'charge' against the light cruisers supporting the High Seas Fleet at the moment the two battle lines, British and German, approached to within striking distance of each other. Admiral Sir Robert Arbuthnot, commanding the 1st Cruiser Squadron in *Defence*, had long contemplated how he would employ his obsolete ships in a clash of dreadnoughts. He had considered the option of manoeuvring on the 'disengaged' side of the battle fleet, that farthest from the enemy, and dismissed it as a 'dull performance'. The more daring tactic of manoeuvring on the engaged side, though it allowed him to pour fire into the crippled German light cruiser *Wiesbaden* in the course of his charge, exposed him to capital-ship fire which brought doom. At 6.20, struck in the magazine by the 11- and 12-inch shells of the German battle line, *Defence* 'suddenly disappeared completely in an immense column of smoke and flame, hundreds of feet high. It appeared to be an absolutely instantaneous destruction, the ship seeming to be dismembered at once.'

Warrior, accompanying *Defence* on her death ride, was also heavily hit. An engineer officer aboard *Warrior* described her last moments of action before disaster overtook her.

Just as I got through the armour door on the main deck, I was met by some people, including the Boatswain, running back, and they said we were being straddled by some 11-inch shell, and they thought it wasn't very healthy out there. As I turned back I perceived that a shell had come into the marines' mess deck, from which I had come. A brown smoke was hanging about and the men of the fire brigade were carrying away three or four poor fellows and laying them down looking dazed and frightened. I therefore went straight down to the port engine-room to see if anything had happened there. [An officer] told me that they had heard an explosion overhead, and some of the lights had gone out, but apparently there was no serious damage below. Finding everything going splendidly there, I decided to return to the starboard engine-room and I looked into the Engineers' office at the top of the ladder on the way. There, for the last time, I saw my Stoker Secretary sitting at his books as if nothing unusual were happening, but he pointed out to me that they had had a shell in a bit further forward, and going out on to the mess deck, I found a great gaping rent in the mess deck overhead, with the daylight falling weirdly through it.

Shortly afterwards *Warrior* was hit by more heavy German shells, crippled, and survived only because the battleship *Warspite*, which simultaneously went out of control, presented a more attractive target to the German battleline. *Warrior* limped away to be taken in tow by the destroyer *Engadine* but foundered through underwater damage before she could make port.

Black Prince, sister ship to *Defence* and *Warrior*, ran foul of the German battleship *Thüringen* during the night action which followed the main engagement, was caught in searchlights and was destroyed with fifteen heavy shell hits. She was the last major loss for either side among the casualties of Jutland. The rest comprised German light cruisers and torpedo-boats and British destroyers, all so fragile that any concentration of shell or torpedo hits, of whatever calibre, consigned them to destruction.

The loss of a few small ships by either side could not alter the outcome of the battle. That turned on the number of capital ships which remained battleworthy after the action was over, and the continuing will of their admirals and crews to take them to sea again. However, the tally of small ship losses contributed to the general impression of victory (or defeat) that the world would gain when the news of Jutland broke; and in that respect the Royal Navy had come out of it better than the

German. Moreover, the losses of small ships and their crews, shipmates to the men who had survived behind the armour and big guns of the capital units, directly affected the morale of the fleets as a whole. In that sense the engagement of the light cruisers, destroyers or torpedo-boats was a significant element in striking the balance of the Jutland encounter.

No fewer than four German light cruisers – *Elbing*, *Frauenlob*, *Rostock* and *Wiesbaden* – five German torpedo-boats and eight British destroyers were lost at Jutland. One of the British destroyers, *Sparrowhawk*, was sunk by a midnight collision with a sister ship, *Broke*. An officer in *Malaya*, watching the manoeuvring of the smaller ships at the start of the battle, had earlier felt 'wonder that so few ships were hit and that there were no collisions', as he saw 'amidst this perfect deluge of shells the light cruisers and destroyers . . . twisting and turning endeavouring to avoid each other and the big ships, which themselves had to perform various manoeuvres . . . the general effect outdid the most perfect picture of a naval battle that I ever saw.' His astonishment at the absence of collisions was well founded. A small space of sea was filled by ships manoeuvring at high speed in close proximity to each other. *Sparrowhawk*'s destruction by *Broke* may be regarded as a delayed outcome of the frantic intermingling of ships he had witnessed at the outset. An officer on the bridge of *Sparrowhawk* 'saw *Broke* coming straight for [us] absolutely end on, at 28 knots. . . . I really don't know why but it was a fascinating sight, I clean forgot about all the Germans and their gunfire. Just as she hit I remember shouting out, "Now", and then nothing more till I found myself lying on the fo'c'sle not of our ship, but of the *Broke* illuminated in a bright light, but in a sort of fog, which must have been due to the clouds of steam escaping from burst pipes.'

There were other collisions. *Sparrowhawk* also managed to collide with the destroyer *Contest* at almost the same time as with *Broke*, though *Contest* survived. HM Destroyer *Spitfire* collided with the German cruiser *Nassau* shortly before midnight, but also survived. The German light cruiser *Elbing* was sunk by collision with the cruiser *Posen*: her engine-rooms were completely flooded and she had to be abandoned.

Most of the other small ship casualties were caused by less direct if more brutal means. The cruiser *Frauenlob* was sunk in the night action by a torpedo fired from HMS *Southampton*. *Rostock* was also torpedoed at night by a British destroyer (either *Contest* or *Ambuscade*) and abandoned when she later encountered the large British light cruiser *Dublin*. *Wiesbaden*, which had been immobilised between the two battle lines early in the action, was overwhelmed by fire. She was hit by fifteen heavy shells and by a torpedo, gradually filled with water and eventually and quite suddenly capsized.

The causes of loss to the German torpedo-boat flotillas were various. V-48 (torpedo-boats had numbers instead of names) was hit by many shells from British destroyers and cruisers. S-35 was sunk by two 13.5-inch shells from Jellicoe's flagship *Iron Duke*. V-27 was scuttled after suffering shell damage in her engine-room and V-4 after striking a mine. V-29 was sunk by a torpedo fired from HM Destroyer *Petard*.

British destroyer losses were almost all caused by shellfire from the German battleships which they attacked during the night action in an effort to cut them off from home. *Tipperary*, *Turbulent*, *Ardent*, *Fortune*, *Nomad* and *Nestor* were sunk in that way; *Shark*, hit by German cruiser shells, was eventually sunk by a torpedo from S-54. The ultimate cause of the loss of *Tipperary*, *Turbulent* and *Nomad* was ammunition explosions in their magazines.

These thin-hulled ships, dependent on their speed and quick handling for any hope of escape in their reckless dashes against dreadnoughts, suffered shattering damage when struck. A survivor of *Tipperary*'s night torpedo run against the German battleships describes the consequences:

> At about 11.45 I suddenly saw and heard a salvo of guns fired from some ship or ships at extremely short range. They were so close that I remember the guns seemed to be firing from some appreciable height above us. . . . The enemy's second salvo hit and burst one of our main steam pipes, and the after-part of the ship was enveloped in a cloud of steam, through which I could see nothing. Losing all their steam, the turbines were brought to a standstill, and we dropped astern out of the action.
>
> The three ships of the enemy that were firing at us could not have fired more than four salvos [all from guns of at least 5.9-inch calibre, far outweighing the destroyer's armament in metal] before they gave us up as done for. . . . Aft we had been hit by only three shells, and only a few of the gun crews were wounded, but when the steam cleared away we found that the majority of the men stationed amidships were killed or wounded, including those ratings who had come up from the engine-rooms or stokeholds, while forward the ship was on fire, with flames coming out of the starboard coal bunkers, and the bridge alight and an absolute wreck.

Tipperary sank, after wallowing two hours awash in a fortunately calm sea, with the loss of 185 men. She was choked with wounded, most of whom quickly drowned. Many of the unwounded survivors drowned also, and others succumbed to exposure as they clung to wreckage or the single raft which was got away from the wreck. 'Of the original 32 men who had been on the raft,' an officer recorded, '2 had died and dropped off during the night, and 4 were found to be dead when hauled aboard the *Sparrowhawk*. Soon after we arrived on board, the bows of the *Sparrowhawk* broke off and floated away, but eventually a destroyer-leader – the *Marksman* – appeared, and after trying to tow the *Sparrowhawk* and finding it impossible, took the crew and ourselves aboard her, and sank what was left of the *Sparrowhawk*. We returned in the *Marksman* to Scapa Flow.'

Ardent, a sister destroyer to *Sparrowhawk*, underwent an even more terrible ordeal after being hit by 5.9-inch shells from the German battleships – chiefly *Westfalen* – in the night action. The captain wrote:

I became aware that the *Ardent* was taking on a division of German battleships. However, we opened fire and ran on at full speed. The next moments were perhaps the most thrilling that anyone could experience. Our guns were useless against such big adversaries; our torpedoes were fired; we could do no more but wait in the full glare of blinding searchlights for the shells that could not fail to hit us soon at such close range. There was perfect silence on the bridge and not a word spoken. At last it came and as the first salvo hit I heard a seaman ejaculate almost under his breath, 'Oh-ooh', as one does to a bursting rocket.

In a few minutes *Ardent* was devastated.

All the boats were in pieces. The funnels looked more like nutmeg graters. The rafts were blown to bits, and in the ship's side and decks were holes innumerable. In the very still atmosphere the smoke and steam poured out from the holes ... perfectly straight up into the air. Several of my best men came up and tried to console me, and all were delighted that we had at length been in action and done our duty. But many were already killed and lay around their guns and places of duty. Most of the engine-room and stokehold brigade must have been killed outright.

Ardent was illuminated and hit by four or five more salvoes shortly afterwards (the time was shortly before midnight), gave several lurches and then went down bows first. 'As the smoke and steam cleared', the captain recalled, 'I could see many heads in the water – about forty or fifty I should think. There was no support beyond lifebelts. ... I spoke to many men and saw most of them die one by one. Not a man of them showed any fear of death, and there was not a murmur, complaint or cry for help from a single soul. ... None of the men appeared to suffer at all; they just seemed to lie back in the water and go to sleep.' *Ardent*'s captain, one of the only two survivors of a tragedy which killed 78 of her crew, may have cast an over-heroic glow across the behaviour of his drowning shipmates in their last moments. The captain of a British destroyer sunk at night off the Normandy beaches in similar circumstances in June 1944 is tormented to this day by the memory of eighteen-year-old sailors calling piteously for their mothers as the sea engulfed them in the darkness.

THE AFTERMATH

By 6.30 am on 1 June most of the High Seas Fleet had reached the safety of the Jade estuary; the last casualty was the battleship *Ostfriesland*, which struck a mine laid by HMS *Abdiel* at 5.30 am but managed nevertheless to limp home. The Battlecruiser and Grand Fleets, with their accompanying shoals of destroyers and cruisers, had returned to

Scapa Flow and Rosyth by 2 June. At 9.45 that evening Jellicoe reported to the Admiralty that his warships were ready to steam at four hours' notice.

That signal writes the strategic verdict on Jutland. Britain's navy remained fit for renewed action, however soon it should come. Germany's did not. The Kaiser, who insisted on christening Jutland 'the North Sea Battle of 1 June', in echo of Howe's immortal 'Glorious First of June', exulted that 'the magic of Trafalgar has been broken', distributed Iron Crosses wholesale to the crews of the High Seas Fleet when he visited it on 5 June and kissed many of the captains. He promoted Scheer full admiral and invested him with the *Pour le mérite*, Germany's highest military honour. Scheer himself, however, was much less convinced of his 'victory'. Shortly after the battle, reflecting on its conduct to fellow admirals, he conceded that 'I came to the thing as the virgin did when she had a baby', and, in his official report on Jutland to the Kaiser of 4 July, he warned that 'even the most successful outcome of a fleet action', which he implicitly conceded Jutland had not yielded, 'will not force England to make peace'.

Germany could publicly celebrate Jutland because the raw 'exchange ratio' was in its favour. The High Seas Fleet had lost only one dreadnought, *Lützow*; the other ship casualties were either pre-dreadnoughts like *Pommern* or secondary units like the four light cruisers and five torpedo-boats. The Royal Navy, by contrast, had lost not only a considerable number of secondary units – three armoured cruisers and eight destroyers – but three dreadnoughts.

Three to one, in crude terms, could make Jutland look like a German victory; but calculated in refined rather than crude terms the 'exchange ratio' was very much more in Britain's favour. Three of her fast battleships, *Warspite*, *Barham* and *Malaya*, had suffered damage requiring dockyard attention, but the battleship fleet itself was almost unscathed; and, despite losses, the Battlecruiser Fleet on 1 June still outnumbered the German 1st Scouting Group, which, moreover, was crippled by damage. The German dreadnought battleships had also suffered grievously. *König*, *Markgraf* and *Grosser Kurfürst* all needed major refits when they returned to port and the German battle line could not have met the British at four weeks', let alone four hours' notice, except at risk of outright defeat.

The human cost, however, had fallen far more heavily on the British. True, her long tradition of 'following the sea' and her large seafaring population made her losses easier to replace; but the truth was that over 6000 British officers and sailors had gone down with their ships or been killed on their decks while the Germans had lost only a few more than 2500.

The casualties of ironclad compared with those of wooden-wall warfare were gruesome. The solid shot exchanged by Nelson's and Villeneuve's ships dismembered or decapitated, and tossed showers of wooden splinters between and across decks. However, if the missiles did not kill outright, their victims retained a chance of clean and quick recovery, even under the hands of surgeons whose only tools were the probe and the knife. The casualties at Jutland suffered wounds almost unknown to an earlier generation of naval surgeons; metal fragmentation wounds, scouring trauma by shell splinter which carved strips of flesh from the body and, most painful and hardest of all to treat, flash and burn effects and flaying by live steam. An officer in *Tipperary* described coming across a sailor 'with a large portion of his thigh removed', probably the result of scouring by a shell splinter. ' "What can I do with this, sir?" asked the torpedo gunner who was attempting first aid. . . . I merely covered the wound with a large piece of cotton wool and put a blanket over him. "Feels a lot better already," said the wounded man.' He was among the majority who drowned when *Tipperary* foundered two hours later.

The wounded who managed to receive some sort of care did not find great comfort. The medical officer of the battlecruiser *Princess Royal* described a surgical centre in which wounded men were wounded again by incoming German shells ('next day about 3 lbs weight of shell fragments . . were swept up from the deck') and where fumes from explosions elsewhere in the ship, sinking through the internal spaces because heavier than air, forced staff and patients to don respirators:

Casualties began to arrive, amongst them a gun-layer from the after turret, which had been put out of action by a direct hit. He . . . had a foot nearly blown away. . . . This gun-layer had developed German measles about two days previously, and should by rights have been landed, but owing to the mildness of his complaint, and because he was an important rating, he had been isolated on board and permitted to come to sea. Later on I amputated his leg. . . . I proceeded to operate on a . . . Marine who had been brought down bleeding seriously from a punctured wound of the face. . . . We had hardly started operating before rapid firing developed, and the tray with all my instruments was deposited on the deck . . . [but] proceeded to operate on the gun-layer. The light was most trying [gunfire had reduced them to dependence on oil-lamps], the securing of arteries during the operation being particularly difficult. . . . The dressing of large numbers of burns, some very extensive ones, now fully occupied the time of the whole staff. . . . Most of the wounded, who numbered exactly 100, were seriously burned.

Aboard the cruiser *Southampton*, a smaller ship, the doctors worked under even more makeshift conditions. One of her lieutenants wrote.

The operating room was the stokers' bathroom . . . about 8 feet high, 12 feet broad and 12 feet long. The centre of the room was occupied by a light portable operating table. A row of wash basins ran down one side and the steel walls streamed with sweat. . . . Stepping carefully between rows of shapes who were lying in lines down each side of the passage-way, I put my head inside the narrow doorway. Bare-armed the fleet surgeon and a young doctor were working with desperate but methodical haste. They were just taking a man's leg off above the knee.... I went aft again and down to the ward-room. The mess presented an extraordinary appearance. As it was the largest room in the ship we placed in it all the seriously wounded [*Southampton* had suffered 40 killed and 40–50 wounded]. The long table was covered with men, all lying very still and silently white.

As I came in [the doctor] signalled to the sick-berth steward to remove one man over whom he had been bending. Four stokers, still grimy from the stockhold, lifted the body and carried it out. Two men were on top of the sideboard, others were in arm-chairs. A hole in the side admitted water to the ward-room, which splashed about as the ship gently rolled. In the ankle-deep flood, blood-stained bandages and countless pieces of the small debris of war floated to and fro... the most dreadful cases were the 'burns' – but this subject cannot be written about.

Both fleets, as they made their way back to harbour from their inconclusive North Sea encounter, were encumbered below decks with 'dreadful cases... that cannot be written about'. The first – it was to be also the last – great clash of dreadnoughts had inflicted appalling human damage. The toll of casualties is not to be compared with the blood-lettings of the Western Front. Exactly one calendar month after Jutland, the British Expeditionary Force was to attack the German trench line on the Somme and suffer 20,000 killed in a single day of action. There had been such massacres earlier and others would follow before the exhaustion of the combatant armies would bring the agony of trench warfare to an end. Set against the 5 million deaths in action suffered during the First World War by the British, French and German armies alone, Jutland is small beer. As a proportion of crew present, some 110,000 in all, the total of fatal casualties, approaching 9000, is high, but must be set against the consideration that the event was unique. The earlier actions – Heligoland Bight and Dogger Bank – had not been costly in life and there were to be no major fleet actions after 31 May 1916.

As a naval battle, however, Jutland ranks among the costliest ever fought. Not until the great Japanese–American clashes of the Second World War in the Pacific would action at sea bring death to so many sailors. There is another dimension to the engagement. It called into question the chief assumptions on which the great ironclad fleets, of which the dreadnoughts were the ultimate embodiment, had been built: that naval supremacy was the direct function of the quality and number of the ship-type which naval thinking deemed dominant at any one time. Those assumptions held good only if that ship-type's dominance was firmly assured, and not threatened by emergent and alternative technology.

Ernle Chatfield, Admiral Beatty's staff commander in the Battle-cruiser Fleet, observed in retrospect:

What would happen [in Nelson's time] when two ships met and engaged was, as far as material was concerned, known within definite limits from handed-down experience and from a hundred sea-fights. [Nelson] knew exactly the risks he ran and accurately allowed for them. He had clear knowledge, from long-considered fighting experiences, how long his ships could endure the temporary gunnery disadvantage necessary in order to gain the dominant tactical position he aimed at for a great victory. . . . We had to buy that experience, for our weapons were untried. The risks could not be measured without that experience. . . . Dreadnoughts had never engaged, modern massed destroyer attack had never taken place.

The passing of the wooden walls and coming of the iron, steam-driven warship had wrenched naval strategy from its foundations. For 200 years admirals had manipulated a naval system in which the fighting qualities of their ships and the rare 'cash transaction' of battle – Clausewitz's term – had been but two among the factors by which the balance of seapower was struck. There were many others: the possession of overseas bases at strategic points, the availability of trained seamen, the distribution of ports adaptable to naval operations, the inter-operability of land with sea forces; and, beside these, the will and capacity of a government to maximise its material advantages for military purpose in great waters.

The British had proved supremely successful at the adjustment of means to ends in the pursuit of national power through the maintenance of a wooden-wall navy. However, the supersession of wood by iron and of sail by steam in the middle of the nineteenth century had consigned the Royal Navy to the working-out of an invisible crisis which, though it would take decades to emerge fully, threatened to undermine all the assumptions on which wooden-wall supremacy had been established. Ironclad navies, vulnerable to defeat 'in an afternoon', as Winston Churchill percipiently put it, were fragile instruments of national supremacy. They were expressions not of the strength of a whole national system – social, financial and industrial –but of no more than a single one of its technological aspects. Germany's naval technology was proved by Jutland to be superior to Britain's. Her ships were stronger, her guns more accurate, her ordnance more destructive. German shells had usually penetrated British armour when they struck; the reverse had not been the case. Because the German navy took second place in national life to the German army, on which the bulk of the state's wealth was spent, Germany's admirals could not transform technological into strategic advantage over their British counterparts; but, because Britain's admirals were themselves the servants of a naval technology supported by a financial and industrial power which had, since the 1870s, been in relative and irreversible decline, their strategic posture was also defective. The Grand Fleet, and its battlecruiser appendix, may have appeared in the years between 1914 to 1916 to be the largest embodiment of naval strength the world had ever seen, as in weight of firepower it unquestionably was. However, it was a pyramid of naval power trembling on its apex, at risk from overtoppling by any new technological development that threatened its integrity. The dreadnought fleet was ultimately a thing of steel – steel ships, steel guns, steel shells. Yet not only was Britain by 1914 third among the world's steelmakers, exceeded in output by both the United States and Germany; steel was a material whose domination of technology had itself passed its apogee. The thrust of industrial innovation had moved to light metals and to alloys, of which the most dramatic expression would be the aeroplane. Aircraft, first committed to warfare in 1912 (by the Italians in Libya), actually made an offstage intervention at Jutland, through the inclusion of the seaplane carrier *Engadine* in the Grand Fleet's order of battle. Her complement of aircraft took no part in the fighting; but their presence was a presentiment not only of the shape of things to come but of the mainstream of development which naval warfare would follow in the post-dreadnought years.

3

MIDWAY

THE COMING OF THE AIRCRAFT CARRIER

The presence of the seaplane carrier *Engadine* with the Grand Fleet at Jutland was, as a portent, an event almost as significant as the battle itself. Alfred Tennyson had written seventy years before:

> For I glimpsed into the future, far as human eye could see,
> Saw the vision of the world and all the wonder that could be . . .
> Heard the heavens fill with shouting, and there raised a ghastly dew
> From the nations' airy navies grappling in the central blue.

The idea of the aeroplane had captured the human imagination long before such a machine approached practicality; and the idea had been imaginatively invested with military purpose almost from the outset. Why should it have been otherwise? The aircraft was a thing of magic, a means of transforming man into bird. While some birds are objects of beauty and sources of pleasure, valued for their plumage and their song, others have always been feared as omens of evil or envied as symbols of power. The taming of birds of prey – kestrels, harriers, even eagles – adumbrated the harnessing of human powers of flight to warfare. Almost as soon as mechanical flight became practicable – for all that Orville and Wilbur Wright clung idealistically to their belief in the aeroplane they had invented as a means of diminishing distance and therefore differences between the families of mankind – its military applications were not merely recognised but rapidly implemented. As early as 1912 the Italians had employed aircraft to bomb Ottoman forces in Libya. Even earlier, in November 1910, an aeroplane had been successfully launched from the bows of an American warship, USS *Birmingham*, as an experiment in the deployment of man's newest medium of movement as an instrument of warfare.

The naval, like the military, aeroplane was originally conceived to be a means of information-gathering rather than of offence, and at the outset there was no agreement as to whether the lighter- or heavier-than-air machine would make the more practicable observation platform. Germany, pioneer of the advanced airship, put its trust in zeppelins, which accompanied the High Seas Fleet to the battles both of the Heligoland Bight in 1904 and of the Dogger Bank in 1915. The British, whose airship experiments proved unsuccessful (perhaps because they lacked an enthusiast for airships as single-minded as Germany's Count Zeppelin), turned necessarily to the heavier-than-air craft, and began to adapt warships as seaplane carriers. The first, a pre-war experiment, was HMS *Hermes*, an old cruiser. At the outbreak of war a merchantman, *Ark Royal*, was converted to the role and then four passenger liners were commandeered, *Empress, Riviera, Campania* and *Engadine*. The last two were with the Grand Fleet in May 1916 and *Engadine* accompanied it to Jutland.

One of *Engadine*'s seaplanes was the first unit of the fleet to sight the Germans; but her report was delayed and did not materially affect the development of the fighting. That was in the pattern of aerial reconnaissance throughout the dreadnought war. Expectations of the usefulness of the aircraft as 'eyes of the fleet' were consistently disappointed, but aircraft enthusiasts had predicated an offensive rather than a merely reconnoitring role for the naval air arm almost as soon as it was conceived. As early as 1913 a British naval officer, Captain Murray Sueter, had foreseen that aircraft could be adapted to carry torpedoes, while, the year before, trials had been conducted by the fledgling Royal Naval Air Service in dropping bombs at sea.

With the marriage of the bomb and the torpedo to a naval aircraft, its emergence as a potent weapon of offence was almost realised. All that was wanted to complete it was the development of a ship from which aircraft could operate safely and regularly in consort with the battle fleet. Seaplane carriers, such as *Engadine*, were not the answer. Launching and recovery required the ship to stop, hoist out the aircraft by crane for take-off, then stop again to hoist it on board when its mission was completed. What was needed was a floating deck from which aircraft could rise and to which they could return as from and to an airfield on land.

Taking off was a great deal easier to arrange than landing. Because a ship's speed through the water, into the wind, actually facilitated an aircraft's rising, *Campania, Engadine* and a third seaplane carrier, *Manxman*, were soon furnished with flight decks which allowed a fighter to take off for a one-way mission. In 1917 the battlecruiser *Furious* – an extreme example of the type, which the experience of Jutland had warned was too fragile for fleet operations – had been given a similar deck, and on 2 August 1917 an intrepid pilot demonstrated that it was also possible to land by side-slipping round the funnel when the ship was steaming upwind at its full speed of 32 knots. (Because aircraft must approach the mother ship from the stern, the traditional centre-line funnel was to remain a major obstruction until, in purpose-built aircraft carriers, the funnel was shifted to the ship's side.)

However, one last stage of adaptation now awaited the inauguration of true flight to and from a ship under way at sea: the construction of an unobstructed flight deck. In 1917 the rebuilding of HMS *Argus*, a seaplane carrier, with such a deck was undertaken. In October 1918, two weeks before the armistice that ended the First World War, she rejoined the fleet in her new guise. Her flight deck, 68 feet wide and 565 long, allowed her complement of Sopwith Camel fighters and Sopwith Cuckoo torpedo aircraft, stored during passage in a hangar below, to take off and land while *Argus* steamed. The age of the aircraft carrier had begun.

Yet there was, at the outset, no consensus among admirals as to what role the aircraft carrier should fulfil. In 1919 Admiral Sir Charles Madden, commanding the British Atlantic Fleet, proposed that three types of aircraft carrier should be built: 'air reconnaissance ships', which were to be complementary to cruisers (themselves of doubtful future value); 'divisional aircraft carriers', which were to observe and correct fall of shot for the dreadnoughts; and 'fleet aircraft carriers', equipped to attack the enemy's battle fleet independently. Only the last can with hindsight be regarded as true aircraft carrier types. The Royal Navy, instinctively committed to the future of the dreadnought, could not even accept that money should be found from its budget to build 'fleet aircraft carriers' from the keel up; the first of the type that it accepted into its order of battle were redundant dreadnoughts rebuilt with flush decks.

Experiments in using aircraft to bomb warships (in the United States German prize ships and in Britain a redundant dreadnought were the chosen targets) nevertheless demonstrated that battleships could be sunk by aircraft in controlled conditions and the experiments foreshadowed their destruction in fleet operations. As a result, carriers were included among the categories of ships whose size and number were limited by the Washington Naval Treaty of 1921. Britain and the United States agreed to be limited to 135,000 tons of carrier tonnage, Japan to 81,000 tons, France and Italy to 60,000 tons; no carrier should exceed 29,000-tons displacement, with a special exception of the units of 33,000 tons to allow for ships building or planned.

The Washington Naval Treaty, however, though hailed as inaugurating an idealistic new era of arms reduction by combatants sickened by war, was in fact a bipartisan device engineered by Britain and the United States to halt a naval race which had been gathering speed between themselves. It was imposed willy-nilly on the other signatories and accepted with bitter reluctance by Japan. The inclusion of aircraft carriers in the provisions was, moreover, dictated not by objective fear of the threat they levelled against battlefleets themselves but by the anxiety that warships might be launched in the guise of aircraft carriers and converted to battleships at a later date – an understandable anxiety, since the best existing aircraft carriers, HMS *Furious* and the second *Hermes*, had begun life as traditional ships of the line.

Salthorse admirals at the head of navies were misinterpreting the future, however, if they believed that the dreadnought could live for ever. Their foreign counterparts might share their emotional commitment to the clash of great guns as the means by which command of the sea would be disputed and exercised in future decades. At a level below the supreme command, however, a generation of new naval leaders, trained in the operation of aircraft from flight decks and persuaded of the revolutionary nature of naval airpower, was emerging. For all the belief of their seniors in the status of aircraft as scouts for the battle fleet, they were convinced that the aircraft carrier was a decisive weapon of war at sea and they would work ceaselessly to achieve recognition of its true status.

Some of these officers were British. Their energies were to be diverted for much of the inter-war years by an internecine dispute with the Royal Air Force over the command of aircraft allocated to the Navy. That was a complication peculiar to Britain. Peculiar to the Royal Navy also was the environment in which its aircraft carriers would work, the narrow seas around Britain's coasts and the confined waters of the Mediterranean, as well as the oceanic spaces. Narrow seas implied a threat from land-based bombers and, with that in mind, the new generation of purpose-built carriers, laid down from 1936 onwards, were given armoured flight decks, as well as heavy anti-aircraft armament. In compensation, their complements of embarked aircraft had to be kept small, as low as thirty; but the high command of the navy justified this restriction on their capabilities by the revealing remark, made by the First Sea Lord at the height of the navy's battle with the Royal Air Force, that aircraft were 'second only in importance to naval gunnery'.

The United States Navy, by contrast, committed itself to a much ampler view of the role of naval aviation. Oceanic in its outlook, with a belief in its mission to exercise command of the sea over not only the Atlantic but also the Pacific, in which it had acquired extensive possessions during the nineteenth century – the Philippines, annexed as a protectorate from Spain in 1898, as well as Hawaii and the islands of Wake, Guam and Midway – it foresaw a pattern of naval operations in which any clash of dreadnoughts would be preceded by a battle for command of the air by its fleet's aircraft. As a result it committed itself to the construction of very large carriers embarking as many as a hundred aircraft. Although its first carrier, USS *Langley*, was, like its original British counterparts, a converted merchant ship, it had by 1927 commissioned two enormous ships, USS *Lexington* and *Saratoga*, with 800-foot flight decks and complements of seventy aircraft each. In their time they were the longest warships in the world, true instruments of independent naval airpower and mothers to naval aircraft almost equal in performance to their land-based equivalents. Outstanding among them was the Curtiss F8C Helldiver, capable of carrying a ship-destroying 500 lb bomb to a range of 720 miles.

The third navy to embrace the aircraft carrier was the Japanese. By 1921 it had three carriers in service, the same number as the United States Navy, and was committed to build more. Like the British and Americans, the Japanese began by converting other types to an air role – *Akagi* and *Kaga* were respectively a former battlecruiser and battleship – but in 1933 they had launched a fourth, *Ryujo*, and in 1936–7 they launched two more, the *Hiryu* and *Soryu*. At the same time they were building four seaplane carriers which lay outside the provisions of the Washington Naval Treaty and would later be converted to become light aircraft carriers. By these varied means, the Imperial Japanese Navy would, at the outbreak of the Second World War, deploy ten carriers, more than any competitor, and would also have embarked the largest naval air force, totalling 500 aircraft. Since 1938, moreover, all the carriers had been grouped in a single striking force, the First Air Fleet, dedicated to independent air operations, an organisation of resources which made the Imperial Japanese Navy potentially the most menacing concentration of naval airpower in the world. Finally, Japanese naval aircraft were markedly advanced in design. The Type 97 (Kate) and Type 99 (Val) torpedo- and dive-bombers, though slower than their American counterparts, had a longer range and were powerful weight-carriers; and in the prototype Zero fighter they had an air-combat weapon without peer among carrier-launched aircraft in any navy.

Carrier flight was still an operation conducted at the extreme limits of practicability. Steam catapults and angled decks lay far in the future. Aircraft were launched under their own power from as far aft as aircraft parking allowed; departure from the flight deck usually entailed a sickening lurch towards the sea as the aircraft cleared the flight deck's end, and crashes under the bows, almost inevitably fatal, were a perpetual hazard of take-off. Safe return to the flight deck depended on picking up one of a succession of arrester-wires stretched across the ship's beam, and missing resulted either in the returning aircraft's falling over the bows, as in a bad take-off, or in its crashing into aircraft already landed but not yet 'struck below'.

Flying skill was therefore at a premium. So too was navigational sense. Without radar, aircrew had to plot their course away from and back to the mother ship with extreme care. The multi-seat torpedo- and dive-bombers of two or three hours' endurance, and with a spare man aboard to calculate bearings and mark charts, had a reasonable chance of plotting a rendezvous. The pilots of single-seat fighters, of short endurance and committed to violent manoeuvre in flight, all too easily lost track of their positions, failed to rediscover the position of the mother ship, which in the nature of naval warfare altered minute by minute, and ran out of fuel on the homeward flight. Carrier flying attracted the hardiest souls among the brotherhood of the air; but it also killed many of the best, however advanced their airmanship.

The majesty of carrier fleets in action was, however, compensation to their air group crews for all the risks they ran. As early as 1929, the USS *Saratoga* demonstrated that a devastation of the locks and air bases of the Panama Canal was theoretically possible by aircraft-carrier attack. And in 1932 *Saratoga* and *Lexington*, in a pre-dawn simulated raid on Pearl Harbor with 152 aircraft, caught the Pacific Fleet base totally by surprise and overwhelmed its defences. Traditionalists in the United States Navy might remain committed to their belief in the future of naval warfare as a contest between dreadnoughts, which it, the British, Germans, Italians, Japanese and even French continued to build as fast as funds allowed; but the Buffalo, Vindicator and Devastator pilots who manned *Lexington, Saratoga, Ranger* and their sister ships as the Second World War approached had a different vision. They foresaw the 'nations' airy navies grappling in the central blue' and were convinced that the future of power at sea would turn on the outcome. Against which opponent they would grapple was, at the end of the 1930s, a development still hidden from them. Britain, though a naval rival, was a friendly state with which war was unthinkable. France and Italy were secondary powers whose interests did not conflict with those of the United States. Germany, clearly bent on aggression, had ambitions in regions too distant from the western hemisphere to impinge on its security. The obvious enemy was Japan. It had already embarked since 1937 on its aggression against China, a country with which the United States had established a special political, commercial and emotional relationship in the nineteenth century. Its national policy was relentlessly expansionist. It clearly nurtured the ambition, rampant for all that it was undeclared, to dominate the western Pacific and its Asian littoral. And it was, after Britain and the United States, the third largest naval power in the world.

THE TWO NAVIES

Japan had risen to naval power by a deliberate act of national will. The circumstances of America's struggle for national independence had caused the embryo United States to build the beginnings of a fleet. Japan had created a navy from nothing out of the conviction that only thus could it outface the foreigners who, in the middle of the nineteenth century, had intruded upon its self-imposed, long-established isolation and thereby threatened its peculiar social order with disruption. Those foreigners were American and they had come in warships, the 'black fleet' which Commodore Matthew Perry brought to the port of Yedo in 1853. Two of his fleet were steamships, vessels totally strange to the Japanese but self-evidently too powerful for any ship at the disposal of the imperial shogunate to challenge.

The Japanese empire might, as the Chinese empire did, have reacted to the phenomenon of Western technological superiority by denying its relevance to their way of life and seeking emotional reassurance in increased introversion. It did no such thing. In the immediate aftermath of Perry's departure, Abe Masahiro, chief counsellor to the emperor and effective ruler of the state, wrote:

> Everyone has pointed out that we are without a navy and that our coasts are undefended. Meanwhile the Americans will be here again next year. Our policy shall be to evade any answer to their request [to open the country to foreign trade] while at the same time maintaining a peaceful demeanour. It may be, however, that they will have recourse to violence. For that contingency we must be prepared unless the country suffer disgrace. Therefore every possible effort will be made to prepare the country for defence.

Mashiro's immediate response was to procure a steamship from the Dutch, with whom the Japanese had maintained tenuous external relations ever since the closing of the country to the West in the seventeenth century. However, this was an interim expedient. If Japan were not to 'suffer disgrace' it would clearly have to acquire the means of meeting foreign navies on equal terms. That meant building a fleet of its own, initially by buying warships from abroad, but in the long term by learning to build its own. In 1868, at the conclusion of a bitter internal struggle between reactionaries and modernisers, the Emperor Meiji proclaimed the policy by which his medieval kingdom would meet the West on equal terms. 'Knowledge shall be sought,' he affirmed, in what would become known as the Charter Oath, 'from all over the world and thus shall be strengthened the foundation of the imperial polity.'

At the time of the Emperor Meiji's 'restoration', that reassertion of the emperor's powers over those of the feudal aristocracy which was the key event in the empire's modernisation, Japan looked to Great Britain (then the world's leading naval power) for the naval 'knowledge' that it needed to put it on a footing of parity with Western fleets. British naval officers were brought to Japan to train the empire's future naval officers. British-built ships were initially bought to equip the navy, denominated a department of state in 1872. From the outset, moreover, the Japanese laid out money for the best. The cruisers *Naniwa* and *Takachiho*, acquired in 1885, were at their launching the largest ships of their type in the world and among the most heavily armed, with two 10.2-inch Krupp guns (just as the Japanese quickly recognised where the best hulls were to be purchased, they had also identified which manufacturer was the leader in artillery design). In 1891 a sister ship to these two cruisers, *Hashidato*, was launched from a Japanese yard.

That initiative was not to end Japanese dependence on foreign building. Capital ships would remain beyond the empire's construction capabilities for another twenty years, until its first dreadnoughts, *Kawachi* and *Settsu*, were laid down at Kure and Yokosuka in 1911–12. It would still look to Britain for the supply of its first example of the novel battlecruiser type, quintessentially a British conception, even while planning to build dreadnoughts of its own. *Kongo*, the navy's original battlecruiser, was bought from the British yard at Barrow in 1910.

By that date, however, the Imperial Japanese Navy had already established its title to stand among the leading fleets of the world. Its victory over the backward and inept Chinese navy in 1894 had attracted little international attention. Its challenging of the Russian navy in 1904 created a world sensation. In that year Japan provoked a war with the tsarist government over the issue of which state should exercise control in the interposed borderlands of Korea and Manchuria. The Japanese navy disposed of the tsar's Far Eastern Fleet in short order at the outset of the war. The tsar's government, heavily committed to a war on land at the end of the Trans-Siberian railway, refused to accept the decision at sea, collected another fleet in European waters and dispatched it to the Far East. Japan's admirals bided their time and laid plans. They knew that the Russian ships must eventually trespass into their operational area and, when they did so by seeking to run the passage of the Straits of Tsushima on 27 May 1905, the Japanese fleet was ready. In the course of a few hours' fighting the Russians were overwhelmed. Nineteen of their thirty-eight ships were sunk; seven were captured, six interned and two scuttled. Only four escaped, to take the humiliating news of the greatest naval disaster since Trafalgar to home ports.

Tsushima, then, established Japan as one of the world's foremost naval powers. It was not the equal of Britain, its ally since 1902, nor even of Germany, but it was the master of Russia, perhaps the equal of Italy and France – itself a power with important Far Eastern interests – and certainly a competitor with the United States, which had only just begun to reach for the place in the maritime firmament that its wealth and location astride two oceans allotted it by right.

From 1905 onwards Japan's actual and potential naval power grew year by year. Throwing in its lot with France and Britain in 1914, it briskly took possession of Germany's Far Eastern possessions both in mainland China and in the Pacific islands, including the Marshall, Carolina and Mariana groups. These archipelagos, insignificant in physical size and economic worth, were of the highest strategic value, lying as they do between Hawaii to the east and the Philippines and China to the west. Their possession endowed Japan at least with a barrier against American naval advances into the far Pacific, potentially with a forward striking position from which the Philippines, the Dutch East Indies, perhaps even the British and French possessions in mainland Asia, including Australia, and ultimately the American mid-ocean bastion of Hawaii, could be brought under threat.

By 1931, when dissident Japanese officers, stationed in Manchuria to guard its extraterritorial railway system, took possession of the province – China's most valuable industrial region – by force, Japan was established as a major mainland Asian power. Six years later that power was enormously enhanced by its invasion of China proper, via the Yangtse and Yellow river valleys, which gave it possession of most of the productive areas of the historic Chinese empire. The mainland war against a weak and divided Chinese army left over an appreciable surplus – at least twelve army and marine divisions – for amphibious operations in oceanic waters. The 'China incident', as the Tokyo government insisted on designating the invasion, diminished the strength of the Combined Fleet scarcely at all. At the outbreak of war between the Western allies and Germany, of which Japan had been an ally itself since 1936, the Japanese fleet comprised ten battleships and ten carriers, forty submarines, some of very great size, a large fleet of modern cruisers and destroyers and some 1500 naval aircraft, of which 500 were carrier-embarked. Japanese naval ordnance was of the highest quality; its torpedoes in particular were the best of any navy's. Its sailors, though conscripts, were as hardened to operational ordeals as the soldiers who had astounded Western observers by their fortitude in the empire's first external war in Manchuria in 1904–5. The Japanese fleet training routine gave them little comfort or rest. An Imperial Navy document of 1937 stated:

In recent years the activities of the fleet have been as follows. Leaving home ports the latter part of January and carrying out intensive training for the greater part of the year in the stormy Pacific or in out-of-the-way gulfs where human habitations are extremely scarce, with hardly a day of rest . . . sometimes more than a month of operating . . . there are no Saturdays or Sundays, especially under way, when one drill follows another – literally a period of no rest and no sleep. This is because if we are not under way we cannot carry out actual battle training, and so with a tenacious and tireless spirit we are striving to reach a superhuman degree of skill and perfect fighting efficiency.

Self-adulatory though this account is, it is generally accurate. In the years before the outbreak of the Pacific War the Imperial Japanese Navy was not only formidable in its material capabilities but also more fiercely hardened to 'following the sea' than any of its competitors. Of no group of Japanese sailors was this more true than its regular officers. Their upbringing and subsequent way of life were more rigorous than those of naval officers anywhere in the world. The British Royal Navy, which recruited naval cadets at the age of thirteen and had sent some fifteen-year-olds to die at Dogger Bank, set an example of professional dedication that was hard to match. The regime at Etajima, the Japanese naval academy, exceeded that of Dartmouth in severity. Founded in 1888 under British supervision, Etajima subjected its entrants, each one selected from as many as eighty applicants, to four years of unremitting academic and physical training. The working day lasted sixteen hours, discipline was enforced by slaps and blows, and the inexpungable shame of expulsion, entailing family disgrace, was held over the head of the cadet throughout his course.

British officers, even with the example of Dartmouth's insularity before them, thought Etajima's products blinkered and narrow-minded, since their main characteristics comprised unswerving loyalty to the emperor and readiness to die in battle. Their seamanship, however, was outstanding, and in some of them Etajima did not wholly extinguish powers of independent thought. Togo, the 'Japanese Nelson' and victor of Tsushima, had entered service before the academy was established and had received his advanced training in Britain. Yamamoto, the outstanding Japanese admiral of the Second World War, had survived his Etajima years and yet retained his independence.

Yamamoto Isoruko, born in 1884, was present as an ensign aboard the cruiser *Nisshin* at the battle of Tsushima, where he had been knocked unconscious by a shell burst and lost two fingers. 'However, when at 2 am the victory was announced,' he recalled, 'even the wounded cheered.' In 1917 he had been sent to Harvard as a language officer, the beginning of his long association with the United States, and on his return in 1921 was appointed to the naval aviation school. Up until then he had been a gunnery specialist. Now on his own initiative he learned to fly and became a believer in airpower as the future medium of dominance at sea. Between 1923 and 1927 he was in the United States again, first as a liaison officer, then as naval attaché in Washington. In 1930 he attended the London Naval Conference at which Japan negotiated an important alleviation of the restriction on ship numbers imposed at Washington in 1921. He was appointed head of the First Air Fleet in 1934 and served again as an arms control negotiator at the London Naval Conference of 1936 when the Washington limitations were effectively brought to an end.

Yamamoto was a fervent Japanese patriot, but he saw the danger into which militarism was leading his country and constantly warned of the danger of challenging America for mastery of the Pacific. 'Anyone who has seen the automobile factories in Detroit and the oil-fields in Texas,' he said, 'knows that Japan lacks the power for a naval race with America.' As a result, and also because of his opposition to alignment with Germany, he attracted the hostility of the 'double patriots' (officers 'more royal than the king') in the lower ranks of the officer corps and for his own safety – since assassination was a favoured expression of 'double patriotism' in the late 1930s – was promoted commander-in-chief of the Combined Fleet in August 1939, a post which took him to sea and kept him beyond the reach of the long knives.

The direction of Japanese policy had been decisively altered in February 1936, when mutinous officers in Tokyo murdered the leading moderates in the imperial government and effectively conferred power on the army, itself under the leadership of generals committed to overseas expansion and to gambling with the risk of war with the Western powers. Konoye, the army's nominee to the succession as premier, was himself a moderate but soon lost control of events. In July 1937 fighting broke out between Japanese troops in northern China and the forces of Chiang Kai-shek, whose success in beginning to rescue his country from warlordism threatened Japanese dominance of the Asian mainland. In August the fighting swelled into a full-scale Japanese invasion and by December the great valley lands of the Yellow and Yangtse rivers had fallen under Japanese control. In the course of the army's advance it had outraged international opinion by its brutality, particularly in the 'rape of Nanking'; it had affronted America by sinking a US Navy gunboat; and it would shortly go to the brink of war with the Soviet Union by provoking a serious border incident in Manchuria.

Japan persisted in its reckless policy for two reasons. One was its association with the European Axis powers, Italy and Germany, whose equally reckless behaviour seemed not only to pay dividends but also to lend assistance and support to their Asian ally's disrespect for international propriety. The other was the relentless urge to Asian mastery fuelled by primal urges within Japan itself. Following the German triumph over France in the spring of 1940, the Vichy government was forced to concede rights of military garrison and transit in Indo-China to Japan. At the same time Britain agreed to interrupt for a period of six months its transport of military supplies to Chiang Kai-shek's armies in southern China across the Burma Road. Meanwhile the United States, in its guise as principal protector of the Chinese republic, sought to inhibit the swelling tide of Japanese expansion, by threatening to restrict her import first of oil, of which she had no domestic reserves, and then of ores and metals, in which she was also deficient.

At a Japanese army–navy conference in August 1941, Colonel Iwakuro Hideo warned of the disparities between Japan's war-making powers and America's. The relevant ratios of American to Japanese capabilities were, he stated: steel production, 20:1; coal, 10:1; aircraft, 5:1; labour, 5:1; shipping, 2:1; oil, 100:1. Overall, he estimated, the war potential of the United States was ten times greater than that of Japan.

No one was more aware of the disparity than Yamamoto, who knew the United States better than any other officer in his country and perhaps as well as any living Japanese. He shrank from war with the United States. At the same time, he could not resist the drive to war which possessed his brother officers. In the summer of 1941, the recently established Imperial General Staff, in which the army and navy combined to plan national strategy, considered four possible plans for the future. They were (1) to seize the Dutch East Indies (Indonesia), then the Philippines and Malaya; (2) to advance from the Philippines to the East Indies; (3) to seize Malaya, via Indo-China, in which Japan had established a military presence, then to capture the Philippines, thus delaying a confrontation with the United States; (4) to attack Malaya and the Philippines simultaneously, then strike into the East Indies. Yamamoto was alarmed by all these proposals, which he was convinced would entail war with the United States, whatever the time-tabling, and on unfavourable terms. 'If,' he had written earlier, 'in the face of such odds [as America offers] we decide to go to war – or rather are forced to do so by the trend of events – I can see little hope of success in any ordinary strategy.'

An extraordinary strategy, if his countrymen persisted down the path to war, might, on the other hand, avert immediate disaster. Such a strategy would be to catch the American Pacific Fleet off guard and destroy it in its base. Since April 1940 the fleet had been transferred, as a precautionary measure, from the American west coast to Hawaii. Hawaii, at mid-centre of the Pacific, lay 1600 miles from the Japanese home islands, a greater distance than any over which a major steam-driven fleet (the Tsushima campaign excepted) had operated before. Early in 1941 Yamamoto, taking up a study made in 1936 by the Naval War College, began to elaborate a plan for a separate attack on Pearl Harbor. At an early stage he turned for advice to Commander Genda Minoru, a 'Young Turk' of Japanese naval aviation. After six weeks' intensive work, Genda reported that the operation was feasible and planning moved to the advanced stage. Kusaka, chief of staff of the First Air Fleet, warned that the operation would be a gamble, but after a fleet critique in September 1941 Yamamoto told him: 'I have resolved to carry out the Pearl Harbor attack no matter what the cost.'

The plan entailed a long and indirect approach, beginning in the Kurile islands, off Siberia, and passing via the isolated island of Midway to reach to within 200 miles of Hawaii from the north. In October 1941 a passenger liner, *Taiyo Maru*, was sent to follow this route and reported it had seen no other ship while on passage. War games confirmed that an operation launched off such an approach might succeed and in October 1941 the chief of the navy, Admiral Nagano, gave consent for preparations to proceed.

The operation would commit six of Japan's ten carriers and 423 aircraft, including 270 bombers, to the attack. The rest of the fleet would simultaneously proceed to attack the Philippines and Malaya. At all target points the object would be to overwhelm the enemy by surprise. But the key to success everywhere was surprise at Pearl Harbor. Yamamoto, to avert objections that the American Pacific Fleet might not be found at home, fixed the attack day on a Sunday, when he knew it always returned to harbour for weekend leave. On 8 November he announced that Y-Day would be Sunday 7 December.

Two days later his chief of staff outlined to the flag-officers of the Combined Fleet the form and purpose of the operation would take:

> A gigantic fleet was massed at Pearl Harbor. This fleet will be utterly crushed at the outset with one blow at the very beginning of hostilities. . . . If these plans should at any stage fail, our navy will suffer the wretched fate of never being able to rise again. The success of our surprise attack on Pearl Harbor will prove to be the Waterloo of the war to follow. For this reason the Imperial Navy is massing the cream of its strength in ships and aircraft to assure success. It is clear that even if America's enormous heavy industry is immediately converted to the manufacture of ships, aircraft and other raw materials, it will take at least several months for her manpower to be mobilised against us. If we assure our strategic supremacy at the very outset . . . by attacking and seizing all key points at one blow while America is still unprepared, we can swing the scale of operations in our favour.

Yamamoto was less optimistic. Knowing the power of the United States as he did, he had already warned that his country's chosen strategy would allow him to 'run wild considerably for the first six months or a year, but I have utterly no confidence for the second and third years. The Tripartite Pact [with Germany and Italy] has been concluded and we cannot help it.' Even as the Hawaii, Philippines and Malay striking forces moved to their attack stations, he was possessed by fear of the 'Detroit automobile factories and Texas oil-fields' and what they meant for Japan's dangerously underdeveloped economy; but, above all, by the latent power of the United States Navy.

The United States, like Japan, was a country that had come late to rivalry with the established naval powers. In the War of Independence and the War of 1812 against Britain it had found the means to construct fleets of formidable frigates. It had also created an effective steam navy to fight the Confederacy in the Civil War and, for a time, had been in the forefront of the naval revolution in technology. However, after 1865 the United States Navy fell into the doldrums. It had no strategic role; in effect the Royal Navy assured the defence of the North American continent's coastline against the European powers, while the Latin American states offered their northern neighbour no strategic threat whatsoever. Consequently it lacked any tactical experience; with no one to fight, its ships fell into obsolescence and its officers stagnated. Alfred Thayer Mahan, who was to become the naval Clausewitz, left the sea to take up his position at the Naval War College in 1855 from the frigate *Wachusett*, whose most notable characteristic was a permanent list to starboard. Mahan was to prove himself an exception among American naval officers of his generation. *Wachusett* was no exception among the navy's ships, which, almost until the end of the nineteenth century, belonged with those of one, if not two, generations earlier among their counterpart fleets.

The United States Navy was not to acquire modern ironclads until the mid-1880s, by which date the condition of the fleet had become a disgrace, and it was not to begin building an ocean-going navy until the 1890s, an initiative then prompted by the theoretical navalist arguments of Mahan – whose international standing made him a prophet – and by America's assumption of the Panama Canal project. So covetous was it thought that European powers would become of the canal that arguments for a 'new navy' found ready support in Washington. The outcome was the fleet which allowed the United States to fight and defeat Spain in the Caribbean and Philippines in 1898–9, from which grew the 'Great White Fleet' that cruised the world in 1908–9. Thereafter the pace of American naval development accelerated. *South Carolina* and *Michigan*, the navy's first modern battleships, had actually anticipated the dreadnought design. By 1917, when the United States entered the First World War on the Allied side, its battle fleet included fourteen dreadnoughts, built or building, all of powerful armament, high speed and advanced design. *California* and *Tennessee* (all American battleships are named after states of the Union) were probably the most advanced of their type in any navy, heavily armoured, of 21-knot speed and carrying twelve 14-inch guns in triple turrets. The attachment of one squadron of America's magnificent new battle fleet to the Grand Fleet in 1917, with the implied threat that the whole might cross the Atlantic in emergency, was one further reason for Germany's not chancing a 'risk theory' battle in the North Sea after Jutland.

However, appetities grow with eating. Exhilarated by its emergence as the second naval power in the world, as it was by 1918, the United States Navy looked forward to becoming the first, a place which federal finance and national industry capacity would easily allow it to take. In May 1918 Admiral William Sims, American naval commander in Britain, proposed a policy of continued expansion: 'The Navy of the United States,' he wrote, 'shall be a self-contained organisation designed to exercise, in the Pacific, a commanding superiority of naval power, and in the Atlantic a defensive superiority of naval power against all potential enemies who may seek to expand their spheres of interest over, or to impose their sovereignty on any portion of the American continent, or Islands contiguous thereto, not now in their [possession], or who may unjustly interfere with our rights of trade expansion.' He calculated that such a policy required the addition of twenty-one battleships and ten cruisers to the fleet, and large numbers of 'fighting scouts', super-destroyers, and submarines.

The programme challenged the Royal Navy to a ship-construction race in which the enfeebled United Kingdom could not possibly hope to compete. An American navy of sixty-nine capital ships – for that was the figure to which the Sims plan was soon raised – would put the Royal Navy's battle fleet of forty-two capital ships at a disadvantage from which it could never recover. The Sims plan, moreover, was wholly in accord with the Naval Act of 1916 which President Woodrow Wilson had sent to Congress with the endorsement that 'no other navy in the world . . . has to cover so great an area . . . as the American navy . . . it ought, in my judgement, to be incomparably the most adequate navy in the world.'

What saved the Royal Navy, temporarily, from the implications of President Wilson's urge to 'adequacy' was his illness, fall from office and replacement by Warren Harding, who was committed to a reduction of international competition between the victors of the First World War and to isolationism in American foreign policy. The result was the Washington Naval Treaty of 1921, which unilaterally restricted America's industrial ability to outbuild Britain but used the military preponderance of the two great maritime powers to impose restrictions on the naval strength of Japan, France and Italy.

The results of the treaty were to hold American naval strength at a level with Britain's throughout the inter-war years. It established between them exact parity in capital ships and aircraft carriers, forced the scrapping of much obsolete and building tonnage and assured the artificial dominance of the British and United States navies over all others in the world.

The logic of the treaty was greatly enhanced by the world slump of 1929–30, which inaugurated policies of severe retrenchment in federal financing. Even had Washington wished to expand the United States Navy in the 1930s, it could not have afforded to do so. However, though the tide of economy bore heavily upon the United States Navy, it could not alter its professional conviction that the security of America rested upon its strength and proper deployment. That could only be against Japan. From 1922 onwards it was Navy Department policy to keep the bulk of the fleet in Pacific waters, with an advanced Asiatic Fleet of small ships based in China and the Battle Force in California, from which it cruised by an annual routine to the Panama Canal and to Hawaii.

The routine did not provide for the fleet to exercise west of the International Date Line, thereby depriving it of operational experience in the waters where it was most likely to deploy in the case of war with Japan, the eventuality recognised by its admirals as the only realistic possibility among the scenarios its planning staff considered. Since before the First World War the planners had annually renewed a series of so-called 'colour' plans, among which 'Orange' predicated the terms of a war with Japan. When, after the First World War, Japan acquired from Germany the Marianas, Marshalls and Carolinas, which together constituted a deep strategic barrier against American naval advance into the western Pacific, early versions of 'Orange' were rendered nugatory. After the First World War 'Orange' was continually revised, the problem of penetrating the Japanese island barrier being rehearsed at Naval War College map-table exercises 127 times. 'Sharp, bloody and confused,' wrote Michel Vlahos, historian of the US Naval War College, 'the

Orange tactical problems often seemed to mirror in grim reality 'the coming war.'

As real war drew near during the late 1930s, however, the problems of penetrating the Pacific island barrier zone began to recede into insignificance beside the complications of a wider strategy. German and Italian naval rearmament threatened British control of Western waters, all the more menacingly because of Britain's economic inability to enlarge its fleet. The Royal Navy of the Munich years, apart from some recently built aircraft carriers, was scarcely more modern than the fleet which had fought at Jutland; many of its first-line battleships had indeed fought at Jutland, while it was deficient in destroyers, submarines and even cruisers, the principal medium of control over its seas of empire to which the Versailles Treaty had very greatly added in extent.

In November 1940, therefore, Admiral Harold Stark, the recently appointed US Chief of Naval Operations, outlined to President Roosevelt a revised estimate of American naval priorities. They were, in lettered order: (a) to concentrate on defence of the Americas; (b) to prepare for an all-out war in the Pacific; (c) to remain on the defensive in the Pacific and Atlantic; (d) to prepare for a major war in the Atlantic while remaining on the defensive in the Pacific. 'Dog', as the revised estimate came to be known, was a radical reversal of the strategy by which the United States Navy had lived for twenty years. It threatened to consign China to Japan's navies and put the Philippines, perhaps even the United States' Pacific island possessions, at risk. However, given the closer proximity of Hitler's Germany to the United States, the growing strength of the German and Italian navies, the doubtful effectiveness of British – let alone French – naval power and the United States' intimate involvement with the security of the European democracies, it was clearly the least undesirable of options. After intense debate between the US Navy and the US Army, it was adopted as national policy in late 1940.

In subsequent discussions with the British in Washington in March 1941, it was formally agreed that 'the Atlantic and European area is considered to be the decisive theatre', but the agreement included provision for the United States Pacific Fleet to 'support Allied operations for the defence of the Malay Barrier by diverting enemy strength through attacks on the Marshall Islands . . . support British naval forces' (based in the supposedly impregnable harbour of Singapore) 'south of the equator and west [to the mid-Pacific] . . . protect Allied territory and sea communications in the Pacific . . . prepare to capture the Marshalls and the Carolines.'

For all that Japan was already bent on a ferocious offensive at the heart of the American Pacific Fleet, the United States Navy clearly conceived itself still to be the dominant naval power in the ocean. A comparison of relative naval strength reveals the basis of this. Taking British, Australian and Dutch ships together with American, and setting them against Japanese, the relevant ratios of Western and Japanese naval units was 10:10 in battleships, 17:16 in heavy cruisers, 27:17 in light cruisers, 93:111 in destroyers and 70:64 in submarines. In only one category did Japan enjoy a decisive advantage, of 10:4. Unfortunately that was in aircraft carriers, which would prove the decisive weapon of the coming oceanic war.

Fair warning of the direction Japanese policy was taking had been given by the imperial government's accession to the Tripartite Pact with Germany and Italy on 27 September, 1940. This recognised 'the leadership of Japan in the establishment of a new order in Greater East Asia', and committed the signatories to assist each other if 'attacked by a power at present not involved in the European war or in the Sino-Japanese conflict'. Since the only potentially belligerent powers to which the pact might apply were the Soviet Union (with which Japan signed a non-aggression treaty in April 1941) and the United States, it was clear that the pact threatened the United States alone. American policy was to attempt to restrain Japanese aggression, even at the risk of accelerating the approach to war. In July 1940 it imposed embargoes on Japanese purchases of strategic chemicals and minerals, aircraft parts and aviation fuel; in September it extended the embargo to scrap metals. These prohibitions were damaging to the Japanese economy, which was entirely dependent for production on the import of raw materials. A year later, on 26 July 1941, one day after Japan had coerced the French Vichy government into conceding garrison rights in southern Indo-China – from which it could strike at Malaya, Burma and the Philippines, indifferently and perhaps simultaneously – President Roosevelt issued an executive order freezing all Japanese assets in the United States and forbidding the export of all commodities to Japan from American ports. The effect was to deny Japan 80 per cent of her oil imports and thereby the means to sustain her war effort against China, while choking at birth any plans she might have to create 'a new order in Greater East Asia'.

'Diplomatic negotiations during the few months of "peace negotiations" that remained after the oil embargo,' wrote Professor Samuel Eliot Morison, official historian of the United States Navy in the Second World War, 'were little more than sparring for time. Civilian elements in the Japanese government tried to find a solution that would satisfy the militarists, who in turn needed a few months to train the carrier groups to destroy the United States Pacific Fleet. America wanted time for new naval construction, for manufacture of munitions and implements of war, and to reinforce the Army in the Philippines.' In the event, Japan won more time than the United States. While President Roosevelt exchanged highminded generalities about the future of the world with Winston Churchill (though also agreeing to the 'Germany first' principle), the Japanese at an Imperial Conference in September

1941 were forging consensus between generals, admirals and ministers on a ruthless scheme of attack:

Determined not to be deterred by the possibility of war with America and England and Holland, and in order to secure our national existence, we will proceed with war preparations so that they will be completed approximately towards the end of October . . . if by the early part of October there is no reasonable hope of having our demands agreed to . . . we will immediately make up our minds to get ready for war.

To this statement the generals and admirals attached a list of specific conditions which required the United States to give Japan a free hand in China, Britain to cease military aid to Chiang Kai-shek, both countries to agree not to reinforce their armies or navies in the Pacific and neither to interfere in Japan's extraction of concessions in Indo-China from Vichy France. 'Thus the military', in Professor Morison's words, 'gave the Japanese government about six weeks to reach a peaceful settlement, and dictated the terms'. The urgency was imposed by the oil embargo, which diminished reserves at a million barrels a month. By September the country (whose domestic production was but 400,000 tons against an annual consumption of 12 million tons) had only a little over a year's supply left and was approaching a threshold minimum it could not afford to cross. As the crisis date of October approached, conflict between the army and Prince Konoye, the civilian prime minister, proved irresolvable. He declined to carry the country to war against the United States; the generals refused to meet the only conditions which they knew would conciliate the United States: an end to the war with China and abandonment of the 'southern movement', via Indo-China, against the British and Dutch possessions in the East Indies. Konoye, defeated, accordingly resigned and on 18 October was replaced by General Tojo.

On 10 November Tojo's military delegates, General Terauchi and Admiral Yamamoto, agreed on a specific plan of operations: '1. Simultaneous landings of amphibious forces in Luzon [Philippines], Guam, the Malay Peninsula, Hong Kong and . . . British North Borneo. 2. Carrier air attack on the United States Pacific Fleet at Pearl Harbor. 3. Rapid exploitation of initial successes by the seizure of Manila, Mindanao [both in the Philippines], Wake Island, the Bismarcks, Bangkok and Singapore. 4. Occupation of the Dutch East Indies and continuation of the war with China.' Admiral-Ambassador Nomura, the Japanese government's special delegate in Washington, continued for the rest of the month in efforts to avert the confrontation which would bring the Terauchi–Yamamoto plan into effect. A moderate of impeccable integrity, his efforts were sincere; but the Tojo government had already set its face against conciliation. Although its day-by-day moves were hidden from the United States government, American capacity to decrypt Japanese diplomatic transmissions warned that a crisis was at hand. On 27 November Admiral Stark signalled his subordinates in the Pacific as follows: 'An aggressive move by Japan is to be expected within the next few days. The number and equipment of Japanese troops and the organisation of naval task forces indicates an amphibious expedition against either the Philippines, Thai or Kra [Malay] Peninsula or possibly Borneo. Execute appropriate defensive deployment.' Stark's 'war warning' was timely, but it failed to alert the Pacific Fleet to the exact nature of the threat.

THE PACIFIC WAR BEFORE MIDWAY

War came to the Pacific on Sunday, 7 December 1941. Shortly after seven o'clock that morning, the American Signal Corps crew of a British-supplied radar station, operating on the north coast of the island of Oahu in the Hawaiian group, detected a formation of aircraft approaching the island at a range of 137 miles. Oahu, whose main port was Pearl Harbor, sheltered the main body of the United States Navy's Pacific Fleet. That Sunday two of its aircraft carriers, *Lexington* and *Enterprise*, with their cruiser and destroyer escorts, were at sea, delivering aircraft to the American outpost islands of Wake and Midway; the third, *Saratoga*, was temporarily in an American west coast port. The battle fleet was at moorings: seven dreadnoughts – *Nevada, Arizona, Tennessee, West Virginia, Maryland, Oklahoma* and *California* – with eighty-nine other warships in attendance; another battleship, *Pennsylvania*, was in dry dock.

The Pacific Fleet was not only at moorings, it was also at peace. Sunday was its day of rest and, despite the wars and rumours of wars which had troubled the ocean and its periphery for the previous four years, the fleet was disposed to rise late and spend the day in relaxation. Headquarters were inert, senior officers ashore, crews straggling to and from breakfast. Ships were permanently at 'Condition 3' of (high) readiness; but it had been in force so long that its conditions were not fully observed. Most of the anti-aircraft guns remained unmanned, while the ready-use ammunition was locked up.

When the Signal Corps radar station's warning reached the information centre at Oahu, the officer on duty interpreted it as an intercept of a flight of B-17 bombers known to be on passage to the island from the continental United States. He told the operator 'not to worry' about the radar signal. Equally, when the destroyer *Ward*, acting as Pearl Harbour guardship – and one of only three units of the fleet in harbour not at moorings – reported at about the same time that it had made contact with a submarine, the harbour control post failed to respond with urgency. The officer in charge telephoned superiors, who ordered those destroyers on standby to get under way or raise steam; but none thought to put the major units on full alert. As a result, though the midget submarine which *Ward* had identified and all four of her sister craft were subsequently destroyed, no anti-aircraft precautions were set in hand. And it was Japanese aircraft, not submarines, which were about to take the Pacific Fleet under attack in numbers.

A first wave of forty torpedo-bombers, fifty-one bombers, forty-nine dive-bombers and forty-three fighters had taken off from the six carriers of the Japanese Air Attack Force at six o'clock that morning, 275 miles north of Pearl Harbor, for their targets lying at moorings in Battleship Row. At 0730 the first-arrived began to orbit overhead and at 0755 the bombs and torpedoes of the concentration began to strike. By 0825 the damage was done. *Arizona*, hit in the forward magazine, was going down with 80 per cent of her crew, *Oklahoma*, hit by three torpedoes, had capsized, *West Virginia* had sunk, *California* was sinking, *Tennessee, Maryland* and *Nevada* were badly damaged. *Nevada*, splendidly handled by her junior officers, got up steam though under fire, and managed to beach down-harbour from Battleship Row. She was the only one of the Pacific Fleet 'battle wagons' to act the warrior during what Roosevelt would call the 'day of infamy'.

Ashore the Japanese were inflicting damage almost as crippling on the American Pacific air force as on the fleet. For fear of sabotage – Hawaii had a large Japanese immigrant population – the island's complement of aircraft, Catalina flying-boats, B-17 bombers. Wildcat and Aerocobra fighters, were parked wherever they were stationed wing to wing, for easier protection. Out of 143 US Army Air Corps aircraft, 56 were destroyed in half an hour of machine-gun passes by the Japanese carrier groups; and losses among Marine corps (23 out of 49) and Navy (27 out of 36) aircraft were similarly severe.

As the second wave of 160 Japanese raiders collected for their return flight to the striking force 200 miles north of the Hawaii islands at ten o'clock on 7 December, they surveyed a scene of devastation. Amid the wreckage of the Navy Yard and its nearby barracks and airfields, nearly 2400 American servicemen lay dead or dying, as many as had been lost by the Germans at Jutland. Five capital ships were sunk or sinking, eight cruisers and destroyers were destroyed or seriously damaged, columns of smoke hundreds of feet high hung over the anchorage, and the garrison of Hawaii was shattered by shock. 'An unwarranted feeling of immunity from attack,' Admiral Ernest King, Chief of Naval Operations, was to charge afterwards, 'seems to have pervaded all ranks at Pearl Harbor, both Army and Navy.' Its insidious influence served to magnify the psychological devastation which the Air Attack Force left behind it.

By contrast, the Air Attack Force was consumed by euphoria. Admiral Chuichi Nagumo, commander of the strike carriers, and his staff agonised for some time over whether or not to renew the attack. They knew they had failed to destroy key targets, including the 'tank farm' which held the Pacific Fleet's fuel reserves, and were particularly exercised by their failure to find the fleet's three carriers at home. Nagumo took hours in conference to persuade himself that the operation had been the success he sought. 'Most of the young flying officers,' recalled Jinichi Goto, a squadron commander from the carrier *Akagi* who had torpedoed USS *Oklahoma*, 'were eager to attack Pearl Harbor again because they wished to inflict as much damage as possible. It was the chance of a lifetime, and many of the pilots felt it should not be passed up.' However, reports from the returning squadrons argued against the command's incertitude. 'Surprise attack successful', 'Every warship torpedoed, outstanding results'; 'Hickham Field attacked; outstanding results'. Persuaded by these estimates of what had been achieved on 'Z-Day' (the Z-flag hoisted on the flagship to initiate operations was the same flown by Admiral Togo at Tsushima), Nagumo eventually ordered the Air Attack Force to turn away to the north and retrace its course into the depths of the Pacific. Of nearly 300 aircraft launched, it had recovered all but 29; 74 had been damaged but returned to their mother ships. In crude attrition terms, Pearl Harbor had been an outstandingly profitable exchange. High on the index of profit and loss hung the state of the striking force itself; not a single Japanese ship was touched in the course of the operation.

Simultaneously, meanwhile, the dispersed striking forces of the Combined Fleet had been taking under attack Japan's other chosen Pacific objectives. Warning of the Pearl Harbor disaster reached American headquarters at Manila in the Philippines some three hours before the Japanese aircraft, launched from bases in Taiwan, arrived, but the same complacency Admiral Stark diagnosed at Hawaii prevailed there also, compounded by indecision and inter-service misunderstanding. While General Douglas MacArthur's chief of staff argued with the commander of the US Army Air Corps about mounting a photographic reconniassance mission against Taiwan, to establish if the Japanese bombers were still at their bases, they arrived over the American airfields, found them crowded with Flying Fortresses and fighters parked wing-tip to wing-tip 'against sabotage' and destroyed half in a single bombing raid. Next day, in conditions of complete air superiority, the Japanese returned to destroy the Navy Yard and several ships in harbour. The following day, 10 December, Japanese amphibious forces began the first of five landings on the islands, which would inaugurate one of the war's bloodiest and bravest defensive efforts by the Allies.

Meanwhile the Japanese had initiated parallel attacks against the British forces in Malaya. On 10 December Japanese bombers based at airfields in southern Indo-China found and attacked the battleship *Prince of Wales* and battlecruiser *Repulse*, recently arrived from Britain to form the nucleus of a Far Eastern Fleet at the Singapore base, and sank both in a brief and onesided battle in the South China Sea. The Japanese army had already crossed the northern Malay border and (supported by seaborne forces landed behind British lines in a series of amphibious hooks) had begun an inexorable advance towards Singapore. The loss of *Prince of Wales* and *Repulse* deprived the defenders of all chances of stemming the onslaught and filled the British government with despair. 'It means,' wrote General Sir Alan Brooke, Chief of the Imperial General Staff, 'that from Africa eastward to America through the Indian Ocean and the Pacific, we have lost control of the sea.'

Wake Island, America's only outpost within striking distance of the Japanese Marshall archipelago, fell on 23 December, despite heroic resistance by its tiny marine garrison. Guam, in the Marianas, had been taken by 10 December; Hong Kong, attacked by Japanese troops from Canton, was to fall on Christmas Day after a brave but hopeless three-week defence. The loss of Wake was particularly galling because it might have been saved. The Japanese neglected to provide their attacking force with air cover and left the landing ships to swing at anchor offshore, unprotected against the carrier force which Pearl Harbor organised to send to its relief. Because of Wake's distance from Hawaii, however, *Saratoga*, whose speed would have allowed it to reach the island before it fell, was forced to take an oiler with it as replenishment ship, whose best speed of 14 knots delayed *Saratoga*'s advance by a crucial two days. On 21 December, fleet intelligence at Pearl Harbor warned that it believed two Japanese carriers were approaching Wake – a true estimate – and next day the Pacific Fleet command, judging that it could not risk the loss of one of its only three carriers in the central Pacific in the cause of a marginal strategic advantage, ordered *Saratoga*'s recall. An American cruiser captain judged afterwards that 'Frank Jack' (Admiral Fletcher, commanding the task force) 'should have placed the telescope to his blind eye, like Nelson'. However, under stringent orders not to hazard his command, Fletcher had no option but to obey. Had he pressed on, 'Wake might have been relieved', in the opinion of Admiral-Professor Morison, 'and there would certainly have been a battle'. The tide of Japanese victory was still flowing strongly, and it might not have been a battle that the United States would have won, but, after three weeks of humiliating defeat, the officers and men of its navy, whatever the strategic calculations of its commanders, sought battle for its own sake. 'By God,' a former fleet admiral exclaimed after his return from Pearl Harbor on a presidential mission at the end of December, 'I used to say a man had to be both a fighter and know how to fight. Now all I want is a man who fights.'

In Admiral Chester Nimitz, appointed to command the Pacific Fleet on 17 December, the United States would find a man – as Lincoln did in Grant – who would fight. Nevertheless, before he could contrive the circumstances in which his slender carrier striking force could take the Japanese at a disadvantage, America still had much humiliation to undergo. In January 1942 the Japanese were advancing fast down the Malay peninsula. They had extinguished the American garrisons inside the perimeter of islands they had delineated as their essential military frontier in the North Pacific, except in the Philippines, which tottered on the brink of capitulation. They were about to begin their assault upon the British base in Burma and the Dutch colonies in the East Indies. Thailand and Indo-China had been incorporated within their sphere of operations. Australia and India, both weakly defended, lay under the shadow of their advance. The only obstacles to the complete realisation of the Terauchi–Yamamoto strategic memorandum were the three American aircraft carriers based on Pearl Harbor and the remnants of the British, Australian and Dutch navies still operating in the East Indies. The latter were about to be brought under attack.

On 15 January 1942, a week before the Japanese launched their amphibious assault against the East Indies, the Australian, British, Dutch and a detachment of American naval forces in the southern Pacific constituted the ABDA command. On the night of 23/24 January part of the ABDA force, under American command, intercepted a vanguard of the Japanese invasion fleet sailing for the Dutch East Indies and destroyed it. However, local disparities of strength were too large to be offset by such a setback. Singapore fell to the Japanese on 15 February, and four days later the East Indies island of Timor, at the extreme eastern end of the Indonesian chain, was invaded and Port Darwin, in Australia's Northern Territory, bombed. Admiral Karel Doorman, the Dutch commander of ABDA's navy, was faced with an imminent descent by superior forces on Java, heartland of Holland's Far Eastern empire. To intercept its approach he had available one American and one British cruiser, one Australian and two Dutch light cruisers, ten destroyers but no more air cover than the ships' own floatplanes provided. The Japanese naval force, protecting an invasion armada of ninety-seven transports, included two heavy cruisers and thirteen destroyers, with two light cruisers as squadron leaders.

Doorman moved to intercept in an engagement which would become known as the battle of the Java Sea. It was to be one of the few purely surface ship actions of the Pacific War, akin in character, if not in numbers and size of ships engaged, to Jutland. Soon after four o'clock in the afternoon of 27 February the two fleets made contact off the north coast of Java. The encounter began with an exchange of gunfire, but Takagi, the Japanese admiral, switched to torpedo attack as soon as he judged the ABDA ships to be within range. Japanese torpedoes, the 'long-lance' model of 50-knots speed, 5000-yards range and 1200-pound warhead, were vastly superior to the enemy's equivalents and lethal even to the best-protected ships, which Doorman's cruisers and destroyers were not. Takagi's first salvo of forty-three were launched too far from their targets to secure hits, but the attack forced the Allied formation to change course, during which manoeuvre HMS *Exeter*, a veteran of the River Plate battle, was disabled by gunfire and a Dutch destroyer blown up. Dusk was falling and the ABDA fleet's cohesion was broken. Takagi pressed home his attacks, while Doorman, covering his movement with a destroyer diversion, steamed in search of the Japanese invasion convoy. The Japanese, keeping fitful contact with Doorman in the gathering darkness, launched more torpedo attacks. Eventually the Japanese, in bright moonlight, caught Doorman's cruisers off guard, and just before midnight fired a final salvo of twelve 'long-lance' torpedoes at their line. Doorman's flagship and its sister cruiser were hit and sunk; following the hard ritual of the sea, Doorman and his cruiser captains went down with their ships. The Australian *Perth* and the American *Houston* survived; but only briefly. On the night after the battle of the Java Sea both cruisers were found by Japanese destroyers while making a last attempt to intercept the Japanese invasion force and were torpedoed. HMAS *Perth* was sunk outright. USS *Houston* put up a brave fight but, damaged by three torpedoes and eventually engaged by Japanese destroyers at machine-gun range, after half an hour's desperate resistance rolled over and went to the bottom.

The battle of the Java Sea brought to an end the opening phase of the Pacific War, wholly to Japan's advantage. In the next two months Nagumo's carrier force would raid as far as Ceylon in the Indian Ocean, sinking a British carrier and two cruisers. Its associated amphibious and ground forces would meanwhile complete the invasion of the Dutch East Indies and Burma, adding those conquests to the capture of Malaya and the Philippines, and would stand poised to strike against New Guinea and the north coast of Australia. In its triumphant advance, the Japanese navy had extinguished the power of the Royal and Dutch Navies in the Far East, driven the United States Navy on to a defensive posture from which its recovery seemed impossible and destroyed five battleships, an aircraft carrier, two cruisers, seven destroyers, 200,000 tons of fleet auxiliaries and merchant ships and hundreds of aircraft. In return, it had lost a few dozen aircraft and suffered no significant damage to any ship of its striking force at all. As the US Navy historian Samuel Eliot Morison, assessing the balance, observed:

> The Malay Barrier was now shattered. Except for isolated pockets of resistance . . . the colonial empires of the United States, the Netherlands and Great Britain, as far east as India and as far south as Australia, had joined that of the French, already liquidated. Within four months of the Pearl Harbor strike, Japan had achieved her Greater East Asia Co-prosperity Sphere. She was poised to move backward into China; or, if America and Britain did not throw in the sponge, forward to the right flank of India or by the left flank into the Aleutians and Hawaii.

The only impediment to Japanese victory was the continued survival of America's Pacific Fleet aircraft carriers, *Lexington*, *Saratoga* and *Enterprise*, together with *Yorktown*, which had joined them from the Atlantic Fleet early in 1942. In February the *Enterprise* group – a carrier and attendant escorts – attacked Kwajalein in the Marshalls and the newly formed *Yorktown* group attacked Rabaul in the Solomons. In April USS

Enterprise and *Hornet*, the latter also a new arrival from the Atlantic Fleet, mounted a daring raid against Tokyo. Loading their decks with B-25 land bombers, barely able to rise from a ship steaming at maximum speed to windward, the two carriers launched their planes at 668 miles' range for the Japanese capital and then rapidly turned away, leaving Doolittle's B-25 force to fly on to landings in areas of northern China outside Japanese control.

Doolittle's Tokyo raid caused an agony of shame among Japan's admirals and generals, to whom protection of the emperor's person and residence was a sacred trust; and it would subsequently influence, with disastrous effect, Japanese strategic decisions over the future of the Pacific War. Meantime the fleet proceeded with planned operations. The Imperial General Staff's war plan required that its defined 'island perimeter' of defence be completed by the capture of New Guinea, off Australia's northern coast, and thence Fiji and Samoa. This effectively cut off the United States' flank of seaward communication with Australia and New Zealand, and thus denied its principal enemy the chance to stage a counter-offensive into the archipelagos of the northern Pacific.

The Japanese fleet was therefore committed to an advance into the Coral Sea, dividing New Guinea from Australia, from which it could dominate its enemies' last remaining area of free strategic sea room in the southern Pacific. The operation would for the first time expose the Japanese navy's precious force of carriers to operations in confined waters, with attendant risks that the Japanese admirals recognised. So critical was the development of the Coral Sea operation to the realisation of their plans, however, that they determined to bite the bullet and proceed. An advanced striking force was split into three divisions, one to seize positions in the Solomons, a second to capture Port Moresby on the southern shore of New Guinea and a third, including the large carriers *Shokaku* and *Zuikaku*, to enter the Coral Sea and fight any enemy force found there.

Nimitz, alerted by signal intelligence to Japanese intentions, could not match the enemy force. Although he had only *Yorktown* and *Lexington* available for battle, he none the less resolutely decided to insert both into the Coral Sea. Early on 7 May a *Yorktown* reconnaissance plane detected a Japanese carrier 175 miles north of the *Yorktown–Lexington* group. Reported as one of a major enemy striking force, it was intercepted and sunk – 'scratch one flattop', the informative signal, became a legendary communication of the US Navy's Pacific War – before Nimitz learned that the casualty, *Shoho*, was a light carrier escort to the Port Moresby invasion force and not part of the main battle formation for which his own should have been seeking. Admiral Inouye, commanding the Coral Sea force, was so alarmed by the loss of *Shoho*, however, that he issued orders to postpone the Port Moresby landing, while dispatching the heavy carriers *Zuikaku* and *Shokaku* to seek out and destroy the *Yorktown–Lexington* group. Aided by heavy weather, which hid them from the Americans, the Japanese pilots found their target and inflicted torpedo damage on *Lexington* which sunk her, after a heroic damage-control struggle, on the evening of 8 May. As a result of the battle between the carrier groups, however, *Shokaku* suffered bomb damage which required her return to dockyard while *Zuikaku* lost so many of her embarked aircraft that she was effectively to be out of action for the next month.

The battle of the Coral Sea electrified America. The sinking of *Shoho* was the first success achieved by the United States Navy since the outbreak of the war and, while not recompense for Pearl Harbor, was sweet revenge. It demonstrated that American carrier aircraft, in particular American carrier aircrew, were the equals of their Japanese counterparts who, in the first six months of war at sea, had won something of the same superman reputation as the Japanese infantry and marines had done in the battles for Malaya and the Philippines. The Japanese, by contrast, persuaded themselves that the Coral Sea was an addition to their string of victories. *Lexington* was better than a fair exchange for *Shoho*, a smaller ship carrying fewer aircraft. To her loss had to be added that of the fleet oiler *Neosho* and the destroyer *Sims*. Although the Coral Sea had forced Japan to postpone the invasion of New Guinea's southern shore, and thus to abandon its intention of making a direct threat to Australia's Northern Territory, the plan's abandonment could be regarded as temporary. In Japanese eyes, the sun was still rising over the waters of the Pacific. Yamamoto's warning that he could guarantee only 'six months or a year' of 'running wild' looked unduly pessimistic. With a push here and a shove there, the empire was at the brink of securing that eastern Pacific island perimeter which would assure it an unassailable oceanic redoubt, consign littoral China and the former European colonies in South-East Asia and the Indies to its economic custody and transform the idea of a 'Greater East Asia Co-Prosperity Sphere' into a world power equal in strength to Hitler's Great Reich, the surviving elements of the British Empire, the Soviet Union and even the United States itself.

THE MIDWAY CAMPAIGN

If in the spring of 1942 Japanese strategic purpose risked distortion it was not by the results of the Coral Sea battle, but by an event of far less substantial strategic substance: Doolittle's Tokyo raid of a month earlier. The Doolittle raid was an early example of a public-relations event. It lacked military purpose altogether and had been conceived purely as a means of depressing Japanese and reviving American hopes for the war's central outcome. President Roosevelt's facetious comment that the raid had been launched from 'Shangri-La' – a post-war American carrier would be named after James Hilton's bestselling novel of

Tibetan romance – perfectly exemplified the spirit in which the operation had been conceived. However, while official Washington might have instantly consigned Doolittle's exploit, for all its foolhardiness, to the propaganda waste-paper basket, official Tokyo chose to regard it with the greatest seriousness. Not only had Doolittle's sixteen B-25s menaced the security of the emperor, thereby shaming the armed services, whose ultimate purpose was to die, if necessary, in his defence; *Enterprise* and *Hornet*, which had carried the bombers to their departure point, had found a way through the Pacific perimeter by which the home islands were supposed to be protected from external attack. The keyhole they had exploited was a narrow one – north of Hawaii, south of the Aleutians, both objectives which Japan eventually intended to attack – but the discovery of its existence was to bring to an end a bitter strategic debate within the Japanese navy – with fatal results for Japan.

The very extent of Japan's success in the first month of the war had complicated rather than simplified its range of strategic opportunities. The future now held much more than the chance merely to proceed at leisure with the dismemberment of China. The whole of Asia seemed to lie at its mercy, Australia under threat and even the Indian Ocean as far west as the British colonies in East Africa, to which the Royal Navy withdrew after the raid on Ceylon, not beyond naval outreach. A junction with the Axis forces operating in the Middle East was not fantasy; nor was an attack on the Soviet Union, trembling apparently on the brink of defeat by the German army, via Manchuria and Siberia.

The navy, alarmed by the army's desire to widen the war so radically, and also by the fear that Britain and America might still find means to build up a counter-offensive base in the southern Pacific, proposed in January that the next large initiative should be an attack on Australia. The generals, calculating the difficulties of supplying such a venture at the far end of immensely long lines of communication, 'absolutely refused to agree to the operations'. At best they were prepared to proceed with the capture of New Guinea, from which Australia's northern coast could be held at risk by aircraft and locally based naval forces.

On that proposal the Naval General Staff showed itself ready to compromise; but it was not the ultimate source of decision within the naval command system. A shore-based headquarters, it was obliged to agree strategy with the seagoing staff of the Combined Fleet which Yamamoto directed. In March he sent an emissary to the Naval General Staff with an alternative scheme. Still troubled by the escape of the American carriers from the Pearl Harbor holocaust, he was anxious to bring them, and the remnants of the American Pacific Fleet, to battle at a place of his choosing, where he could be sure of putting them at a disadvantage. The isolated island of Midway, a thousand miles north of Hawaii and in itself a potential thorn in the Japanese side, was an ideal focus for mounting such a trap. The example of Wake, where the

Americans had been ready to use one carrier, suggested that they would respond to an invasion threat by committing all three carriers – even though more than twice outnumbered by the Japanese – to its defence. Yamamoto believed his case inconstestable.

The Naval General Staff contested it none the less. Its officers pointed out that Midway was beyond the range of Japan's land-based aircraft, which had played such a key role in the capture of the Philippines and the destruction of *Prince of Wales* and *Repulse*, but within that of Flying Fortresses based in Hawaii. They doubted whether a surprise of the magnitude of Pearl Harbor could be sprung on the Pacific Fleet a second time. They also thought that the operation overstretched; and they warned that Midway, even if captured, could be taken back again when the Americans chose. If Yamamoto sought a decisive action with the enemy's carriers, far better, they judged, to provoke it in New Guinea waters, where the same results could be achieved as in action at sea around Midway but with the added advantage of furthering the 'southern advance' into the last Anglo-American Pacific stronghold.

The debate stalemated. The army objected that a successful Midway operation would draw the forces into a battle for Hawaii itself, which the generals feared would be lost. The Naval General Staff, intimidated by Yamamoto's prestige as the victor of Pearl Harbor, temporised. Even some of Yamamoto's subordinates argued the difficulties: Nagumo, who had commanded the Pearl Harbor carriers, spoke (though not to Yamamoto's face) of 'an impossible and pointless operation'. Then, on 18 April, came the Doolittle raid on Tokyo. 'All opposition to the Midway operation', in Professor Ronald Spector's words, 'abruptly ceased . . . Admiral Yamamoto regarded the raid as a mortifying personal defeat'. Not only Yamamoto: admirals and generals combined to reproach themselves for the affront that had been offered to the emperor. The Midway 'keyhole' through which the *Enterprise–Hornet* group had approached Tokyo become overnight the focus of every strategic concern among Japan's military leaders. Inoue, the admiral charged with leading the carrier strike force into the Coral Sea, was notified that his operation would be allowed to continue, but would be brought forward in date. Thereafter all air groups would be concentrated in the North Pacific for a strike against Midway with the object not only of closing that 'keyhole' but also of destroying for good the American carriers which were the last impediment to Japan's unrestricted control of the ocean.

'Midway Island acts as a sentry for Hawaii,' Admiral Nagumo was to write when the battle was over. So much geography demonstrates; but in the weeks of preparation leading up to the battle the American Pacific Fleet's difficulty was to know where the Japanese carriers would strike next – south, east or north – in the broadest strategic spectrum. The identification of a precise objective was a secondary consideration. Nevertheless, the Japanese succeeded in providing some clues. On 3/4

March two of their flying-boats resumed offensive operations against Hawaii by dropping bombs, and on 10 March another was detected near Midway and shot down by US Marine Corps fighters. 'Back bearing' intelligence – calculations based on tracking the departure point of the aircraft by reference to their known line of flight – identified their base as French Frigate Shoals, a patch of dry ground in between Hawaii and Midway. The flying-boat mission implied, perfectly correctly, that the Pacific area north of Hawaii was now an active Japanese operational sector and that Midway atoll should be regarded as an objective under risk of Japanese attack.

The American cryptanalysts accordingly began to listen out. The advantage was with them. The Japanese were not able to read American naval ciphers. Thanks to the work of the US Army's Signal Intelligence School before the war, however, the Americans could read theirs (though the Pearl Harbor plan had been hidden from them by radio silence and contradictory indicators). Like the Germans, the Japanese had consigned the safety of their military communications to a ciphering machine, known to the Americans as 'Purple'. Less sophisticated in design than the German Enigma, its security was further compromised by the Japanese habit of repeating enciphered communications on an earlier model, 'Red', to outstations which had not yet been equipped with 'Purple' (introduced in 1939). 'Red' transmissions had been broken even earlier than 'Purple', with the result that, by comparing identical texts sent on both, the American cryptanalysts were able to read 90 per cent of all Japanese 'secure' transmissions, and could fill in the meaning of the missing portions by inspired guesswork, alternative intelligence and interception of low-level (Y) transmissions, such as ship-to-ship messages.

Such ease of reading was interrupted by the normal practice, observed by the Japanese, of changing cipher settings, though not the basic cipher system, at regular intervals. However, here the ocean-wide dispersion of Japanese forces, and its attendant state of mind, 'Victory Disease', worked to Japan's disadvantage. Difficulties in distributing the new setting, known as JN 25b, until the end of May 1942, and a complacent Japanese belief in the ability of their militarily incompetent enemies to penetrate the existing one, JN 25, gave the Hawaiian cryptanalysts an extra two months to work on the current messages. Those yielded a good deal of precious information, particularly the indication that an operation (codenamed MI) was planned against a target designated only as AF.

Captain Jasper Holmes, a Hawaiian cryptanalyst, was tantalised by MI and in early May became possessed, as others were at the cryptanalytic centre, by the conviction that AF designated Midway and MI Japanese invasion of the atoll. He accordingly devised a cipher trap. Midway retained a secure undersea telegraphic link with Hawaii, which allowed messages to pass between the two islands without violation of radio silence. Choosing a subject he believed of significance to the Japanese, he instructed the Midway end of the telegraphic link to signal in clear by radio that the island – dependent on a distilling plant for supply – was running short of fresh water. Listening out under strict instructions to do so, an American intercept station in Australia plucked from the ether an Imperial General Headquarters message from Tokyo that AF reported a shortage of fresh water, decrypted it and signalled to Hawaii, 'This will confirm the identity of AF.'

So it did. All that was then needed to mount a timely riposte to Operation MI was an indication of its date. Circumstantial evidence had already fixed the chronological brackets each side of 1 and 10 June. However, needing for safety to refuel every seven days, the carrier captains required a more precise fix of the Japanese approach date than that. Calculations of an intercept disclosing the departure day of a Japanese oiler of known speed, which it could be guessed was a component of the attack force, moved its estimated arrival off Midway to 30 May or after, which thereby shortened the time bracket at the other end – since the attack force certainly would not linger near the island longer than necessary to deliver its attack. It was not until 25 May that the Hawaii cryptanalysts intercepted a message on which detailed planning calculations could be forwarded. That message revealed Japanese intentions to attack the Aleutians on 3 June, Midway on 4 June. Nimitz could now manoeuvre his task force.

Nimitz had three carriers available for the coming battle – *Enterprise*, a Pacific fixture, *Hornet*, a recent arrival, and *Yorktown*. However, *Yorktown*'s availability was marginal. Damaged at the Coral Sea, she had limped into Pearl Harbor on 27 May for what Admiral Fitch, the Coral Sea task force commander, estimated would be a 'ninety-day refit'; an 800 lb bomb had penetrated amidships to her fourth deck in the battle, killing sixty of her crew and starting a serious fire. Splinters from near misses alongside had penetrated her hull and started leaks. She entered the largest Pearl Harbor dry dock at 1430 hours on 27 May. At 1100 hours on 29 May she was flooded out of the dock ready for sea, 1400 men having worked around the clock to repair damage aboard and stop holes outboard. During the afternoon, with hundreds of men still working on her, she embarked replacement aircraft for those lost at the Coral Sea. At nine in the morning of 30 May she put to sea for her next engagement with the enemy.

Nimitz's Midway striking force was thus just brought to a strength of three carriers, but of them only *Enterprise*'s air groups – four squadrons of torpedo-, surface- and dive-bombers and a squadron of fighters – were battle-experienced. *Yorktown*'s had not worked together before, the Coral Sea having dispersed its veterans, and *Hornet*'s had never been in action. As escorts to the carriers Nimitz had eight cruisers and seventeen destroyers, together with two oilers; nineteen submarines, another separate command, were to patrol on the Midway approaches.

It was a revolutionary assembly of naval power, notable for a total absence of traditional 'capital ships'. Cruisers and destroyers were present solely to protect the carriers from surface-ship and submarine attack. All offensive potential was concentrated within the air groups of the carriers themselves, a concentration that determined that the battle, like that of the Coral Sea (though in much greater force), must be fought at long range; such long range, indeed, that, if conducted according to plan, the major units would never come within sight of each other.

Yamamoto's Midway force was far more elaborately subdivided than the American. In accordance with Japanese preferences for confusing and surprising the enemy, it comprised five main groups: an advanced force of ten submarines, which was to set traps in the Midway area; the Midway Occupation Force, including not only transports and escorts but a powerful covering screen of two battleships and four cruisers; the Carrier Striking Force, under Nagumo, with four of the fleet's large carriers; the main body, commanded by Yamamoto himself, comprising three battleships – including *Yamato*, the largest warship in the world – and a light cruiser; and Northern Area Force targeted against the Aleutians. In all, the Combined Fleet totalled eleven battleships, five carriers, twelve cruisers, forty-three destroyers and a swarm of transports, oilers, seaplane tenders and patrol boats. Departing from three main bases, in the Marianas, and the north and south home islands, it was to operate over an enormous triangular area of ocean, the sides – from Japan to Midway and the Aleutians – stretching over more than 2000 miles of sea.

Yamamoto's plan was as elaborate as his dispositions and required the closest co-ordination in time of his various fleet elements. It was to begin with a bombardment of Dutch Harbor in the Aleutians on 3 June, intended to deceive the Americans as to his intentions. Next day the Carrier Striking Force was to bomb Midway and engage the American carriers if they arrived on the scene. Yamamoto's covering force, standing nearby, would join in the battle as it developed. On 5 June the Midway Ocupation Force would commence the landings. Meanwhile the Northern Area Force would station itself between Midway and the Aleutians to intercept any American units detached from the Pacific Fleet to go to the American Aleutian garrison's relief.

American naval strategists, in the aftermath of Midway, were to puzzle without conclusion on the over-elaboration of Yamamoto's plan. Since he enormously outnumbered the Pacific Fleet, while the Americans, given their lack of resources, had no option but to remain concentrated, it seemed inexplicable that he did not concentrate also, thereby confronting his enemy with a mass of force that could not possibly be defeated. That was not only the simple solution of his strategic purpose – to knock out the Pacific Fleet for good and all; it was also, in orthodox naval strategic terms, the right solution. However, the Japanese were not orthodox naval strategists. For all its enormous size, they regarded the Pacific Ocean – 64 million square miles in extent, twice the size of the Atlantic – as a forum of amphibious rather than purely maritime operations. In all their previous wars, as early as those against China and Russia in 1894 and 1904, they had combined fleet with army deployments, the one intended to support the other, exactly as if the Pacific were, like the Mediterranean, an inland sea rather than the largest ocean in the world. The Mediterranean littoral powers – Spain, Venice, the Ottoman Empire, even France – had always devised plans in which sea and land operations, the former usually hinging on fortified points secured by the latter, interconnected. It was a strategy validated by results. The Japanese saw no reason in 1942 to depart from their well-tested routine. Samuel Eliot Morison analyses their thinking thus:

> Yamamoto, counting on surprise, expected no opposition to his invasion of Midway. He knew that the Pacific Fleet had no fast battleships, underestimated the number of carriers at its disposal (believing that two had been sunk at the Coral Sea), and, never expecting that Nimitz would be wise to his movements, anticipated no challenge to develop until several days after Midway had been secured. By that time substantial forces in Pearl Harbor might be tearing up to Dutch Harbor (in the Aleutians) and even if Nimitz had decided to let the situation develop he would be unable to reach Midway until 7 or 8 June at the earliest. Nagumo's carriers would then be in readiness to strike the challenging Fleet; perhaps get between it and Midway, which by that time would be a Japanese fixed airplane carrier, then Yamamoto's Main Body, and the various battleship and heavy cruiser divisions that had accompanied the outlying forces, would close for the kill. His carrier pilots would have been rested, every ship would have had a big drink of oil [from their accompanying replenishment ships], and the numerically inferior Pacific Fleet would have been annihilated. Alternately if Nimitz refused to bite in the first week of June, he would certainly try to recapture Midway within a month or two, and the Combined Fleet would be ready in the Marshalls to pounce on him.

'The vital defect in this sort of plan,' Professor Morison concludes, 'is that it depends on the enemy's doing exactly what is expected. If he is smart enough to do something different – in this case to have fast carriers on the spot – the operation is thrown into confusion.' Nimitz was indeed 'smart enough' to have devised such a difference; and he had, of course, three advantages which the Japanese had not taken into account: the first, via cryptanalysis, was foreknolwedge of the enemy's intentions; the second was an unsinkable air base in Midway for a powerful force of Flying Fortresses; the third was radar. Midway had two powerful radar sets, and all Nimitz's carriers and some of his cruisers were equipped with radar also. The seaborne sets gave a fix only at short ranges but the Japanese had no radar at all. The material advantages of this disparity were significant, the psychological advantages substantial.

Nimitz, however, was in no doubt that he would fight at severely disadvantageous odds. He had no battleships whatsoever and fewer units of all other ship types. It was therefore crucial to strike for the jugular: 'to inflict maximum damage on enemy by employing strong attrition tactics', as he put it in his operational instruction to his two carrier group commanders, Admirals Frank John Fletcher (*Yorktown*) and Raymond Spruance (*Enterprise* and *Hornet*). To this he added: 'In carrying out the task assigned . . . you will be governed by the principle of calculated risk, which you shall interpret to mean the avoidance of exposure of your force to attack by superior enemy forces without good prospect of inflicting, as a result of such exposure, greater damage on the enemy.' In brief, the air groups of the carriers were to press home their attacks on the Japanese fleet, and its carriers in particular, without regard for losses; but the precious trio, *Yorktown*, *Enterprise* and *Hornet*, were not to be exposed to risk themselves. Pilots and aircraft could be replaced, carriers – in immediate terms – could not.

As to preliminary dispositions, he ordered the carrier groups to take position 700 miles north-east of Midway in the great waste of the ocean and on the far side of the island from which the enemy could be calculated to approach. Preliminary search for the Japanese would be conducted by aircraft from Midway itself – by 4 June there were 121 aircraft crowded on to the tiny island's airstrip and, in the case of floatplanes, in its lagoon. Once located, the enemy formations would be tracked by scouts from the carrier and by radar and then brought under attack.

Enterprise and *Hornet* set sail from Pearl Harbor on 28 May, *Yorktown* two days later. Nagumo had taken his carriers out of the Inland Sea of Japan on 26 May, steaming south-east for Midway, and Yamamoto followed him, also on 28 May. The other elements of the fleet, which the covering force of submarines had preceded earlier in the month, departed northern Japan and the Marshalls at the same time. By 3 June the Midway Occupation Force was some 700 miles west of the island, moving inside one of those weather fronts which the Japanese were so adept at using as cover to disguise their deployments. It was within such a front that they had made their approach to Pear Harbor six months earlier. Then American reconnaissance arrangements had been so lackadaisical that they had been missed. Now, on full alert and with the scent of approaching danger strong in their nostrils, the Americans were on guard. At nine in the morning of 3 June, a Midway-based Catalina flying-boat, at the very end of its patrol, decided – like the Signal Corps radar operator at Pearl Harbor six months before, but with more profitable result – to continue his search for a few minutes longer than its allotted span. At a little after nine, the pilot, Ensign Jack Reid, suddenly exclaimed, 'Do you see what I see?' to his co-pilot. 'You're damned right I do,' was the answer. Spread out thirty miles ahead of the Catalina was an enormous formation of ships which could only belong to the enemy and appeared to be his main fleet.

The formation was in fact the transport and seaplane group of the Midway Occupation Force. It was escorted only by cruisers and destroyers, its accompanying battleships lying beyond the horizon and out of view of Ensign Reid's Catalina. The sighting was real enough to prompt Captain Cyril Simard, commanding Midway's defences, to action. He at once dispatched nine Flying Fortresses to bring the Japanese formation under attack; bombing from high altitude, they returned with the report that they had sunk 'two battleships or heavy cruisers' and two transports, a not uncommon mistake by army pilots attacking from height against ships at sea. They had in fact hit nothing. However, early next morning, 4 June, four Catalinas, armed with torpedoes and guided by radar, made another contact with the Midway Occupation Force and scored a hit on one of its accompanying oilers, the *Akebono Maru*. The explosion killed twenty-three men and forced the oiler temporarily out of formation, though – as was too often the case with the inferior and sometimes defective American torpedoes of that vintage – failing to sink the ship. But the battle of Midway had definitely begun.

THE BATTLE OF MIDWAY

The battle now opening would repeat the pattern of operations, already well established in the Pacific War but not yet before exemplified on so wide or large a scale, of fleets engaging at distances which hid them from each other throughout the course of the action. Mutual invisibility was a strategic difficulty with which admirals had grappled since great fleets first took to the high seas. It had tantalised Nelson, who, in the great campaigns of the Nile and Trafalgar, had for weeks flogged the waters of the Mediterranean and Atlantic in his efforts to find, fix and fight his opponent, aided only by the constants of prevailing wind, distances and sailing-ship speeds, to help him calculate where the enemy might be brought to battle. The same difficulty, within confines narrower than those which had determined Nelson's plotting but entailing ship speeds far higher than any for which he had had to allow, had similarly exercised Jellicoe and Beatty. For all three admirals, however, the solution of strategic difficulty paid off in tactical certainty. At the end of their chases and surveys, they had the reassurance of catching the enemy clear in view, within range of their gunfire and at distances where estimation of damage inflicted could be readily established – more readily, it is true, by Nelson and his captains than by Jellico and his; but in both cases they had before their eyes the fall of shot and strike of salvoes to substantiate their success in bringing on a fight.

To strategic difficulty the Pacific War added the dimension of tactical uncertainty. At the Coral Sea none of the carriers on either side sighted the enemy's; and so fragmentary was the judgement which returning attack pilots could make of the results of their bomb and torpedo strikes that, as we have seen, Yamamoto went to Midway persuaded that he had sunk two of his carrier opponents in the earlier battle when he had sunk only one. These obscurities were to persist and ramify. At Midway the fleets would fight at 200 miles' range of each other, filling the skies with aircraft of the deadliest offensive power but manned by crews so consumed by the effort to find their targets, deliver their weapons and make their way back to the moving home of their mother ships that exact observation of the state in which they had left the enemy, even the spot of sea room in which that enemy had been located, would frequently be beyond their powers. The Midway admirals were in a sense to fight blind, counting on a kingdom of the one-eyed to guide them towards each other for the lethal blow.

Four types of aircraft, of which the Japanese possessed only three, were to determine Midway's tactical character. The first was land-based: the American Flying Fortresses and other bombers, and their associated fighters and reconnaissance floatplanes, based at Midway. Their presence conferred on the Americans an important advantage. Midway was a fixed point, to which bomber and fighter crews operating against ships could find their way back without navigational complication. It was also unsinkable. Moreover, the bombers based there, particularly the Flying Fortresses, were of longer-range, heavier armament and greater bomb-load than any shipborne type. The Midway air force was not, in practice, to inflict crippling damage on Yamamoto's fleet; but its existence was to invest American capabilities with a psychological menace that troubled the Japanese throughout the battle, while its intervention, on one if not two occasions, was to distort their decision-making with disastrous effect.

The second type of aircraft was shipborne, embarked in both Japanese and American carriers, and this was also a high-level bomber. The Japanese version was the Aicha D3A, or Type 97, known to the Americans as the Val; its American equivalent was the Douglas Dauntless. Val's speed was about 200 mph and its range 800 miles; the American Devastator, an inferior aircraft, had the same range but was much slower. Both could be used as dive-bombers, in which configuration the pilot aimed his aircraft directly at the target, pulling out of the dive at minimum height as he released his bomb. Val was a notoriously deadly dive-bomber, delivering a 900 lb projectile with great accuracy; but, though dive-bombing excelled as a means of ship destruction, it was highly dangerous, even against the skimpy anti-aircraft defences mounted by warships in 1942, and returned heavy losses for uncertain results.

Even more risky was torpedo-bombing, which required pilots to fly straight and level, at minimum altitude, while the torpedo was lined up on target. The manoeuvre greatly simplified the anti-aircraft gunners'

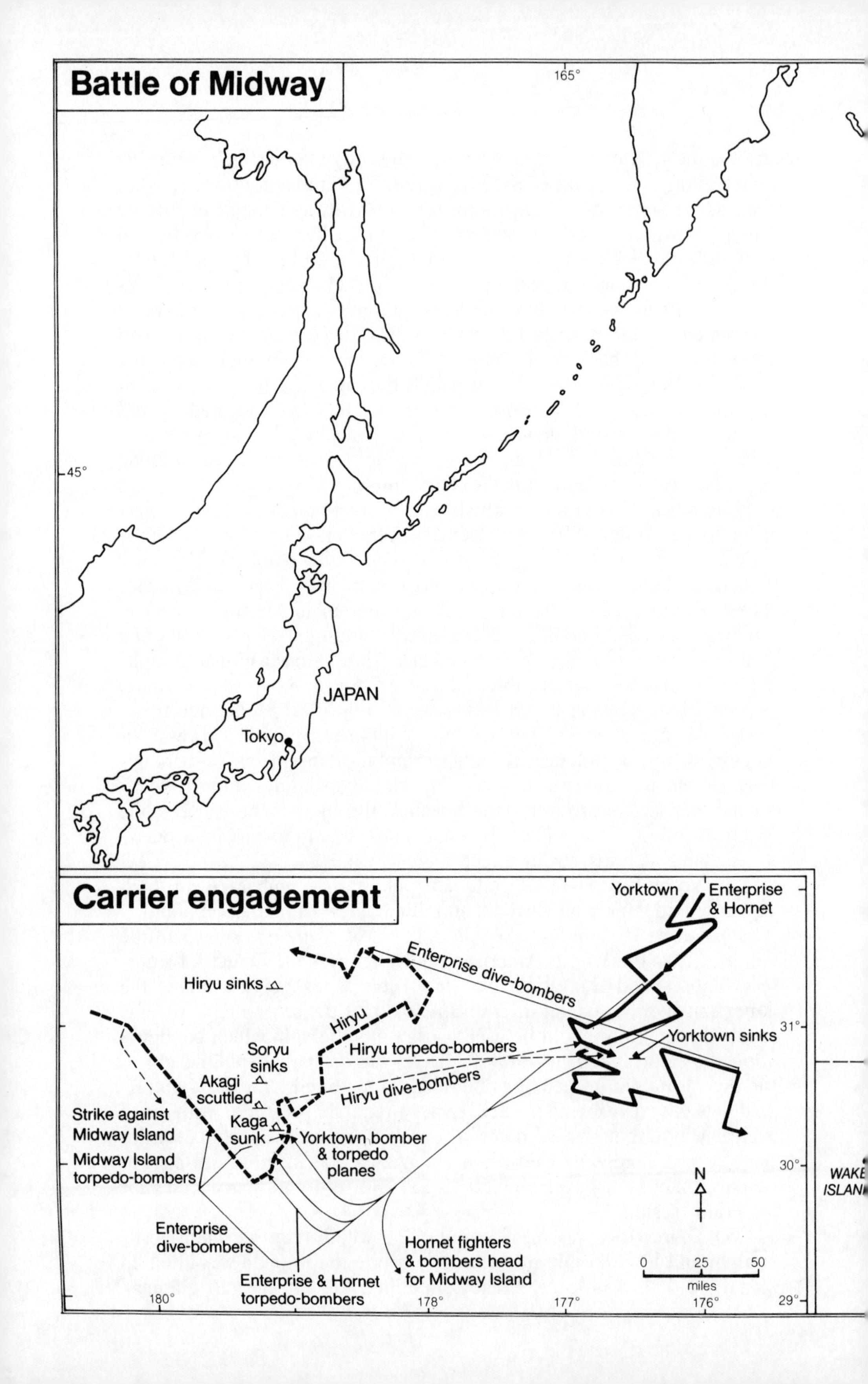

Battle of Midway
165°
45°
JAPAN
Tokyo
Carrier engagement
Yorktown
Enterprise & Hornet
Enterprise dive-bombers
Hiryu sinks
Hiryu
31°
Yorktown sinks
Hiryu torpedo-bombers
Soryu sinks
Akagi scuttled
Hiryu dive-bombers
Strike against Midway Island
Kaga sunk
Yorktown bomber & torpedo planes
Midway Island torpedo-bombers
30°
N
WAKE ISLAN
Enterprise dive-bombers
Hornet fighters & bombers head for Midway Island
0
25
50
miles
Enterprise & Hornet torpedo-bombers
180°
178°
177°
176°
29°

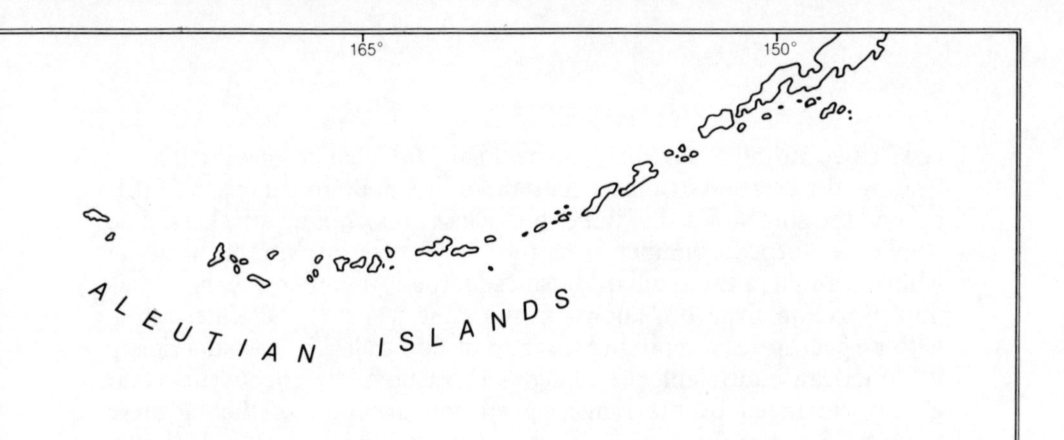
165°
150°
ALEUTIAN ISLANDS

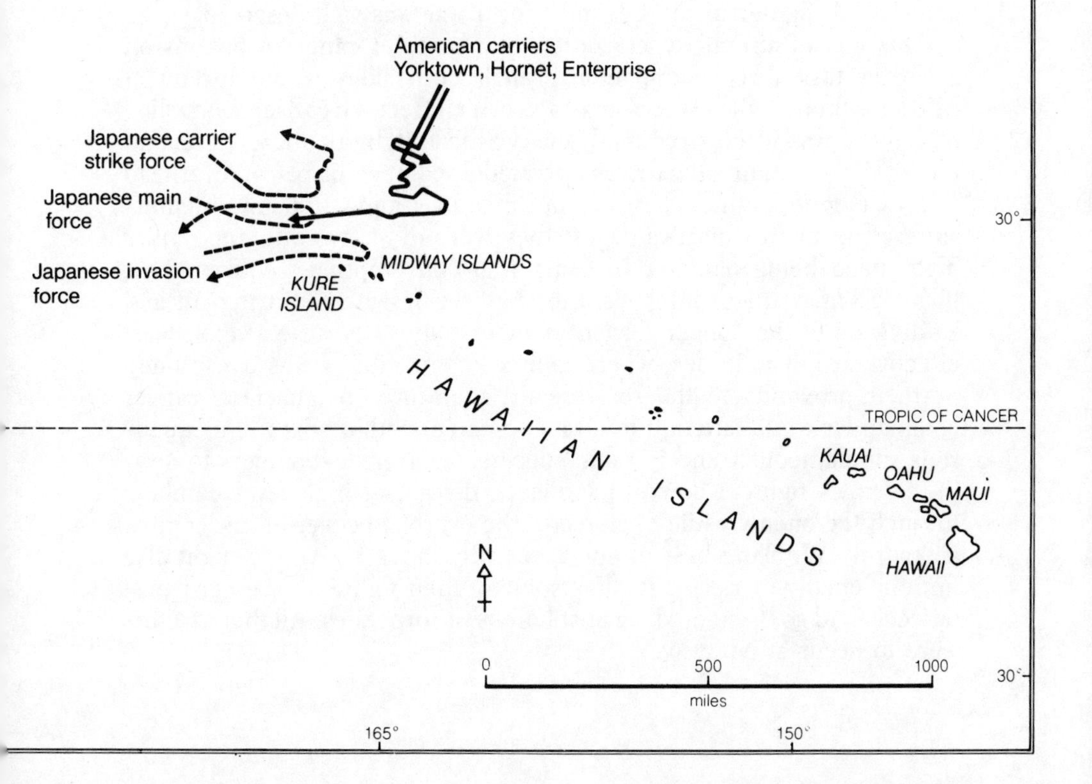
45°
PACIFIC
OCEAN
American carriers
Yorktown, Hornet, Enterprise
Japanese carrier
strike force
Japanese main
force
30°
Japanese invasion
force
MIDWAY ISLANDS
KURE
ISLAND
HAWAIIAN ISLANDS
TROPIC OF CANCER
KAUAI
OAHU
MAUI
HAWAII
N
0
500
1000
miles
30°
165°
150°

task, since no allowance had to be made for change of elevation or bearing; the creation of a mere 'curtain of fire' at up to a thousand yards beyond the ship sufficed to inflict heavy loss on incoming attackers. The shipborne torpedo-bomber was the third type of aircraft used at Midway. In 1942 the standard Japanese torpedo-bomber was the Nakajima B5N, or Type 99, known to the Americans as the Kate; again, with a speed of 200 mph and a range of 600 miles, it was superior to its American equivalent, the Douglas Devastator. Its effectiveness was greatly enhanced by the range, speed and accuracy of the Japanese torpedo; American torpedoes, launched at the end of recklessly daring approach runs in the battle of New Guinea a month before Midway, had consistently run under their targets or failed to explode on impact.

The fourth type of aircraft to fly at Midway was the shipborne fighter (though the Americans also operated some land-based fighters from the island). The standard American version was the Grumman Wildcat. Heavily armoured and with self-sealing tanks, it was cherished by its pilots as 'rugged', being difficult to shoot down and providing a steady gun platform for 'deflection' shooting, at which they excelled. However, it was 20 mph slower than its Japanese equivalent, the Zero (Mitsubishi A6M), already famed as the most elusive dogfighters in the Pacific skies. Though the fragile Zero disintegrated if struck hard by a Wildcat's guns, the American pilots' difficulty was to get it in their sights; its reputation as the most advanced and versatile seaborne, though also land-based, fighter of the Second World war was well deserved.

This mix of aircraft types conferred a complex range of options on a carrier task force commander, which both sides would exploit at Midway, though the Americans to greater effect. A carrier's first line of defence was its elusiveness. If that was lost, fighters offered a second line of defence, and all carriers operated a 'combat air patrol' overhead as a matter of routine when within range of a known enemy. Fighters suffered from two disadvantages: they were of short endurance, their high speed being paid for in heavy fuel consumption, requiring that they land at frequent intervals, thus interfering with the flying-off and landing-on of the 'longer-legged' bombers; and they were at their least effective at low altitudes, where their manoeuvrability was constrained by their proximity to the sea. Ideally, therefore, an attacking carrier commander would attempt to hit an opponent with a mixture of squadrons simultaneously and in rapid succession: torpedo-bombers to draw the enemy's fighters down to sea level, dive- and high-level bombers to catch the enemy while deprived of the overhead cover of his 'combat air patrol'. With the best of good luck, the incoming strike might also find the enemy carriers refuelling some of their fighters (or other types) on deck, and so 'flatfooted' against bombs or torpedoes. All these factors were to occur at Midway.

The battle over Midway island

Admiral Nagumo, in command of the Japanese Carrier Striking Force, was ebullient, direct and uncomplicated. He was a sea dog, happier afloat than ashore, absorbed by shipboard routine, devoted to his sailors and loyal to old shipmates. 'Generous and outgoing,' a contemporary recalled, he was 'the sort to greet a friend with a shout of welcome and a stunning clap on the shoulder.' He was also oddly sentimental. A false report that Admiral Kimmel, the US fleet commander, had 'lost his head' over the Pearl Harbor disaster brought tears to his eyes and expressions of self-reproach. Patently likeable and unreflectingly brave, he was none the less, in the judgement of his friend, Admiral Nichizo Tsukahara, commander of the Eleventh Air Fleet, 'wholly unfitted by background, training, experience and interest for a major role in Japan's naval air arm. [He] was an old line officer, a specialist in torpedo attack and large-scale manoeuvres. . . . He had no conception of the real power and potentialities of the air arm when he became commander-in-chief of the First Air Fleet' in April 1941.

He had learned a great deal in the intervening year and had commanded with almost flawless success so far; not a single ship of his had been scratched in the Pearl Harbor operation and, though Coral Sea might be judged an American strategic success, it had cost the Pacific Fleet one of its precious carriers, while his own striking force still remained intact. Nagumo, none the less, was not truly 'air-minded'. Raised in the tradition of ship destruction by close combat with guns and torpedoes, his mind grappled uneasily with the spatial and time dimensions of engagement over long distances. He thought in terms of massing an overall superiority – which his numbers easily allowed him to do – rather than of keeping the right 'mix' of aircraft types, ready for action, airborne over his own ships and heading for the enemy, which was the secret of successful carrier command.

Before the two carrier fleets drew into range of each other and were still nearly 400 miles apart, the Americans north-east, the Japanese north-west of the island respectively, Nagumo – still ignorant of his enemy's presence – decided to make the first strike against the island itself. At half past four in the morning of 4 June, nine squadrons of aircraft, thirty-six Val and thirty-six Kate bombers escorted by thirty-six Zero fighters, left his four carriers – *Akagi* ('Red Castle'), *Kaga* ('Increased Joy'), *Hiryu* ('Flying Dragon') and *Soryu* ('Green Dragon') – and set off for Midway.

They had 276 miles of sea to cross and had covered nearly half the distance when, at about 0530, they appeared on the screen of one of Midway's search radars. The interception was then lost and an alert postponed until at seven minutes to six it was confirmed by a report from one of the navy's shipborne radars: 'Many bogey aircraft bearing 310 degrees, distance 93 [miles].' Midway's force of six Wildcats and twenty Buffaloes was instantly scrambled to intercept, climbed to 17,000 feet and found the 108 Japanese aircraft bearing in on the bombers in a formidable, self-protecting 'Vee of Vees' with Zeros flying cover overhead. The American fighters, most of them with Marine pilots, found themselves hopelessly outnumbered and outclassed. Drawn into dogfights, which only nine of the twenty-six planes survived, they failed in attempts to check the bombers, which pressed on over Midway, destroyed the command post, oil fuel tanks, hospital and service buildings, wrecked floatplanes in the lagoon and departed, twenty minutes after arrival, at 0650. Some thirty of the intruders had been hit by the Marine pilots or ground fire but the exchange ratio was very much in the Japanese favour.

Lieutenant Joichi Tomonaga, leader of the Midway attack force, nevertheless signalled *Hiryu* as he began the return flight, 'There is need for a second attack', thereby unsettling Nagumo, who was reluctant to sanction landings while the Midway air defences remained active. However, Tomonaga had underestimated the gravity of the situation. Unknown to him, Midway's air reconnaisance force had detected Nagumo some twenty minutes before he himself had taken off from *Hiryu*. A Catalina on dawn patrol, searching 200 miles to the north-west, broadcast at 0534 the single cipher group, 'Enemy carriers'; then at 0545 a plain-language transmission, intercepted by *Enterprise*, 'Many enemy planes heading Midway bearing 320 degrees distant 150 [miles]'; finally, at half past six, the message, 'Two carriers and battleships bearing 320 degrees distant 180 [miles] course 135 degrees speed 25 [knots]'. Admiral Fletcher, the senior carrier commander aboard *Yorktown*, at once ordered Admiral Spruance, with *Enterprise* and *Hornet*, to 'proceed southwesterly and attack enemy carriers when definitely located'. Meanwhile Nimitz signalled Commander Cyril Simard, who was commanding at Midway, 'to go all out for the carriers'.

Thus, even while Tomanaga was leading his damaged but still relatively intact Midway strike group back to *Hiryu* and her sisters, the island's full complement of fifteen Flying Fortresses, four medium Marauder bombers and six Avenger torpedo aircraft were making their way by parallel but separate courses towards the Japanese carriers. Shortly after seven o'clock, the Marauders and Avengers, wholly unescorted, began their attack on *Hiryu* and *Akagi*, dropping torpedoes and bombs. Four Avengers and two Marauders were shot down over their targets. The Flying Fortresses, which arrived overhead at 20,000 feet at 0810, suffered no loss and returned home with firm reports of having inflicted four hits on two carriers; but, as with most high-altitude bombing against fast ships taking evasive action, it had done no damage at all.

The bombing had, however, shaken Nagumo's resolution, since it confirmed Tomonaga's judgement on the need for a second attack on Midway. Such an attack would require his torpedo- and dive-bombers,

USS *Yorktown*, flagship of Admiral Fletcher, commander of Task Force 17, the only American aircraft carrier sunk at the Battle of Midway, 4 June 1942.

ABOVE LEFT Admiral Chester Nimitz (1885–1966), Commander-in-Chief, Pacific Fleet (left) and Vice-Admiral Raymond Spruance (1886–1969), commander of Task Force 17.
TOP Vice-Admiral Frank Jack Fletcher, commander of US carrier forces and of Task Force 17.
CENTRE Admiral Chuichi Nagumo (1887–1944), commander of the Japanese carrier fleet.
LEFT Admiral Isuruku Yamamoto (1884–1943) commander of the Japanese Combined Fleet 1939–43.

crowding the decks of *Hiryu*, *Kaga*, *Akagi* and *Soryu* in readiness against any American carriers detected within striking distance, to be stripped of their anti-ship weapons and rearmed as high-level bombers for a land mission. Tomonaga's message had been received at seven o'clock, and at ten past seven Midway's Avengers and Marauders had made their attack, ill fated but confirming his warning that Midway still showed fight. At 0715, therefore, Nagumo issued the order to 'strike below' the torpedo aircraft waiting for dispatch against an American fleet, and for their torpedoes to be replaced with bombs in the hangars while Tomonaga and his Midway survivors were landed on.

The great carrier battle

The balance of advantage so far rested in the Japanese fleet's favour. It had destroyed more aircraft than it had lost and beaten off the three attacks the Americans had launched against it. However, intellectual advantage and strength of morale – of such key significance in the clash of navies and armies alike – rested with the Americans. The morale of neither fleet had yet been touched. Sailors in the main bodies of the two navies had no physical evidence of impending triumph or disaster before their eyes to suggest how the course of action ran. By this stage in the morning of a contemporary land battle, or of a sea battle of old, there would have been a wrack of broken men and material strewn about the field of engagement to speak of its ebb and flow. None strewed the sunny waters of the north-west Pacific either side of Midway. Flames and ruins on the island itself were testimony to the violence of the early morning engagement, but apart from a scar on the flight deck of *Akagi* – inflicted by the impact of a crashing Avenger before it tipped over the side into the sea – neither fleet was scratched.

Yet the integrity of Nagumo's carrier group gaped as if from a wound not yet inflicted but which it must inevitably suffer. Not only did Nagumo remain in ignorance of the brooding presence of *Yorktown*, *Enterprise* and *Hornet*; he had already, by his decision to 'break the spot' – 'spot' was American carrier jargon for the state of aircraft readiness prevailing at any moment – and strike his torpedo aircraft away, compromised his ability to hit at an American carrier force should it be located. Worse was to follow. At 0728, thirteen minutes after his order to 'break the spot', he received word from the spotter floatplane of one of his cruisers, *Tone*, that it had sighted an American surface force. The pilot's message, infuriating in its imprecision, read that he had 'sighted what appeared to be ten enemy surface ships in position bearing 10 degrees, distance 240 miles, from Midway. Course 150 degrees, speed over 20 knots.'

Nagumo prevaricated, a dangerous mental set for an admiral to adopt in a sea battle at any time, and disastrous in the fast-moving conditions of carrier warfare. His initial thought was that 'ten ships' offered his armada of carriers and battleships little threat and that he needed, in any case, time for his returning Midway strike group to land on. Then he changed his mind. At 0745 he ordered that those embarked aircraft not yet rearmed with bombs for the second Midway strike should retain their torpedoes in preparation for action against enemy fleet units. Meanwhile he wirelessed *Tone*'s floatplane with an urgent request for clarification of its first sighting report: 'Ascertain ship types.' At 0809 the *Tone* search pilot advised that the ten ships comprised five cruisers and five destroyers, thereby allaying Nagumo's anxiety, but at 0820 the pilot added the amplification, 'Enemy is accompanied by what appears to be a carrier'. He had sighted the *Yorktown* task force, from which Admiral Fletcher, alerted by Midway's Catalina and the fleet's own radar sighting, was just about to launch twelve torpedo- and seventeen dive-bombers for a search and attack mission against *Hiryu*, *Soryu*, *Kaga* and *Akagi*.

Nagumo, who might still have recovered from his error if given an opportunity to think – for flight time over the 150 miles of sea space still separating the two carrier fleets was an hour at contemporary aircraft cruising speed – was next distracted by another strike from Midway. Delivered at 0820 by eleven old and slow Marine Corps Vindicators, it was driven away from the carriers by concerted Zero attacks and did no damage to them or their escorts. Nevertheless it had the effect of confusing Nagumo's capacity to analyse time, speed and distance at a moment when he most needed to think clearly.

Between 0840 and nine o'clock, Nagumo's carriers recovered Tomonaga's Midway formations, hastened the rearming of the bombers with torpedoes and landed on as many of their Zeros as was possible, to refuel them for return to combat air patrol. Tamon Yamaguchi, the admiral commanding the *Hiryu–Soryu* group, argued with Nagumo by signal blinker that, such was the operational urgency, he should dispense with the rearming procedure and dispatch the bombers towards *Tone*'s scout plane, even if they arrived over the American carrier with fragmentation weapons instead of armour-piercing bombs and torpedoes. Nagumo rejected his submission. He sensed that, after an initial period of confusion, he was now recovering his power to strike. Confident of the numerical superiority of his fleet, he was not even shaken by the reception, at 0855, of a final baleful message from *Tone*'s scout: 'Ten enemy torpedo planes heading towards you.' As the message arrived he was signalling Yamamoto, in *Yamato* 450 miles to the north, 'Enemy composed of one carrier, five cruisers and five destroyers sighted at 8 am in position bearing 10 degrees, distance 200 miles from AF' (as if the cipher fiction still had use). 'We are heading for it.' Simultaneously by lamp from *Akagi*'s bridge he was instructing her sister carriers: 'After completing recovery operations, proceed northward. We plan to contact and destroy the enemy task force.' However, superiority of ship numbers counted for nothing in long-range carrier encounters if the more numerous fleet were caught without its combat air patrol aloft and threw away its strike aircraft in serial and uncoordinated attacks.

Admiral Raymond Spruance, commanding *Enterprise* and *Hornet* towards which Nagumo was now heading, had been thinking exactly as a carrier commander should in those fateful minutes while his opponent had dithered between the choice of ship or shore strikes. Spruance's original plan had been to launch his Dauntless and Devastator aircraft at nine o'clock, when they would have less than a hundred miles of sea to cover to reach Nagumo's estimated position. News of the Japanese attack on Midway had suggested to him, however, that an earlier launch might catch the two Japanese carrier groups recovering and refuelling their aircraft, a particularly desirable moment to launch bombs and torpedoes, for the flight decks would be cluttered with inflammable fuel lines; he could not, of course, guess that they would also be heaped with bombs torn from the returned aircraft and left to lie while torpedoes were hooked on to the weapon release racks. Accordingly, and even though it meant committing his pilots to a flight of 175 miles, with the attendant danger that some would 'splash' for lack of fuel on the return journey, he decided shortly after six o'clock to launch at seven.

He also decided to make the strike 'all or nothing', launching every dive-and torpedo-bomber, so that the Japanese would be hit simultaneously by a concentrated mass. This decision increased the hazard of the mission. Launching 'a full load' took an hour, and required the first aloft to wait overhead until all were in the air, each plane consuming fuel as it circled. It was an added disadvantage that the prevailing wind required *Enterprise* and *Hornet* to reverse course for flying off, thereby further opening the gap the pilots would have to cross. However, he judged all these risks necessary. Between 0702 and 0806, sixty-seven Dauntless dive-bombers and twenty-nine Devastator torpedo-bombers, with an escort of twenty Wildcat fighters (leaving thirty-six for combat air patrol), drove down the decks of *Enterprise* and *Hornet* and climbed to altitude. At 0745 an onset of anxiety about the risk of his aircraft running out of fuel over the sea prompted Spruance to order those already aloft away towards their targets; the last two squadrons followed in their wake. There were now six in the air altogether: Bombing 6, Scouting 6 (also bombers) and Torpedo 6 from *Enterprise*, Bombing 8, Scouting 8 and Torpedo 8 from *Hornet*, together with parts of Fighting 6 and 8.

All cleared the decks successfully, revving up engines to full revolutions, releasing brakes and accelerating the full length of the flight deck to lurch off the bow, under their maximum load of fuel and weapons. 'To get off a carrier deck', a pilot recalled, 'one does have a lot of mechanical preparation on deck and a never-failing audience which means that the beginning of every strike involves fulfilment of

Walter Mitty dreams. I'd say the actual take-off forced one into some self-confidence and bravado, unlike the infantry situation where no one was watching.' Yet this was also a moment for which the regular and reservist pilots of Task Force 16 air group had trained long months, first ashore to master the art of putting an aircraft down on to the two-football-field space of a carrier deck, then afloat to feel the toss and pitch of a moving hull, the tug of an arrester-gear landing, the surge of power which kicked an aircraft aloft, finally in the depths of the ocean to learn the anxieties of searching for a mother ship across apparently empty horizons. The skills of the carrier pilot were now theirs; but for many this was the first day on which they would fly them against the enemy.

Samuel Eliot Morison, a direct observer of the great Pacific air battles, was to write:

> This fourth of June was a cool and beautiful day, perfect for carrier war if the wind had only been stronger and from the enemy's direction. At 19,00 feet the pilots could see all around a circle of 50 miles' radius. Only a few fluffy cumulus clouds were between them and an ocean that looked like a dish of wrinkled blue Persian porcelain. Small consolation, to be sure, for these young men who were to fall that day in flames or drown in the broad ocean whose mastery they would win for their country. Yet, if a sailor must die, the air way is the fairest. The tense, crisp briefing in the ready rooms; the warming up of the planes which the devoted 'ground crews' have been checking, arming, fuelling and servicing; the ritual of the take-off, as precise and ordered as a ballet. Planes swooping in graceful curves over the ships while the group assembles; hand-signalling and waving to your wing man, whom you may never see again; a long flight over the superb ocean; first sight of your target and the sudden catch at your heart when you know that they see you, from the black puffs of anti-aircraft bursts that suddenly appear in the clear air; the wriggling and squirming of the ships, followed by wakes like the tails of white horses; the dreaded Zeros of combat air patrol swooping down on you apparently out of nothing; and suddenly the tight, incredibly swift attack, when you forgot everything but the target so rapidly enlarging, and the desperate necessity of choosing the exact moment – the right tenth of a second – to release and pull out.

This moment of contact the pilots of *Enterprise* and *Hornet* had been briefed to expect at 0920. At 0905, however, Nagumo ordered a 90-degree alteration of course, under pressure of further warnings from his reconnaissance aircraft of approaching enemy aircraft. This change put him on a north-easterly instead of south-easterly course and carried his convoy away from the Americans' indicated contact point at over 20 knots. When *Hornet*'s dive-bombers reached it, accordingly, they found the sea empty, and their leader, deciding that the Japanese carriers must be closing on Midway, turned due south towards the island over a hundred miles away. Soon many were out of the fuel necessary for the return journey and were forced to press on to try to land on the island. Fifteen found it; those – the last departed from the flight decks – with sufficient fuel returned to *Enterprise* and *Hornet*. All the escorting Wildcat fighters, which had the shortest range among the American aircraft deployed, ditched in the open sea and were lost. This large element of Task Force 16's air group therefore missed the battle altogether.

The dive-bombers had also become separated by cloud from their accompanying torpedo-bombers, whose leader was Lieutenant-Commander John Waldron. When Waldron found empty sea at the nominated contact point with Task Force 16's other aircraft and five minutes after the expected moment of sighting saw funnel smoke on the horizon, he decided to turn north. Wiggling his wings, he gathered his group around him and 'just went as straight at the Jap fleet as if he'd had a string tied to them', as one of his pilots, Ensign George Gay, recalled. Waldron had long abandoned any illusion about the survivability of his old and slow aircraft in the face of Japanese gun and fighter defence. 'My greatest hope,' he had written to his crews the evening before, 'is that we encounter a favourable tactical situation, but if we don't . . .' The tactical situation was as unfavourable as could be. *Hornet*'s fifteen torpedo-bombers had no fighter cover, were clear in view of a combat air patrol of quadruple strength and had to fly low, straight and level for their approach torpedo run. One by one they went down until only Gay's Devastator was left. At 800 yards from a carrier he could not identify, the automatic release of his torpedo failed. He flew on to drop it manually, passed below the carrier's bridge, on which he saw the Japanese captain 'jumping up and down raising hell', crossed the flight deck, which he noticed draped with refuelling hoses, and then, his controls shot away by an attacking Zero, crashed into the sea. He was to inflate his life-raft and be picked up by a Catalina the day after the battle, the only survivor of the thirty aircrew of *Hornet*'s Torpedo 8.

The leader of Torpedo 6, *Enterprise's* squadron, had like Waldron decided to turn north when they found the sea empty at the contact point. Soon after 0936, when *Akagi* signalled her sister carriers to cease fire, he spotted them on the horizon and lined up his fourteen Devastators for a torpedo run. The Japanese carriers manoeuvred to present their sterns, forcing Torpedo 6 to make a wide swing for a beam shot, and so giving time for the combat air patrols to concentrate. During the flight from *Enterprise* Torpedo 6's fighter escort had become separated. It was entirely unprotected. Pressing on as Torpedo 8 had done, pitting its speed – little better than 100 mph – against the 25 knots of the carriers racing away from it, the squadron reached their bombing position with painful slowness. While it did so the Zeros began to attack and one by one the Devastators fell into the sea. Only four of the fourteen planes survived, and they failed to score a hit.

Yorktown, operating apart from, though in consort with, Task Force

16 (she and her escorts constituted Task Force 17), had launched later than her sisters, at the time Spruance had originally chosen. Fletcher was worried that there might be Japanese carriers unaccounted for within striking range, and did not want to be caught with empty decks if an attack came out of the blue. Finally at 0830 he decided he could wait no longer. Unlike Spruance, however, he did not launch a 'full load' but sent Bombing 3, Torpedo 3 and part of Fighting 3, keeping Scouting 5 and the rest of Fighting 3 with the ship.

Torpedo 3, the slowest squadron, started first, making a course to allow for a long Japanese advance towards Midway since the last sighting report; the attack plan was that, if contact was not made at the expected point, all squadrons would then reverse course and fly up the path the Japanese had been predicted to follow until they were found. The fighters would be flying at the extreme limit of their range, 175 miles, 'really giving a lot', as Lieutenant-Commander Max Leslie, Torpedo 3's leader, put it; but Lieutenant-Commander John Thatch, the fighter commander, was willing to take the risk. They were the last to join the formation circling above *Yorktown*, but at 0905 reached the dive-bombers' altitude and set out after the slow Devastators.

The Devastator torpedo-bombers were overtaken by the Dauntless dive-bombers and Wildcat fighter group in mid-flight and they proceeded for a while together, until cloud hid the low-level torpedo aircraft from the dive-bombers and fighters 14,000 feet far above. The courses of Torpedo 3 and Bombing 3 then diverged; and by chance Torpedo 3 chose the better heading. About ten o'clock it sighted smoke on the horizon, turned right 'to get a better look' and prepared to attack. They were some fourteen miles from what they had now identified as the four Japanese carriers (somewhat scattered by Task Force 16's attack) and squaring up for a torpedo run when they were surprised by two Zeros of the combat air patrol and began to suffer losses. At ten miles' range, two more Zeros attacked, and then waves of six or eight attacked in series, driving the pilots of the torpedo aircraft down to 150 feet while the rear gunners tried to fight back with their inadequate swivel-mounted machine-guns. The squadron split into two, to make convergent beam attacks, but as they reached torpedo range they – and their escorting fighters – were overwhelmed. Seven of the twelve Devastators went down. 'Any direction I was able to look,' recalled a survivor, Chief Petty Officer Wilhelm Esders, 'I could see five, six, seven or more aircraft on fire, spinning down, or simply out of control and flying around crazily.' None of the torpedoes launched scored hits. The attack was as fruitless as all those already launched from Midway and Task Force 16.

Mitsuo Fuchida, aboard *Akagi*, watched the attack develop from the flight deck:

The raiders closed in from both sides, barely skimming over the water. Flying in single columns, they were within five miles and seemed to be aiming straight for [us]. I watched in breathless suspense, thinking how impossible it would be to dodge all their torpedoes. But these raiders, too, without protection escorts, were being engaged by our fighters. On *Akagi*'s flight deck all attention was fixed on the dramatic scene unfolding before us, and there was wild cheering and whistling as the raiders went down one after another. . . . Both enemy groups reached their release points, and we watched for the splash of torpedoes aimed at *Akagi*. But . . . at the last moment the planes appeared to forsake *Akagi*, zoomed overhead and made for *Hiryu* to port and astern of us. . . . Seven enemy planes finally succeeded in launching their torpedoes at *Hiryu*, five from her starboard side and two from port. Our Zeros tenaciously pursued the retiring attackers as far as they could. *Hiryu* turned sharply to starboard to evade the torpedoes, and we watched anxiously to see if any would find their mark. A deep sigh of relief went up, no explosion occurred, and *Hiryu* soon turned her head to port and resumed her original course. . . . Most of the credit for this success belonged to the brilliant interception of our fighters. . . . No less impressive was the dauntless courage shown by the American fliers, who carried out the attack despite heavy losses. Shipboard spectators of the thrilling drama watched spellbound, blissfully unaware that the worst was yet to come. . . . As our fighters ran out of ammunition, during the fierce battle, they returned to the carriers for replenishment, but few ran low on fuel. Service crews cheered the returning pilots, patted them on the shoulder and shouted words of encouragement. As soon as a plane was ready again, the pilot nodded, pushed forward the throttle and roared back into the sky.

Commander Fuchida and his shipmates had reason for their elation. 'A total of 40 [aircraft]', as he reckoned it, 'had been thrown against us . . . but only seven American planes had survived long enough to release their missiles, and not a single hit had been scored. Nearly all the raiding aircraft had been brought down.' In fact, counting the first torpedo attack from Midway, the Flying Fortress attack and two dive-bomber attacks from the island, involving forty-two aircraft, and the torpedo-bomber attacks by *Hornet*, *Enterprise* and *Yorktown* involving forty-one, there had been seven attacks altogether by eighty-three aircraft, of which thirty-seven had been destroyed, *Hornet*'s Torpedo 8 in its entirety.

Yet the attacks had some effect. At ten o'clock, as the sea closed over the wreckage of the last of *Yorktown*'s torpedo aircraft, the Japanese First Air Fleet's carriers found themselves more widely dispersed than fleet routines or safety permitted. Instead of steaming in a self-protecting box at 1300-yard intervals, they were scattered, *Kaga* and *Soryu* at 6000 yards from *Akagi*, and *Hiryu* out of sight of the flagship altogether. Moreover, their combat air patrols, dragged down from altitude by the torpedo attacks, were at sea level – the worst position for a fighter escort. Further, the flight decks were crowded with refuelling and rearming aircraft, draped with high-octane petrol hoses and littered with the high-explosive bombs discarded after Nagumo's change of mind an hour and a half earlier.

Still, ninety-three aircraft – Vals and Kates – were ready to depart. The time for the decisive strike against the American carriers, whose location was now known within close limits, had been fixed for 1030. The Japanese air groups were intact, greatly outnumbered the American groups even before they had suffered their recent losses and must certainly succeed in devastating *Hornet*, *Enterprise* and *Yorktown*, at latest by noon. 'At 1020', as Fuchida described the scene, 'Admiral Nagumo gave the order to launch when ready. On *Akagi*'s flight deck all planes were in position with engines warming up. The big ship began turning into the wind. Within five minutes all her planes must be launched.'

Those five minutes were to constitute one of the few truly crucial 'moments of decision' which can be isolated in the whole course of warfare. At 1025 Nagumo stood poised on the brink of perhaps the greatest naval victory ever promised an admiral, certain to be spectacular in itself and destined to alter the balance of power between the Western and the Asian world for decades to come. At 1030 he confronted not victory but disaster. This change of fortune was the result of two accidents. The first was the course chosen, quite by chance, an hour earlier, by *Yorktown*'s torpedo-bombers, which gave them sight of the Japanese carriers and so called their combat air patrol down to sea level. The second was the random intervention of an American submarine *Nautilus*, whose straying into the First Air Fleet's path caused a destroyer, *Araski*, to be detached from the carriers to drop depth charges. *Araski*'s depth charges missed; but the white ribbon of its wake, as it worked up speed to rejoin Nagumo's covering screen, caught the eye of the leader of *Enterprise*'s dive-bomber group at 0955 and sowed a seed of suspicion.

Enterprise's Bombing 6 squadron had, like others, lost its way when Nagumo altered course. Now its leader, Lieutenant-Commander Wade McClusky, detected, even from 14,000 feet, that *Araski* was in a hurry and guessed that she was steaming to rejoin the Japanese main body. The stream of her wake was a perfect indicator of the main body's position. McClusky now lined up his formation – thirty-seven Devastators – on *Araski* and headed north-east. Shortly after 1020 he sighted *Akagi*, *Soryu* and *Kaga* steaming north-west in a 'circular disposition [of] roughly eight miles'. *Hiryu* was further ahead. McClusky turned to attack and led his bombers in from 14,500 in a 70-degree dive at 280 knots. The sky was empty of Zeros, all at sea level or on their mother ships' decks, and nothing impeded the trajectory of their 500 lb and 1000 lb bombs.

Akagi was the first to go. Fuchida recalled:

Visibility was good. At 1024 the order to start launching came from the bridge by voice-tube. The Air Officer flapped a white flag, and the first Zero fighter gathered speed and whizzed off the flight deck. At that moment a lookout screamed, 'Hell-divers'. I looked up to see three black enemy planes plummeting towards our ship. Some of our machine-guns managed to fire a few bursts but it was too late. The plump silhouettes of the American Dauntless dive-bombers quickly grew larger and then a number of black objects suddenly floated eerily from their wings. Bombs! Down they came straight towards me. I fell intuitively to the deck and crawled behind a command post mantlet.

Taijiro Aoki, captain of *Akagi*, noted in the log he made up afterwards: 'Three bombers dive on *Akagi* from positions bearing 80 degrees to port. . . . At about 500 metres altitude, bombs were loosed. First was a near-miss about 10 metres abeam of bridge; second hit the near elevator amidships (fatal hit); third hit the flight deck on the port side, aft. This third hit exploded in the aircraft park, among machines still rearming. The second penetrated to the hangar and detonated a torpedo store.' 'A terrific fire . . . which was just like hell' broke out, reported Nagumo's chief of staff, Ryunosuke Kusaka, and in seconds the ship's centre section was engulfed. Nagumo refused to leave the bridge and had to be dragged down. Kusaka's report continues: 'When I got down, the deck was on fire and anti-aircraft and machine-guns were firing automatically having been set off by the fire aboard ship. I had my hands and feet burned. . . . Bodies were all over the place. . . . That is the way we eventually abandoned *Akagi* – helter-skelter, no order of any sort.' The only routine observed was the ceremonial transfer of the ship's official portrait of the emperor into the destroyer whence Nagumo shifted his flag.

Nagumo was forcibly transhipped at 1047, only twenty minutes after the first bomb strike. The ship by then was a ruin. 'There was a huge hole in the flight deck, just behind the midship elevator,' Fuchida wrote. 'The elevator itself, twisted like molten glass, was drooping into the hangar. Deck plates reeled upwards in grotesque configurations. Planes stood tail up, belching livid flame and jet-black smoke.' Below decks there were more horrors. A damage-control crewman, going down to discover why the engine-room would not supply power to the pumps, found the boilers still working and the engines turning, but the crew of the starboard section all dead, killed by flames sucked down through the ventilating system.

Kaga was meanwhile suffering attacks that would do worse damage. She was hit by four bombs: one, landing just forward of the bridge, exploded a fuel-cart which sprayed the bridge party and burned them all to death. The rest set fire to aircraft and penetrated the hangars, detonating bomb stores and fuel lines. In its passage one of the bombs 'disintegrated' the ship's chief maintenance officer, who was running for cover. A brother officer who saw him disappear was surprised to hear himself framing the poetic thought, 'Those who vanish like dew will surely be quite happy.' The emperor's portrait was extracted from the inferno and transferred to a destroyer. In a few minutes the carrier had taken fire from end to end and, though some hardy souls remained aboard to attempt damage control, was clearly beyond salvation. She remained afloat until early evening until, shortly after seven o'clock, a tremendous internal explosion sent her to the bottom.

Last to be hit was *Soryu*, the victim of the *Yorktown*'s dive-bombers, which Admiral Fletcher had dispatched last against the Japanese carrier formation. Their leader, Lieutenant-Commander Maxwell Leslie, had made his own calculation as to where the Japanese might be heading and it proved to be correct. Shortly after 1020, and from a height of 20,000 feet, he spotted smoke on the horizon, descended to 14,500 and commenced his attack against the nearest carrier, which happened to be *Soryu*, while the *Enterprise* bombers were engaging *Akagi* and *Kaga*. Between 1025 and 1028 his aircraft inflicted three hits. The first penetrated *Soryu*'s forward hangar and folded the elevator back against the bridge. The second exploded in the aircraft park, tossing a Zero overboard and starting a major fuel fire. The third hit near the after elevator. Within twenty minutes the ship was ablaze from stem to stern. The fire, however, took less fierce hold than in *Kaga*, and damage-control parties which had been put back aboard managed to subdue the worst of the outbreak and got the ship back under way for an escape. At 1145 she was proceeding at 2 knots on an even keel when another of Midway's 'accidents' intervened. USS *Nautilus* had already launched torpedoes against Nagumo's escorting battleships and cruisers – the episode which had sent the destroyer *Araski* to take her under depth-charge attack. It was that conjunction which had attracted the attention of *Enterprise*'s dive-bombers with such disastrous results. Now the captain of *Nautilus* was to make his third eventful sighting of the morning – more than most submarine commanders might make in a whole career beneath the waves. At 0820 Commander W. H. Brockman put up his periscope to find 'ships on all sides . . . moving across the field at high speed and circling away', as his after-action report described it. 'A cruiser had passed over us and was now astern. . . . A battleship was on our port bow and firing her whole starboard broadside battery . . . flaghoists were being made, searchlights were trained at the periscope.' Brockman sat out the resulting depth-charge attack and beat a speedy retreat on the surface after the enemy had departed. Three hours later, however, he again sighted enemy ships, submerged and, when he put up his periscope, found *Soryu* in his field of vision at short range. He stalked the stricken ship for three hours until he reached a range at which even American torpedoes could not miss, fired three and watched *Soryu*, hit by all of them, break in half and go to the bottom.

The retreat from Midway

Between 1115 and 1145 the American torpedo-bombers and their escorting fighters began to reappear over their mother ships – which was their own ship was less important to pilots, some on the point of running out of fuel (one landed with only two gallons in his tanks), than reaching any ship at all. Many expended all fuel on the return flight and were forced to ditch, some within sight of their own carriers. When the score was reckoned, *Enterprise* was found to have lost fourteen of her thirty-seven dive-bombers and *Yorktown* two of her thirty-seven, to add to their losses of torpedo-bombers; there had also been heavy casualties in Wildcat fighters – sixteen – mainly due to ditching.

The Task Forces nevertheless were intact and now outnumbered the Japanese First Air Fleet by three to one; only *Hiryu* survived. In the five minutes between 1025 and 1030 that morning the balance of advantage in the Pacific War had been shifted, as it would prove for good. Despite catastrophic losses, however, the Japanese still showed fight. Almost as soon as he reached his new command post in the destroyer to which he had shifted his flag, Nagumo reiterated orders for *Hiryu*, last of his carriers, to attack the Americans, and at eleven o'clock eighteen dive-bombers and six fighters took off. They were followed at 1331 by ten torpedo-bombers and six more fighters.

The first group headed west towards the position in which it was now all too clearly established Task Forces 16 and 17 must lie. Shortly after noon it found *Yorktown*, still landing on its dive-bombers, but with twelve Wildcats overhead on combat air patrol. Half *Hiryu*'s Vals were shot down as they approached; another two fell to anti-aircraft fire from *Yorktown*'s escorts. However, eight survived the fighters and shells to drop their bombs and score three hits. Of these, one penetrated the flight deck, a second went down the funnel, started fires and put out five of the six boilers, and a third exploded at the fourth deck, igniting a rag store. By 1220 *Yorktown* was stopped dead and ablaze.

Brilliantly co-ordinated damage control got her started again at twenty to two, and she worked up to 20 knots and prepared to fly off fighters. Then, ten minutes later, *Hiryu*'s second wave arrived. *Yorktown*'s combat air patrol was short of fuel, the radar had been knocked out and her escorts, mistaking enemy for friendly aircraft, delayed opening fire until too late. Within two minutes *Yorktown* had suffered two torpedo hits and quickly assumed a list of 26 degrees. The damage extended to the power system, making it impossible to counter-flood, and at three o'clock, when capsize threatened imminently, Captain Elliott Buckmaster ordered 'Abandon ship'.

Before the first attack on *Yorktown* arrived, however, Admiral Fletcher had followed a hunch that a Japanese carrier survived in his vicinity and had sent off a reconnaissance mission of ten bombers to sweep the ocean to his west. At 1445 one of the pilots of Scouting 5, Lieutenant

Samuel Adams, sighted wakes on the horizon, closed to verify his sighting and saw *Hiryu*, with two battleships and numerous other escorts, in a position a hundred miles from the Task Forces. While *Yorktown* listed from the damage her adversary had inflicted, twenty-four dive-bombers, whose crews had all taken part in the morning attacks on *Hiryu*'s sister ships, took off from *Enterprise*, found their target at five o'clock and inflicted four hits. One blew the forward elevator platform against the bridge, destroying all controls. The other three started massive fires. *Hiryu*, its engine-room undamaged, raced forward at 30 knots, shrugging off a final attack by Midway-based Flying Fortresses at six. Even so, her wounds were mortal. The fires eventually became uncontrollable. In the early hours of 5 June, after the ceremonial transhipment of the emperor's portrait, the captain ordered the crew to abandon and went down with his ship.

Yorktown, also abandoned, survived longer. Twenty-four hours after she had been given up as lost, she was found afloat and in little worse condition than she had been left. A salvage crew was placed on board, which put out the last fire and passed a tow to an escort. A destroyer which took station alongside supplied power to counter-flood and the list was corrected. *Yorktown*, though low in the water and down by the bow, had recovered her seaworthiness and begun to limp for the safety of Pearl Harbor. It was at this moment that Nagumo made his last intervention. Early the day before one of his floatplanes had detected *Yorktown* abandoned and drifting. He had ordered a submarine, I-168, to search for her and, after twenty-four hours, contact was made. Four torpedoes were fired, two hit *Yorktown*, and she had again to be abandoned. So strong and complex was her interval construction that she hung on, her list only slightly increasing, until six in the morning of 6 June. Then she suddenly rolled over and sank. I-168, like USS *Nautilus*, had inflicted a deadly tit-for-tat on the carrier fleet.

The great losses of Midway had now been nflicted, and the count stood increasingly in America's favour; one of her carriers to four Japanese. With the Japanese carriers over 2200 seamen had been lost – 221 from *Akagi*, 800 from *Kaga*, 416 from *Hiryu* and 718 from *Soryu* – as well as 250 aircraft and at least 90 pilots. The loss of carriers, of course, necessarily entailed that of their aircraft, since with the sinking of *Hiryu* there was nowhere for any of the survivors to land. A large number had been shot down or ditched, with resulting heavy casualties among their aircrew; such aircrew survivors as there were had escaped only because they had been aboard when their mother ships foundered and had been picked up by escorts or, in a few cases, had been plucked from the sea after being shot down or having ditched. As the Japanese fleet air airm had no more than 1500 pilots trained to operate from carriers, and perhaps as few as a thousand, and was producing only 100 replacements a year, the loss of 90, which may be a low estimate, was disastrous to its efficiency. In a single day at Midway it lost a whole annual graduating class. The coming months were to reveal that the loss could never be made good and was as serious as that of the destruction of the carriers themselves.

Yamamoto, stationed to the north-westward behind the 18-inch guns of the giant *Yamato*, refused to be cast down. At quarter past seven on the evening of 4 June he was boldly signalling his subordinates that the enemy had been 'practically destroyed' and that the Combined Fleet was 'preparing to pursue the remnants and at the same time to occupy Midway'. In reply, Nagumo bleakly warned: 'There still exist four [*sic*] enemy carriers . . . six cruisers and sixteen destroyers. They are steaming westward [towards Japan]. None of our carriers is operational.'

Nor was this the end of the Japanese ordeal. In their retirement from the vicinity of the island, two cruisers of the Midway Occupation Force (a now redundant designation), *Mogami* and *Mikuma*, rammed each other while manoeuvring and suffered damage that lost them vital speed. Early next morning they were found, unprotected by air cover, by six Dauntless and six Vindicators from Midway, guided to their targets by a scouting Catalina. *Mikuma* was hit on its after turret by a stricken Vindicator, whose Marine pilot crashed it there in his death agonies. Next day, 6 June, both cruisers were attacked again by three air strikes from *Enterprise* and *Hornet*. *Mogami* survived, despite incurring severe damage; but the second and third strikes started such serious fires in *Mikuma* that she had to be abandoned, thus becoming the last of Midway's casualties. It was a feature of this attack, unique to Midway and perhaps to the whole Pacific War, that the closing of the range between mother ships and targets allowed the carrier pilots to have both friendly and enemy ships, at a distance of ninety miles from each other, in view at the same time. The weather remained as perfect as it had been since the battle began two days before.

COUNTING THE COST

Yamamoto's vast tentacular plan had not failed in its entirety. Kiska and Attu, his objectives in the Aleutians, had fallen to his Northern Area Force without loss; but, as both were undefended, and of the tiniest strategic value, this success was no recompense for the destruction of his Carrier Striking Force. He had preserved intact the battleships of the Combined Fleet, the heavy cruisers – formidably strong ships, as *Mikuma*'s long resistance had shown – and two light carriers which had not been under Nagumo's command. There were other carriers building; a new fleet carrier had just been commissioned, and another would be commissioned in July and a new light carrier in November. Five fleet carriers were being laid down and would join the fleet in 1944.

However, the Midway losses had lent awful substance to Yamamoto's pre-war warning of the fundamental disparity between Japanese and American industrial capacity. Fourteen American fleet carriers would be commissioned in the same period, nine light carriers and no less than sixty-six escort carriers, a class of cheap but versatile warships to which Japan could produce no equivalent because it lacked the resources to equip them with aircraft or train the pilots to fly them. By mid-1944 the total of Japanese embarked carrier aircraft would stand below 1000, while America would deploy over 3000. 'Such was the scale of American industrial power', by H. P. Willmott's analysis, 'that if during the Pearl Harbor attack the Imperial Navy had been able to sink every major unit of the entire US Navy and then complete its own construction programmes without losing a single unit, by mid-1944 it would still not have been able to put to sea a fleet equal to the one the Americans could have assembled in the intervening thirty months.' Even with the command of the Pacific such a victory would have given it, it could not, of course, have undertaken an invasion of the continental United States.

It is symbolic of the extent of the Midway disaster that the captains of two of the four carriers destroyed should have insisted on going down with their ships. Aboard *Hiryu*, Tomeo Kaku and Admiral Tamon Yamaguchi took station on the bridge, as the flight deck tilted towards the water, exchanging poetic reflections, overheard by an officer who had been ordered to abandon ship. 'Let us enjoy the beauty of the moon,' Yamaguchi suggested. 'How bright it shines,' Kaku agreed. 'It must be in its twenty-first day.' Ryusaku Yanagimoto of the *Soryu* remained on his bridge after ordering the crew into the sea. When Chief Petty Officer Abe, a navy wrestling champion, reboarded to beg him, 'on behalf of all your men', to be taken to safety, if necessary by brute force, he was met with silence. 'Abe guessed the captain's thoughts,' recalled Mitsuo Fuchida, one of the survivors, 'and started towards him with the intention of carrying him bodily to the waiting boat. But the sheer strength of will and determination of his grim-faced commander stopped him short. He turned away and as he left the bridge he heard Captain Yanagimoto calmly singing "Kimigayo", the national anthem.'

The majority of those Japanese who took to the sea inevitably shared their captain's fate. A survivor of *Soryu*, swimming in the water alongside, 'could look "downhill" ' when a swell lifted him and 'see hundreds of heads dotting the water all around. In the distance he could see the *Soryu* and further off the burning *Kaga*.' Despite the warmth of the Pacific summer water and the ministrations of rescuing destroyers, hundreds of those fugitives from their sinking ships were to perish in the darkness of the night of 4 June.

Their number greatly exceeded the total of American casualties. *Yorktown*'s crew made an easy escape, dropping over the side to be picked up by waiting escorts. Apart from the men aboard the destroyer

Hamman, sunk by the same salvo of torpedoes as *Yorktown* herself, they were the only shipwreck victims of the US Pacific Fleet in the Midway battle, and most of both crews survived. So too did more of the ditched American airmen than might have been expected. Of 163 pilots and air gunners shot down, 27 were rescued from their life-rafts by patrolling Catalinas in the next ten days, and others managed to attract the attention of passing ships and even make their way to Midway.

The sick berths of both Japanese and American ships had a stream of casualties to deal with, some appalling in nature. The aviation fuel which was the lifeblood of carrier operations caused terrible burns when ignited, as it had been in all five carriers hit by torpedoes and bombs. Face and hand burns were a common consequence, and worse burns had been suffered by men doused in burning petrol. There had also been severe conflagrations in several of the carrier engine-rooms, notably *Yorktown*'s and *Hiryu*'s, with effects on the 'black gangs' familiar since the beginning of steamship warfare.

Nevertheless in human terms Midway had been a 'cheap' battle for vanquished and victors alike. The Japanese had lost not more than 3000 dead, the Americans fewer than 1000 – a total of fatalities lower than at either Trafalgar or Jutland The aeroplane, though deadly as a ship-killer in precision strikes, spared crews the terrible battering of repetitive gunnery salvoes in the flank-to-flank engagements of the battle line. This was not to mean that the great Pacific War would be a 'cheap' campaign. As it swelled in intensity, and Japanese resistance to the Americans' inexorable counter-offensive grew in desperation, crew losses would rise in horrifying number. Resort to kamikaze (suicide) tactics, forced on the Japanese by the destruction of their trained carrier air groups, would entail the immolation of dozens of American radar picket destroyers, as well as many larger ships, while orthodox American surface-ship, submarine and aircraft strikes would sink Japanese ships by the score – a fleet carrier, three battleships, six heavy cruisers, four light cruisers, eleven destroyers and five submarines in the month of October 1944 alone. In that perspective, Midway was indeed an 'incredible victory', as great a reversal of strategic fortune as the naval world had ever seen, before or since, and a startling vindication of the belief of the naval aviation pioneers in the carrier and its aircraft as the weapon of future maritime dominance.

4

THE BATTLE OF THE ATLANTIC
Convoys SC122 and HX229

THE EMERGENCE OF THE SUBMARINE

Six years before Orville and Wilbur Wright coaxed their *Flyer*, the world's first practicable aircraft, into flight at Kittyhawk, North Carolina, a fellow American, John Philip Holland, perfected another machine, whose design had been almost as long in gestation, and which was to have an effect on the course of naval warfare quite as revolutionary and even more immediate than that of the aeroplane – the submarine.

The idea of the submarine is as old as the ocean-going warship. It exercised, inevitably, the fertile mind of Leonardo da Vinci and appeared in embryo form as a working model as early as the sixteenth century when a Londoner, William Bourne, experimented with a watertight boat which could be propelled and held beneath the surface by the power of oars. An American inventor, David Bushnell, produced an oared submersible to help the United States fight the Royal Navy in the War of American Independence, and a fellow countryman, Robert Fulton, offered a similar contrivance to Napoleon in 1801. Both craft delivered their offensive weapon, christened a torpedo (named after the torpedo fish or electric ray), by attaching a fused explosive charge, with a hand-cranked screw, into the wooden bottom of the target ship. On 6 September 1776 Bushnell's submersible almost succeeded in sinking HMS *Eagle* with such a device.

The attractions of the sumbersible and the torpedo to weak naval powers need no elaboration. Here was a truly secret weapon, potentially deady and physically indetectable, which could reduce an overbearing surface fleet to impotence at negligible cost – provided always that the submersible and its torpedo could be made to work. The early submersibles were defective in both respects. Oars (which were worked in the vertical plane) provided an erratic means of keeping a submersible submerged, while the ship-to-ship contact that placement of the original torpedo entailed was risky and difficult. The Americans nevertheless persisted, attempting submersible operations against the British Navy in the War of 1812 and, on the Confederate side, actually sinking an enemy ship, USS *Housatonic*, in the Civil War.

The essential elements of a submarine offensive arm remained inadequate, moreover, until the 1860s, when an Englishman, Robert Whitehead, in the employment of the Austrian government, developed a machine which foreshadowed the design of the truly submersible and self-propelling submarine of the future. Designated 'The Secret', it was in effect an unmanned underwater projectile and took the form of a metal fish, driven by compressed air working counter-rotating propellers, and incorporated a depth-keeping device and a contact fuse actuating an explosive charge in the nose. First used in anger, ineffectively, by the Royal Navy against a Peruvian ironclad in May 1877, it actually sank a target in January 1878 when fired by a Russian at a Turkish warship in Batum harbour.

Until a submersible which replicated Whitehead's design on a scale large enough to be manned by seamen could be designed, however, 'The Secret' would remain a weapon of surface warfare. In that guise it spawned two new families of ships, the torpedo-boat, and its antidote, the torpedo-boat destroyer; their appearance was greatly to alter both the design and the tactics of capital ships in the last two decades of the nineteenth century. To their armaments of heavy, armour-piercing guns were added batteries of light quick-firers, intended to destroy torpedo-boats at ranges longer than their missiles could travel, originally less than 2000 yards; to their lines of battle were attached screens of escorts – light cruisers and torpedo-boat destroyers (the latter fulfilling both a defensive and later an offensive role, when equipped with torpedo tubes themselves) – as a means of holding the torpedo launchers at a distance. Anti-torpedo nets, swung out on booms, were also for a time incorporated in the battleships' defences; but the devices proved so cumbersome and ineffective that, well before the outbreak of the First World War, they had been discarded.

By that time, in any case, the menace of the surface torpedo-boat, though still a reality, had been overtaken by that of its submersible counterpart – the 'Holland boat'. This had become not merely an arresting development but a component of every advanced fleet. By 1914 true submarines, able to hold their depth at will, travel long distances under water and launch torpedoes with accuracy at their targets, were a factor in fleet engagements with which every admiral had to reckon. They were no longer merely the nostrum of weak powers confronted by strong; all advanced navies included them in their orders of battle and wrote rules of engagement to provide against their presence in the opposing fleet. With reason: submarine torpedo attack was to account for the sinkings of eight major warships, as well as damage to many more, during the First World War. The founderings were of the British armoured cruisers *Cressy*, *Hogue* and *Aboukir* in the North Sea in September 1914, of the battleship *Formidable* in the Channel in January 1915, and of the battleships *Triumph* and *Majestic* off the Dardanelles in May 1915; of the French cruiser *Gambetta* in the Mediterranean in April 1915; and of the German armoured cruiser *Prins Adelbert* in the Baltic in 1915.

These were remarkable accomplishments by a weapon originally conceived by a political fanatic as a means of humiliating British imperial might. John Philip Holland, a British subject but an Irish nationalist and subsequently an American citizen, dedicated himself in the 1870s to the development of a practicable submarine with which the Irish Fenian Brotherhood was to sink British warships as a terrorist sensation. Fenian money supported his early experiments; subsequently, when the wider application of his design became apparent, he accepted American government funds to finance its completion. American official interest was generated by the realisation that a submarine force would provide a cheap and effective means for the defence of its harbours against foreign naval attack, fear of which was current in the 1880s; Holland cunningly played on it by writing an article entitled 'Can New York be Bombarded?' Its publication prompted the US Navy Department to offer funds for the submission of an effective submarine design. Holland won the design competition and, after several false starts, presented the Navy Department with *Holland VI*, a boat which met the specifications. Its characteristics were those of all submarines which were to fight at sea until the very end of the Second World War. Propelled on the surface by an oil-fuel engine, which recharged the batteries of the electric motor used when the boat was submerged (electrical power, needing no oxygen supply, was not a competitor for its air reserves), *Holland VI* dived by filling 'ballast' tanks with sea water and rose by expelling it from them by compressed air. The compressed air bottles were filled by a compressor working off the engine-room power supply. Changes of depth were achieved by working 'hydrofoils' which acted as horizontal rudders, when the boat was in motion, below the surface. Changes of direction, above or below the surface, were made by applying the rudder as in a normal ship. The armament comprised a single torpedo tube, from which the 18-inch torpedo was expelled by compressed air. Targets were identified by means of a retractable periscope from which the captain could also 'con' (direct) the boat when it was submerged. Speed on the surface was 8 knots, speed submerged 5 knots – not enough to draw ahead of a target under way but sufficient to allow a secret approach against a warship on an attacking bearing, and therefore to achieve the defensive capability stipulated in the Navy Department's terms of competition. Maximum diving depth was 100 feet, as much as the strong internal 'pressure' hull could stand, but it was rarely attained.

The Holland boat was so obviously revolutionary that shortly every advanced navy wanted one. Since it was the product of a private company in an era when commercial sovereignty was a paramount principle, it came rapidly on the market. The Royal Navy bought the design in 1900, the Japanese and Swedish navies in 1905, the Dutch in 1906, the Russian in 1907. The French and German navies at first persisted with experimental models of their own but later came round to Holland's principles. By 1914 Holland boats, armed with (greatly improved) Whitehead torpedoes, equipped the submarine arms of the sixteen navies which had taken them into service. Altogether they numbered some 400.

As weapons of naval warfare, however, the early submarines proved ineffectual. Despite their capacity for invisible manoeuvre, their underwater speed, by 1910 about 8 knots, and endurance, about twelve hours, was too limited to allow them to accompany surface fleets or to work against them with any large chance of success. The British E-class boats, and their German equivalents, U-9 to U-15, had grown to a displacement of about 600 tons and could dive safely to 200 feet ('crushing depth' was about 350 feet). They achieved speeds of 15 knots on the surface with their diesel engines, a much safer power plant than the early petrol engines, and had an operational range of up to 5000 miles. However, unless opportunely positioned, they could not 'acquire' a warship target submerged and could not overhaul one on the surface.

Submarines, in consequence, were confined to operating against the approaches to naval ports and in what naval strategists called 'pelagic' areas – confined waters in frequent use by the enemy where his movements obeyed laws of probability, such as the Baltic, Black Sea, Channel, North Sea and parts of the Mediterranean. All the early submarine successes, like the sinking of the *Cressy*, *Aboukir* and *Hogue*, were achieved in that way. Submarines none the less succeeded in greatly influencing the handling of battle fleets. Both the British and Germans deployed them in their North Sea operations, stationing them on 'patrol lines' which the enemy fleet was expected to cross, and apprehension of underwater attack was a potent factor in Jellicoe's command of his fleet at Jutland. On its return from the engagement, two British battleships, *Marlborough* and *Warspite*, both damaged and therefore presenting easy targets, were attacked by the U-boats U-51 and U-63, but the torpedoes missed. U-66, which had been stationed off Rosyth to intercept Beatty's battlecruisers, sighted them in their outward passage but failed to get close enough to attack. Scheer's scheme of 'trapping' could not be made to work when surface and submerged speeds were so disparate.

British submarines, confronting navies like the German and Turkish which were confined to narrow waters, continued to fight an active and orthodox naval war. The German U-boat fleet, denied anything but the rare shot at a warship by the distance at which British naval bases lay from their own home ports – and by the laying of elaborate minefield and barrier defences – had to look elsewhere for targets. They found them in the swarms of merchant shipping on which their island enemy depended to supply his war effort. Justifying this form of commerce raiding as a riposte to Britain's highly efficient blockade of their own maritime trade, they conducted between January and September 1915 an effectively 'unrestricted' campaign against merchant shipping in the seas around the British Isles. However, the small tonnage sunk and the number of U-boats lost – about one for every twenty ships destroyed – as well as the international odium the campaign provoked, notably after the sinking in May of the liner *Lusitania* with large numbers of Americans aboard, eventually forced the German admiralty to desist.

It did not resume unrestricted sinking until 1 February 1917, when the military situation on land had descended to such a level of stalemate that the German high command decided only desperate measures at sea could break it. During 1916, while adhering to the letter of international law governing commerce raiding – that merchant ships must be stopped and the crews allowed to take to the boats – U-boats had sunk up to 300,000 tons a month; but these losses did not reduce the intake of necessities below minimum levels of support for the war effort, while the sunken ships were being replaced out of new launchings. Calculations fixed the level at which sinkings would cripple British, and to a lesser extent French, operations at 600,000 tons monthly. As the number of available U-boats had reached over a hundred, it was also calculated that such a total was within the underwater fleet's capability. The Germans accordingly decided to bear the renewed odium that a resumed unrestricted campaign would provoke and strike for a quick decision.

The results were remarkable. In the early 1915 campaign, U-boats had sunk only fifty ships. In February 1917 they sank 250, in March 330 and in April 430, most by torpedoes fired without warning from submerged positions. Further, the 'exchange ratio' proved very much in the German favour; monthly U-boat losses were four, five and three respectively, in all cases the result of chance rather than of concerted and effective anti-submarine action. Anti-submarine vessels, operating only with primitive hydrophone listening devices and the occasional spotting assistance of aircraft and airships, simply could not find their enemy beneath the surface.

By July, with sinkings running at the predicated 600,000 tons a month, Admiral Henning von Holtzendorff, Chief of the Naval General Staff, believed that his forecast of January was about to be realised. He had written then: 'basing our calculations on 600,000 tons of shipping sunk by unrestricted U-boat warfare and the expectation that at least two-fifths of neutral traffic will at once be terrorised into ceasing their voyages to England, we may reckon that, in five months, shipping to and from England will be reduced by 39 per cent. England would not be able to stand that.' Mysteriously England seemed to be standing it very well. Her imports had been reduced by only 8 per cent, and, though it meant belt-tightening at home, her armies in France, the Middle East and Africa were suffering not at all; nor were those of her allies, France, Russia and Italy, which depended indirectly on her import trade. The reason for this paradox was, in the immediate instance, that the 'neutral traffic' had not been decisively 'terrorised' into rejecting British charters. Impelled in part by financial need, in part by energetic British diplomacy, the neutrals, after an early fright, had resumed their traffic as before. Building to replace losses had accelerated, and interned German merchant ships had been seized abroad to add to the fleets plying into British harbours. The U-boats, in an effort to heighten the terror factor, had had to devote much of their activity to attacks on neutral ships, sparing the British merchant fleet, then by far the largest in the world, from that concentrated offensive which Holtzendorff had planned to direct against it.

There was a second, longer-delayed compensation to offset the results of the unrestricted campaign. From May, and after an acrimonious domestic debate about its efficacy, the British had begun to experiment with a convoy system. Convoy was as old as organised naval warfare. It was practised by the Romans, against Mediterranean piracy, and had been a standby of the Spaniards in the heyday of their American empire and of the British in the Napoleonic wars. Wiseacres in the British Admiralty argued in 1917 that convoy would improve the U-boats' chances by presenting them with large targets rather than with a haphazard pattern of individual sailings. However, such a view failed to consider the limitations under which U-boats operated. Their principal difficulty lay not in hitting targets when they found them but in finding targets at all and in being in a favourable position to engage such targets when they did. Many individual sailings improved their chances in both respects. Some targets would elude attack, but in manoeuvring against one that was missed a U-boat would enhance its likelihood of being in the correct position to attack the next and the one after that. Convoy, by contrast, diminished attack opportunities by reducing a large number of individual ship targets, presenting themselves in widely spaced succession, to effectively one only. If a U-boat was not in the correct position to attack the compact mass of a convoy when sighted, it would miss all the ships in it, and then have to wait for an extended period before another appeared; and, even if then favourably placed, it could not, in its time-defined attacking span, sink any more ships than it would have done if presented with a series of individual targets during the same lapse of time. All this was simple mathematics; and, though there were British admirals who argued against the sums, mathematics both proved them wrong and progressively robbed the unrestricted U-boat campaign of its point.

Mathematics worked even if the counter-attack of a convoy's escorts was ineffective. However, convoying naturally enhanced the power of escorts, by multiplying the number of naval ships keeping company with merchantmen; and it also improved the escorts' chances of finding a U-boat target in a variety of ways. Convoying drew the U-boats to warships, instead of forcing the latter to embark on almost always fruitless searches; and it directed an escort towards a U-boat, at a range close enough to lend counter-attack the chance of success once a torpedo was fired. The torpedo might hit home; but calculations about whence it had been fired were simplified by noting the position of the attacked ship and the arc of exposure it occupied at the moment of the torpedo alarm. Working with hydrophones (an underwater listening device which 'heard' the submarine's engines), and simply by rule of thumb, the escort could track back along the estimated torpedo course – speed and range of the underwater missile being known – and deliver depth charges into areas of the sea where U-boats were likely to be found. Depth charges, invented in 1915, work by driving hydraulic pressure waves, generated by the detonation of their explosive filling, against a submerged submarine's hull. If detonated close enough, they crack the hull, allowing sea water to enter under pressure. Since depth-charging is an unpleasant experience – even if it does not damage the hull – it was the bold submarine captain who, surviving the first attack, decided to elude the second by shortening rather than lengthening the range from his convoy target. Depth-charging therefore tended to drive U-boats away from convoys and thereby to diminish their initial losses and improve their chances of eventual escape.

The struggle between convoy and U-boat consumed almost all the energies of the Royal and Imperial German navies in the last twenty months of the First World War. Advantage lurched between one and the other. By the end of 1917 British imports had been reduced by 20 per cent and there was particular concern for the guarantee of oil fuel supplies. At the same time the British began to lay fields of an improved model of mine which effectively closed the Dover Straits to submarine passage and forced U-boats seeking the rich Atlantic targets to pass round the north of Scotland to enter the 'pelagic' zone. By the end of 1917 the 'exchange ratio' had fallen to only sixteen merchantmen destroyed for one U-boat; and between July and December 1917 forty-six U-boats were eliminated and only forty-two built, an attrition rate that offered no chance to the German Naval General Staff of increasing its fleet to a war-winning strength.

During the last nine months of the war, with 120 U-boats at sea, German sinkings averaged four merchant ships for each U-boat on station each month, the majority of the casualties being individual targets; of 1133 casualities only 134 were sunk in convoy. Sixty-one

U-boats were sunk in the same period, fourteen fewer than were delivered from the shipyards. The German navy was planning to increase its output to twenty-two per month in 1919 and thirty-two in 1920; but the German army, whose chief of staff, Ludendorff, was now effectively head of government, had already concluded that the Holtzendorff campaign would not win the war. By April, when the unrestricted sinking campaign reached its height, he had already launched the first of his 'war-winning' offensives against the British and French, with troops released from Russia by the collapse of Russian resistance. By July, when his fifth offensive had failed, the campaign had passed its apogee and, in May, U-boat losses had actually exceeded launchings. It was an index of failure that, of thirty-six convoys which crossed the patrol line maintained by eight U-boats off Ireland in the middle of May, only five were intercepted and only three merchant ships sailing in those convoys were sunk.

The November armistice brought the U-boats' struggle to win the war by mercantile strangulation to an end. Of 373 which had put to sea, 178 had been sunk, primitive though the counter-measures available to the defenders were, with the loss of 5000 of the 13,000 seamen belonging to the U-boat service. For each U-boat lost, 32 merchant ships had been sunk – 5708 ships in all, or a quarter of the world's tonnage. Half of it was British, equivalent to one-third of their merchant fleet at the time of the war's outbreak. However, despite the depredations, building had kept pace with losses and the world's merchant marine was actually larger in 1918 than it had been in 1914. At the cost of great national anxiety in all importing countries and high human suffering, the U-boat campaign had failed.

Set beside the U-boat campaign, the operation of other submarine forces, of which the British was the most important, had been a marginal affair. The British submarine force had lost fifty-four boats, mostly to mines, had damaged four German capital ships and a light cruiser in the North Sea and had sunk a light cruiser and four destroyers. They had better success against merchant shipping in the Baltic and Sea of Marmora, though it was also there that most of their submarines were lost. Warships were emphatically proved a tougher target than merchantmen. However, as the German mercantile campaign had also turned out in the end a failure, the verdict on the submarine as a weapon of war in November 1918 might appear to be that its worth was unproven. Such was absolutely not the judgement of the victors. They had been severely shaken by the 'First Battle of the Atlantic', appalled by its cost and severely stressed by the effort needed to fight it. Of all the weapons they had met in the hands of the enemy, it was the submarine that frightened them most, and it was a central provision of the Versailles Treaty imposed on Germany in 1919 that it should not possess submarines in the future. Military, though not civilian, aircraft were forbidden it; the building or possession of submarines of any sort, even commercial models for underwater salvage and exploration, was outlawed categorically. The British, Americans, Japanese, French and Italians retained sizeable submarine fleets; it was one of Britain's failures at the Washington Naval Conference of 1921 that it failed to achieve agreement on limiting their size and that of the boats comprising them. However, all the Western ex-combatants were united in determining that Germany should never sail a U-boat again.

DÖNITZ AND THE U-BOAT SERVICE

The prohibitions on German submarine building did not last long. Germany had not participated in the Washington Naval Conference and was therefore not bound by the prohibition promulgated there on the use of the submarine in the 'wholesale destruction of commerce'. During the 1920s the German navy set up a design office in Holland to plan future submarine building and two separate experimental models were constructed in Spain and Finland. One of Hitler's first military initiatives on coming to power was the ordering of twenty-four of the Finnish and two of the Spanish versions. In 1935, following his repudiation of the Versailles Treaty, he concluded an Anglo-German Naval Agreement that allowed him, among other provisions, to build up to 45 per cent of the Royal Navy's submarine tonnage. The treaty was linked to another, called the London Submarine Agreement of 1936, by which both parties bound themselves to sink merchant ships only in accordance with the provisions of international law – that is, with warning if merchant ships were sailing unescorted, and without warning only if they were escorted or in protected convoy. However, the Submarine Agreement was, by its nature, unenforceable.

In 1935 Hitler appointed to the command of the new U-boat fleet a veteran of the unrestricted campaign, Admiral Karl Dönitz, who had already experimented with a novel system of U-boat tactics which he was convinced would win a further anti-shipping war for Germany. Karl Dönitz was an epitome of the officer-type which built the Tirpitz navy. Of modest origins – his father was an engineer with the famous optical firm of Zeiss – he secured entry to the naval cadet school not by family background, which counted for so much in the contemporary German army, but by personal qualities and intellect. He was a successful cadet, was elected without difficult to the 'officer corps' of his first ship, the cruiser *Breslau*, and cruised in her in the Mediterranean in 1913–14. At the outbreak of the First World War he was transferred to the battlecruiser *Goeben*. *Goeben* was, of course, the 'gift ship' by whose transfer to the Turkish navy Germany helped to coax the Ottoman Empire into the war on its side. In *Goeben* he operated against the Russian navy in the Black Sea, and he was awarded the Iron Cross First Class in May 1916 for his part in an action with the dreadnought

Imperatriza Maria. Shortly afterwards he was ordered to leave her company and report to Kiel for training as a U-boat officer. His confidential reports marked him as a potential leader – 'Dönitz is a charming, dashing and plucky officer, with first-rate character, qualities and above-average gifts.' At a moment when the tide of war was setting against the High Seas Fleet, he was an obvious choice for transfer to the submarine arm on which the German Naval General Staff was counting to reassert the fleet's power at sea.

Dönitz's first appointment, on completing training, was to the U-39, commanded by Walter Forstmann, already one of the most famous submarine captains in the navy and holder of the *Pour le mérite*, Germany's highest military decoration. Operating at the mouth of the Adriatic, against Italian shipping, and off the North African coast, U-39 sank eight ships on Dönitz's first patrol. One was a troopship with a thousand Italian soldiers on board, all of whom drowned in the resulting panic. It was Forstmann's second troopship sinking. Of the first he had written: 'And yet to be honest I am not quite satisfied. Again and again the thought goes through my head that when the steamer sank only 150 soldiers were lost out of 900. . . . However hard it may seem to sentimental minds in time of war, one must energetically put aside all sympathy, all pity and every other feeling of the kind . . . the object of war is to annihilate the armed forces of the enemy whether it be on the battlefield or in a fight at sea.'

Dönitz was thus confronted at the outset with the barbarity of surprise torpedo attack at its starkest. In Forstmann's next cruise fourteen ships were sunk, a success the Naval General Staff judged put him 'at the head of all U-boat commanders'. On Dönitz's third time out with U-39, Forstmann was less successful: the boat was nearly sunk by collision with a target and was then driven down by air attack. However the fourth patrol was again a success and won Dönitz a command of his own, the UC-25, a combined torpedo and mine-laying submarine.

Dönitz, despite Forstmann's tutelage, proved to lack the master's touch. Although he sank one large steamer, for which he was awarded the Knight's Cross of the Hohenzollern Order, UC-25 only barely survived a depth-charge attack off Sicily and he returned to port in deep gloom. On his next patrol in a new boat, UB-68, he mismanaged a dive in attacking a convoy, was forced to surface, was attacked by gunfire and had to abandon ship. Picked up and made prisoner, he fell into a mood of depressed self-reproach. 'He was very moody and almost violent at times,' reported his British interrogating officer, 'and it seems he was not very cordial even with his fellow countrymen as he had previously said he was done with the sea and ships.'

On his return to Germany the mood passed. Assured by his former commander that the Versailles ban on U-boats would not 'remain for ever', he decided to keep his commission and serve the tiny navy Germany was allowed by the peace treaty. He was, he later wrote, 'under the spell of this unique U-boat camaraderie' and ready to wait his chance. In the meantime he secured command of the next best thing, one of the torpedo-boats in the Baltic flotilla. Torpedo-boats were, of course, surface ships but, since the torpedo was their principal arm, they provided a means of simulating U-boat surface attacks which, provided they were delivered under cover of darkness, German commanders had come to believe might be more profitable than the slow and half-blind submerged method. 'In future,' one of Dönitz's brother officers in the flotilla wrote in 1922, 'it will be essential for convoys to be hunted by sizeable numbers of U-boats acting together.' At that time Dönitz's flotilla had begun training 'to surprise the enemy under cover of darkness, fire their torpedoes and escape rapidly; for this they had to find the enemy by day, hang on to him at the borders of visibility without themselves being seen, and approach gradually as visibility drew into twilight. This tactic of finding and holding touch with the enemy until the attack could be launched at night was the principal feature of the "pack" tactics with which Dönitz's name is associated.' It remained the central scheme of training throughout Dönitz's time with the flotilla in 1922–6 and the subject most frequently set as a staff problem to its officers during the winter seasons. In 1927 Dönitz was promoted to command a half-flotilla of his own, and in 1929, during the autumn manoeuvres, he scored a training triumph by 'destroying' a whole enemy convoy by night torpedo attack.

He was now marked out for promotion, filled a senior staff appointment from 1930 to 1934 and was then given command of one of the navy's few large surface ships, the cruiser *Emden*, which he took on a world cruise. In July 1935, shortly after his return, he was nominated to command the first flotilla of new German U-boats which Hitler was about to bring into being, through repudiation of the Versailles Treaty and with the reluctant agreement of the British, whose politicians' commitment to the policy of appeasement of Germany, then at its height, overcame the cautionary instincts of their admirals. At first Dönitz's command consisted of only three small coastal craft. But by the following year, when promoted *Führer der U-boote* (U-boat Leader), he had six, divided into two flotillas, and could look forward to the delivery in the near future of ocean-going types. He opposed the construction, advocated by other former U-boat officers at the German admiralty, of large, long-range cruising submarines, designed to operate as individual commerce raiders in distant waters. His philosophy called for the creation of a large fleet of medium-size boats, groups of which could act in a 'pack' (*Rudel*) against enemy convoys. Their tactics should be those he had tested as a surface torpedo-boat commander in the Baltic in the previous decade.

It was the U-boats' low submerged speed that had driven Dönitz to this conclusion. To compensate for it, he advocated concentration against concentration, a means of reinsuring against one U-boat's missing a convoy by backing it with several. In early 1939 he wrote:

The disposition of boats at the focal points of the seaways in the Atlantic has to follow these principles: (a) at least three boats form a group. Disposition of the boats in [an area with] a breadth of some 50 and depth of 100–200 miles; (b) further groups according to the number of operational boats available – dispersed in the direction of the reported steamer track at some 200–300 miles; (c) command of all groups basically through C-in-C U-boats at home; (d) in the case of a sighting by one of the boats of a group, all the others are to attack independently without further orders; (e) direction of other groups on to the enemy through C-in-C U-boats.

In short, the U-boats were to form a net across the Atlantic steamer routes, attack on sight but meanwhile call up all others disengaged and report sighting by wireless to the home command; it in turn would, if the attack proved profitable, concentrate additional 'packs' against the target by its own wireless communications. The idea would have been instantly comprehensible to Nelson, who had been tantalised by the difficulty of 'concentration against concentration' in fleet warfare, however he might manipulate his frigate signalling screen. Wireless supplied the means by which the new signalling screen was to be extended and co-ordinated; but what lent it real menace was the U-boats' formidable powers of attack and the ruthlessness – perhaps first generated by Forstmann's pitiless destruction of the Italian troopship – with which Dönitz was prepared to direct it against defenceless merchantmen and their inadequate escorts.

The practicality of pack tactics was given its first test in May 1939 when a token force of German merchantmen (including, significantly, a tanker) sailed the Bay of Biscay as a target for fifteen of the new Type VII and IX U-boats. The convoy was soon sighted by one of the boats in the signalling screen which brought three more to contact. Their attack failed, but a second group acquired contact next morning. Heavy weather foiled 'sinkings', but that afternoon the third and largest group intercepted and began to achieve a high rate of success. By the end of the exercise the convoy was surrounded by thirteen U-boats and had theoretically been overwhelmed. In his after-action critique Dönitz wrote: 'The simple principle of fighting a convoy of several steamers with several U-boats . . . is correct. The summoning of U-boats was under the conditions of the exercise successful. The convoy would have been destroyed . . . gradually even more U-boats could come on to the convoy, its position would become even more difficult and also the strength relationship, the cover afforded by its escort would become even less, so that great losses from the convoy could be expected.' In a separate communication to another admiral shortly after the exercise, he drew further on the results of the exercise to argue: 'It is clear that the attack on British sea communications alone can have a "war decisive" effect in a naval war against Britain.' He was now intellectually as well as emotionally committed to the philosophy of unrestricted U-boat warfare. He was persuaded, and tried to persuade others, that with a fleet of 300 U-boats the German navy could bring Britain to defeat by its own efforts, quite apart from those of the army and the Luftwaffe. By 28 August 1939, when those calculations were submitted in an official memorandum to the admiralty in Berlin, the end of the era of theoretical exercises was at hand. War with the Royal Navy was less than a week distant, and the Battle of the Atlantic was about to begin.

THE BATTLE OF THE ATLANTIC

Dönitz's belief that Britain lay vulnerable to defeat by the interruption of her sea communications was demonstrable by the simplest statistical exercise. As with that other island empire, Japan, her military and economic power rested on her ability to import raw materials, oil and food in enormous and regular quantities. Britain, though self-sufficient in coal, produced no oil and less than half her food requirements, and was dependent on imports for some of her low-grade and almost all her high-grade metal ores, much finished metal, all her rubber and significant proportions of key manufactured goods like machine tools. Her total annual import requirements were 55 million tons, of which 42 per cent was carried from ports within the British Empire – a trade pattern that imposed unusually long hauls on the British merchant fleet; typically, twice as long as those over which French imports had been carried before the war.

The import trade was chiefly supported by Britain's fleet of 3000 ocean-going merchantmen, with a carrying capacity of 17 million tons. It was still the largest in the world, though about a quarter smaller in number of ships and tonnage than it had been before the 'First Battle of the Atlantic' twenty years earlier. The officers and crews employed aboard numbered 120,000, an asset as precious and difficult to replace as the ships themselves. Both were highly vulnerable to loss by U-boat attack. Dönitz's projected figure of 300 U-boats, providing a force of fifty on the patrol lines at any one time, would, if each sank three merchant ships a month – an average that First World War experience validated – destroy over half the fleet in a year, a rate of sinking nearly twenty times that of replacement building.

These were raw figures, unlikely to be achieved in practice, since they made no allowance for U-boat losses (which could not be avoided), for the addition of neutral ships to the British fleet or for troughs in the sinking graphs imposed by bad weather and the frictions of war. Nevertheless, to anticipate events, by early 1941 Dönitz, with a hundred U-boats under command, of which six were operational in the Atlantic at any one time, had sunk 400 ships in the previous eight months, a rate of sinking twice that of new construction. The effect on the British war and domestic economy was crippling. Annual imports of all commodities had decreased from 55 million tons (in 1939) to 35 million tons by January 1941; by March imports were running at an annualised rate of no more than 30 million tons. Food imports were at an irreducible minimum of 15 million tons, which provided the individual British citizen with, for example, two ounces of tea a week and one egg per fortnight. The slaughter of livestock, to economise on imported foodstuffs, had made meat a rarity; bread, potatoes and vegetables were the everyday staples. 'How willingly,' wrote Winston Churchill, 'would I have exchanged a full-scale attempt at invasion for this shapeless, measureless peril, expressed in charts, curves and statistics.'

'The only thing that ever really frightened me during the war,' he recorded in his memoirs, 'was the U-boat peril.' It had presented itself as soon as he became First Lord of the Admiralty in September 1939 and was to grow in menace throughout his five years as Prime Minister. At the outset the campaign was a 'restricted' one, since Hitler was anxious not to provoke neutral, particularly American, hostility while Britain and France remained undefeated; the experience of the First World War had proved that the institution of an 'unrestricted' campaign aroused international outrage. The German navy was also apprehensive of the Royal Navy's capacity to track U-boats with the underwater ranging and direction-finding device, Asdic (from Allied Submarine Detection Investigation Committee), developed in 1918 by the Canadian scientist, R. W. Boyle, for the Admiralty's Anti-Submarine Division (it would later be known as sonar). It consoled itself with the calculation that even a 'restricted' policy would force the British to adopt convoy. Because the rigidity of convoying limited the total number of sailings, this would reduce British import capacity; moreover, convoying would permit sinking without warning, since according to the German interpretation of international maritime law merchantmen accompanied by warships could be deemed legitimate targets.

A flagrant breach of international law was nevertheless committed by a U-boat captain, Lemp of U-30, on the very first day of the war when in the Atlantic off Ireland he sank the liner *Athenia*, which he claimed to believe was a troopship but which was in fact loaded with civilians, including 316 Americans. Half the thirty U-boats on patrol, which had been sent to war stations before the outbreak, were hastily withdrawn. U-30's log was doctored to disguise the incident, and the rules against sinking without warning sternly reinforced. As a result, the anti-shipping campaign achieved little success in the first nine months. Britain's escort fleet of sixty destroyers succeeded in sinking eleven U-boats – which, with other losses, set the 'exchange ratio' at 12½ merchant ships sunk to every U-boat lost. By April, when the fifteen remaining U-boats were withdrawn from the Atlantic to take part in the Norwegian campaign, the size of Dönitz's operational fleet had slightly fallen.

With the fall of France the balance of advantage was to shift dramatically to the German side. That catastrophe for the anti-Hitler alliance put the French Atlantic ports into Dönitz's hands and established the front line of U-boat operations in the Bay of Biscay at the eastern edge of the Atlantic. At a stroke the distance which U-boats were obliged to travel to their patrol stations was halved and the dangers of the passage eliminated. Instead of having to negotiate the minefields of the Dover Straits, use of which the Germans had abandoned after three U-boats had been sunk, or make the long traverse round the north of Scotland, U-boat captains could launch themselves from Lorient – later also from Saint-Nazaire, Brest, La Pallice and La Rochelle – direct into the convoy tracks. Some convoys, sailing from American and Canadian ports, ran far to the north of the French Biscay ports, though still a great deal closer than they did to the former operating bases in Kiel and Wilhelmshaven. Others passed the doorstep, particularly those bound for the Indian Ocean, West Africa and the Mediterranean, taking reinforcements and supplies to the British armies in Egypt, India and the Far East. As the British escort fleet of destroyers had suffered heavily in the Norwegian campaign and Dunkirk evacuation, such convoys were ill protected – Britain, in any case, was desperately short of escorts – and sinkings increased, alarmingly for the British, gratifyingly for the Germans. Between June and September 1940 U-boats sank 274 ships, for the loss of only two of their own number. Ten new U-boats were coming off the slips each month – fewer than Dönitz hoped, but enough to compensate for losses and add to the strength of his fleet as well – so that the theoretical aim of the outright destruction of the British merchant marine was, at last, within grasp.

By June 1941 tonnage sunk totalled over 300,000 tons, though only thirteen U-boats were at sea at any one time. The British sensed a crisis at hand. They began to route North American convoys much further northward towards Iceland, which they had occupied in October 1940, despite the worse weather to be encountered there. The escort fleet was enlarged by the acquisition of fifty American First World War four-funnelled destroyers known as 'four-stackers' (the price for which was the British concession of US basing rights in the British West Indies), while a considerable number of long-range aircraft were diverted from the strategic bombing campaign against Germany to convoy protection.

These measures produced some success. In March five U-boats were lost in attacks on two North American convoys, because, it was judged in retrospect, captains were becoming over-confident. The Royal Navy had also managed to increase the size of their escort fleet to some 400, by incorporating auxiliary vessels, designing new and cheaper ships and drawing on the resources of the Royal Canadian Navy. With these additions, it became possible to provide escorts to a convoy for its whole transatlantic voyage, instead of handing over charge in mid-ocean with consequent loss of efficiency. The range of aircraft, based on Iceland and Canada as well as Britain, was also extending – an escort medium which deprived U-boats of much of their freedom of action by forcing them to operate submerged in the proximity of convoys in daylight. However, an 'air gap' of several hundred miles still yawned in mid-Atlantic, in which U-boats could motor on the surface in the torpedo-boat style Dönitz had practised in the Baltic twenty years earlier.

Dönitz was also putting his patrols ever further from base. Captains, with growing experience, were learning to extend the range of their vessels by economic management of fuel, and were increasingly also to resupply themselves from supply ships at sea. U-boat headquarters regularly dispatched captains to the West African coast and as far afield as South America, to intercept the beef, wool and mineral trade from Argentina and Brazil. In the last half of 1941 the need to intervene in the Mediterranean naval war, where the Italian submarine fleet's inefficiency caused the Germans to despair, reduced Atlantic sinkings; but by December of that year Dönitz could count 236 U-boats in his fleet, knew that the exchange ratio stood at about thirteen merchant ships sunk for every U-boat lost overall (eighty-one to one in the South Atlantic), had firm evidence that he was sinking British shipping at a rate faster than it was being replaced – the British merchant fleet was smaller by 3 million tons than at the beginning of the war – and still retained the prospect of putting 300 U-boats to sea.

At the start of 1942, moreover, he was suddenly presented with a plethora of new and easy targets. The United States, on a basis of 'armed neutrality', called a 'short of war' policy, had been providing escorts to Atlantic convoys since the previous September. The Japanese attack on Pearl Harbor – and Hitler's unilateral declaration of war on 11 December – pitched it headlong into the battle of the Atlantic and by January 1942 U-boats were operating freely off the American coastline. Dönitz had wanted to send twelve but, because of the Mediterranean commitment, was allowed to release only five. Those, however, catapulted sinkings in American waters from 200,000 to over 300,000 tons in two months, and by June the total for 1942 exceeded 600,000 tons. This 'happy time', in the U-boat captains' gruesome phrase, was the product of a variety of factors, particularly the reluctance of American merchant skippers sailing in coastal waters to accept convoy, the dearth of escorts to accompany convoys in any case, the brilliant background illumination that American seaboard lighting provided, particularly off the Florida resorts, and the fixed pattern of routing which American coastwise shipping followed. A high proportion of the sailings were among tankers shipping oil between the Gulf loading points and the refineries and tank farms on the Atlantic seaboard. In January about twenty-nine tankers were sunk in American waters, without any loss whatsoever to their U-boat attackers. American anti-submarine patrols were provided, if at all, by weakly armed cutters of the US Coast Guard; air patrols were almost never flown. As Samuel Eliot Morison recorded:

> Some of the details of these sinkings, especially of tankers, are pitiful to relate: oil scum ignited by signal flares on life preservers, men knocked out by cork life preservers, attempting to swim in a heavy viscous layer of fuel oil, and ducking to avoid flames. Tanker *O. A. Knudsen* was attacked three times in twelve hours off Hole-in-the-Wall, Bahamas, and finally sunk by two U-boats without her radio distress signals having attracted a single rescue vessel or plane. The loaded tanker *Gulftrade* was torpedoed and sunk off Barnegat, only 300 yards from a Coast Guard cutter. Chilean freighter *Tolten* was torpedoed and sunk 30 miles off Ambrose Channel, New York and only one man survived . . . tanker *Tiger* was sunk off Cape Henry while manoeuvring to pick up a pilot; on the following night, between Cape Charles and Cape Henlopen, the unarmed collier *David H. Atwater* was sunk by gunfire at a range of about 600 yards. Her crew of 27, given no opportunity to abandon ship, were riddled by machine-gun fire; only three men survived.

Such pitiless action by submarine crews against seamen on unarmed merchant vessels was strictly the letter of Dönitz's commands. In instruction no. 154, written as early as November 1939, he had ordered his crews: 'Rescue no one and take no one with you. Have no care for the ships' boats. Weather conditions and the proximity of land are of no account. Care only for your own boat and strive to achieve the next success as soon as possible. We must be hard in this war. The enemy started this war in order to destroy us, therefore nothing else matters.' Only one U-boat captain would be subsequently convicted by an Allied court of deliberately killing survivors in the water (Eck of U-852), but Dönitz's attitude, from the outbreak of the war, encouraged a harshness in his crews of which the destruction of the *David H. Atwater* was a direct result.

By June 1942 the United States Navy, benefiting from an escort building programme which Roosevelt had set in train as early as July 1941, had introduced a convoy system on the eastern seaboard, while blackout measures also reduced the illumination of targets at night. In July three U-boats were sunk in those waters and two damaged; Dönitz accordingly brought the distant Atlantic campaign to an end. His capacity to resume the mid-Atlantic battle was, however, by now greatly enhanced. He had 331 U-boats under command, of which 140 were operational and 50 permanently on the patrol lines. With these numbers, close control exercised from his Brittany headquarters at Château Kerneval, copious intelligence of convoy movements supplied by the naval B-Dienst ('B' for *Beobachtung*, observation) and a fleet of refuelling U-boats ('milch cows') at sea from which successful patrol captains could replenish, he was well placed to return sinkings on the North American–British convoy routes to their level of mid-1941.

In practice his crews were to exceed that level. In November 1942, a month when escorts were drawn away from the North Atlantic waters to protect the troopships sailing to North Africa for the Torch landings, sinkings reached 729,000 tons, 119 ships in all. The operation of the 'pack' (to the Allies, 'wolf-pack') system underlay this success. Disposed at twice visibility distance from each other – the interval Dönitz had advocated in his 1939 paper – and directed towards the convoys by the transmitters at Kerneval, which in turn were alerted by B-Dienst cryptologists, the U-boats were often able to concentrate large numbers against a single target, overwhelm the escort and inflict many sinkings. Convoy SC94, for example, attacked by eighteen U-boats in August, lost twenty-six ships; in November SC107 lost fifteen ships. U-boat losses also rose, for the escorts were gathering skill and acquiring more effective detection equipment and anti-submarine weapons. However, by the end of the year, with sinkings running at an average of a hundred ships every month, building (at 7 million tons) not quite replacing the 7¾ million tons sunk that year, an exchange ratio of ten ships sunk for every U-boat lost, and U-boat numbers rising absolutely through replacement from the shipyards, Dönitz was able to sense that the crisis of the battle of the Atlantic was at hand. By January 1943 he had 400 U-boats under command, 200 operational and 100 at sea, ten more than he had argued before the war would bring Germany victory. The relentless concentration of his wolf-packs in the coming months, as the North Atlantic winter storms relented to offer attacking weather, promised to win him the 'war-decisive battle' he believed would bring Germany victory.

A crisis was indeed at hand, and would be marked by a dramatic see-saw of advantage from one side to the other. The Allies, with 500 escorts at their disposal, were now able to strengthen the screens provided to convoys and would soon organise 'support groups' to come to the help of convoys severely stricken. Their means of electronic warfare had been greatly improved, making night attack on the surface increasingly dangerous for any U-boat. The numbers and range of their surveillance aircraft had increased, so that the 'air gap' in mid-Atlantic trembled on the brink of closure. Their improved ability in radio direction-finding greatly facilitated the rerouting of convoys away from sea areas in which wolf-packs lay. Moreover, their access to German naval ciphers, allowing them to read Dönitz's instructions to his captains accurately and in 'real time' (as quickly as the intended recipients could read them), was on the point of perfection. To set against these technical advantages, the Germans were also benefiting from access to 'real time' cipher intelligence, were manipulating packs of U-boats of improved offensive quality manned by crews of growing experience and had developed an electronic device which warned U-boats of the approach of radar-equipped search aircraft and allowed them to dive before they became targets.

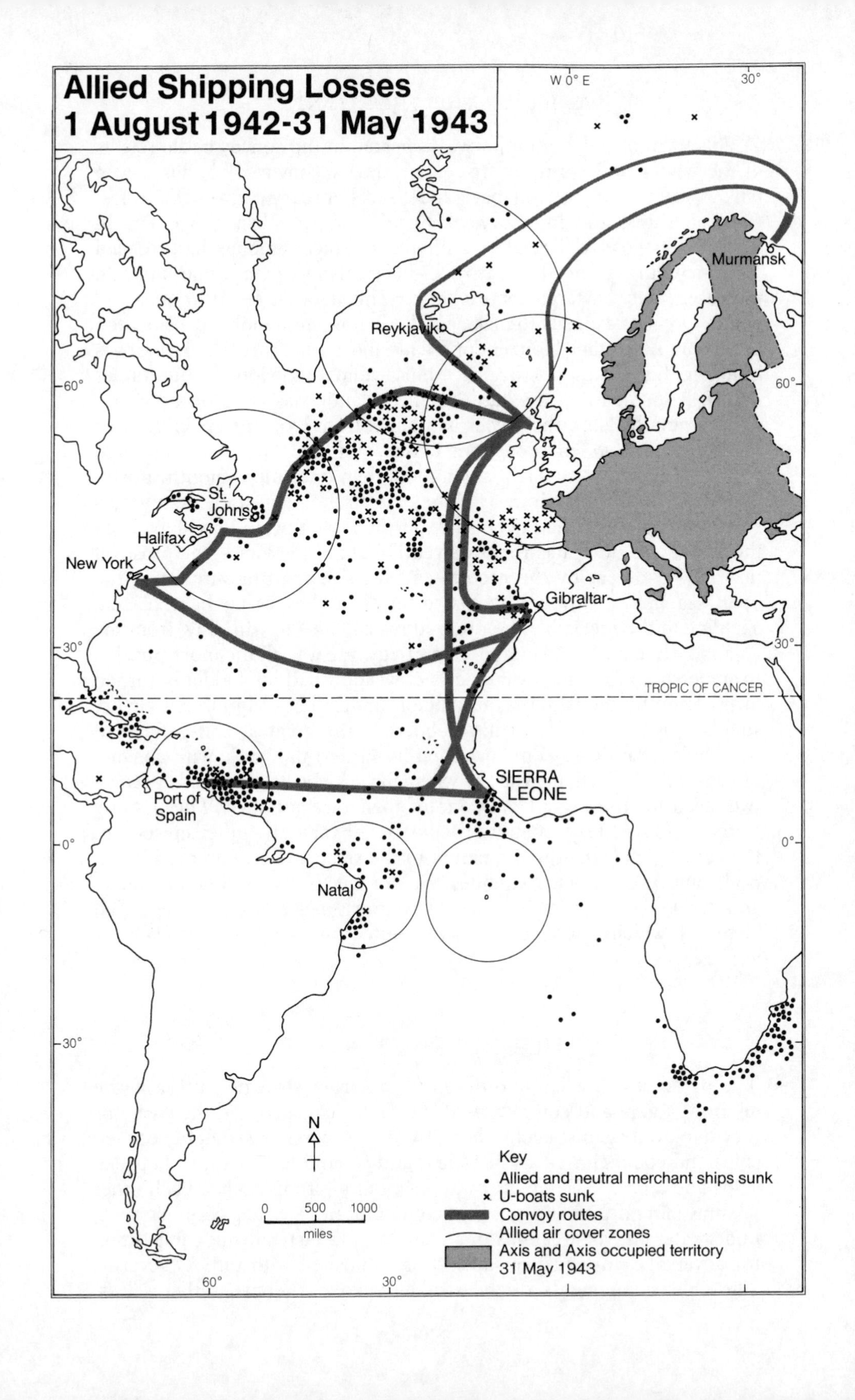
Allied Shipping Losses
1 August 1942-31 May 1943
W 0° E
30°
Murmansk
Reykjavik
60°
St. Johns
Halifax
New York
Gibraltar
30°
TROPIC OF CANCER
SIERRA LEONE
Port of Spain
0°
Natal
30°
N
0
500
1000
miles
60°
Key
Allied and neutral merchant ships sunk
U-boats sunk
Convoy routes
Allied air cover zones
Axis and Axis occupied territory 31 May 1943

This technological interplay was repeated in the convoy battle results of the winter and spring of 1943. In January convoy TM1 lost seven tankers out of nine to wolf-pack attack. In February convoy ON16 lost fourteen ships, and in one week thirty-four were lost altogether. In April ON55 lost twelve, after a month in which sinkings had totalled 108, including 72 not in convoy. U-boat sinkings meanwhile had also increased, but in March the exchange ratio stood at seven to one, well within Dönitz's capacity to make good. He now contemplated a situation as favourable as that Holtzendorff had enjoyed in April 1917, and was inflicting his losses not against ships sailing individually but under escort. It seemed that the battle of the Atlantic was about to be won.

Two months later, the pieces had fallen from Dönitz's grasp. In May the exchange ratio fell to only one to one, and the U-boats, even though 118 were at sea, were each sinking less than one ship a month. Forty-one U-boats were lost in May alone, and in the biggest of the month's battles twenty-seven had been sunk for the loss of twenty-six ships from the target convoy. Catastrophe stared Dönitz in the face – the prospect not only of defeat by the escorts and their supporting aircraft in the open sea but of losing U-boats faster than they could be replaced. Yielding to the inevitable, he ordered his captains to withdraw from the Atlantic while he reconsidered his strategy. He was all the more puzzled to understand how his 'war-decisive' weapon had so suddenly turned in his hand by the wholly contradictory indication of imminent victory supplied by the success of his U-boats in the greatest engagement of the whole Atlantic war only two months earlier: the battle with convoys HX229 and SC122 in March, when forty U-boats had sunk twenty-two ships for the loss of only one of their own number. The fighting of the HX229/SC122 battle explains better than any other episode of the battle of the Atlantic the nature of the struggle between the U-boat packs and their surface enemies. Before we turn to follow its course and development in detail, however, we must pause to assess the varied elements which supplied the two contestants with their means of warfare.

THE UNDERWATER WAR

The battle of the Atlantic differed from earlier struggles at sea above all in the range and complexity of the forces engaged and the weapons they deployed against each other. It was not merely a struggle between ships and commanders, as Trafalgar and Jutland had been, or between ships and aircraft also, as Midway was, but a pitting against each other of ships, aircraft, intelligence and communication systems, and surface, underwater and air weapons in a complex and fast-moving competition for advantage, in which mistakes were punished with pitiless severity. The chief components of the struggle were the convoys themselves, their U-boat enemy, the surface escorts, surveillance and attack aircraft, anti-submarine weapons, radio intelligence and command systems and cryptanalysis. Let us look at each in turn.

Convoy

Samuel Eliot Morison explains:

A convoy is the supply train and reinforcement column of the sea. A group of merchant vessels or troop transports, highly vulnerable to surface and submarine attack when alone, steam in company escorted by warships of types able to ward off the anticipated attack. . . . The typical Transatlantic convoy . . . consisted of 45 to 60 merchant ships steaming in nine to twelve columns, with 1000 yards between columns and 600 yards between ships. A nine column convoy would, therefore, present a frontage of four nautical miles and a depth of one and a half miles or more . . . fast and quickly turning destroyers and corvettes were, equipped with sound gear and depth charges as well as guns, essential. These formed the screen, each unit having a definite segment of a circle on the periphery of the convoy which it patrolled by day if the weather was clear; at night or in thick weather it kept station, closing occasionally with the nearest merchantman to establish position. Each convoy was routed by the Admiralty though designated one position before it sailed; the escort commander was given discretion whether to steer evasive courses, to zig-zag or to steer straight ahead. Troop convoys . . . were always faster (12 to 15 knots) than merchant ship convoys (7 to 9 knots) and were heavily escorted.

The convoy itself was under the command of a commodore, usually a retired naval officer embarked in one of the faster merchantmen; and, as the system developed, at least one rescue ship and tug, to take damaged but salvable ships in tow, was also included. The commodore, who had briefed the merchant captains before departure, exercised control of his charges by visual or sound signal, always seeking to impose formation and maximum speed of advance. As Morison recalled:

A convoy is beautiful, whether seen from a deck or from the sky. The inner line of stolid ships in several columns is never equally spaced, for each has her individuality; one is always straggling or ranging ahead until the Commodore signals angrily 'Number so-and-so, take station and keep station!' Around the merchant ships is thrown the screen like a loose-jointed necklace, the beads lunging to port or starboard and then snapping back as if pulled by a mighty submarine elastic; each destroyer nervous and questing, all eyes topside looking for the enemy, sound gear below listening for him, radar antennae like cats' whiskers feeling for him. On dark nights only a few shapes of ships a little darker than the black water can be discerned; one consults the radar screen to ascertain that the flock is all there. To one coming topside for the dawn watch, it is a recurring wonder to see the same ships day after day, each in her appointed station, each with her characteristic top-hamper, bow-wave, lift and dip; the inevitable smoker, the inevitable straggler, the vessel with the old shellback master who 'knew more about shipping forty years ago than any goddam gold-braid in a tin can' and whose sullen fury at being convoyed translates itself into belated turns, unanswered signals and insolent comebacks. When air cover is furnished there are darting, swooping planes above the convoy; upon approaching [an American] port, the stately silver bubble of a blimp comes out, swaying in the breeze and blinking a cheery welcome.

From the start of the war, the Admiralty assigned code letter groups to convoys, indicating their nature and direction. PQ and QP, for example, signified, after June 1941, convoys running to and from Russia by the Arctic routes; HG Gibraltar to Britain; MG Malta to Gibraltar; on the North Atlantic routes the most important designations were ON convoys outward bound from Britain to Halifax, Nova Scotia, and HX convoys homeward bound in the opposite direction; ONS and SC were slower versions of ON and HX respectively. All followed broadly defined oceanic tracks, which were moved progressively northward towards Iceland (base for mid-oceanic air patrols) as the U-boat operations from French ports extended in range; exact routings, and reroutings away from the established positions of wolf-packs, were frequently and rapidly changed by signals from the convoy control centre in the Royal Navy's Western Approaches Headquarters, and later also by the Convoys and Routing Section of the US Navy Department in Washington.

As the war progressed, U-boat depredations had the effect of increasing convoy speeds and improving their station-keeping. Early losses were suffered by the slower and smaller ships. Their replacements were larger, faster and handier. By 1943 a significant proportion of convoys consisted of the American war-emergency Liberty ships, based on the design of the British Sunderland tramp steamer, built at astonishing speed (the record in a public-relations exercise was four days) by prefabrication at the Kaiser organisation shipyards. Fifty a month were being delivered by the end of 1942. Their speed was 11 knots, tonnage 4300, and they carried 6000 tons of cargo. An improved version, the Victory, had a speed of 18 knots. The Liberty's tanker equivalent was the T2, with a speed of 14 knots; the improved T3 could reach 18 knots. The predominance of the Liberty ship, however, still lay in the future in early 1943. The size of convoy ships still ranged between 1000 and 9000 tons, and convoy speeds rarely exceeded 9 knots. As the Type IX U-boat cruised at 17 knots on the surface, merchantmen were easily headed and outrun by their hunters.

U-boats

The Germans were to build nine U-boat types during the war, twenty-two altogether if variants are included. The last were highly advanced, running on a closed hydrogen-peroxide fuel system and ventilating through a 'schnorkel' breathing tube, thus avoiding the need to surface, except at will, altogether. However, the two standard types of the battle of the Atlantic, the Type VII and Type IX, were much less refined, scarcely an improvement on the boats in which Dönitz had sailed in the First World War. Their propulsion was by diesel engine on the surface giving a speed of up to 17 knots and a range, at lower average speed, of 16,000 miles on electric motors. Submerged speed, driven by batteries which the diesel recharged, was 7 knots; submerged endurance, limited by air reserves, was about twelve hours. The boats' main armament was an electrically driven torpedo, which left no wake and thereby averted the danger of being attacked 'up the track', the means by which U-boats commonly fell victim to escorts in the First World War. The Type VII carried fourteen, the Type IX nineteen, launched through four bow and one (for the Type IX two) stern tubes.

U-boat crews numbered about fifty, jammed into sleeping space wherever it could be found among machinery and torpedo tubes; they shared a single lavatory and typically gave up washing and shaving as soon as they put to sea, because of the shortage of fresh water. By compensation, U-boat rations were excellent and boats rapidly developed that intense 'camaraderie', memory of which Dönitz had cited in 1919 as his reason for wishing to return to naval service. It was generated in part by forced intimacy, more powerfully by shared danger, which, whether imposed by the perils of the sea, the terror of depth-charging or the brooding menace of air attack in surface cruising, was a condition with which U-boat men lived every hour of their lives between setting out on patrol and returning to harbour in the Biscay ports. Oberleutnant Helmut Dauter explained:

> The life aboard our Atlantic operational boats was very hard because of the constricted space and the proximity of the sea; even on the bridge we were only five metres above the water. As every man on board was visible to everyone else and regardless of rank and position exposed to the severe hardships, sacrifices and dangers, there had to clearly quickly be a strong feeling of togetherness, of sharing the same fate. It fulfilled us completely even when we were not at sea. It was our whole life. We had been put into it [U-boat men were not volunteers] with all its glory and terror and we accepted it, often with anxiety and fear, often with joy and enthusiasm.

U-boat crews clearing Brest and Saint-Nazaire were still making passage across the Bay of Biscay on the surface in early 1943; the RAF's Coastal Command, though it ran regular anti-U-boat patrols on the U-boats' outward routes and had scored significant successes by searchlight and depth-charge attack at night in July–September 1942, currently lacked a search radar whose emissions were undetectable by the targets' warning receiver. As a result, the U-boats, by diving at the approach of aircraft, were able to make safe entry to the Atlantic within two days of leaving base (by then protected by bomb-proof concrete shelters) and to reach their patrol lines within five days, there to remain on station for up to forty days.

Almost all their time at sea would be spent on the surface, watching for convoys from positions designated by U-boat headquarters (moved from Kerneval to the Hotel am Steinplatz in Berlin in March 1942, following a British commando attack on Saint-Nazaire) and manoeuvring against one as directed by signal transmission; the need to sustain communications with home was another reason for patrolling surfaced. Boats usually submerged only when they had taken position ahead of a convoy's predicted track, there to lie in wait until darkness allowed them to surface again and initiate attacks – and, of course, when driven down by escorts, when they might go as deep as 600 feet. British depth charges were set to operate as deep as 550 feet, and some U-boat captains claim to have gone below 800, but that surpassed the 'crushing depth' of the pressure hull.

The U-boat captains' model tactic, though not always risked by the less daring, was to make a first attack from beyond the escort screen, penetrate the gap opened by the escorts' counter-manoeuvres and deliver subsequent attacks from within the convoy itself, where the radar echoes of the merchantmen would be confused with its own. The merchantmen also interfered with the escorts' attacking runs when the U-boat eventually dived to escape and might duplicate sonar echoes while it moved away through the convoy. The mounting of attacks from within the convoy had the added advantage of shortening the range of torpedo runs and improving identification and observation of the target.

Escorts

The U-boat's principal enemy was the convoy's close escort, exclusively British or Canadian (or Allied – Norwegian, Belgian, Polish, Free French) until September 1941, then alternatively American also. At the outset the escort was typically a destroyer of one of the older classes, unsuitable for fleet operations but capable of over 30 knots and, when a boiler was removed at the expense of some reduction in speed, able to cross the Atlantic without refuelling (refuelling of shorter-range escorts, from an accompanying oiler, was by this time standard convoy practice). These destroyers, usually of the V and W classes, to which the famous fifty American First World War 'four-stackers' were added in September 1940, were excellent in close support, being fast and manoeuvrable. However, with their narrow hulls and low displacement (about 1000 tons), they were miserable sea boats, wet above decks and violent in motion; while their configuration, designed for heavy gun and torpedo armaments, made them difficult to adapt for the emplacement of anti-submarine weapons.

They were also expensive and slow to build. From the outset, therefore, the Admiralty added to the escort fleet by constructing cheaper, smaller but more seaworthy and specialist craft – initially corvettes and sloops, with speeds as low as 16 knots, but with large batteries of depth-charge launchers. Some of the bigger deep-sea trawlers were also added to the oceanic escort groups, their excellent sea-keeping qualities making up somewhat for their low speed.

By 1942, however, the Admiralty had recognised the need for a specialist class of anti-submarine warship, intermediate in size and speed between the destroyer and the corvette, having something of the former's performance and the latter's armoury. The result was the frigate, a true ocean-going escort, able to make over 20 knots, cross the Atlantic without refuelling, deploy a full battery of underwater weapons including forward-firing depth-charge launchers, and accommodate a crew of a hundred men in reasonable comfort.

Escorts were formed into groups, usually of three destroyers, one of which acted as command ship, and six other ships comprising corvettes, frigates and trawlers. The B5 Group, which was to sail with convoy SC122, comprised two destroyers (one of which was American), five corvettes, a frigate, a trawler and a large United States Coast Guard cutter, the latter an excellent type which had already achieved notable success in anti-submarine operations. By early 1943, in addition to the close escort groups the Admiralty had succeeded in finding enough extra warships to begin forming a number of so-called 'support groups'. These, operating by the same principle as the U-boat wolf-packs, though in a contrary direction, were to cruise the trade routes under independent command, ready to intervene against the enemy whenever a convoy came under an attack too concentrated for the close escort to repel by its own efforts.

Escort crews were chiefly drawn from 'hostilities only' seamen, conscripted from civilian life during the course of the war, and reserve or volunteer reserve officers whose experience of the sea derived either from the merchant service or from yachting, if from any practical field at all; many reserve officers of the Atlantic escorts were naval novices. The British war historian Martin Middlebrook calculates that of 127 officers who sailed with the escorts of HX229/SC122 only twenty-four were regulars; all the rest were reservists, the majority of whom had never been to sea before 1939.

As with the U-boat men, however, escort crews rapidly forged powerful bonds of loyalty among themselves. The dangers they faced – and consequent losses – were not as acute as those oppressing the submariners; but they were 'little ship' sailors also, inhabitants of a world in which individual virtues and vices were known to all, mistakes could not be hidden and successes brought a universal thrill of achievement. 'I relished gales and never minded how much green water, rain and hail came over me,' one of them recalled afterwards. 'This, I felt, was what the Atlantic was supposed to turn on and I'd have been disappointed if it had been different.' The exhilaration of a successful attack on a U-boat, validated by the wreckage that an accurate depth-charging brought to the surface, was further compensation for all the hardship and boredom of weeks of keeping station with a convoy.

Anti-submarine weapons

The principal means by which an escort achieved a successful anti-submarine attack was through its 'sound gear' known as Asdic to the Royal Navy, sonar to the Americans (the latter term eventually became standard). Sonar worked by directing an electrical impulse, generated in a retractable 'dome' fitted under a ship's bottom, in a search arc towards the suspected position of the U-boat. When the impulse struck the target, the return of the echo could be heard through microphones, and the operator, by calculating the time lapse between transmission and reception and noting the angle of the sonar relative to the heading of the ship, was able to fix both the bearing and the distance of the target (though initially only up to 1 000 yards); these calculations, in the machinery fitted in British anti-submarine escorts by the outbreak of the war, were achieved automatically and displayed on an illuminated screen.

The only deficiency in the system was in depth-finding. The sonar principle would return depth values, but only at near-perpendicular angles from stationary targets, such as the sea bottom; it was early depth-finding devices, working on the returned-echo principle, which had set the pioneers of sonar on their course. Sonar had another deficiency: it would not work at short ranges, typically directly ahead of the ship in the last stage of its attacking run. Attacks, it was accepted, therefore, were 'blind' over the last 200 yards, a gap in sonar's effectiveness which captains of submerged U-boats learned to exploit by 'breaking' violently to port or starboard as the escort neared its weapon-release point.

The effects of this deficiency were compounded by the limitations of the early anti-submarine weapons, depth charges of medium weight dropped in groups of five over the stern of the ship. In consequence, an escort had to cross its target's position before it could release, and its pattern of slow-sinking charges, detonated by a pre-set 'depth pistol' actuated by water pressure, had to be accurate in both placing and fusing if the U-boat was to be damaged. The difficulties of the procedure, akin to those of precision bombing by aircraft on land, resulted in a low ratio of sinkings to attacks throughout 1939–40. In order to improve probabilities, the Admiralty increased the weight of depth charges so that they would sink faster, enlarged their explosive filling and increased the number of charges that could be released in a salvo to ten. It also experimented with throwers, which projected depth charges to port and starboard so as to enlarge the 'spread', and increased the intervals at which depth charges entered the water.

It rapidly became clear, however, that the real need was for a weapon which would project anti-submarine missiles ahead of the ship, into the 'blind' area which sonar could not cover at the culmination of a ship's attacking run, fused by a device that would detonate the charge in direct proximity to the submarine. The result, introduced at the end of

1941, was the so-called 'Hedgehog' anti-submarine mortar, which fired a pattern of twenty-four bombs, activated by contact fuses, into the sonar's blind area, at intervals from each other slightly less than that of a U-boat's beam. The bombs detonated only if they touched the U-boat's hull but with sufficient explosive force, it was calculated, to penetrate and so destroy it.

Hedgehog, however, proved to have limitations almost as severe as those of the old-fashioned free-sinking depth charge. Its use required a skill which few escort crews were given the time to acquire; and its charges were too light to be certainly destructive. A heavier mortar, codenamed Squid, became available in 1944 and proved much more effective. Analysis after the war revealed that a single depth-charge attack had a 6 per cent chance of causing sinking, Hedgehog (when properly used) 20 per cent and Squid 50 per cent. However, the introduction of Squid also coincided with that of a depth-estimating sonar, derived from a device that tilted the sonar dome, allowing the operator to aim its sound impulse through a calculable arc. Neither aid was available in 1943, when escort captains still had to depend on their judgement in setting the depth pistols which exploded their depth charges and on the skill of their crews correctly to operate the Hedgehog, where fitted. Attacks were commonly made with a combination of both weapons, the Hedgehog often being used only when all depth charges had been expended.

Effective depth-charge and Hedgehog attack was nevertheless always terrifying and often lethal to submarine crews. Puncture of the hull, even when all internal watertight doors were closed, would admit water at pressures which at worst would sink the ship, at best force it to the surface, either through threatening it with sinking or by shorting out its electrical system, damaging its depth-keeping and steering gear, and causing torpedoes to start their self-detonating mechanisms and thus 'run wild' in the forward and aft compartments. A U-boat caught in a resolutely conducted depth-charge trap fought for its life against the probabilities. Operational analysis showed that its chances of survival after the delivery of a sixth close attack rapidly diminished, probably because the U-boat captain lost his capacity to think his way out of danger; and by 1943 expert escort commanders, like Captain F. J. Walker of 2nd Escort Group, had devised a method of 'playing' a U-boat between two surface warships, one listening, the other repeatedly depth-charging – which made escape particularly unlikely for a U-boat whose captain did not early break out of the search pattern.

Aircraft

Hostile aircraft terrified the seamen of the Atlantic battle, those of the convoys as much as the U-boat crews who were their enemy. As soon as the Biscay ports fell to the Germans, a force of long-range Focke

Wulf 200, Gruppe 40 of thirty aircraft, was based in Brittany to undertake reconnaissance and strike missions against the convoys; and, though it was initially unsuccessful in guiding U-boats to distant targets, it quickly demonstrated how lethal bombing attacks against merchant ships could be. Early in 1941 the Admiralty reacted by equipping some merchant ships with catapult-launched Hurricane fighters, 'one shot' aircraft, since the pilots had to ditch once launched, but effective in shooting down the FW 200, chasing them away or deterring them from interfering altogether. By April of that year it had been decided that every convoy should include a catapult fighter (CAM) ship, and in June another expedient appeared: *Audacity*, a merchantman adapted to launch several fighters, out of which would develop the escort carrier, most potent of all anti-submarine weapons.

The U-boats, when operating beyond the range of shore-based fighter cover, had to brave out encounters with aircraft single-handed. Until 1942, however, aircraft were of little direct threat to them, the types in Allied service lacking the range and the offensive equipment to find them in distant waters or to damage them closer to home. The only aircraft of extended range were the British Sunderland and American Catalina flying-boats, which were few in number (only fifty-four were available to Coastal Command in June 1942, of which twenty-eight flew in any one day). Even when operating from all three Allied base areas contiguous to the North Atlantic – the North American coast, Iceland and the British Isles – the aircraft could not meet in mid-ocean; the area not covered by their patrols was known as the 'Greenland Gap' and offered a rich hunting ground for those U-boats that could reach it. It would not be closed until May 1943 when VLR (very long range) Liberator four-engined bombers, carrying large loads of depth charges, came into service in numbers.

Between May and October 1942, however, Coastal Command had temporarily succeeded in making the Bay of Biscay a place of danger for U-boats by deploying against them a combination of new weapons. These were the torpex depth charge of improved explosive power, an airborne search radar and a powerful searchlight, the Leigh Light. Tracking their target by night on radar, the aircraft illuminated a surfaced U-boat in the last moments of the plane's attacking run and released a pattern of depth charges around the boat as it tried to dive. Two U-boats were damaged in this way in May and two sunk in July. Dönitz was forced to order his captains to make the Biscay passage into the Atlantic submerged, thus delaying their arrival at the convoy routes and shortening their patrol times. In October, however, a receiving device which detected airborne radar emissions came into U-boat service and the Atlantic boats resumed their practice of traversing the Bay of Biscay on the surface, diving only when warned of an aircraft's approach. It was not until a higher-frequency radar, the 10-centimetre set, began to be fitted to anti-submarine aircraft in January 1943 that Coastal Command recovered its advantage – for a time at least.

The tactical to-and-fro of the Bay battle drove Churchill to institute a strategic bombing campaign against the U-boat bases. Despite Bomber Command's reluctance to divert aircraft from its effort against German cities, in January 1943 it was obliged to divert a proportion of its strength, eventually rising to 20 per cent, against Lorient, La Pallice, La Rochelle, Brest and Saint-Nazaire. The effort proved ineffective. With remarkable foresight, Hitler had already had enormous bomb-proof concrete shelters for the boats constructed in all these ports. Even direct hits on their roofs, 12 feet thick, failed to penetrate, and although 9000 tons of bombs were dropped in January and February, causing appalling 'collateral' damage to surrounding buildings and hundreds of French civilian casualties, not a single U-boat was touched. The Admiralty and the US Navy Department were reinforced in their belief that the Battle of the Atlantic could only be won at sea.

Radio intelligence

Yet the central struggle for control of the Atlantic was conducted on land. 'Command of the sea' is never achieved in a haphazard fashion. Nelson's recurrent complaint of 'want of frigates' spoke of every admiral's chronic need to find the enemy in the waters of the ocean, follow his movements and bring him to battle at a time and place of his choosing. Until the coming of radio that search could only be conducted afloat. Radio, with which a fleet commander manoeuvred his dispersed units, betrayed information of positions, speeds and movements which could be intercepted and collated ashore and retransmitted to the commander of the hunt; and such 'radio intelligence' contributed – misleadingly, as we have seen – to the British conduct of the battle of Jutland.

However, radio intelligence lay at the heart of the waging of the U-boat campaign by both sides. The theory of U-boat pack operations (*Rudeltaktik*) which Dönitz had developed before the war was based on the principle of massing U-boats against a convoy target by control from a central, shore-based headquarters. It required transmissions from headquarters to captains; it equally required transmissions in the opposite direction, and it was those which presented the U-boats' enemies with the raw material of the radio war. Two principles were in conflict here: that of the necessity for 'radio silence' and that of the overriding importance of strategic command. Because strategic command was so vital, radio silence had to be violated, and on a regular and frequent basis. The U-boat transmissions provided the British and, later, American listeners with the direction-finding 'fixes' which determined where danger areas in the Atlantic lay and so how convoys should be routed to avoid them.

U-boat headquarters had taken trouble to reduce the length of transmissions to a minimum. The Atlantic map was 'squared' and the squares allotted short code groups, so that a U-boat captain could indicate his current position by the briefest of letter groups. All other standard elements of a message were similarly compressed. Nevertheless, as Jürgen Rowehr, the German historian of the U-boat war, has pointed out, there were six forms of transmission which a U-boat captain could not avoid making at regular intervals. They were: (1) convoy position reports; (2) warnings of enemy submarines and mines; (3) operational situation reports; (4) weather reports; (5) own position reports; (6) responses to transmissions from headquarters. Even when confined to the briefest encoded groups, such transmissions provided material for an enemy 'fix', and so put at risk the transmitting U-boat and any others its message called towards it.

Between January and December 1942 particularly, for reasons to be discussed, British and American radio direction-finding of such transmissions provided the most important intelligence for the waging of the U-boat war; but it was at all times of high value. Fixes, particularly if they revealed a massing of U-boats, allowed the convoy control centres to route their charges away from areas thus established to be of high risk. And early warning, imposing long, high-speed surface chases by the U-boat captains after their quarry, was often enough to spare a convoy attack altogether. Between July 1942 and May 1943 the British directors of the direction-finding service, Commanders Hall and Winn, and their American counterpart, Captain Knowles, managed to reroute 105 out of 174 North Atlantic convoys, some 60 per cent, clear away from identified wolf-pack traps. Partial identification of traps spared another twenty-three, and kept losses in thirty to low figures. Only sixteen convoys ran into large wolf-packs and suffered heavy damage.

Convoys themselves, which observed radio silence as a staff of life, provided little direction-finding intelligence to the enemy; signals between merchantmen and escorts were made by directional light, flag or siren. U-boats themselves also minimised radio intercommunication in the operational area, but transmissions from U-boats to headquarters were monitored by escorts and sometimes provided attack intelligence; in June 1942, for example, an escort of ONS102 detected contact reports signalled by the 'Hecht' ('Pike') wolf-pack to base, as a result of which U-94 and U-590 were depth-charged and damaged.

Decryption

Vital though direction-finding was to both sides, however, the 'great game' of radio warfare was played between the two sides' cryptographers. The Ultra story is now part of the folklore of the Second World War; how the British, building on the achievements of their Polish and

French allies, succeeded in reconstructing the machinery and mathematics of the German Enigma cipher system, ultimately to read it in 'real time' – as quickly, that is, as enciphered radio messages could be read by a German message-taker himself.

Less well known is the pattern and extent of the British success at the Government Code and Cipher School at Bletchley. Success depended heavily upon German users of the Enigma machine breaking the rules for its setting; experienced and well-trained users – those, for example, at German air force headquarters operating what Bletchley codenamed the 'Pink' setting – only rarely committed the errors which allowed the British cryptanalysts to break into their traffic. Traffic transmitted by teleprinter and land-line evaded attack, while even radio traffic, as long as very careful signallers used the key, was rarely penetrated; the Gestapo key was never broken. Naval keys, necessarily transmitted by radio, often by young and inexperienced operators working under difficult conditions – and none was more difficult than in a U-boat at sea – yielded more frequently. That likelihood was known to German naval headquarters and it took appropriate precautions: one was to establish an *Offizier* key, which could be used only by an officer; another was to supply U-boats with the most advanced models of the Enigma machine.

Both these precautions were greatly to complicate Bletchley's part in the battle of the Atlantic. However, the principal impediment to its establishing cryptological dominance over the U-boat command had a different origin: for long and significant periods of the war the German B-Dienst could read the Royal Navy's codes, sometimes when the reverse was not the case. In particular the German navy's 'Shark' key, used to control U-boats in the North Atlantic between February 1942 and May 1943, was not broken until December 1942. At times thereafter 'Shark' resisted attack again, and, by the worst of bad luck, it did so completely during the nine days, 10–19 March 1943, in which the Admiralty was trying to enable convoys HX229 and SC122 to fight their way through an exceptionally strong U-boat patrol line.

The Royal Navy's no. 3 cipher, on the other hand – that used for convoy control in the North Atlantic, both within the British service and for communication with the US Navy – was broken by the German B-Dienst in February 1942, by painstaking reconstruction (from a host of clues and loose ends) of the book from which ciphers were made up. Despite a setback in December when the book underwent change, no. 3 cipher was regularly read again from February until June 1943. 'From February,' as the British official history of intelligence discloses, the B-Dienst 'was sometimes obtaining decrypts about convoy movements between 10 and 20 hours in advance. Throughout the period February 1942 to 19 June 1943 it frequently decrypted in this cipher the daily signal in which the Admiralty issued its estimate of U-boat dispositions.' Given these two pieces of daily information, U-boat headquarters was theoretically enabled to manoeuvre its boats away from identified locations and towards convoy tracks when and as it chose; in practice, bad weather, difficulties of communication and the intervention of chance prevented it from 'playing' the battle of the Atlantic as a mere radio game. Like the British, moreover, the Germans were obliged to forego the use of much valuable information out of prudent concern to protect the secret of their cipher-reading success. Nevertheless, at sea if nowhere else, German cryptanalysts must be recognised as having been on equal terms with their British adversaries for long and critical periods of the war, to the Allies' great disadvantage; in the critical battle for convoys SC122 and HX229, the B-Dienst took and held the ascendancy.

THE BATTLE FOR CONVOYS HX229 AND SC122

HX229 and SC122

SC122 and HX229, which were to provide the focus for the largest of all U-boat engagements of the Atlantic battle, were respectively slow (7-knot) and fast (9-knot) convoys which sailed from New York on 5 and 8 March 1943 for the United Kingdom. Their component ships had been gathering in the Hudson river for some weeks beforehand. SC122 would consist when formed of sixty-five ships, HX229 of forty; but SC122, because it initially included vessels bound for other North American ports, would set off into the Atlantic at a strength of fifty. SC122 included a large number of general cargo types, old and slow freighters carrying steel, iron ore, bauxite, copper, sugar, wheat, cocoa, meat, timber and, in a few cases, explosives. The freighters' ports of origin were various: some had already crossed the Atlantic from Africa to join, others had come up from South America and the Caribbean, but the majority had loaded in the United States. HX229 also included numbers of general freighters, but a higher proportion of tankers, a number of fast refrigerated ships and five Liberty ships. It carried much fuel oil, lubricants and aviation spirit and a great deal of meat.

Both convoys were to follow closely aligned routes, somewhat northward of the Great Circle Line between New York and Northern Ireland, but SC122 was to clear harbour on 5 March, three days earlier than HX229, and the two were to proceed independently. On the first leg, each was protected by a local escort group. The ocean escorts were to be picked up off Nova Scotia and Newfoundland. SC122's consisted of five Royal Navy corvettes, HMS *Buttercup*, *Godetia*, *Lavender*, *Pimpernel* and *Saxifrage*, a frigate, HMS *Swale*, the US Coast Guard Cutter *Ingham* (to join later), a trawler, HMS *Campobello*, and two destroyers, USS *Upshur* and HMS *Havelock*; the escort commander, Commander R. C. Boyle, sailed in the last. HX229's escort comprised four corvettes, HMS *Abelia*, *Pennywort* and *Anemone* and HM Canadian

Ship *Sherbrooke*, and seven destroyers, HMS *Volunteer, Beverley, Mansfield* (the last two ex-American four-stackers), *Witherington, Highlander, Vimy* and USS *Babbitt* (some of these were to join on passage); the escort commander, Lieutenant-Commander G. J. Luther, sailed in *Volunteer*. No support group was available to either, no catapult aircraft were embarked in either convoy, and air cover from the North American shore terminated at a range of 850 miles, 800 miles short of the point at which it would be resumed from Northern Ireland. The shortest possible crossing time was calculated at seventeen days, of which four would be spent in the North Atlantic 'air gap'.

The wolf-packs

Dönitz's U-boats on his North Atlantic patrol lines in early March 1943 were restoring their formations after a four-day battle with SC122/HX229's predecessors, SC121 and HX228, in which seventeen merchantmen and a destroyer had been sunk for the loss of one U-boat. Fourteen U-boats formed an advanced screen, 750 miles from the Newfoundland coast, codenamed 'Raubgraf' ('Robber Baron'). The others, with new arrivals, were re-forming into two lines in the air gap, 'Dränger' ('Harrier') of eleven and 'Stuŕmer' ('Attacker') of seventeen. Forty-two U-boats in all were therefore on station at the outset of the battle, together with two tanker 'milch cows' to replenish those running low on fuel. Many of the U-boat crews were inexperienced in North Atlantic warfare or were outright novices. A few captains, notably Gerhard Feiler of U-653, Helmut von Tippelskirch of U-439 and Hans-Gunther Brosin of U-134, had made half a dozen or more patrols. The majority were on their second or third, and thirteen were at sea for the first time. However, there was no necessary correlation between experience and success: Paul-Karl Loeser of U-373 was on his eighth patrol but played little part in the coming battle; Manfred Kinzel of U-338, on his first patrol, was to sink four ships and damage a fifth.

Dönitz's concentration of numbers against SC122/HX229 was formidable, outnumbering their escorts by two to one. Even more important than numerical superiority was operational foreknowledge. On 12 March the B-Dienst deciphered the sailing orders, four days old but good for several more, of a secondary convoy, HX229A, whose route aligned closely with those of both SC122 and HX229. By a lucky chance, the German cryptanalysts confused HX229A with HX229, a much larger target which, by monitoring the cycle of convoys, they were expecting to leave New York in any case. Subsequent listening out for signals, and rapid decryption of eight made by SC122 and HX229 on passage between New York and Halifax, provided confirmation of the convoys' speed, composition and heading. By 12 March information was firm enough for U-boat headquarters to decide that it had a rich

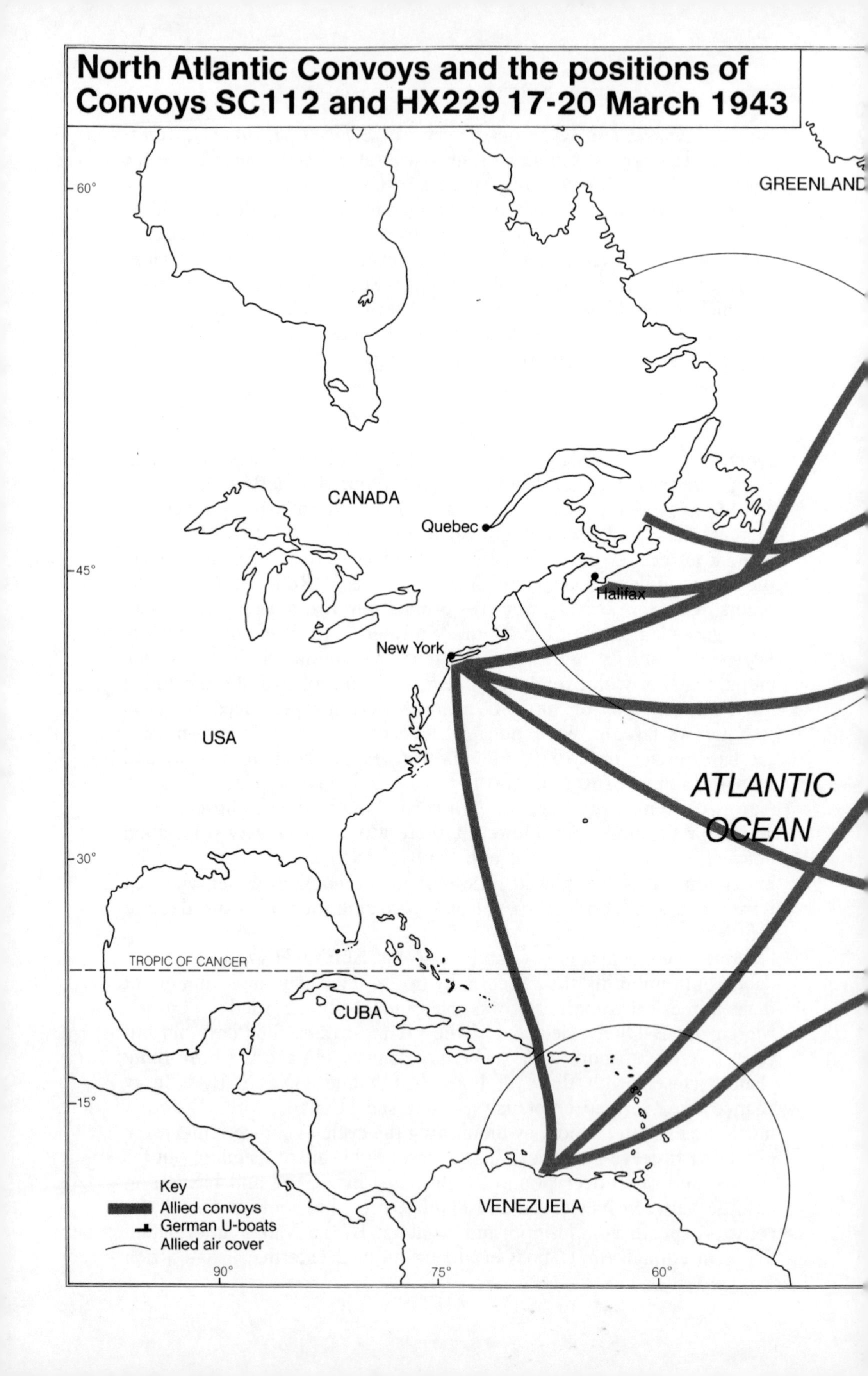
North Atlantic Convoys and the positions of Convoys SC112 and HX229 17-20 March 1943
GREENLAND
60°
CANADA
Quebec
45°
Halifax
New York
USA
ATLANTIC
OCEAN
30°
TROPIC OF CANCER
CUBA
15°
VENEZUELA
Key
Allied convoys
German U-boats
Allied air cover
90°
75°
60°

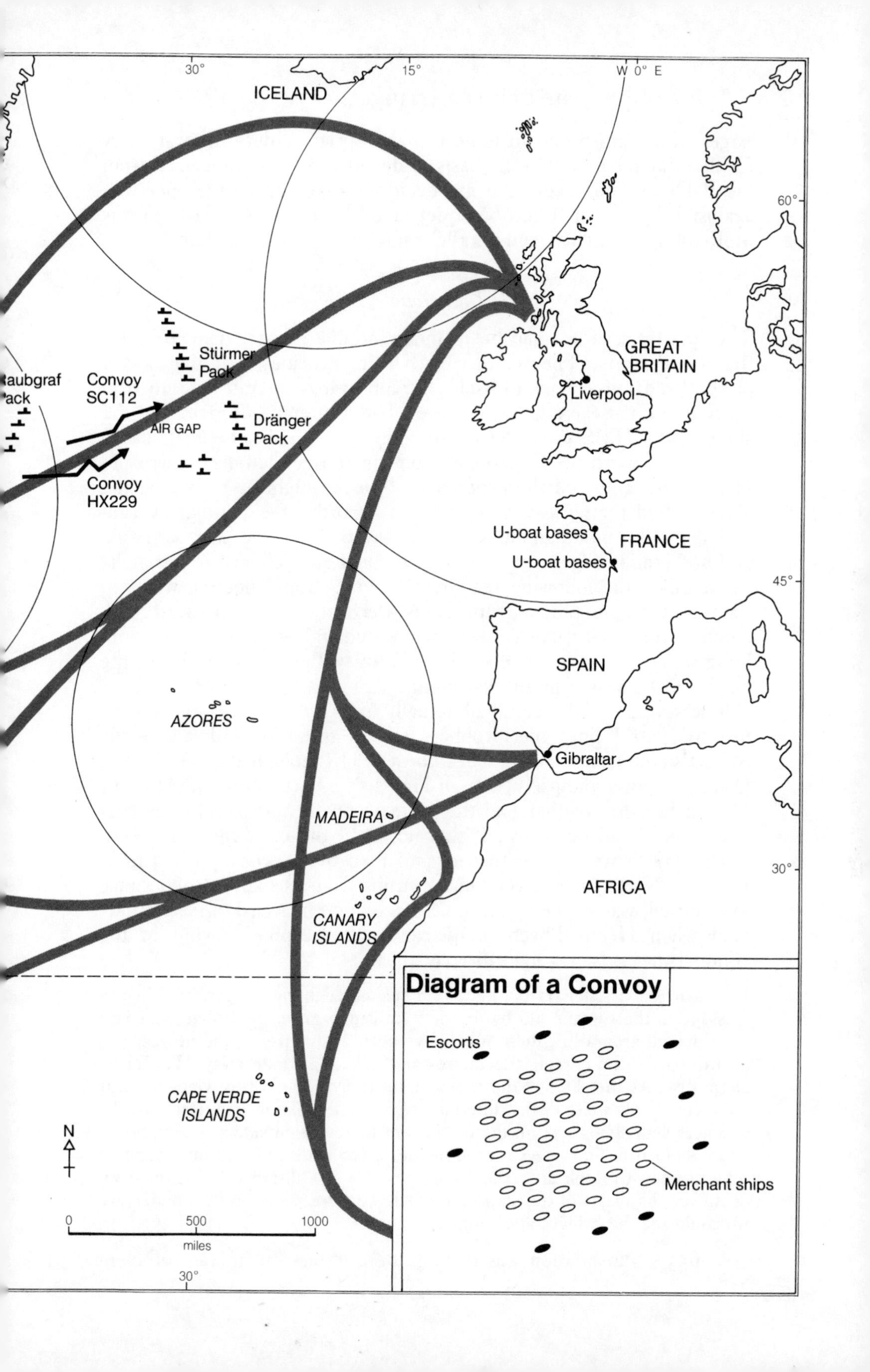
ICELAND
GREAT BRITAIN
Liverpool
FRANCE
U-boat bases
U-boat bases
SPAIN
Gibraltar
AFRICA
AZORES
MADEIRA
CANARY ISLANDS
CAPE VERDE ISLANDS
Stürmer Pack
Dränger Pack
Convoy SC112
Convoy HX229
AIR GAP
Diagram of a Convoy
Escorts
Merchant ships
30°
15°
W 0° E
60°
45°
30°
N
0
500
1000
miles
30°

target within grasp and to issue the appropriate orders. Its war diary for that day records: 'On the basis of decoded messages received from the B-Dienst, the leadership has decided to commence the operation against HX229; which has been detected.' SC122, which HX229 was overhauling on a close and parallel route, was to share its fate.

The encounter

The first week at sea had been uncomfortable but not dangerous for the two convoys. The weather had been atrocious, but that was a protection against attack in itself, and long-range aircraft continued to provide cover. Severe gales, however, had scattered and damaged the ships, one – HMS *Campobello* – so badly that it had to be abandoned. An officer aboard SS *Coracero*, a 7000-ton refrigerated meat-carrier in HX229, remembered the experience: 'On the night of 15 March the gale reached the peak of its ferocity . . . shortly after midnight we hit and shipped a mountainous sea which swept down our starboard side and broke amidships, smashed No 3 lifeboat and reduced it to matchwood which the following sea smartly removed and nothing was left. As was common practice our boats were always swung overboard, hanging from their davits ready to be lowered and, when in that position, hung some forty feet above sea level. This will give you an idea of the height of the seas running that night.'

The severity of the gale had actually hidden HX229 from Dönitz's forward patrol line, the 'Robber Baron' group of U-boats, while SC122's course, a hundred miles north of HX229's, had taken it clear. U-91 had got a glimpse of one of HX229's escorts on the night of 15 March; but the weather had then swept convoy and patrol line apart and contact had been lost. It was not until the early morning of 16 March that it was re-established, and then by the convoy's bad luck. U-653, a North Atlantic veteran, returning from its sixth patrol because low on fuel, was travelling on the surface 800 miles east of Newfoundland when Heinz Theen, a quartermaster keeping lookout in the conning tower, 'saw a light directly ahead':

> I think it was a sailor on the deck of a steamer lighting a cigarette. I sent a message to the captain and by the time he came up on the bridge we could see ships all around us, there must have been about twenty, the nearest was on the port side between 500 metres and half a sea mile away. We did an alarm dive. As the ships of the convoy went over the top of us we could hear quite clearly the noise of the different engines – the diesels with fast revs, the steamers with slow revs and the turbines of the escorts made a singing noise. After about two hours we surfaced behind the convoy and sent off a sighting report. Then we took up a shadowing position at a distance from which we could see the masts of the ships and when we were taken up by a high wave we could see the bridges and funnels.

U-653's transmission was of only three letters but it was sufficient to place HX229 in grid 14 of square BC on U-boat headquarters' map of the North Atlantic. By conflation of intelligence, the B-Dienst now confused SC122 with HX229 and believed it had found the former. SC122 was in fact 150 miles to the eastward and moving on a slightly northerly course, but the effect of the confusion was unimportant in the light of the orders Dönitz at once issued. These were for the ten boats of the 'Robber Baron' line to turn east and motor at top speed on the surface to intercept while eleven boats of the 'Stürmer–Dränger' line 400 miles away in mid-Atlantic turned west to join them. Both convoys – though Dönitz thought he had only one in the trap – must now certainly be caught between the upper and lower jaws within the next forty-eight hours. So certain was even the Admiralty of this inevitability that it abandoned thoughts of routing the victims away from their gathering predators and signalled the Convoy and Routing Section in Washington to urge that both SC122 and HX229 steer the most direct course they could for the United Kingdom, trusting to the capacity of their escorts to fight them through. Since the next two days' voyage lay through the epicentre of the 'air gap' into which aircraft from neither Iceland nor Britain could reach, this was desperate counsel.

The massacre of HX229

Even by this stage HX229's situation was desperate. Badly scattered by the storm of 15–16 March, it had only just recovered formation as dusk drew in on the evening of 16 March. It was now steaming in eleven parallel columns, the more vulnerable ships, carrying oil and explosives, in the centre, the escorts disposed ahead and to the flanks at 4000 yards (torpedo range) from the perimeter. Only six escorts were present: *Mansfield, Volunteer, Witherington, Anemone, Beverley* and *Pennywort*; the promised reinforcements, *Highlander, Babbitt, Abelia, Vimy* and *Sherbrooke* had not yet joined. There were already seven U-boats in contact, clinging to the convoy at the limit of visibility, and many more motoring at high speed to intercept. The bad news had percolated to the merchantmen crews and set teeth on edge. 'Myself and some of the catering staff were off duty having a cup of tea on deck,' recalled Able Seaman H. J. Brinkworth in SS *Nariva*, a refrigerated-meat ship sailing at the head of the third column from starboard, 'when I think it was a destroyer sped through the convoy flying [a flag signal] and I asked them if they knew what the signal meant. None of them did know and I told them that from my previous experience I understood it to mean that enemy submarines were in our vicinity.' Second Officer J. D. Sharp, in SS *Zouave*, described how the same sense of impending danger had communicated itself to the merchantmen of nearby SC122: 'Just at sunset a two-flag signal crept up to the masthead of the Commodore ship and you did not need to look at it to know it was W.C. – Enemy submarines in the vicinity . . . immediately we had a terrible feeling of apprehension and of nervous tension which increased as darkness set in – which of us will be afloat in the morning and, if we "get it", who will be with us in the morning?'

HX229 and SC122 were to be twelve fewer at the next dawn; the worst of the disaster was to fall on HX229, whose ordeal began shortly before midnight on 16 March. At ten o'clock U-603, commanded by Lieutenant Hans-Joachim Bertelsmann, found a gap in the escort line and moved into the attack. U-603 belonged to the 'Robber Baron' group and was on its second North Atlantic patrol. It had overhauled the convoy the previous afternoon and now, in clear visibility and calm sea, got a clear sight of the convoy in the interval, 10,000 yards wide, between *Beverley*, one of the ex-American four-stacker destroyers, and *Pennywort*, a Flower-class corvette. It fired first a salvo of three FAT torpedoes and then a single G7e. The latter was a conventional missile; the FAT were programmed to reverse course at a predetermined time and then make several passes across a convoy's track. Which found its target Bertelsmann did not establish, but at five minutes past ten a detonation was heard in the U-boat and, as *Beverley* and *Pennywort* turned towards it to commence a search, Bertelsmann submerged.

His victim was the Norwegian *Elin K*, carrying wheat and manganese; the ship was hit in the after hold and began to sink fast. Fortunately it had an experienced and disciplined crew who launched their lifeboats without panic and got clear away in the calm sea. 'It was very dark,' remembered Motorman John Johannessen, 'but somebody had a torch and within a minute everybody was getting the lifeboats launched. . . . I remember the boat was banged against the ship's side two or three times before we managed to get clear; by that time, the aft deck was awash. The ship sank very fast and, when we found the other lifeboat and heard that everybody had been saved, we all shouted a hurrah.'

Elin K's crew was almost immediately picked up by HMS *Pennywort*, whose captain was 'most impressed by the calmness and efficiency of the Norwegians. . . . I'm afraid I cannot say the same of some of our later survivors.' Later survivors, however, were to experience a long-drawn-out agony of apprehension which those of the *Elin K*, for all their ordeal, were spared. Shortly after eleven o'clock, U-758 entered the gap between *Pennywort* and *Beverley*, enlarged by their departure to search for U-603, and fired four torpedoes at short intervals. The Dutch frigate *Zaanland* and the American Liberty ship *James Oglethorpe*, carrying meat, wheat, zinc, steel, cotton and food between them, were both hit. *Zaanland* began to settle at once; from the lifeboats her crew heard 'a rumble like thunder – probably the boilers crashing through the bulkheads – we saw sparks on the forecastle probably caused by the anchor chains running away and then it was all over.'

The Dutchmen aboard *Zaanland* were as disciplined as the crew of the *Elin K*. *James Oglethorpe*'s men behaved differently, some panicking, others showing stoical fortitude. At the torpedo strike there was a rush for the boats, and thirteen out of fifty were drowned when one upended. Thirty men stayed with Captain A. W. Long, who believed the ship could be saved; its engines were still running and the cotton in the hold had swelled to check the inflow of water. While the ship departed on a wide circling course, caused by the helm jamming at the moment of impact, Captain Long gathered his stalwarts and, as the convoy left him to its rear, started to try making course for Newfoundland. He was not to arrive; somewhere in his desperate voyage, storm or undetected damage sank the ship and no trace of it or its crew was ever seen again.

Commander Luther's warships were now detached far from their escort positions, rescuing survivors or trying to start attacks against the U-boats, whose locations they could sense but not precisely fix. Only one had luck. A lookout on *Anemone*, one of the Flower-class corvettes disposed on the convoy's port flank, spotted a surfaced U-boat (it was U-89 on its seventh patrol, and so perhaps over-confident) at a range of 3000 yards. For twelve minutes, as *Anemone* exerted all its inadequate speed (16 knots), the U-boat remained in clear view, obviously unaware of the approaching danger. When eventually it crash-dived the corvette was only 300 yards short, so close that the captain, Commander P.G. A. King, did not dare fire his full pattern of depth charges at the shallow setting such a near-instantaneous attack required; to do so would have damaged his own ship. Accordingly he dropped five out of ten, although the force of the explosions upset both his radar and his radio telephone. After sixteen minutes U-89 surfaced again and tried to make a run for it – its surface speed and *Anemone*'s almost coincided – but was forced below and depth-charged a second time, an attack which put the corvette's sonar temporarily out of order. When it recovered, Commander King made five depth-charge attacks on strong sonar contacts, heard sounds that persuaded him he had hit home, but was then recalled to his escort position. In fact he had only slightly damaged U-89, but it was already short of fuel and suffering engine trouble, and it now left the vicinity of HX229 to make its way home.

Anemone was needed because there had been another sinking. At half past midnight the *William Eustis*, a Liberty ship carrying sugar – enough for three weeks' ration for the British population, an escort crew calculated – was torpedoed by U–435, abandoned by its crew (prematurely, the captain of HMS *Volunteer* thought) and sunk by *Volunteer*, to avert the risk of a U-boat capturing the confidential cipher books which the captain, who was saved with all his crew, had left aboard.

At and shortly after half past two, another attack developed, delivered by U-435 and U-91 of the 'Robber Baron' line. Between them they fired eight torpedoes, of both circling and direct-shot type, one of which hit the American freighter *Harry Luckenbach* and sank her quickly. Three lifeboats got away, but the ship had been at the rear of one of the columns and so they were quickly left behind. No less than four escorts subsequently came across them, but, either because, like *Penny-*

wort, they were already overloaded with survivors or because, like *Volunteer*, they were on a close escort mission, none was able to stop. *Harry Luckenbach*'s survivors drifted away into the Atlantic wastes and were never seen again.

Between half past two and five o'clock there were no attacks; the escorts' frenzied scurrying away from the convoy's perimeter had held some U-boats at bay, while others were reloading torpedo tubes and seeking an advantageous attack position. Just before five o'clock one was found by U-600, which had been dodging escorts and closing the range for four hours. It fired five torpedoes, four of circling type, in quick succession and heard five explosions. It later claimed to have hit five ships. The reality was bad enough. Three of the most valuable ships in the convoy – the freighters *Irénée du Pont* and *Nariva*, carrying general cargo and meat, and the 12,000-ton tanker *Southern Princess* – had been struck, *Irénée du Pont* twice. She began to go down at once and her crew panicked, twelve drowning close to lifeboats which had cast off too soon. *Nariva* floated upright longer, with a huge gash in her side, into which survivors in the lifeboats saw one of the rafts disappear. 'I can still hear the screams of the men inside the hull,' wrote Second Officer G. D. Williams. 'But then, thank God, the same rush of water that had drawn them into the hull of the ship, at the next roll swept them out again by which time we were so much closer and could grab the lifelines and drag the men to safety in our boat, one of whom turned out to be our dear elderly chief engineer who, as if in gratitude for our rescue, became violently sick all over me.'

The *Southern Princess*, placed for safety in the convoy's centre, exploded and took fire. 'We watched in stupefying silence and fascinated horror, hardly believing it was real,' wrote a spectator, who, like everyone else in the convoy, particularly those near enough to hear the crew's screams, thought that all in her must perish. Fortunately the fire had taken hold aft, away from the crew quarters, and ninety-six of the hundred aboard got off. They were picked up by one of the rearmost ships, *Tekoa*, which had been nominated as rescue ship and bravely stopped to fulfil its duty in the glaring illumination of the tanker fire. 'The outlook at this time,' Commander Luther later wrote in his report, 'was not encouraging, with the possibility of more attacks to come and so few escorts to deal with them. I ordered escorts to act offensively by making frequent dashes outwards at high speed, dropping occasional single depth-charges in the hope that it might deter an intending attacker.' At half past six, the destroyer HMS *Beverley* detected a surfaced U-boat while making one of these excursions, held it in her radar until the boat dived at a range of 1200 yards, and then depth-charged after a sonar approach. The U-boat manoeuvred sharply, inside the destroyer's turning circle, but one or more of the seven depth charges dropped exploded close: U-228, on her first patrol, sprang a leak and withdrew from the battle, not to rejoin it.

The sky was now beginning to lighten, driving the U-boats to the limit of visibility and bringing the convoy and its escorts a hope of intermission. Air cover was still a day away, but the escorts, to which five reinforcements were hurrying, would not have to deal with close-range surface attacks during daylight hours; and submerged U-boats, unless already positioned ahead of the convoy's track, lacked the speed to intercept it. The packs had, however, already inflicted harrowing losses. Eight of the thirty-seven merchantman which had set out on the North Atlantic crossing (three had been dropped off in Canada) had been torpedoed, and, though 447 of their crews had been rescued, 143 had been drowned or were adrift in boats that the ocean would soon engulf. No U-boat had been seriously damaged and only twenty-eight torpedoes had been expended. Since it was torpedo stocks rather than fuel which determined a pack's endurance, the night's work left the 'Robber Baron', 'Attacker' and 'Harrier' groups well placed to resume their offensive as soon as darkness fell again.

In the meantime one of their number, U-91, completed the night's work by scavenging the debris. *Nariva* and *Irénée du Pont* remained afloat astern of the convoy into daylight, close to the burning tanker *Southern Princess*. The tanker had capsized; but the freighters, though down in the water, appeared salvable. The corvette *Anemone* had *Nariva*'s crew aboard and, when light broke, put the captain, second officer and second engineer back on board to see if way could be got in her. 'She looked a bit pathetic,' recalled Second Engineer H. W. Brophy, 'with her bows deep in the water and the foredeck awash as she rose and fell in the heavy swell. I noted the battery-powered red distress light was still burning and there was still a wisp of steam and smoke pouring out of the funnel. The surface of the sea all round the ship was littered with still-frozen carcasses of lamb and mutton which had obviously been washed out of the lower hold spaces through the enormous hole blown open by the torpedo.' While the visitors were inspecting the engine-room, and deciding that it would take hours to raise steam in the boilers, *Anemone* suddenly departed, leaving them marooned. It was an uncomfortable moment; the corvette, however, had moved to avoid a torpedo track and then to attack the U-boat which had launched it. When it failed to make contact, it returned to the *Nariva*, took off the three officers, made an attempt to sink the two casualties still afloat (the tanker had finally gone under) – abandoned ships were a menace to others – and worked up speed to rejoin the convoy. As soon as she was over the horizon, U-616, the boat which had attacked her, made its own attempt to sink the hulks, but failed. It fell to U-91, which had been trailing the convoy at a distance, to send both to the bottom in the early afternoon.

At one o'clock in the afternoon of 17 March, two U-boats, U-384 and U-361, arrived in attacking positions on HX229's starboard flank. They were two of ten boats hanging at the limits of the convoy, which had been regrouped into nine columns to close the gaps left by sinkings. Two escorts were in close company; the other three were still detached on search and rescue. In the circumstances, U-384 and U-361 comfortably reached submerged attacking positions and found easy targets. The Dutch ships *Terkoelei* and the British *Coracero* were the victims. *Coracero*'s crew, except for five killed instantly in the engine-room by the torpedo explosion, all got away. *Terkoelei*'s men, many of whom were Asian, were shocked into inactivity by the disaster; two lifeboat parties would not row away from the sinking ship's side and were carried down when it capsized on top of them.

Mansfield and *Volunteer*, the close escorts, made token attacks against the enemy but quickly returned to rescue those in the water. 'Some particular survivors,' wrote Engine Room Artificer G. T. Smith of *Volunteer* 'were in a capsized lifeboat. All managed to negotiate the scrambling nets except one who was in the water and clinging to the bilge grab rail. He didn't have the strength to pull himself from the water and he stared with unblinking eyes at the people safe above him. One of our leading stokers scrambled down and, with Lieutenant-Commander Hill [anxious] to get under way, the survivor was hauled to safety only to die within five minutes of being rescued.' The fatality was a young soldier of the Maritime Regiment Royal Artillery which provided gun crews to the merchantmen of the convoys.

Mansfield and *Volunteer*, loaded with survivors, now departed to rejoin the convoy. Their fellow escort, the destroyer *Beverley*, an ex-American four-stacker with a turn of speed, was meanwhile achieving one of the group's few successes of the battle. Positioned ahead of the convoy, it spotted first one, then another U-boat lying in wait, worked up to 25 knots, forced both below and quickly got a firm sonar contact on one of them. *Beverley*'s crew were experienced. They had sunk a U-boat the previous month and damaged another on the morning of 17 March. They were about to subject U-530 to a submariner's nightmare: a prolonged and accurate sonar and depth-charge attack. For two and a half hours *Beverley* made one run after another, six in all, damaging the U-boat so badly, even when it went below 600 feet, that all its lights went out and water started to enter through the torpedo tubes. 'The younger men were very steady,' a crewman recalled, 'but the married ones looked scared.' Another, more convincingly, said, 'We were all in terrible fear.' *Beverley*'s final attack was with its single one-ton depth charge, which would certainly have sunk U-530 but for the firing mechanisms failing to operate. The destroyer was then obliged to return to close escort of the convoy, leaving the U-boat to struggle away, its pressure hull creaking under strain and water sloshing over the terrified crew's feet. The boat had lost almost all buoyancy, the pumps had been damaged too badly to shift liquid outboard, and it was only by violent use of the electric motors that its captain, Kurt Lange, was eventually able to force it to the surface. Not one of Dönitz's more aggressive commanders – he was the second oldest in the fleet – he turned U-530 for home.

Beverley's sustained depth-changing of U-530 – she had dropped twenty-seven charges and fired two Hedgehog salvoes – had had the indirect effect of frightening away several other U-boats which were shadowing. In consequence, HX229 passed a quiet night. The crews of the merchantmen and escorts spent the hours of darkness keyed up for a renewal of the attack; but the enemy had temporarily lost them. The B-Dienst was enveloped in a blanket of radio silence. The U-boats, radarless and hampered by the bad visibility of a gathering storm, got no glimpse of the convoy as it jogged eastward through its patch of ocean; a focus of many eyes though it must have seemed to HX229's crews, the convoy was no more than an elusive speck to a hunter in the great Atlantic wastes.

HX229's invisibility continued throughout the morning of the following day, 18 March, the penultimate of the nine days during which the Enigma 'Shark' key defied Bletchley's efforts to break U-boat headquarters' communications with its captains. Shortly after one o'clock that afternoon, however, one of the 'Harrier' group U-boats, U-221, which had come up from the east, found itself ahead of the convoy's track. Submerging, the captain found a gap in the escort screen, fired five torpedoes (two of the circling type) and heard three detonations. He had hit two ships. One was the *Walter Q. Gresham*, an American Liberty ship loaded with powdered milk – then a staple of British children's wartime rations, which the rising sea stirred into a thick white froth as the ship settled – the other the *Canadian Star*, a refrigerated ship with twenty-four passengers aboard, including a number of service families which had earlier escaped from the Japanese at Singapore. The *Gresham* lost twenty-seven out of its sixty-nine crew, some of them gunners who bravely manned their weapon as the ship settled under them. *Canadian Star* lost thirty out of eighty-seven, including seven passengers. Four formed a complete family; the father of another, who had seen his wife and son swept away in a capsized lifeboat, died in the water while waiting to be picked up. Those surviving were picked up by the corvette *Anemone*. One of her officers, Lieutenant D. C. Christopherson, recalled that 'there was a little boy; an RAF officer threw him up on to the deck like a rugger ball and one of our stokers caught him. He was still breathing but completely numb. The little boy's mother came up all right but the RAF officer's wife got trapped between the lifeboat and *Anemone*'s side and was badly crushed.' (She died aboard the corvette.) 'Then there was a very pretty girl with long hair. She grabbed the net but slipped back. A sailor, with split-second timing, leaned over, grabbed her hair and swung her right up and on to *Anemone*'s deck.' *Canadian Star*'s captain, in his anxiety to ensure that all aboard had left before him, missed the lifeboats and rafts and went down with his ship.

The ordeal of SC122

While HX229 had been undergoing mass attack, SC122, which U-boat headquarters had mistaken for it, was suffering also, though at the hands of only a single U-boat, U-338, commanded by Manfred Kinzel. U-338 belonged to the 'Attacker' group, which had been ordered westward from its mid-Atlantic patrol line on 15 March. At about two in the morning of 17 March, Kinzel's lookouts reported many ships at less than a mile's range dead ahead. Although they were in the 'wrong' place – HX229 was 120 miles away to the south-west – Kinzel ordered an immediate attack.

'We could only see four columns of ships,' recorded Lieutenant Herbert Zeissler; the convoy was in eleven columns of fifty ships, with six escorts close in ahead and on the flanks and a seventh, the fast frigate *Swale*, at a distance. 'We fired the first two torpedoes at the right-hand ship we could see; we then had to turn to port to aim the second pair of torpedoes at the lead ship of the second column. By then we were very close indeed, about 150 metres, from another ship – I could see a man walking along its deck with a torch. We heard two torpedo explosions and our quartermaster, Trefflich, an enthusiastic Saxon, embraced me. Some of the ships fired at us with machine guns but the fire fell short. We turned hard a'starboard and fired the stern torpedo at the ship at the head of the column but we never heard whether it hit or not. We dived then and the convoy came over the top of us.'

The stern torpedo had indeed struck. It travelled through several columns of the convoy before hitting *Fort Cedar Lake*, a brand-new 7000-ton freighter in general cargo. Three of the other four torpedoes also hit, on *Alderamin*, a Dutch freighter carrying oil and seed, the British *Kingsbury*, carrying soya, bauxite and timber, and the *King Gruffyd*, also British, carrying steel, tobacco and explosives. *Alderamin* sank at once, leaving many of her crew in distress; the only lifeboat safely launched left many behind and its officer-in-charge was later arraigned for neglect of duty. By contrast, the captain, C. L. van Os, spent much time swimming in the water to see all his men aboard the corvette *Saxifrage* which had come to the rescue; before being picked up, he insisted on swimming right round the corvette to ensure that no one had been overlooked, an epically responsible act in March sea temperatures. By an extraordinary coincidence, *Saxifrage* was to rescue Captain van Os from his next ship when it was sunk in the Mediterranean in 1943.

Despite van Os's bravery, eighteen of his men died of drowning or exposure, as did half of *King Gruffyd*'s crew and two from *Kingsbury*. *Fort Cedar Lake*'s company were all picked up by the convoy's rescue ship *Zamelek*, one of the hero ships of the North Atlantic, which sailed with sixty-four convoys and rescued 611 survivors; its tiny size – 1567 tons – may have persuaded U-boats that it was not worth a torpedo.

U-338's success – the crew ate a celebration breakfast of sausage and strawberries and cream almost under the devastation they had caused – provoked intense excitement at U-boat headquarters in the Hotel am Steinplatz in Berlin. Dönitz, away on an inspection in Italy, had a signal sent in his name – 'Bravo. Stick to it. More of the same.' His staff, at first perturbed that U-338 might have mistaken its position but then discounting the possibility, now ordered six boats from the 'Attacker' line to home on U-338 and reinforce Kinzel's efforts. Captain Heinz Bonatz, head of the B-Dienst (his son was aboard one of the 'Harrier' group boats) could identify several of the merchant ships from their distress calls and so convince the operations staff of the reality of SC122's existence and the exactitude of U-338's sighting report.

On the morning of 17 March SC122 comprised forty-four merchantmen and six escorts. Two corvettes, *Saxifrage* and *Godetia*, were still detached on rescue missions, the former with the gallant little *Zamalek*. The trawler *Campobello* had had to be abandoned after springing a leak; its crew were rescued by *Godetia*. A reinforcement, the US Coast Guard Cutter *Ingham*, was on its way from Iceland but had not yet joined. Two U-boats, U-338 and U-666, were in contact, another, U-439, would shortly make touch (by chance, as it happened) and a fourth, U-355, was closing from its earlier station on the 'Attacker' patrol line.

The commander of SC122's escort group, Commander S. C. Boyle (his wife was one of the plotters at the Admiralty Operational Intelligence Centre in London), was rather better placed than Commander Luther of HX229, because he had more escorts under command and fewer U-boats with which to deal.

One of them, however, was the highly aggressive U-338, which, although or because it was on its first patrol, clung doggedly to SC122's flanks and sought to press home attacks. About two o'clock in the afternoon of 17 March, after the arrival and departure of the first patrolling aircraft that either convoy had seen (of which more later), Captain Kinzel achieved an attacking position ahead of the convoy and to port, and fired four torpedoes. Two were not spotted; one was seen by the convoy and avoided; the fourth, after missing one ship (on which ten American Red Cross women were passengers), hit the Panamanian freighter *Granville*, loaded with military stores for Iceland, and damaged her so badly that she quickly broke in two. Twelve of her crew were lost in abandoning her.

USS *Upshur*, the only American ship in the escort, at once began an attack. 'I well remember the huge cloud of dust – rather than smoke – rising amidships in broad daylight,' recorded one of her officers, Lieutenant John White, 'and [the captain] rushing to the bridge' (from lunch) 'and with some exasperation asking, "What's the matter now,

Johnny?" I felt like answering, "It's not my fault. It's those goddam Germans." But I just pointed to the merchantman breaking up half a mile away.'

Upshur was joined by the corvetta *Godetia*, manned by a Belgian crew, in making three sonar attacks, during which they dropped twenty-seven depth charges. They drove U-338 'into the cellar' at beneath 600 feet, lower than the last setting on the British depth pistols; and *Godetia*, which kept up the attack after *Upshur* rejoined the escort, also succeeded in frightening U-666, which got into her sonar search pattern and heard depth charges exploding in her vicinity. However, at about three o'clock, having failed to observe any effects from her attacking runs, *Godetia* broke contact and rejoined the convoy.

SC122 had not seen the back of Kinzel and U-338, nor had it suffered its last losses. Soon after ten o'clock on the evening of 17 March, the corvette *Pimpernel* picked up a radar echo from a U-boat surfaced on the convoy's starboard flank at a range of 6000 yards and turned to attack; but the boat, U-305, had already fired four torpedoes. 'We had steamed hard at 16 knots to get round to the front of the convoy,' Midshipman Wolfgang Jacobsen recalled, 'then we stopped about seven miles ahead and waited. We could see the convoy coming down on us quite clearly in the bright moonlight and watched carefully to pick up which targets we should go for. When the four ships that we were aiming for were overlapping, we fired . . . we dived then and got under the convoy. One of the ships we had hit sank almost at once and we could hear the boilers blowing up under water. We had the feeling that it was coming down all around us.' U-305's four torpedoes had found the large refrigerated ship *Port Auckland* and the smaller *Zouave*. '*Zouave* sank in a very few minutes,' wrote Cook S. Banda, 'not only because we had an extra heavy cargo [iron filings] but also because she was a rattling old tub and I can hear her to this day heaving a sigh of relief as she sank. She literally fell to bits – there were rivets flying about like machine-gun bullets. There were no real regrets at her going down, none of us was aiming to rejoin after this voyage.'

Port Auckland stayed afloat longer and while the corvette *Godetia* was pulling in survivors – some of whom had been trapped for a time in the engine-room in a terrifying swirl of inrushing water – U-305 fired another torpedo to speed her sinking. The corvette at once turned to attack and began a stern chase after the surfaced U-boat; but its top speed was a knot less than the enemy's and it failed to reach an attacking position before U-305 dived. The Belgians then returned to complete the rescue operation, watched unbeknown by Kinzel, who was lying with U-338 ahead of the convoy. At midnight he moved in to reopen his own attack but was driven down by *Havelock* and had to lie submerged until the convoy had passed over him. He then resurfaced and at two o'clock fired a torpedo which sent *Port Auckland* to the bottom. Eight of her crew, already dead in the engine-room, went with her; another thirteen men had been lost in *Zouave*.

The coming of the aircraft

About half past seven in the evening of 18 March *Anemone* and its sister corvette, *Pennywort*, turned to rejoin convoy HX229. They were loaded with survivors from the most recent and earlier sinkings, and had been able to mount no attacks against the U-boats which had sunk the ships they had tended. However, to the heartfelt relief of Commander Luther, protection of HX229 was no longer exclusively in surface-ship hands. Thirty-six hours earlier a U-boat captain, Helmut von Tippelskirch of U-439, had been alarmed to detect an aircraft overhead, had dived to hide from it and spent the rest of the day submerged. The aircraft, a Liberator, was approaching the limit of its endurance and had to return to its Northern Ireland base before half the day was out; but it succeeded in driving down another U-boat, Kinzel's U-338, before it departed and it left behind the warning that the packs' freedom to manoeuvre at will on the surface around the convoy's flanks was now at an end.

The Liberator which had frightened U-439 was at the extreme limit of its operating range, nearly a thousand miles from base, and its Australian pilot brought his crew back to Aldergrove, near Belfast, after eighteen hours in the air. Next day, 18 March, however, both SC122 and HX229 were sufficiently far advanced eastward to have put themselves within easier range both of the Liberators from Aldergrove and of others from Iceland, and close to the operating radius of Flying Fortresses based in the Hebrides and Sunderland flying-boats from County Londonderry. The effect of their intervention in the convoys' battle against the U-boats was to be dramatic.

The Aldergrove Liberator's appearance had so surprised the U-boats of the 'Attacker' and 'Harrier' groups, none of which expected to be seen by an aircraft so far from land, that three were spotted on the surface and two attacked. An officer on the American escort *Upshur* recalled 'the joy when we first saw an aircraft with us. At about the time they came out to cover us we had decided that this convoy experience would last forever and that the Atlantic really had no "other side". We gave a loud cheer when the first aircraft was spotted.'

Soon after the Aldergrove Liberator, from 86 Squadron, was obliged to leave the convoy, another from 120 Squadron in Iceland appeared overhead. Its navigator, Flight Sergeant T. J. Kempton, had persuaded his pilot to ignore standard search procedures and fly direct to HX229's estimated position; 'We did this and picked up the convoy on radar twenty minutes later . . . nearly 1000 miles from base.' With the time saved, the Liberator was able to attack and force below no less than six

U-boats in the next hour, several of which it depth-charged or machine-gunned.

In the morning of the next day, 18 March, two Liberators found SC122 and held U-boats at bay. They were replaced by three more in the afternoon, one of which played cat and mouse with U-642 and twice forced it to submerge. HX229 was not found by any of the five Liberators which flew to look for it, and it was during this interruption of direct air cover that *Canadian Star* and *Gresham* were sunk by U-221. Two Liberators attacked U-boats nearby on the surface, however, and one of the boats was temporarily disabled by depth-charge attack.

The steady arrival and departure of the Liberators, moreover, broke up the U-boat concentrations, so that only one more ship, *Carras* of SC122, fell victim to torpedo attack while in formation; the last convoy casualty, *Matthew Luckenbach*, was to be hit on 19 March after it had disobeyed orders and used its 15-knot speed to make its way to supposed safety. The appearance of the aircraft had the additional indirect effect of enhancing the protective capacity of the escorts. Spared the need to patrol at a distance from the convoys' perimeters, since aircraft were now forcing the U-boats down, and reinforced by a destroyer and a Coast Guard cutter (two more destroyers and two corvettes were also steaming to join), the escort groups began to exert a degree of retaliation. At midnight on 18 March, the overworked *Anemone* caught U-615 trying to attack from behind HX229. Lieutenant von Egan Knieger reported that 'when we were at last in the attack position, an escort came immediately upon us at high speed. Our only salvation was "in the cellar" [of maximum diving depth].' *Anemone* and *Volunteer* made seven attacks in ninety minutes, probably including U-134 and U-440 in their depth-charge patterns, *Pennywort* made a separate attack, and *Highlander* nearly sank a U-boat which failed to detect its approach. 'It was very close,' Lieutenant D. G. M. Gardner recalled, 'and, from our bridge, the U-boat captain could be seen on the conning tower watching the convoy through his binoculars; his stern lookout must have been asleep.' By the end of the night engagement four of HX299's escorts had attacked and three U-boats had been damaged by Hedgehog missiles and depth charges, of which seventy-one had been dropped. The action closed at dawn when *Anemone*, whose crew must have had reason for thinking that theirs was almost a lone battle, found two U-boats surfaced at HX229's rear perimeter and forced both below by threat of gunfire.

It was now the morning of 19 March and both SC122 and HX229, twenty-two fewer in number than they had been four days before, were in waters as safe as convoys could be while still on oceanic passage during the battle of the Atlantic. The escort groups had been swelled by reinforcements to a strength of nineteen, with two more still to join. The Liberators, Fortresses and Sunderlands of seven squadrons of aircraft were patrolling in relays overhead to keep the tracking U-boats

British merchant under convoy by a Royal Navy destroyer (foreground) at the outset of the Battle of the Atlantic, 1940.

TOP An Atlantic convoy changing course under orders of its commander as it approaches British waters during the Battle of the Atlantic.
BELOW U-39, a Type VII U-boat, on exercise in the Baltic before the Battle of the Atlantic; it was sunk in 1939 attacking the British aircraft carrier *Ark Royal.*

TOP A United States Navy Submarine chaser depth-charging a U-boat off the coast of Florida in early 1942.

LEFT The crew of a sinking U-boat swimming for their lives, Battle of the Atlantic.

A conference of merchant captains at Liverpool, Summer 1941, before setting out in convoy for North America during the Battle of the Atlantic.
TOP LEFT Admiral Sir Max Horton, Commander, Western Approaches, a former submarine officer who directed the Battle of the Atlantic from the British side, 1942–5.
TOP RIGHT Grand Admiral Karl Dönitz (1891–1981), commander of the German U-boat fleet and from January 1943 of the German Navy, here congratulating Lieutenant Otto Kretschmer, a U-boat 'ace' of the Atlantic battle.

at a distance and drive them below should they surface. Twenty-four U-boats had been maintaining contact during the night of 18/19 March; by the evening of 19 March only fifteen were still in the fight. Two had been damaged, including the overbold Kinzel's U-338; one had been sunk. A Flying Fortress from Benbecula in the Hebrides, patrolling the rear of HX229, had guessed that a squall might conceal a surfaced U-boat. It accordingly flew into the rainstorm, found a target, dropped four depth charges and saw large gouts of oil colour the surface where the boat disappeared. It had sunk U-384, which two days earlier had torpedoed the *Coracero*. The report of its sinking was deciphered by the B-Dienst, thus adding to the evidence that advantage in the battle for HX229/SC122 had finally been reversed.

U-boat headquarters had already come to its own conclusions about the continuing value of the operation. Balancing losses known to have been inflicted against those likely to be suffered as Allied escort reinforcements and aircraft entered the battle, it decided on the evening of 19 March to order its U-boats to break contact by first light on 20 March and return to patrol stations or, if stores were expended, to base. There were to be no more attacks except by boats which found targets of opportunity or against stragglers and hulks.

Aboard the surviving ships of HX229 and SC122, now in close company, the relaxation of tension brought by the continued presence of aircraft overhead translated itself into a sort of euphoria, the common reaction to sudden departure of danger. 'Chaps would be giving haircuts to their chums, whistling, skylarking and looking at the future and not giving a thought to the weeks now behind them. The whole ship bore a carefree air,' recalled a veteran. This was despite the presence of 1100 survivors from twenty-two sunken ships who were aboard the escorts, the rescue ship *Zamalek* and the New Zealand refrigerated ship *Tekoa*, of HX229, which had rescued 146 from the burning tanker *Southern Princess* and the freighter *Narive* and *Irénée du Pont*. The majority of the survivors, whether they had undergone sinking or merely lived in terror of it over the previous five days, had escaped explosion and the freezing sea and lived to sail again. Many of them were to be outward bound within the month.

THE BALANCE OF THE BATTLE

The battle of HX229/SC122 was the largest and longest-sustained of the Atlantic war. It involved at least forty U-boats, the greatest number ever concentrated for an engagement, against ninety merchantmen and other ships escorted by twenty destroyers, frigates, corvettes and Coast Guard cutters (and an armed trawler which foundered in the foul weather). Twenty-two merchantmen were lost to attack by the U-boats, which fired ninety torpedoes, and 372 seamen and passengers from the convoys died, the majority drowned or killed by exposure in the cold seas of a March Atlantic. There was one naval casualty, a seaman washed overboard from HMS *Mansfield*.

Some 161,000 tons of cargo went down with the torpedoed ships. It included, as we have seen, wheat, steel, tobacco, explosives, timber, bauxite, meat, iron ore, butter, cheese, manganese, fuel oil, sugar and powdered milk. Three of the ships carrying these cargoes were Liberty ships, out of six in the ten convoys, a disturbing rate of sinking even against that at which Libertys were being launched. Overall the rate of sinking in the mid-March battle, 146,000 tons in less than a week, almost exceeded the capacity of the burgeoning Anglo-American, particularly American, shipbuilding programme – 7½ million tons a year – to replace it.

Yet, if all the elements of the HX229/SC122 battle are drawn into the equation and its factors analysed, the solution by no means favoured the U-boats. They had 'run wild', to borrow Yamamoto's phrase, for two days in the 'air gap', strewing the Atlantic with sinking ships, crowded lifeboats and the bodies of seamen and civilians for whom rescue came too late or not at all; but they had not sunk or even touched a single escort, overpressed and overexposed though those little ships had been. They suffered significant damage and loss themselves. Frustrated though the escort captains were by lack of visible result from all their depth-charging, they in fact frightened off three U-boats and damaged seven: U-134 (*Anemone* and *Volunteer*), U-190 (*Babbitt*), U-338 (*Lavender* and *Upshur*), U-439 (*Highlander*), U530 (*Beverley*), U-440 (*Anemone*), U-86 (*Mansfield*) and U-228 (*Beverley* again). The aircraft did even better, frightening two U-boats, damaging U-305, U-338 (the daring Kinzel), U-527, U-598, U-631, U-666 and U-441, and sinking two: U-384, close to the convoys, and U665, caught by a Wellington crossing the Bay of Biscay on its voyage home and depth-charged. There were no survivors from either sinking.

There was worse for the U-boats in store. The German state radio would hail the attacks of HX229/SC122 as 'the greatest convoy battle ever fought', and Dönitz's headquarters war diary would note 'the greatest success so far obtained in a convoy battle'. However, his opposite number, Admiral Sir Max Horton, commanding Western Approaches, reviewed the result in a different light. 'The real trouble,' he wrote to a friend on the same day, 'has been basic – too few ships [escorts], all too hard worked with no time for training. . . . The Air, of course, is a tremendous factor – it is only recently that the many promises that have been made show signs of fulfilment so far as shore-based aircraft are concerned, after three and a half years of war. . . . All these things are coming to a head just now and although the last week has been one of the blackest on the sea, so far as this job is concerned, I am really hopeful.'

The cause of his optimism was a fivefold conjunction of promised advantages: the resumption of the breaking of the 'Shark' Enigma key, which would be read on 90 out of 103 days from 19 March until 30 June and, despite German refinements to the machine, consistently thereafter; the installation of the 10-centimetre radar in ships and aircraft, against which the Germans were not to develop a detector until August; the reinforcement of the long-range aircraft squadrons, which would eliminate the Greenland 'air gap' and provide both defensive and offensive cover over all the U-boats' main operating areas; the creation, out of the accelerated warship building programme, of 'support groups' of escorts, able to lend assistance to hard-pressed convoys – four became available in May; and the appearance of the escort carrier, a convoy's own floating airfield and the ultimate antidote to the U-boats' brazen tactics of surface attack.

Horton's hopefulness was validated on the very next west–east run. SC122/HX229's successors, SC123/HX230, sailed in company with an escort group formed around the carrier USS *Bogue*. Dönitz concentrated two new patrol lines, 'Seawolf' and 'Seadevil', of seventeen and fifteen boats, in their path, but *Bogue*'s Avengers and Wildcats, only twenty in number, held them at bay and only one merchantman was lost. HX231 suffered worse, and ONS176, a westbound convoy, lost HMS *Beverley*, the veteran of HX229, as well as four merchant ships. The April convoy battles were bitterly contested, and 313,000 tons of shipping were lost, but the figure was half that for March and fourteen U-boats had also gone under.

The climacteric of the Atlantic war came in May, when three packs, 'Woodpecker', 'Blackbird' and 'Ram', totalling sixty boats, attacked the westbound convoy ONS5 and were in contact with it for ten out of its sixteen days' mid-Atlantic passage. Six ships were sunk by 5 May, and on the night of 5/6 May, urged on by Dönitz – 'Immediately after the onset of night the drumroll must be timed to begin. Make haste, as there are forty of you there will be nothing of the convoy left' – the packs closed in for the kill. However, by then a support group had joined, fog had gathered, giving the escorts a radar advantage, and the U-boats found the tables turned. Two rammed and sank each other manoeuvring around the convoy's flanks in poor visibility. Five were destroyed by the escorts, two by ramming, one by Hedgehog, two by depth-charging. Next day U-boat headquarters called off the attack. Twelve merchant ships had been sunk, but the destruction of seven U-boats in a single night's engagement was an intolerable rate of loss.

'Intolerable' was the word Dönitz used in his retrospect of the month: 'Losses, even heavy losses, must be borne when they are accompanied by corresponding sinkings. In May in the Atlantic the sinking of about 10,000 tons had to be paid for by the loss of a boat, while not long ago a loss came only with the sinking of 100,000 tons. Thus losses in May have reached an intolerable level.' He thought U-boat losses totalled thirty-one; in fact, when the non-arrival of others destroyed by aircraft in the Bay of Biscay were added in, it was found the final tally was thirty-four. In consequence he ordered 'a temporary shift to areas less endangered by aircraft', a recognition that he could no longer pit the wolf-packs against the escorts, escort carriers and long-range aircraft. In effect, he accepted defeat.

The Allies had not seen the last of the U-boats. Dönitz would resort both to expedients and to radical solutions of his difficulties. The former included the arming of U-boats to 'fight it out' with aircraft in the Bay and the sailing of boats in groups to resist air attack. Both achieved temporary successes against aircrew who attacked imprudently; but U-boats were at an intrinsic disadvantage against air weapons, as Kinzel, the tormentor of HX229, was to be one of the captains to discover. On his return from his first triumphant patrol he had shot down a Halifax. On his third, stalked by a Liberator, he decided to 'stay up and fight' as he signalled U-boat headquarters; when at length he tired of waiting and submerged, his Liberator adversary dropped an acoustic torpedo and destroyed him and all his crew.

Acoustic torpedoes were a new weapon, of which the German themselves were shortly to have the secret: by homing on the sound of a ship's propellers they were peculiarly deadly to escorts, though the danger was eventually overcome by the towing of noise-makers astern. Less easy to deal with was the schnorkel – a pipe allowing air to be drawn into a submarine when submerged – with which U-boats began to be fitted in the spring of 1944. Although it permitted an underwater speed of no more than 5 knots, too slow for Atlantic operations, it allowed boats to operate almost indetectably and so to increase their rate of sinkings in coastal waters, to the Allies' perturbation. Anti-submarine aircraft were almost powerless against schnorkel boats, and escorts, of which the Allies deployed over 400 in Atlantic waters by 1945, began to suffer a significant rate of loss.

Dönitz's ultimate effort to reinvest his fleet with offensive power was through an entirely new technology. The course of the battle of the Atlantic, when reviewed in May 1943, had revealed that the submarine could defeat escorts working in combination with aircraft only if it could hide itself from the aircraft by operating submerged at all times and outrun the escorts by achieving a higher speed underwater than they could on the surface. An interim realisation of these qualities was found in the Type XXI and XXIII boats, which were large, streamlined and of great battery endurance. However, the true submarine of the future, the 'Walther' boat, so-called after its inventor, harnessed a new fuel, hydrogen peroxide, which delivered power sufficient to achieve 25 knots without the need to replenish air supplies by surfacing at all.

By May 1945, after two years in which Dönitz's crews had sunk only another 337 merchantmen for the loss of 534 U-boats – a reverse exchange ratio of 1.5:1 – four 'Walther' boats were undergoing trials and a 'round-the-world boat', under development from the experimental models, promised to be a truly 'war-decisive' weapon. By then, however, the war was at an end and Dönitz, appointed by Hitler in his political testament to succeed him as the Third Reich's second head of state, was skulking in the naval academy at Mürwik where he had begun his career as an imperial cadet thirty-five years before.

He left behind a terrible legacy. The Tirpitz navy into which he had been apprenticed was born from a naked and selfish rivalry for power and died in frustrated rancour. The Hitler navy, of which Dönitz was the chief architect, had forsworn every principle of the sea's fellowship – mutual help in the face of nature, instant assistance to the shipwrecked, magnanimity in victory and fair play at all times – against a code of 'hardness' justified by the appeal to national survival. The consequences for Atlantic seafarers had been appalling. Over 30,000 British, American and Allied merchant seamen died in the sinking of 2603 merchant ships. However, the consequences for his own men had been proportionately worse. The pool of seamen on which Dönitz's U-boats had inflicted their losses numbered several hundred thousand. His own U-boat crews totalled no more than 40,900 from war's beginning to war's end, and of those 28,000 had gone down with their boats, a casualty rate of 70 per cent, unapproached by that of any branch of any other service in any country.

The reality achieves graphic force when the tally of loss is reckoned against the U-boats' order of battle in their fight with HX229/SC122. Forty-five U-boats belonged to or were associated with the packs which attacked those convoys. Two survived the war, one interning itself in Argentina in May 1945 when on a South Atlantic patrol, another surrendering off Canada at the same date; two were damaged in harbour by bombing and not used again; another was so badly damaged that it was written off; one was scuttled; the other thirty-nine were all sunk at sea, most without survivors. One was sunk at sea in collision with another U-boat, one was mined, eleven were sunk by escorts, twenty-two sunk by aircraft. Four were sunk in co-operative attacks by ships and aircraft, including U-616, destroyed by eight US Navy ships and aircraft of 38 Squadron RAF on 17 May 1944 after a three-day hunt, the longest of the U-boat war. The roll-call is remorseless: 'rammed', 'depth-charged', '13 survivors', '9 survivors', '2 survivors', '37 survivors', 'no survivors', 'no survivors', 'no survivors', 'no survivors'. Among those who did not survive the U-boat war were Dönitz's own two sons. Neither had taken part in the battle of HX229/SC122, but Peter Dönitz died beneath the North Atlantic in U-954 on 19 May 1943, sunk by a Liberator, and Klaus, whom his father had withdrawn from the Atlantic battle by use of privilege, was killed in a patrol-boat action in the Channel on 14 May 1944. Over neither death did Dönitz permit himself the smallest interruption of his daily routine. The hardness he so often urged on his captains had entered into his soul.

Conclusion

AN EMPTY OCEAN

By the end of the Second World War, indeed well before its end, the submarine and the aircraft carrier had established themselves indisputably as the dominant weapons of war at sea. Of the two types, it was the aircraft carrier whose rise was the more dramatic. The Soviet Union had built none, the two laid down by Germany and France, *Graf Zeppelin* and *Béarn*, had not been completed, but the British had seven fleet carriers, five light fleet carriers and thirty-eight escort carriers, and twenty fleet or light fleet carriers building; the Japanese had two of thirteen fleet carriers and two of eight light fleet carriers still afloat; the United States Navy, which had begun the war with seven carriers, deployed in August 1945 twenty fleet carriers, eight light fleet carriers and seventy-one escort carriers, providing deck space for nearly 4000 embarked aircraft of a multiplicity of types – fighter, torpedo, bomber, anti-submarine and reconnaissance.

British aircraft carriers, built with armoured decks to resist air attack from land in the confined waters where they had been designed to operate, provided a robust addition to Allied naval airpower in the concluding stages of the Pacific War. However, it was the inexorable advance of the American task forces – units of destroyers and cruisers grouped around one, two or three carriers – which had brought the Japanese navy to defeat. In the battles of the Philippines Sea and Leyte Gulf in 1944, its striking power was destroyed for good; and, to oppose the advances of the task forces to Iwo Jima and Okinawa in 1945, Japan was reduced to the desperate expedient of massing against them waves of kamikaze suicide aircraft – in effect, piloted flying-bombs. In the Okinawa campaign, 1900 kamikaze aircraft were flown at targets, some 250 got through the air defence screens and twenty-five ships were sunk; 150 ships were damaged, including four aircraft carriers and two battleships. None the less the suicide offensive could not check the remorseless onset of the carrier task forces, whose power not only assured the capture of any of the island fortresses the Americans chose to attack but also allowed their embarked aircraft to attack the home islands directly in a series of fast incursions into Japanese sea room designed to destroy the kamikaze squadrons at their bases.

The majority of the American carrier groups manoeuvring at sea exceeded even that of the dreadnought fleets. The spectacle of those great floating airfields steaming upwind at 25 knots under the vast Pacific sky to launch and recover up to a hundred aircraft in a single sortie, surrounded by the cruisers, destroyers and radar-pickets of their air defence screens, left an indelible impression of grace and power on all who witnessed it. Here, it seemed beyond doubt, was the supreme instrument of command of the sea, unapproachable by surface ships, self-defending against aircraft and able to strike at will for hundreds of miles in any direction beyond the circle of ocean they directly occupied.

Yet the defeat of Japan was not solely to be ascribed to the aircraft carrier; in the opinion of Tojo, the Japanese war leader, the submarine played an equal part in the American victory. Statistics bear out his analysis. Submarines not only destroyed one-third of the Japanese fleet, including two of its last aircraft carriers; they also destroyed two-thirds of the Japanese merchant navy. At the beginning of the war Japan owned 6 million tons of merchant shipping; by the end of 1944 that tonnage had declined to 2,500,000 tons, despite the requisition of 800,000 tons by capture and the addition of another 3,300,000 from new construction. Eight months later the figure had fallen to 1,800,000 tons, chiefly representing small ships of the Inland Sea fleet. This toll of belated destruction was largely inflicted by American submarines, which by mid-1945 were operating with impunity in the Sea of Japan itself, and had brought most traffic between the home islands to a halt. Since the beginning of the war over 2000 Japanese merchant ships were sunk, 60 per cent of them by American submarine-launched torpedoes.

In short, what Dönitz tried but failed to achieve in the Atlantic the Americans succeeded in doing in the Pacific. Their submarines locked a stranglehold about the enemy economy and squeezed it into paralysis. For Japan, to an extent even greater than Britain, was a country dependent upon seaborne imports for its raw materials and means of subsistence. Its population was larger than Britain's but its agricultural product was smaller, as was its domestic product of fuel and basic minerals. America's threat to interdict its import of oil and metals was the pretext it had chosen for making war in 1941; America's actual interdiction of their supply in 1945 ensured that, had Japan not accepted defeat by nuclear bombardment, it would have shortly had to give up war-making in any case.

The American submarines which destroyed Japan's means to import were superior in type to those with which Dönitz fought the battle of the Atlantic, being faster on the surface and twice the size, with a larger complement of torpedoes and a greater cruising range. The Americans did not, moreover, seek to orchestrate their submarines' operations by radio orders from land, thereby denying the enemy the opportunity to locate and attack them through intercepts. But these were marginal superiorities. The American submarine of 1945 differed little from the American submarine of 1941. It was still essentially a submersible, able to submerge when need be but operating to best advantage on the surface as a torpedo-boat and losing most of its speed and endurance when it sought invisibility in the deep.

Expert prognosis, had it been sought in 1945, might well have held that the submarine's potential for development lagged far behind that of the aircraft carrier. True, the German Walther boat, with its closed hydrogen-peroxide fuel system, offered the promise of prolonged submerged cruising, and of high underwater speed for short periods; but no Walther boat had been brought to an operational state and the experimental models that existed were small in size. Schnorkel boats were also able to cruise submerged on their diesels at speeds better than electric motors could deliver; but the schnorkel imposed unpleasant pressure changes on the crew, which effectively limited underwater endurance, while cruising range was still determined by fuel capacity. The submarine's offensive capacity, moreover, continued to reside in the torpedo, of which even the best models, like the heavyweight, high-speed Japanese 'Long Lance', were comparatively short-range and inaccurate.

The aircraft carrier, by contrast, was a ship-type undergoing sensational improvement. The first 'supercarrier', USS *Forrestal*, was, when launched in 1954, the largest warship in the world, at 86,000 tons far outweighing the Midway class of 1942, then thought to be giants at 55,000 tons, and dwarfing the 14,500-tons USS *Ranger*, laid down in 1931 as America's first purpose-built aircraft carrier. *Forrestal* admittedly carried fewer aircraft than the Midways, but hers were jet-powered, little inferior in performance to their land-based equivalents and capable of delivering nuclear weapons. The US Navy's carriers in fact acquired their first nuclear-capable aircraft in 1951. With the launching of the supercarriers, the navy put itself at the forward edge of the American strategic system. Supercarriers embarking high-altitude bombers of the Savage, Skywarrior and Vigilante series and deployed to the Mediterranean and western Pacific complemented – competed with – the air force's Strategic Air Command in holding the Soviet Union at nuclear risk. The reality of the risk was enormously enhanced in 1958 with the laying down of a carrier that was nuclear-powered, the new USS *Enterprise*. *Enterprise*, if replenished under way with stores and aviation fuel, could in theory keep the seas indefinitely, using its mobility to hide from an enemy and its air group and supporting screen of escorts to defeat any attacker that chanced to find it.

Four years before the keel of USS *Enterprise* was laid, however, the launching of USS *Nautilus* achieved a modernisation of the submarine revolutionary enough to imply that the aircraft carrier might not, after all, persist in its apparently ordained role as mistress of the twentieth-century oceans. For *Nautilus* was also nuclear-powered, thereby dispensing altogether with the old and bulky duplication of engines for submerged and surface cruising, and travelled at the same speed – more than 20 knots – below and above the surface. Its considerable size, over 3000 tons, and its advanced air-purification system allowed it, moreover, to remain submerged for days at a time.

Nautilus, in short, realised the dream of the submarine pioneers, being a true submarine and not merely a submersible boat. Even so, it was not yet a dominant weapon of war. Its armament consisted of conventional torpedoes and, though it would certainly have eluded the escorts which fought the battle of the Atlantic and slaughtered any convoy they sought to protect, it did not in itself represent the 'war-decisive' weapon into which Dönitz had hoped to transform the U-boat. Pitted against a high-speed carrier group and its formidable array of anti-submarine aircraft, *Nautilus* would not necessarily have inflicted crippling losses and might have been at considerable risk of survival itself.

In the next decade, however, the successors to *Nautilus* grew in size, power and capability. The experimental USS *Triton*, of 5500 tons, circumnavigated the globe submerged in 1960. *Skipjack*, first of a class of nuclear-powered attack submarines, achieved an underwater speed of 30 knots and regularly dived below 1000 feet. Trials with the Regulus missile mounted in USS *Halibut* also validated the submarine's ability to launch nuclear-capable missiles, though *Halibut* had to surface to do so, while Regulus was a relatively primitive subsonic cruise missile.

With the launching of the first of the George Washington class in 1959, a year after the launching of the nuclear supercarrier *Enterprise*, half-measures in the revolutionisation of the submarine disappeared and it moved in a single step to the first rank among units of naval power. *George Washington* was unquestionably a capital ship, if that dated term still had validity; indeed, it exceeded the capital ship's status, being an instrument of national strategy at the direct disposal of the head of state. For *George Washington* represented a marriage between two dynamic technologies: that of the true submarine and that of the long-range ballistic nuclear missile. The boat deployed no specifically marine weapon at all, no gun and no torpedoes. Its armament consisted of sixteen Polaris missiles, representing a new seaborne element in the United States' nuclear deterrent system, to be launched, if at all, not at the direction of the boat's captain but only by specific instructions from the President of the United States.

George Washington was the first of a ballistic-missile fleet which was to grow to forty-one units, a figure to be fixed by Soviet-American agreement in 1972. Meanwhile the direct descendants of *Nautilus*, now known as nuclear attack submarines, were also multiplying. By 1980 they numbered nearly a hundred, of which the most advanced achieved underwater speeds of 30 knots – higher, that is, than that of any but the fastest escorts – and dived to below 1000 feet. At such depths conventional anti-submarine weapons, even if motor-propelled to increase their rate of sinking, were erratically effective; the attack submarine's own counter-escort weapons, particularly the wire-guided torpedo, were actually a more effective weapon. Further, escorts laid themselves open to counter-attack if they used active sonar as a means to locate underwater targets, while passive sonar, which simply monitors the noise of surface ship movements, did not expose a submerged submarine to retaliation.

Passive sonar could, of course, be used by surface escorts to detect submarines below the surface; but so rapidly could a nuclear-propelled submarine manoeuvre at depth that precision attack, either by motor-propelled depth charge or by guided torpedo, was an uncertain means of achieving a hit on one of them. In consequence anti-submariners came to reckon only two weapons as dependably effective against their adversary: one was the nuclear-warhead torpedo, in the American form called the Subroc, a rocket-propelled diving missile which killed a submarine by creating heavy shock waves in a wide area of sea; the other was the wire-guided torpedo – steered by signals transmitted along a thin cable unreeled between torpedo and ship – fired from an aircraft, a submerged mine or another submarine.

Of the three, the submarine-hunting submarine seems potentially the most deadly instrument of anti-submarine warfare. Submarine captains are alarmed by aircraft because they lack the means with which to bring them under attack, even if they are alerted to their presence by active-sonar echoes (aircraft-borne passive sonar does not betray itself at all); but aircraft are relatively feeble anti-submarine weapon platforms, and they must track their prey by indirect means. Typically they acquire targets by dropping patterns of sonar buoys which retransmit echoes to the parent aircraft, and by 'dunking' (dipping) sonar transponders on a cable into the sea surface. By contrast, an attack submarine can chase its quarry through the sea's depths, hiding in the 'cone of silence' created by the quarry's propeller wash until it has reached an attacking position from which its homing torpedoes can be launched. Guided by acoustic data processed by the submarine's computers and retransmitted along the torpedo's wire-control system, such homing weapons are deadly to a submarine which has failed to evade its pursuer.

The significance of the developing dialectic between submarine and anti-submarine – replicating underwater the nineteenth-century surface contest between torpedo-boat and (torpedo-boat) destroyer – is nowhere better demonstrated than in the growing diversification of submarine types. Forty years ago, in the aftermath of the Second World

War, all submarines were 'attack' vessels, dedicated to the offensive against surface ships. By 1960 the class had separated into three: ballistic-missile submarines, belonging to the 'central strategic system' of the nuclear powers; nuclear attack submarines designed to win a third 'battle of the Atlantic' should it break out; and conventional submarines for operations in confined water. The third type has today almost disappeared from the naval order of battle of advanced states. The second continues to increase its underwater speed, safe limit of submersion and offensive power; boats of the later Los Angeles class, for example, travel at 35 knots, dive to nearly 1500 feet and mount submarine-launched cruise missiles, as well as torpedoes, which endow them with strategic as well as tactical capability. The first and truly strategic type has begun to diversify in a highly significant manner. The American Ohio class mounts twenty-four intercontinental missiles and displaces 19,000 tons, as against the sixteen shorter-range missiles and 8000 tons of the earlier Lafayette class; the Soviet Typhoon class, mounting twenty missiles, displaces 25,000 tons, considerably more than any of the dreadnoughts which fought at Jutland.

It requires little prescience to foresee that submarine types will continue to diversify in exactly the same way as ironclads did in the last century. That diversification was among the most striking of all developments in the naval architecture of steam and iron. The wooden world knew only one category of ship, differentiated by size alone; but size differentiation ensured that the larger were not a threat to the smaller, and vice versa, since the low speed and manoeuvrability of the heavily gunned ship ensured that it could not bring the more lightly armed to battle, while the more lightly armed ship dared not use its superior sailing qualities to challenge a heavier adversary. Frigates, in short, fought frigates, and line-of-battleships fought each other. The coming of the ironclad, of the weapons coeval with the ironclad and particularly the torpedo, altered that stratification. The torpedo-boat was designed specifically to challenge the largest ships in an enemy's fleet. Its appearance called forth the torpedo-boat destroyer, which in turn required the multiplication of light cruisers, then of heavy cruisers and ultimately the creation of the battle cruiser. Fleet actions, in consequence, imposed on admirals a bewildering duty to orchestrate diverse ship-types which, as Jutland demonstrated, not even the worthiest and most dedicated could always get right. The later addition of submarines and aircraft carriers to the simultaneous equation admirals were called upon to solve in their heads, against the time-urgency and space variables of battle, compounded their difficulties still further.

These difficulties of orchestration are now threatening to transfer themselves underwater, as the efficient parts of fleets progressively acquire diverse submarine forms: larger and smaller ballistic types, cruise missile types, mixed cruise missile/attack types, and pure attack types, all of them nuclear-powered. Tennyson's image of 'the nations' airy navies grappling in the central blue' threatens to be replaced as a vision of the future by something akin to an underwater Jutland, involving fleets as large and variegated as Jellicoe's and Scheer's, and beset by difficulties of command and control as acute as afflicted either of those admirals. For it remains an unsolved weakness of modern submarine operations that communication, both to submerged submarines from the surface and between one submerged submarine and another, is a problem which scientists are still struggling to solve. Surface-to-submarine communication is possible when the submarine deploys a large enough trailing aerial, though that automatically limits its manoeuvrability and restricts its depth-keeping; inter-submarine communication, because of the conductivity of water, is intrinsically indirectional and insecure. The consequence is that submarine fleets, though undoubtedly the most powerful instruments of naval forces ever sent to sea, are unamenable to either tactical or strategic control. As the history of naval warfare, over the 500 years in which it has been waged in an oceanic dimension, is essentially the story of an effort to impose first tactical and then strategic control over fleets, it is clear that admirals have far to go before they can resume the powers of command which ironclad and wooden-wall predecessors exercised with some degree of certainty.

Yet command of the sea in the future unquestionably lies beneath rather than upon the surface. If that is doubted, consider the record of the only naval campaign fought since 1945, that of the Falklands in 1982. From it two salient facts stand out: that the surface ship can barely defend itself against high-performance, jet-propelled aircraft; and that it cannot defend itself at all against the nuclear-powered submarine. Traditionalists would undoubtedly invoke 'special circumstances' to argue otherwise. They would argue that the eleven out of twenty-seven British surface warships sunk or damaged by Argentinian aircraft bombs or guided missiles were hit in exceptional circumstances, defined by the narrowness of the Falkland Sound, in which the escorts had to cover the landing of the task force's embarked troops, and the constriction of the 'exclusion zone' within and around which the fleet operated at sea. That the fleet's freedom of action was limited by its need to land and support its embarked troops is undeniable. What traditionalists overlook in arguing constriction as an explanation of the losses the task force suffered is that almost all naval battles, throughout the history of war at sea, have been fought in close proximity to land. The deep oceanic encounters of the Pacific War – and they are few enough in number, the battles of Midway and the Philippines Sea standing alone in terms of distance from any considerable land mass at which they were fought – remain exceptional events.

Even in the vastness of the Pacific in the Second World War, most encounters between fleets, or between fleets and maritime aircraft, took place close to the mainland, to large islands or to archipelagoes. That holds true of Pearl Harbor, the battles of the Java and Coral Seas, Savo Island, the eastern Solomons, the Santa Cruz islands, Guadalcanal, the Bismarck Sea, Leyte Gulf and Iwo Jima and Okinawa. The same is also true of all the naval battles of the First World War, including even the distant actions of Coronel and the Falklands. All nineteenth-century naval battles – Navarino, Sinope, Lissa, Manila Bay, Tsushima – were fought in confined waters. The record of action in 'classical' naval operations between the wooden walls of Britain, Holland, France and Spain discloses the same pattern. Only Howe's Glorious First of June ranks as a deep-sea engagement. All the other 'decisive' battles between ship-of-the-line navies, including the Armada fight, the Texel, Beachy Head, Barfleur, the Saints, Camperdown, Cape St Vincent, the Nile, Copenhagen and even Trafalgar itself were fought close to, within sight of or actually directly offshore of land.

It was not, indeed, until the appearance of the submarine and the aircraft carrier that deep-sea operations acquired strategic point. Thitherto, the intrinsic difficulty of locating an enemy fleet or profitable concentrations of merchant shipping in great waters had always argued for the necessity of bringing on fleet engagement as close to home, or to major overseas bases, as possible; that logic was reinforced by the fact that most naval operations were an adjunct of land warfare and that fleets were bound by amphibious considerations to hold close to the operational areas of the armies they were supporting. The aircraft carrier and the long-range submarine altered the terms of that argument. The first, by taking to sea what essentially was an instrument of land warfare, the aeroplane, opened up the possibility of striking over a wider area of strategic space than any admiral had previously sought to dominate. The second, by its power to establish broad lines of surveilllance across sea routes deep within the ocean, confronted surface navies with the need to fight at a distance from land greater than any over which they had before ventured outreach.

Between the upper pincer of the aircraft carrier and the lower of the submarine, the conventional surface ship of whatever size – battleship, cruiser, escort – awaited an inevitable constriction. Without the protection of the carrier-borne aircraft it could not survive in a surface engagement; equally, it could not safely engage its submarine enemy unless aircraft were at hand – at first to keep that enemy submerged, later to enlarge and reinforce its own capacity to detect and attack the submarine keeping to the deeps. The ultimate effect of the operation of these two pincer jaws has been to bring them into immediate opposition. The conventional surface ship is now a marginalised instrument of military force, while the submarine and the aircraft carrier directly challenge each other for command of the sea.

What shall be the outcome? Proponents of the one and of the other sea system are each convinced that their favoured weapon commands the future. Enthusiasts for maritime airpower emphasise the degree of risk at which the submarine is held by the anti-submarine aircraft and the carrier group's formidable ability to defend itself through the deepening of its escort screen, against torpedo and missile attack. Submariners, by contrast, argue that the escort screen is no stronger than its component units, that they are themselves surface ships (though some are also attendant attack submarines) and that those surface escorts face inevitable erosion by sustained submarine assault. The destruction of the carrier group's heart, the carrier itself, must come by inexorable process, and the long reign of the surface capital ship will then be ended.

Foresight is the riskiest of all means of strategic analysis. It must nevertheless be said that the forecasts of the submariner are intrinsically the more convincing. For it is with the submarine that the initiative and full freedom of the seas rests. The aircraft carrier, whatever realistic scenario of action is drawn – that of operations in great waters or of amphibious support close to shore – will be exposed to a wider range of threat than the submarine must face. In a shoreward context it risks attack not only by carrier-borne but also by land-based aircraft, land-based missiles and the submarine itself. The experience of the Falklands rubs home how menacing only two of these elements proved to be: the Argentinians' land-based aircraft and land-based missiles inflicted losses which narrowed the British aircraft carriers' protective screen of escorts to the slenderest of margins; had they been able to deploy either an effective carrier or submarine offensive effort – or both – against the task force it must have been driven into retreat.

The British attack submarines, by contrast, operated at will, sinking the Argentinian navy's largest conventional surface ship, driving its aircraft carrier and the whole of its escort fleet ignominiously into harbour, and risking in the process no effective retaliation whatsoever. That the Argentinian navy was an ineffective anti-submarine force does not invalidate the conclusion to be drawn from the encounter. Given equal numbers and an equivalent allocation of ship-types between the two fleets, it would have been the Royal Navy that operated at a disadvantage, with inevitably disastrous consequences for the outcome of the expedition to the South Atlantic. It would have suffered all the losses that it did; and to them would have been added the sinkings that a nuclear attack submarine force must certaintly have inflicted.

The era of the submarine as the predominant weapon of power at sea must therefore be recognised as having begun. It is already the instrument of ultimate nuclear deterrence between the superpowers, holding at risk their cities, industries and populations as it circles their shores on its relentless oceanic orbit. It is now also the ultimate capital ship, deploying the means to destroy any surface fleet that enters its zone of operations. Five hundred years ago, before the sailing-ship pioneers ventured into great waters, the oceans were an empty place, the only area of the world's surface in which men did not deploy military force against each other. In a future war the oceans might appear empty again, swept clear both of merchant traffic and of the navies which have sought so long to protect it against predators. Yet the oceans' emptiness will be illusory, for in their deeps new navies of submarine warships, great and small, will be exacting from each other the price of admiralty.

GLOSSARY

all-big-gun ship a battleship, or battlecruiser, armed exclusively with heavy guns of the same calibre; *Warspite*, 1906, was the first of the type

arrester-wires wires stretched across the landing deck of an aircraft carrier to catch the hook of an arriving aircraft and stop it

Asdic from Allied Submarine Detection Investigation Committee (1917): a sound-emission device carried under the hull of an anti-submarine vessel which also received the echo when sound was returned from a submarine hull. The time interval allowed the submarine's range and bearing to be estimated; after 1944 depth could be estimated also

battlecruiser a ship of battleship size and armament, but sacrificing armoured protection for superior speed

battleship the largest class of fighting ship in a fleet, carrying the heaviest guns and armour; in wooden warship days, the ship of the line or line-of-battleship, then of several 'rates' (see *first-rate*)

bowsprit the spar projecting from the bow of a sailing ship, by which the fore-top mast (q.v.) was stayed and on which the jib-sails were set

breaking the line the action of passing one fleet's line of battle through the enemy's, with the object of destroying his cohesion

cable-bitt large vertical timbers, morticed into the keel, to which anchor and mooring cables were attached

capital ship term first coined in 1909, denoting the largest fighting ships in the fleet – battleships and battlecruisers; now obsolete

carronade a shortened ship canon, invented by the Carron Company about 1790, and favoured by the Royal Navy for its ease of handling at close ranges

clean copper (bottom) copper sheathing of the underwater hull of wooden ships was adopted by the Royal Navy in 1761 as a protection against the wood-boring teredo worm; copper-bottom ships still needed regular cleansing of weed, which reduced their speed

'command of the sea' the free use of the sea and its denial to the enemy; the term was coined by Admiral A. T. Mahan in 1890 and defined by him as the proper object of naval strategy

companion way a ladder between decks

corvette a wooden warship with a single deck of guns, smaller than a frigate (q.v.); in the Second World War, an anti-submarine escort, again smaller than a frigate

crosstrees short transverse spars at the head of the topmast, to which the top galiant mast was stayed

cruiser a warship next in size below a battleship or battlecruiser, used to cruise in distant waters and to scout for and protect the battle fleet

cutter (1) a large open boat carried by a sailing warship; (2) a single-master sailing warship, with 6–10 light guns; (3) a patrol vessel of the US Coast Guard

declination from the truck the angle observed between the deck of one ship and the top (truck) of another's mainmast

destroyer originally torpedo-boat destroyer (TBD); a type of fast warship, smaller than a cruiser, developed about 1886, to protect the battle fleet from torpedo-boats; later itself a torpedo-boat, escort and maid-of-all work, distinguished by its high speed

'doubling' placing one's own ships on both sides of the enemy's line, by sailing some round its rear or van (head)

downwind relatively further from the source of the wind than another ship; the opposite is 'upwind'

dreadnought an 'all-big-gun' battleship (q.v.) and more loosely battlecruiser, after HMS *Dreadnought*, first of the type; obsolescent after 1918

Enigma the machine on which the German armed forces enciphered and deciphered confidential radio and telex traffic, 1939–45; loosely also the traffic itself

escort carrier the smallest class of aircraft carrier, embarking 20–35 aircraft, often converted from merchant ships and intended particularly to escort convoys

first-rate the largest line-of-battleship in sailing navies, according to a system introduced in Britain in the 1750s; first-rate, 100 guns or more; second-rate, 84–98; third-rate, 70–80. Only these rates were normally deemed fit to 'stand in the line of battle'. Fourth-rates (usually 64 guns) were rare. Fifth- and sixth-rates were frigates

float plane also known as a seaplane; an aircraft with floats in place of wheels, allowing it to operate from water. Some flying-boats and seaplanes were also 'amphibians', with wheels

flying-boat an aircraft with a fuselage of hull form, allowing it to put down on and take off from water

fore-and-aft sail a sail set along the central bow-to-stern line of a ship, as opposed to a square sail; fore-and-after rigging runs likewise

foremast the mast nearest the bow

foresail the largest and lowest sail set on the foremast

fore-top the platform on the foremast into which the fore-topmast was stepped; some times used as a fighting platform

fore-topmast a separate spar extending the foremast upward from which the fore-topsail was set

foreyard the yard on which the foresail was set

frigate see *first-rate:* a fifth- or sixth-rate warship, mounting respectively 36–50 guns and 28–32 on a single deck; frigates were fast sailers, used as scouts and cruisers (q.v.)

gaff the spar at the top of the fore-and-aft sail (q.v.) on the mizenmast of a square-rigger (q.v.)

'go aboard' to place a ship alongside an enemy ship

hardtack ship's bread, baked into hard biscuit for durability

Hedgehog a mortar firing depth charges ahead of an anti-submarine vessel

Holland boat the first practicable submarine, after its inventor, J. P. Holland

ironclad loosely, a warship built of iron, or of wood protected by iron; more properly a ship protected by iron or steel armour. The first ironclads appeared in 1853; the term fell out of use with the appearance of the dreadnought (q.v.)

jib-boom an extension of the bowsprit (q.v.)

jury spar (or **rig**) an improvisation, after storm or battle damage

kamikaze a suicide aircraft, packed with explosives and flown by its pilot as a manned missile against a ship; Japanese, from the word for 'divine wind'. Kamikazes were used by the Japanese in 1944–5 after they began to run short of trained pilots and first-line aircraft

leeward see *downwind*; when two ships or fleets are sailing parallel, that furthest from the source of the wind is 'to leeward'

light carrier an aircraft carrier of size intermediate between an escort (q.v.) and a fleet carrier, embarking 40–50 aircraft
line abreast a formation in which ships sail side by side rather than following bow to stern
line ahead a formation in which ships sail following each other bow to stern; in sailing warfare, a fleet in line ahead was conventionally divided into van (head), centre and rear
lose way to slow down a ship's passage through the water, by sail-handling or use of the engines; a sailing ship may also lose way when the wind drops or wind or tide changes
luffing to luff is to handle a ship or its sails so that wind is spilled from the sail(s); a method of losing way (q.v.)

mainmast the tallest mast in the ship, next behind the foremast (q.v.)
mainsail the largest and lowest sail on the mainmast
main-top see *foretop*
main-top mast see *fore-topmast*
mainyard see *foreyard*
massing a manoeuvre in early sailing-ship warfare when one fleet concentrated a superior number of its ships against an inferior number of the enemy's
mizen the last mast in the ship (from the bow)
mizen-top see *fore-top*
mizen-topmast see **foretopmast**

navalism a strategic theory; derived from the writings of the American Admiral Alfred Thayer (1840–1914); which holds that the possession of an oceanic navy is an essential attribute of a great power

orlop deck the lowest deck in the ship, below waterline, and so not a gundeck

poop a short deck nearest the stern, raised above the quarterdeck
powder monkey a young seaman who brought gunpowder cartridges from the magazine to the guns during battle
prize crew a crew put aboard a captured vessel, usually to sail it to a friendly port

quarterdeck the deck raised above the maindeck and running towards the stern; the station of the captain and officers, unless otherwise employed, at sea and in battle; loosely, the officers' deck
quarter-rail the rail round the quarterdeck

rabbeted a method of fastening one timber at an angle to another; from 'rebate'
'real time' a term from the world of intelligence: information about

the enemy received in 'real time' arrives with the interceptor either at the same time as with the intended recipient or soon enough afterwards for the interceptor to act usefully upon it; the importance of the British Ultra (q.v.) intelligence system was that it decrypted much German Enigma (q.v.) traffic in 'real time'

sail 'by the wind' to sail into the wind or with the wind abeam (at right-angles to the ship); sailing 'on the wind' the ship has the wind behind

scantlings the timbers of a ship, apart from the keel, before it is planked

scarfed a method of joining two timbers end to end, by a diagonal joint

schnorkel a tube, protruding above the surface from a submerged submarine, which allows its diesel engines to continue working without exhausting the crew's air supply; a Dutch conception, it was perfected by the German navy in the Second World War

sea-keeping staying at sea and the ability safely to do so

seaplane see *floatplane*

sea room safe distance from the land

shot wads wads of paper or other fibre rammed into a gun to hold the ball in place before firing

sloop a warship smaller than a corvette (q.v.) or a frigate (q.v.), of two or three masts and mounting a few guns; later a small escort vessel

slow match a chemically impregnated length of cord, kept smouldering in action, with which the gunpowder charge of a cannon or early firearm was detonated

sonar the American term for Asdic (q.v.), which it has now replaced

spritsail a fore-and-aft sail set on a diagonal spar; in sailing warships, a square sail set on a yard under the bowsprit

squadron a number of warships, less than a fleet; more recently a unit of warships of prescribed number, four, six or eight, all of the same type – the larger the warship the smaller the number

square-rigger a ship rigged with square sails

standing rigging the fixed ropes which support a ship's main spars-masts, bowsprit, jib-boom; the most important parts of the standing rigging are the shrouds and stays

strike (colours) to lower the ship's national or military flag; in battle, a gesture of surrender

strike below to send equipment, particularly aircraft, below decks; aircraft are 'struck below' by mechanical elevator

stringers timbers running horizontally along a ship's frame to lend structural strength

stay a part of the standing rigging (q.v.) of sailing ship; see also *tack*

studding sails auxiliary square sails, set outside the ordinary square sails in fine weather for extra speed

tack to turn a sailing ship by moving its bow towards and then past the source of the wind; in square-rigged ships, the manoeuvre entailed changing the angle of the sails to the mast at the moment of turning, to avert the wind's playing on the front of the sail and 'taking (the ship) aback', which stopped it; ships 'taken aback' were said to have 'missed stays'

topgallant the topgallant mast was that stepped above the topmast on which the topgallant yard and sail were set

tophamper generally, the masts, yards, sails and rigging of a ship; loosely, everything above the upper deck of a ship of an insubstantial nature

torpedo-boat a small fast steam warship, equipped with torpedoes, for the attack of larger vessels; in the German navy the term for destroyer (q.v.)

trunnion small projections from the barrel of a cannon, integral to it and slightly forward of its point of balance, by which it is suspended in its carriage

turret (A, B etc.) turrets are lettered from bow to stern; in a four-turret ship A, B, X, Y; Q is the midship's turret in a five-turret ship

Ultra the term given by the British Code and Cipher School at Bletchley during the Second World War to the material intercepted and decrypted from German Enigma (q.v.) traffic; see also *'real time'*

upwind see *downwind*

waisters men working in the waist – central upper deck – of a sailing ship, who did not go aloft

wales broad planks running horizontally along a ship, outside the covering planks, for extra strength and protection, e.g. gunwale

wear to turn a sailing ship by moving its bow away from the source of the wind; it entailed turning through three-quarters of a circle and was therefore slower than tacking (q.v.) but safer, since it averted the danger of missing stays (q.v.). Wearing was judged unseamanlike, except in heavy weathers

weather gage see *downwind*; a fleet or ship having 'the weather gage' of another is upwind of it

windward see *leeward*

yard the transverse spar on the mast of a square-rigged (q.v.) sailing ships from which a square sail is set

yard arm the outer end of a yard

SELECT BIBLIOGRAPHY

Naval Warfare

Albion, R. G., *Forests and Sea Power*, Hamden, Conn, 1965
Anderson, R. C., *Naval Wars in the Levant, 1559–1853*, Princeton, 1952
Oared Fighting Ships, London, 1962
Brodie, B., *A Guide to Naval Strategy*, New York, 1965
Sea Warfare in the Machine Age, Princeton, 1941
Callender, G., *The Naval Side of British History*, London, 1924
Cipolla, C., *Guns and Sails in the Early Period of European Expansion*, London, 1965
Clarke, I. F., *Voices Prophesying War*, London, 1970
Corbett, J., *Some Principles of Maritime Strategy*, London, 1918
Graham, G. S., *Empire of the North Atlantic*, Toronto, 1950
Guilmartin, J., *Gunpowder and Galleys*, Cambridge, 1974
Kennedy, P., *The Rise and Fall of British Naval Mastery*, London, 1976
Landström, B., *The Ship*, New York, 1961
Lewis, M., *The Navy of Britain*, London, 1948
The History of the British Navy, London, 1957
Lloyd, C., *The Nation and the Navy*, London, 1961
Mahan, A. T., *The Influence of Sea Power upon History*, (London, 1965 ed.)
Marcus, C. J., *A Naval History of England*, 2 vols, London, 1961–71
Marder, A. J., *The Anatomy of Sea Power*, Hamden, Conn., 1964 ed.
Padfield, P., *Tides of Empire*, London, 2 vols, 1979, 1981
Pares, R., *War and Trade in the West Indies*, London, 1963 ed.
Parkinson, C. N., *War in the Eastern Seas 1793–1815*, London, 1954
Parry, J. H., *The Age of Reconnaissance*, London, 1963
Potter, E. and Nimitz, C., *Sea Power*, New Jersey, 1960
Richmond, Admiral Sir Herbert, *Statesmen and Sea Power*, Oxford, 1946
Rodger, A. B., *The War of the Second Coalition*, Oxford, 1964
Rodger, N. A. M., *The Wooden World*, London, 1986
Roskill, Captain S. W., *The Strategy of Sea Power*, London, 1962
Schurman, D. M., *The Education of a Navy*, London, 1965
Sherwig, J. N., *Guineas and Gunpowder*. British Foreign Aid in the War with France, 1793–1815. Cambridge, Mass., 1969
Williamson, J. A., *The Ocean in English History*, Oxford, 1941

Trafalgar

Bennett, G., *Nelson the Commander*, London, 1972
Corbett, J., *Fighting Instructions*, 1530–1816, London, 1905
The Campaign of Trafalgar, London, 1910
Desbrières, E, tr. C. Eastwick, *The Campaign of Trafalgar*, 2 vols, Oxford, 1933
Fraser, E., *The Enemy at Trafalgar*, London, 1906
Fitchett, W. H., *Nelson and his Captains*, London, 1902
Howarth, D., *Trafalgar*, London, 1969
Hughes, Q., *Britain in the Mediterranean*, Liverpool, 1981
Lewis, M., *England's Sea Officers*, London, 1939
A Social History of the Navy, 1793–1815, London, 1960
Longridge, N., *The Anatomy of Nelson's Ships*, London, 1965
Kennedy, L., *Nelson's Band of Brothers*, London, 1951
Mackenzie, R. H., *The Trafalgar Roll*, London, 1910
Mackesey, P., *The War in the Mediterranean, 1803–10*, Oxford, 1957
Masefield, J., *Sea Life in Nelson's Time*, London, 1905
Nicholas, Sir H., *Dispatches and Letters of Lord Nelson*, London, (vol II) 1844–6
Oman, C., *Nelson*, London, 1947
Pocock, T., *Horatio Nelson*, London, 1987
Pope, D., *England Expects*, London, 1960
Smyth, Admiral W., *A Sailor's Word Book*, London, 1878
Walder, D., *Nelson*, London, 1978
Warner, O., *Nelson's Battles*, London, 1965

Jutland

Bacon, Admiral Sir Reginald, *The Jutland Scandal*, London, 1925
Berghahn V., *Der Tirpitz-Plan*, Dusseldorf, 1972
Campbell, N. J. M., *Battle Cruisers*, London, 1978
Jutland, London, 1986
Chalmers, Rear Admiral W. S., *The Life and Letters of David Earl Beatty*, London, 1951
Corbett, Sir Julian and others: *Naval Operations*, vols I-V, London, 1920–31
Fawcett, H. W. and Hooper, G. W. W., *The Fighting at Jutland*, London, 1921
Gibson, L. and Harper, J. E. T., *The Riddle of Jutland*, London, 1934
Goldrick, J., *The King's Ships were at Sea*, Annapolis, 1984
Groos, O., *Der Krieg zur See*, vol V, Berlin, 1925
Hase, G. von, *Kiel and Jutland*, London, 1921
Holger, H., *Luxury Fleet*. The Imperial German Navy, 1888–1918, London, 1980.
Hough, R. *The Great War at Sea 1914–18*. Oxford, 1983
James, Admiral Sir William, *The Eyes of the Navy*. A Biographical Study of Admiral Sir Reginald Hall, London, 1955
Marder, A. J., *Fear God and Dread Nought*. The Correspondence of Admiral Lord Fisher, vol III, London, 1959
From Dreadnought to Scapa Flow. The Royal Navy in the Fisher Era, vols I–III, London, 1961–6
Parkes, O., *British Battleships*, London, 1960
Patterson, A. T., *Jellicoe*, London, 1969
Roskill, Captain S. W., *Admiral of the Fleet Earl Beatty*, London, 1980
Scheer, Admiral Reinhard, *Germany's High Seas Fleet in the World War*, London, 1920
Steinberg, J., *Yesterday's Deterrent*, London, 1965
Taylor, J., *German Warships of World War I*, London, 1969
Woodward, E. L., *Great Britain and the German Navy*, London, 1935

Midway

Agawa, H., *The Reluctant Admiral: Yamamoto and the Imperial Navy*, Annapolis, 1979
Beloto, J. and W., *Titan of the Seas*, New York, 1975
Brown, D., *Carrier Operations in World War II*, vol II, London, 1974
Butow, R., *Tojo and the Coming of War*, Princeton, 1961
d'Albas, A., *Death of a Navy*, London, 1957
Dull, P., *A Battle History of the Imperial Japanese Navy*, Annapolis, 1978
Friedman, N., *Battleship Design and Development*, Greenwich, Conn., 1978
Fuchida, M., and Okumiya, M., *Midway*, London, 1957
Hagan, K., *In Peace and War*, Westport, Conn., 1978
Hezlet, A., *The Aircraft and Sea Power*, London, 1970
Ito, M., *The End of the Imperial Navy*, London, 1956
Kahn, D., *The Code Breakers*, London, 1966
Lewin, R., *The American Magic*, New York, 1982
Marder, A., *Old Friends, New Enemies*, New York, 1981
Morison, S. E., *The Rising Sun in the Pacific*, Boston, 1968 ed.
Coral Sea and Midway, Boston, 1980 ed.
O'Connor, R., *The Imperial Japanese Navy in World War II*, Annapolis, 1969
Okumiya, M. and Horikoshi, J., *Zero*, London, 1957
Potter, E., *Nimitz*, Annapolis, 1976
Reynolds, C., *The Fast Carriers*, New York, 1968
Roskill, Captain S. W., *Naval Policy Between the Wars*, 2 vols, London, 1968, 1976
Sprout, H. and M., *The Rise of American Naval Power*, London, 1967
Storry, R., *A History of Modern Japan*, New York, 1960
Thorne, C., *Allies of a Kind*, London, 1978
Watts, A., and Gordon, B., *The Imperial Japanese Navy*, London, 1971

The Battle of the Atlantic

Beesley, P., *Very Special Intelligence*, London, 1977
Bekker, P., *The German Navy*, New York, 1974
Hitler's Naval War, New York, 1974
Bennett, G., *Naval Battles of the Second World War*, New York, 1975
Gretton, P., *Convoy Escort Commander*, London, 1964
Hezlet, A., *The Submarine and Sea Power*, London, 1967
The Electron and Sea Power, London, 1975
Hinsley, F. and others, *British Intelligence in the Second World War*, vol 2, London, 1981
Jones, R., *The Wizard War*, New York, 1978
Lewin, R., *Ultra Goes to War*, New York, 1979
Medlicott, W., *The Economic Blockade*, 2 vols, 1952, 1959
Middlebrook, M., *Convoy*, 1976
Padfield, P., *Dönitz*, London, 1984
Rohwer, J., *The Critical Convoy Battles of 1943*, London, 1977
Roskill, Captain S. W., *The War At Sea*, vol II, London, 1960
Showell, J., *The German Navy in World War II*, Annapolis, 1979
U-Boat under the Swastika, London, 1974
Werner, H., *Iron Coffins*, New York, 1979
Willmott, H., *Sea Warfare*, Chichester, 1982

INDEX

Compiled by Gordon Robinson

Fort Matagorda
Carraca
Chiclana
Couil
C. TRAFALGAR
Puntal Road
CADIZ BAY
I. of LEON
S. Pedro Channel
Puntal Fort
CADIZ
C. Rocha
Shoals
Shoal
St. Pedro Shoals
Fort St. Sebastian
Cadiz N. 30 E. distant about 38 Miles out right or Land.
(The Coast is not laid down by Scale)
ENEMY'S VAN
Temeraire, 98.
Neptune, 98.
Sirius, 36.
Naiad, 38.
Euryalus, 36.
Phoebe, 36.
Conqueror, 74.
Leviathan, 74.
Ajax, 74.
Entreprenante Cutter.
Africa, 64.
Orion, 74.
Agamemnon, 64.
Minotaur, 74.
Pickle Schooner.
Spartiate, 74.
Britannia, 100.
EVER MEMORABLE BATTLE OFF
Published 12th Dec 1805, by ROBERT LAURIE